ALSO BY RICHARD RHODES

ARSENALS OF FOL

ARSENALS
OF FOLLY

THE MAKING OF THE
NUCLEAR ARMS RACE

**SIMON &
SCHUSTER**

London · New York · Sydney · Toronto

A CBS COMPANY

RICHARD RHODES

First published in Great Britain in 2008 by
Simon & Schuster UK Ltd
A CBS COMPANY

1 3 5 7 9 10 8 6 4 2

Simon & Schuster UK Ltd
Africa House
64–78 Kingsway
London WC2B 6AH

www.simonsays.co.uk

Simon & Schuster Australia
Sydney

A CIP catalogue for this book is available
from the British Library.

ISBN: 978-1-84737-118-8

Printed and bound in Great Britain by
Mackays of Chatham Ltd

For Chuck Hansen, 1947–2003

A grant from the Alfred P. Sloan Foundation supported the research and writing of this book.

Reality is that which, when you don't believe in it, doesn't go away.

PETER VIERECK

CONTENTS

PART ONE **A RIGID SYSTEM**

PART TWO **APES ON A TREADMILL**

PART THREE **COMMON SECURITY**

PART ONE	A RIGID SYSTEM

What happened in this country was that a rigid system was created, and then life was herded into it.

MIKHAIL GORBACHEV

ONE TO THE CHERNOBYL SARCOPHAGUS

ON THE SATURDAY MORNING IN APRIL 1986 when the alarms went off at the Institute for Nuclear Power Engineering of the Byelorussian Academy of Sciences, in a forest outside Minsk, the nuclear physicist Stanislav Shushkevich thought the institute's reactor was bleeding radiation. Its fuel assemblies, sealed inside aluminum cassettes at the bottom of a deep, stainless-steel tank full of distilled water, might have sprung a leak. Or something might have spilled in the institute's radiochemistry lab. Dosimeter operators began working their way methodically through the labs and offices and found radiation everywhere. It was in people's hair and clinging to their clothes. It registered two hundred times normal on the air filters. It was near danger levels at the front door.

The dosimetrists moved outside and discovered it there as well: on the sidewalk, on the grass, on the periwinkle crocuses pushing up through the dark litter of the forest floor. So the institute wasn't the source. An order over the public-address system warned everyone to stay indoors. Someone called the Lithuanian nuclear-power complex at Ignalina, one hundred miles northwest, and radiation was everywhere there too. Chernobyl, in the Ukraine, was farther away, two hundred miles southeast, where four big RBMK* thousand-megawatt reactors were lined up end to end in a building almost a mile long. Hundreds of people worked there, but the phones rang unanswered. Something was wrong at Chernobyl.

By afternoon, institute chemists had found radioactive iodine in the fallout, which confirmed that a reactor had exploded. For radioactive gas and

---

* In Russian, an acronym for "reactor, high-power, boiling, channel type." The RBMK reactor is essentially a large block of graphite drilled with hundreds of channels into which uranium fuel elements are inserted. Water also circulates through the channels to cool the fuel elements and transfer heat out of the block. Reactors use light elements to slow and reflect neutrons to sustain a slow-neutron fission chain reaction, the source of their energy; in the RBMK design, both the graphite (carbon) and the circulating water (hydrogen) moderate the reaction.

smoke from Chernobyl to have reached Minsk, the explosion must have occurred sometime during the night. How much radioactivity had been released? How much more would follow? Why had no one warned them?

Shushkevich, fifty-two, a solid, ample man with a ruddy face and a high, domed forehead fringed with graying brown hair, was friendly and avuncular but shrewdly intelligent. He was vice-provost of the Byelorussian University in Minsk, a liberal humanist in the tradition of Andrei Sakharov. The Soviet Union's change of direction since the death of Konstantin Chernenko in March 1985, just thirteen months before, had filled him with hope. Chernenko, an emphysemic general secretary with the soul of a retired file clerk, had served as a placeholder between the reform-minded but ailing former KGB chief Yuri Andropov and his vigorous young heir apparent, Mikhail Gorbachev. At Chernenko's death his private safe had turned up no personal diary or other intimate record, only a large cache of money no one could account for. Good riddance, Shushkevich had thought: "I was the first at the university to put a portrait of Gorbachev on the wall."

The night of Chernenko's death, Raisa Maksimovna, Mikhail Gorbachev's wife and partner, pacing beside him in the garden of their country house near Moscow, heard him say resolutely, "We just can't go on like this." The next day, 11 March 1985, Gorbachev had been elected general secretary at a meeting of the Communist Party Central Committee. In his acceptance speech immediately after his election he had called for open government and accountability: "I emphasized the need for transparency (*glasnost*) in the work of Party, Soviet, state and public organizations," he wrote later. He had laid out in detail his other fundamental goal, perestroika—economic restructuring, salvaging the nearly moribund Soviet economy—at a Central Committee plenum the following month, stressing "the elimination of everything that interferes with development."

The huge Soviet military-industrial complex, which insinuated itself into every corner of the Soviet economy and consumed at least 40 percent of the state budget, headed his list for cutbacks, and in a letter delivered to President Ronald Reagan on 15 January 1986 he had broached a proposal without precedent across the four dangerous decades of the U.S.-Soviet nuclear-arms race: "A concrete program," as he described it during a press conference in Moscow later that day, ". . . for the complete liquidation of nuclear weapons throughout the world . . . before the end of the present century." Opening to such unprecedented initiative, 1986 had seemed a year of immense possibility. Now a disaster loomed, of consequences yet unknown, and radiation blew north from Chernobyl.

At 2:30 on Saturday afternoon someone finally called the institute to report an accident at Chernobyl. In the early hours after midnight, Chernobyl Reactor Number Four had run away in four seconds from 7 percent of maximum rated power to about one hundred times maximum rated power, an event called a prompt critical excursion that had flashed the reactor's thousands of gallons of circulating water to high-pressure steam. The graphite core of the massive, concrete-encased reactor was an enclosed cylinder forty feet in diameter and twenty-three feet tall, set on end, with blocks of concrete and a water pool beneath it to absorb the fierce radiation its zirconium-clad uranium fuel elements produced, and a two-million-pound, disk-shaped upper biological shield of concrete blocks set over it like a lid to protect workers from radiation exposure. In the same spirit of bravado that had prompted the scientists at Los Alamos during the Second World War to nickname the atomic bomb they were building the "gadget," the men who operated the RBMKs called the upper biological shield the *pyatachok,* Russian for one of the smallest Soviet coins, the five-kopek piece.* When the water flashed to superheated steam and the reactor's steam pipes started exploding, an eyewitness reported later, the *pyatachok* "began to bubble and dance."

Then two explosions in the space of less than four seconds tore open the reactor and blew out the building. The reactor core was sealed within a metal tank filled with a mixture of helium and nitrogen to prevent the graphite moderator—four million pounds of pure carbon—from burning. The prompt critical excursion had heated the graphite red hot. The first steam explosion lifted the two-million-pound *pyatachok.* At the same time the steam burst down through the metal tank and penetrated the red-hot graphite. Steam combines ferociously with hot carbon to make carbon monoxide, liberating hydrogen; the second and more powerful explosion combined steam and exploding hydrogen gas, tilted up the *pyatachok* nearly vertical, shattered the upper half of the reactor core, and blew tons of its red-hot radioactive debris—a rubble of highly irradiated uranium-oxide fuel as well as radioactive graphite and zirconium—past the *pyatachok,* through the roof, and half a mile into the air.

It fell out by size. Big blocks of hot graphite landed on the roofs of Number Four's turbine hall and Reactor Number Three. To lower construction costs, the roofs had been covered with flammable asphalt; the hot graphite set them on fire. Blocks and smaller pieces of graphite landed on the grounds

---

* One hundred kopeks equal one ruble.

around the building and splashed hissing into the four-mile-long cooling pond that lay between the plant and the Pripyat River. The cooling pond was fed by and drained into the river, which drained in turn into the big reservoir downstream that stored the water supply of the city of Kiev, the Soviet Union's third-largest city, with a population of some 2.5 million people.

Graphite pieces and soot-like particles scattered across a stand of pines southeast of the complex; several weeks later, when the radiation had killed the trees and their chlorophyll had faded, people started calling the dead stand "the Red Forest." About half the total radioactive fission products jettisoned from the reactor fell within a two-mile radius of the building. The gases released in the explosion diluted and dispersed into the upper atmosphere, but the wind carried the finest aerosols and hot, intensely radioactive particles (which lofted on their own heat like microscopic hot-air balloons) northwest toward Minsk, on to Ingalina and then across the Baltic Sea to Finland and Sweden. The explosions also blew out the shield elements below the reactor; with the water channels through the graphite blocks drained, the hot graphite chimneyed air up the channels through the remaining lower half of the reactor core and the graphite began to burn. It burned efficiently, the soot and ash carrying more and more radiation high into the air.

A containment structure such as the concrete-and-steel dome that protects all Western and Japanese power reactors would probably have confined the Chernobyl explosions and their radioactivity, but Soviet reactors of the RBMK type lacked such containment.

In the 1950s, when the RBMK design was developed and approved, Soviet industry had not yet mastered the technology necessary to manufacture steel pressure vessels capacious enough to surround such large reactor cores. For

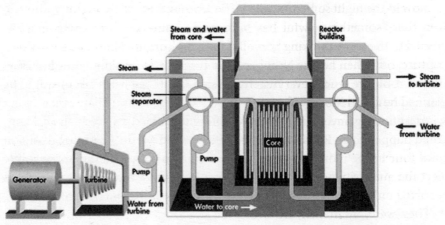

Source: Nuclear Energy Institute

that reason, among others, scientists, engineers, and managers in the Soviet nuclear-power industry had pretended for years that a loss-of-coolant accident was unlikely to the point of impossibility in an RBMK. They knew better. The industry had been plagued with disasters and near-disasters since its earliest days. All of them had been covered up, treated as state secrets; information about them was denied not only to the Soviet public but even to the industry's managers and operators. Engineering is based on experience, including operating experience; treating design flaws and accidents as state secrets meant that every other similar nuclear-power station remained vulnerable and unprepared.

Unknown to the Soviet public and the world, at least thirteen serious power-reactor accidents had occurred in the Soviet Union before the one at Chernobyl. Between 1964 and 1979, for example, repeated fuel-assembly fires plagued Reactor Number One at the Beloyarsk nuclear-power plant east of the Urals near Novosibirsk. In 1975, the core of an RBMK reactor at the Leningrad plant partly melted down; cooling the core by flooding it with liquid nitrogen led to a discharge of radiation into the environment equivalent to about one-twentieth the amount that was released at Chernobyl in 1986. In 1982, a rupture of the central fuel assembly of Chernobyl Reactor Number One released radioactivity over the nearby bedroom community of Pripyat, now in 1986 once again exposed and at risk. In 1985, a steam relief valve burst during a shaky startup of Reactor Number One at the Balakovo nuclear-power plant, on the Volga River about 150 miles southwest of Samara, jetting 500-degree steam that scalded to death fourteen members of the start-up staff; despite the accident, the responsible official, Balakovo's plant director, Viktor Bryukhanov, was promoted to supervise construction at Chernobyl and direct its operation.

Now in the night someone called Bryukhanov from the power plant to tell him that "something awful has happened—some sort of explosion." He rushed to the scene thinking he would have to deal with another steam-valve rupture, but when he saw Number Four ruined and smoking, fires burning on the roof, fire trucks everywhere, he said later, "my heart stood still." He claimed he called Moscow for permission to order an immediate evacuation, without finding anyone in authority willing to believe that such an accident could happen to an RBMK. Whether he contacted Moscow or not, he waited until four in the morning—three and a half hours after the explosions—to alert the authority nearest the plant, Kiev Regional Civil Defense, and then reported only the roof fires, which he told Kiev would soon be extinguished.

They were, by firemen from Pripyat and from Chernobyl town, eleven miles from the power station. Firemen arrived within seven minutes of the explosions; by four a.m. eighty-one engines and 186 firemen had joined the first responders, most of the men working on the roof in ordinary fireman's gear, directing water onto the fires and moving intensely radioactive blocks and chunks of graphite over the side with wheelbarrows, shovels, and their bare hands. Despite the danger, no one ordered Reactor Number Three shut down. Doing so might have been unsafe. It continued operating through the night, the control-room operators wearing respirators for the little protection they gave. Saving Number Three's roof from collapse became the firefighters' first priority. By seven a.m. they had extinguished all the roof fires, but Number Four was still a red-hot crater, billowing smoke.

The first information known to have reached Moscow was a coded signal, "1-2-3-4," sent to Soviet civil-defense headquarters about two hours after the explosions. The numbers invoked the highest state of emergency, an accident involving nuclear, radiation, fire, and explosion effects. The Soviet nuclear-power industry was managed by the Ministry of Medium Machine Building, the branch of the Soviet military-industrial complex that was also responsible for producing nuclear weapons. That ministry contacted Nikolai Ivanovich Ryzhkov, the Politburo member responsible for Soviet industry, and he in turn alerted Gorbachev. Gorbachev hastily assembled the Politburo in an emergency meeting. By noon on Saturday, just as Shushkevich, in Minsk, was learning that a reactor had exploded, the Politburo had appointed a government fact-finding commission whose members—scientists, physicians, engineers, and high Party officials—were instructed to meet at Moscow's Vnukovo Airport at four p.m. From there they flew to Kiev, where a long line of black government ZIL limousines waited to deliver them to Pripyat. It was eight o'clock Saturday evening before they arrived. A member of the commission, a fifty-year-old physicist named Valery Legasov, the first deputy director of the Kurchatov Institute of Atomic Energy in Moscow and a former member of the RBMK reactor design team, described the conditions they found: "The reactor premises were destroyed, several hundred people had received radiation injuries, two people had been killed and the remainder of the shift of workers on duty at the time of the accident were hospitalized."

Legasov was detailed by the commission leader to organize putting out the reactor fire. He saw immediately that the station managers and local officials were unprepared for a disaster on such a major scale and had no idea what to do; "they had no guidelines written earlier and were incapable of making any decisions on the spot." The government commissioners improvised, discussing options among themselves and consulting by phone with the Kurchatov Institute and the Ministry of Energy in Moscow. With the roof fires out, they could confirm that the reactor itself was burning, "a *white pil-lar* several hundred meters high," Legasov emphasized, "consisting of burning products constantly flying from the crater of the reactor," and down in the reactor itself "individual spots of deep crimson luminescence." A large mass of graphite burns at the rate of about 2,200 pounds per hour; since there were about 5.5 million pounds of graphite in the reactor, if it was allowed simply to burn itself out it would continue to spew its radioactivity into the environment for more than ten days.

In some desperation, lacking any other means of limiting the fire—water would dissociate in the intense heat into oxygen and hydrogen, feeding combustion—Legasov and his colleagues decided to try to smother it from the air. The only immediately available material with which to do so was sand from a riverside quarry. The Pripyat town committee was delegated to round up 150 spades and an equivalent number of local young people. At around eleven on Saturday evening a truckload of sacks arrived at the quarry, but the load included no twine for tying the sacks once they were filled. Someone remembered a stock of red calico the town kept for festival decorations, and strips of red calico soon brightened the mounting pile of sandbags.

Early on Sunday morning, 27 April, the Kiev district chief of air staff, Major General N. T. Antoshkin, arrived by car to supervise the assault. Antoshkin called in a squadron of big Soviet Mi-8 workhorse helicopters. The drops began on Sunday afternoon. "The first flights were the most difficult," Antoshkin told the Tass news service later. "Picture a crater of very limited proportions, to which one must first select the shortest possible route, after which one must try to drop a bag of sand in a precise spot, all in a matter of seconds. The pilots proved to be topnotch in these peaceful bombing runs." A flight engineer, speaking of his pilot, described a grimmer scenario:

> [At 110 meters (360 feet) above the blown-out reactor] the radiometer registered 500 roentgen* per hour.... The helicopter hung over the crater ... he opened the door. He could feel the heat from below. A mighty torrent of radioactive gas ... rose up. All this without respirators. The helicopter was not protected underneath with lead. They only began to think about that later,

---

* Roentgen, rad, and rem are roughly comparable measures of radiation. A whole-body exposure of 20–100 rem will result in a temporary reduction in white blood cells; of 100–200 rem, vomiting, diarrhea, fatigue, and reduction in resistance to infection; of 200–300 rem, serious radiation sickness with symptoms as with 100–200 rem and 10 to 35 percent mortality in thirty days; of 300–400 rem, serious radiation sickness, destruction of bone marrow and gastrointestinal tissue, and 50 to 70 percent mortality in thirty days; of 400–1,000 rem, acute illness and 60 to 95 percent mortality in thirty days. Above 1,000 rem, 100 percent of the victims will die within days. (Source: The Atomic Archive.)

when hundreds of tonnes [i.e., metric tons] had already been off-loaded. At first, however, they stuck their heads out through the open door to aim at the nuclear crater and threw the sacks. . . .

Pilots protected themselves by stuffing lead plates under their seats. They coined a slogan to suit the circumstances: "If you want to be a dad, cover your balls with lead."

Despite the late start, the helicopter crews flew ninety-three drops on that Sunday, dumping about one hundred thousand pounds of sand into the crater. Each crew member received 20 to 80 rads of radiation on each flight. "The first twenty-seven crews," the flight engineer concludes, "soon had to be sent to Kiev for treatment" of radiation sickness. Chernobyl death and disability figures have never included military personnel, even though as many as 340,000 would participate in the resulting area-wide cleanup by the end of 1986; despite the promises of glasnost, the number of those who died or were disabled has not been revealed. "They flung us there," one soldier said, "like sand onto the reactor." Helicopter dumping operations continued throughout June, with several other materials added to the formula: clay to quench the fire and absorb hot particles; boron carbide to capture neutrons to slow what was presumed to be a continuing chain reaction; crushed dolomite, a soft marble that releases carbon dioxide when heated, to blanket the fire with inert gas; lead shot to melt and boil (at 3,172°F.) to absorb heat. Up to 10 May, more than eleven million pounds of material were dumped into the reactor; another twenty-six million pounds were dumped through the end of June.

NOT ONLY PREPARATIONS FOR HELICOPTER DROPS began on Saturday night. Pripyat, with a population of forty-five thousand, was only two miles northwest of the burning reactor. No one had warned the people to stay indoors that day; many had gone about their business, shopping, walking dogs, encouraging their children to play outside in the warm spring sunlight. Radiation levels were low in the morning in Pripyat, about 0.1 rem per hour. But as the burning reactor got hotter, the melting fuel elements vaporized an increasing inventory of radionuclides. By nine p.m., the level in the Pripyat street nearest the power station had reached 1.4 rem per hour. Physicists on the government commission warned of higher levels to come, and at about eleven p.m. the commissioners decided to order the town evacuated. Not long after midnight a column of 1,216 large city buses—most of them yellow Icarus double buses—and about three hundred trucks left Kiev for Pripyat, a column of transport almost ten miles long. The drivers had been sworn to secrecy.

On Sunday morning, the evacuation was announced four times on local radio. It was set for two p.m. "Have your papers, indispensable things and, if possible, rations for three days, with you," the townspeople were told. The evacuation turned out to be permanent, as the authorities who ordered it probably knew in advance it would be; whatever was left behind—savings passbooks, family photographs, clothing, furniture, family pets—was lost. By the time the townspeople boarded the buses, many of the women wearing only light dresses or even bathrobes, the radiation level in the streets had reached a dangerous 10 rem per hour. The convoy carried them west into the villages of the Polissia and Ivankiv districts of the Ukraine, where they were housed uncomfortably among the population. Someone realized the buses would have to be decontaminated before they could be returned to Kiev; in a day and a half the Ukraine Republic Motor Repair and Construction Association assembled a fully equipped open-air decontamination center in a field outside the city to receive them. Chernobyl town (with a population of 12,000), the rural countryside and, eventually, an exclusion zone thirty kilometers (nineteen miles) out in every direction from the power station were permanently cleared of people and livestock. Family pets that were left behind in the zone either suffered the depredations of a burgeoning population of wolves or were shot.

During the morning of the Pripyat evacuation, the town council sent high school girls door-to-door dispensing potassium-iodide tablets to the townspeople. The tablets came from civil-defense supplies. They were meant to protect the population from a radioactive form of iodine that made up fully half the volume of the radionuclides boiling out of Reactor Number Four in the first days after the explosions—iodine-131 (^{131}I), a fission product that emits beta and gamma radiation when it decays. The half-life of ^{131}I is only eight days (meaning that half of the atoms in a given quantity decay away every eight days, transmuting into xenon), but the shorter half-life indicates that its radiation is correspondingly more intense. The thyroid gland, wrapped around the neck below the larynx, takes up iodine from the bloodstream and uses it to make thyroid hormone. The gland does not discriminate between stable and radioactive forms of iodine. In theory, then, flooding the thyroid with stable iodine from potassium-iodide tablets should protect the gland from taking up radioactive iodine, being irradiated and irradiating the surrounding tissue. Thus the Pripyat Sunday morning distribution.

It was well intended, but it was probably too late. Potassium iodide administered up to two days before exposure to ^{131}I protects the thyroid gland almost completely. But potassium iodide taken more than eight hours after exposure is only marginally effective, especially if normal dietary iodine intake is inadequate—as it was in the Chernobyl region, where goiter (thyroid enlargement) is still common because low levels of iodine in the soil leave locally grown food and milk deficient.

Potassium-iodide prophylaxis had been one of Stanislav Shushkevich's urgent first thoughts when he and his colleagues at the institute had confirmed on Saturday afternoon that a reactor had exploded at Chernobyl. "In every civil-defense shelter in the Soviet Union there was information on what to do to deal with radioactive fallout," he told me, "and a supply of potassium iodide tablets. They were supposed to be distributed as quickly as possible in appropriate doses, especially to children." The director of the institute, Valery Nesterenko, happened to be visiting Moscow when he learned of Chernobyl. "I called Nikolai Slyunkov, the general secretary of the Central Committee of the Byelorussian Communist Party in Minsk," Nesterenko said later. He kept calling for two hours before Slyunkov's assistant put him through. He told Slyunkov the accident was serious and a radioactive cloud was moving toward Byelorussia. "We need to immediately perform an iodine prophylaxis of the population," he warned, "and evacuate everyone near the station."

Slyunkov was unimpressed. "I've already received reports," he informed Nesterenko. "There was a fire, but they've put it out."

Nesterenko exploded. "That's a lie! It's a blatant lie!" Slyunkov wouldn't budge. Greatly worried, Nesterenko took the first train home. In Minsk he measured his son's thyroid—"that was the ideal dosimeter then," he told the journalist Svetlana Alexievich bitterly—and found it slightly radioactive. He, Shushkevich, and the other scientists at the institute began warning people.

When Nesterenko finally got to see Slyunkov in person, the following week, the Party boss challenged him: "Why are your men running around town with their dosimeters, scaring everyone? I've already consulted with Moscow, with Professor Ilyin, chairman of the Soviet Radiological Protection Board. He says everything's normal. And there's a government commission at the station, and the prosecutor's office is there. We've thrown the army, all our military equipment, into the breach."

"Every political entity had a civil defense unit," Shushkevich explained, "that was supposed to know what to do with a radiation incident. They had rules developed by scientists and supported by government agencies. But everybody waited for an order, and none came, only a statement that it had been 'an insignificant accident.' "

Nesterenko discovered that the Byelorussian leadership was secretly taking iodine. "When my colleagues at the institute gave them checkups, their
thyroids were clean. Without iodine that's impossible. And they quietly got
their kids out of there too, just in case." At the same time, he said, "they took
away all the institute's radiation-measuring equipment. They just confis-
cated it, without any explanations. I began receiving threatening phone calls
at home. 'Quit scaring people, professor. You'll end up in a bad place.' "

Shushkevich and Nesterenko both blamed Gorbachev. "I'd bet there'd
been a call from the Kremlin," Nesterenko speculated, "right from Gorbachev, saying, you know, 'I hope you Byelorussians can keep from starting a
panic.' . . . And of course if you didn't please your higher-ups, you didn't get
that promotion, that trip abroad, that dacha." Shushkevich underwent what
he calls "a sad evolution." If he had been the first at the university to hang
Gorbachev's portrait on the wall, the attempted cover-up of Chernobyl in
those first days and weeks after the accident made him furious: "I understood that was treason." When Gorbachev finally spoke publicly about Chernobyl in mid-May, claiming that "the worst is over" and "the most serious
consequences have been averted," Shushkevich was appalled. "That was the
end of my respect for Gorbachev. His advisers had to have told him of the
seriousness of the accident. From that day on I hated him." In time, Shushkevich's "sad evolution" would lead him into politics, and his loss of faith in
Gorbachev would have the largest consequences.

THROUGH SATURDAY AND SUNDAY, despite the frantic efforts at Chernobyl, the evacuation of Pripyat's entire population, the extensive casualties,
and the plume of radiation advancing into Finland and Sweden, no public
announcement issued from the Kremlin. In his memoirs, Gorbachev implicitly blames the government commission for the delay, writing that its reports
"consisted mainly of preliminary fact-finding, with all kinds of cautious
remarks but without any conclusions at all." Whether or not Gorbachev was
misled, a better measure of the Soviet government's initial response is that
sometime on Sunday, the editors of *Izvestia*, the government-controlled
newspaper, were ordered to suppress a story about the accident. Kiev went
unwarned. So did Minsk. So did Europe. "In those first days," a village teacher
in Byelorussia wrote later, "there were mixed feelings. I remember two: fear
and insult. Everything had happened and there was no information: the government was silent, the doctors were silent. The regions waited for directions
from the *oblast* [i.e., province], the *oblast* from Minsk, and Minsk from

Moscow. It was a long, long chain, and at the end of it a few people made the decisions. We turned out to be defenseless. That was the main feeling in those days. Just a few people were deciding our fate, the fate of millions."

Curiously, a U.S. spy satellite had passed over the Chernobyl complex on Saturday morning only twenty-eight seconds after the explosions and had imaged it. American intelligence thought at first that a missile had been fired, reports health physicist and Chernobyl expert Richard Mould. When the image remained stationary, "opinion changed to a missile had blown up in its silo." Consulting a map corrected the mistake. By Sunday the British government had been informed, but neither the United States nor Britain warned the public.

The plume of radionuclides from Chernobyl had continued moving northward and westward throughout the weekend of 26 to 27 April, its fallout dusting Poland, the Baltics, and Finland. Finland detected plume radiation early Sunday afternoon, when Helsinki recorded levels of six times normal background,* but the Finns decided to investigate more thoroughly before announcing their finding. At about the same time, the plume crossed into Sweden. It went undetected until early Monday morning, 28 April, when staff arriving at a Studsvik corporation energy research laboratory on the Baltic coast about fifty miles southwest of Stockholm measured radiation levels higher than normal. Morning arrivals at the Forsmark nuclear-power plant sixty miles north of Stockholm made a similar discovery, measuring radiation levels 150 times background. Forsmark contacted the Studsvik lab midmorning, and samples retrieved from air filters, Studsvik scientists later reported, "combined with a knowledge of the wind direction, allowed us to confirm . . . that the contamination was caused by a release from a nuclear reactor east of Sweden and not from nuclear weapons." Though the Soviet government might prefer to keep its nuclear accidents secret, the plume of radiation pouring out of Reactor Number Four was broadcasting the truth.

The samples ruled out an exploding nuclear weapon because nuclear weapons and nuclear power plants each produce a characteristic and distinct spectrum of fission products. Studying filter samples, Studsvik determined that the reactor fuel had been in active use for about four hundred days.

---

* Radiation occurs everywhere on Earth. It issues from long-lived elements such as uranium and thorium that permeate the earth's crust and are dissolved in seawater. Cosmic rays continually rain down from space, their intensity varying with altitude. The human body carries a load of radioactive potassium acquired from food and drink. Radon gas, a natural decay product of radium (itself a decay product of uranium), spills from house foundations and granite walls. These and other sources produce "background" radiation—naturally occurring rather than man-made (the two kinds are indistinguishable)—that varies at different locations across the earth from extremely low levels below 1 millisievert (0.1 rem) to above 280 mSv (28 rem). (One sievert equals 100 rem.) (Source: Jaworowski, 1999, p. 25.)

(Chernobyl Reactor Number Four had reached the end of a fuel cycle and had been scheduled for a maintenance shutdown the week after the accident.) The lab found highly radioactive microscopic particles of fallout—"hot spots"—contaminating the grounds, some of which consisted of spheres of pure ruthenium, a silvery metal fission product. Ruthenium melts at 4,082°F.; uranium at 2,070°F.; and zirconium, the metal of the fuel's cladding, at 3,360°F.; all three had melted and vaporized. That morning, Sweden announced to the world that a Soviet reactor had melted down and was spreading its radiation across Europe. The world media responded; for the next weeks Chernobyl was the lead story of print and broadcast news.

The government commission had reported to Moscow on Sunday. Ryzhkov carried the report into the regular Monday morning Politburo meeting. What to do about the report occasioned intense debate. In the past, every nuclear accident had been treated as a state secret; acknowledging the accident publicly would be an unprecedented change of policy. Eduard Shevardnadze, Gorbachev's foreign minister and old friend, had quoted the general secretary at a public event just the previous week speaking out in favor of glasnost: "We categorically oppose those who call for releasing public information in doses," Gorbachev had said; "there can never be too much truth." Denying Chernobyl was absurd, Shevardnadze argued, an affront to common sense: "How can you conceal something that can't be hidden? How could people complain about 'washing our dirty linen in public' when it was radioactive and had slipped out in spite of us?" From the standpoint of politics, Shevardnadze thought that trying to maintain secrecy would be "outright sabotage of the principles of the new thinking."

The Soviet system's seemingly pathological obsession with secrecy had emerged from its messianic conception of authority. "Possessed by a unique sense of its own destiny," the former Soviet military economist Vitaliy Shlykov wrote, "and hoping to establish a new world order 'free of capitalistic exploitation,' the communist leadership of the country saw a military confrontation with the rest of the world as inevitable. To be prepared for that confrontation, the Soviet State had to be turned into a permanent military camp." This ideological interpretation of reality, which emerged in the 1920s, had far-reaching consequences:

> It was decided that the equipment of the Red Army had to be based on dual-use technologies, i.e., those applicable to both military and civilian needs. The civilian aviation and automobile and tractor industries were expected to provide the basis for mass production of military aircraft and tanks, and they were explicitly organized and equipped to do so. For instance . . . new types of auto-

mobiles were allowed to go into production only if [the factories] could meet the standards of tank production. This was supposed to make the mobilization of civilian industry in wartime relatively easy.

The RBMK reactor was a dual-use design. It was developed in the 1950s as a production reactor to produce plutonium for nuclear weapons, then adapted for civilian power operation in the 1970s; Like its graphite core, its *pyatachok* was punctured with multiple channels from which irradiated fuel rods could be removed via an overhead crane while the reactor was operating. If the military needed plutonium, on-line refueling would allow fuel rods to be removed early to maximize their bloom of military-grade plutonium.* A safety containment structure around such a reactor, which would probably have prevented an accident like the one at Chernobyl, would have also greatly reduced its military value. Military needs thus competed with civilian needs in the choice of the RBMK design when the Soviet Union decided to greatly expand electricity production with nuclear power in the early 1970s; a competing light-water reactor design, the Soviet VVER, was safer but less suitable for the production of military-grade plutonium. The RBMK design was adapted for civilian use primarily for economic and logistic reasons—the concrete and graphite reactors drew on different industrial resources than the steel VVERs did—but their dual-use potential weighted the decision as well. From the perspective of the Politburo's old guard, then, publicly discussing an accident at a Soviet nuclear power plant, especially one that revealed such serious design flaws, would be no less subversive than revealing the location and fitness of an army in the middle of a war.

Unfortunately, Gorbachev knew very little about nuclear physics or the Soviet nuclear-power industry. His adviser Anatoly Chernyaev, who attended every Politburo meeting on Chernobyl that year, insists that the champion of glasnost made no effort to cover up the accident but made the mistake, common to the Soviet leadership, of trusting the experts. Faced with what Shevardnadze would call the "unsheathed . . . claws" of the Politburo opposition, Gorbachev relied on the advice of senior scientists and managers such as Anatoly Alexandrov, the eighty-three-year-old president of the U.S.S.R.

---

* Uranium-238, the bulk of the uranium in a nuclear reactor, does not undergo fission under slow-neutron bombardment and does not chain-react; the active portion of natural uranium is a rare isotope, uranium-235. When ^{238}U absorbs a neutron, however, it can transmute to a man-made element of atomic number 93, neptunium, which transmutes further within days to a man-made element of atomic number 94, plutonium, which does chain-react and is an even more efficient explosive for atomic bombs than the rare fissile form of uranium, ^{235}U. A ton of natural uranium fuel in the American World War II–era graphite-moderated production reactors produced, after several months' operation, about a dime's volume of plutonium.

Academy of Sciences and the physicist who had directed RBMK design. Gorbachev complains bitterly in his memoirs that immediately after the accident Alexandrov and the powerful minister of Medium Machine Building, Yefim Slavsky, misled the Politburo, claiming (in Gorbachev's sarcastic parody): "Nothing terrible has occurred. These things happen at nuclear reactors. Just drink a little vodka, have a bite to eat, have a good night's sleep—forget it."

Confronted with stiff resistance within the Politburo, ill-informed himself, and badly advised by his experts, with the Swedish ambassador clamoring for more information, Gorbachev compromised and agreed to the broadcast of a simple, misleading statement on national television at nine p.m. that Monday night:

> From the USSR Council of Ministers: An accident has occurred at the Chernobyl nuclear power plant—one of the atomic reactors has been damaged. Measures are being undertaken to liquidate the consequences of the accident. Those affected are being given aid, and a government commission has been created.

It was a grudging beginning, but it opened a crack in the monolith that the full flood of world attention soon forced wide.

Hans Blix, the Swedish diplomat, who had trained at Columbia University in international law, was the director-general of the United Nations' International Atomic Energy Agency (IAEA) at that time. Blix, in Vienna, remembers hearing about the Chernobyl accident on the same Monday that the Politburo met. "I was phoned by the Swedish minister of energy," he told me. "I then phoned around to Poland and other places, and on about Monday evening I heard from the Russians. Then they went public about it." One outcome of the Monday Politburo meeting was the appointment of a strategic group to follow and direct Chernobyl recovery operations from day to day. The group met for the first time on Tuesday. Its chairman was Nikolai Ryzhkov, a Gorbachev ally. Another prominent member was Central Committee secretary Alexander Yakovlev, one of the principal theoreticians behind Gorbachev's ambitious program of reforms. They more than counterbalanced Yegor Ligachev, a conservative who favored Gorbachev's reforms only so long as they sustained the Communist Party's leadership over the U.S.S.R. Blix told the Soviets that the IAEA was prepared to help in any way possible. Before the week was out, he was invited to travel to Moscow with a team of experts. Whether he and his team would be allowed to view the accident scene he did not yet know, but he prepared to pack his bags.

Pravda began publishing regular reports on the Chernobyl accident on 30 April—a major breakthrough for glasnost. On 1 May, Thursday, it reported that "the emission of radioactive substances has decreased, and radiation levels in the area of the atomic power station and in the station settlement [i.e., Pripyat] have gone down," which was true—temporarily. *Pravda* also claimed that as a result of the accident "two people died and a total of 197 were hospitalized; 49 of them have been discharged from the hospital after examination. Enterprises, collective farms, state farms and other institutions are operating normally." But evacuations of the rural areas around the Chernobyl plant were ongoing that week, so that by the next day, Friday, a ten-kilometer (6.2-mile) exclusion zone had been emptied of people and domestic animals, and there would soon be evidence that more casualties had been sustained than the numbers cited in official reports.

Ryzhkov and Ligachev traveled to Chernobyl that Friday to review the situation firsthand. They were just in time to hear of a new and imminent threat. By then the helicopters had dumped more than eleven million pounds of materials onto the reactor. The tons of sand, clay, lead, dolomite, and boron piled into the crater failed to seal it completely, however; the reactor was still sufficiently exposed to allow the chimney of air pulled up through the core's empty water channels to continue fanning the graphite fire. And since the pile of material was now so massive that it held in the heat, the temperature of the core had begun to rise, eventually reaching about 4,500°F. Superheated gas and particulates filtered up through the ruins, renewing the radioactive plume, and the level of radioactivity, which had been declining steadily, began again to increase. (On Monday it reached a level nearly as high as it had been on the first day of the accident.) Ryzhkov and Ligachev acted immediately: they ordered the exclusion zone enlarged from a ten-kilometer to a thirty-kilometer (nineteen-mile) radius, increasing the area to be evacuated by more than 1,000 square miles, including the town of Chernobyl, which dated back to the twelfth century and was a center of Hasidism. The journalist Svetlana Alexievich later interviewed a soldier who participated in the evacuations and remembered them vividly:

> At first there was disbelief, this sense that it was a game. But it was a real war, an atomic war. We had no idea—what's dangerous and what's not, what should we watch out for, and what ignore? No one knew.
>
> It was a real evacuation, right to the train stations. . . . We helped push kids through the windows of the train cars. We made the lines orderly—for tickets at the ticket window, for iodine at the pharmacy. In the lines people were swearing at one another and fighting. They broke the doors down on stores and stands. They broke the metal grates in the windows. . . .

great in emergen-
in those times the
Dutch or German.
But there'll always

Ir   six thousand head of
c   haphazardly, because
h   scarce. "We didn't just
l   ole lives."

ourning reactor intensi-
the globe, it also threat-
n the reactor core. The
d it against the weakened
the water-filled shielding
torian Zhores Medvedev

r pool of water which was
ore powerful explosion and
um, plutonium and large
only about 3 or 4 percent of
released into the environ-
ore was blown out and scat-
e destroyed reactor core was
en greater catastrophe there
pool and to freeze the earth

its had brought in oil-drilling
oil below the reactor. Through
at the rate of about one thou-
s—per day to freeze the soil
trogen injected into the spaces
around the core vap   at soon smothered the fire. But
putting out the fire had no effect on the increasing heat generated by the
decaying fission products in the reactor's remaining fuel. Over the night of 6
to 7 May, sharply shadowed in floodlights, sweat-soaked in dark green ZZK
protective suits and echoing gas masks that allowed only twenty-four min-

utes each of exposure to the intense radioactivity of the blown-out reactor, the engineers pumped five million gallons of water out of the bubbler pool. In the coming days they used shaped-charge explosives to blow holes through the concrete foundation, laid pipe into the empty pool, and pumped in enough concrete to fill it to a solid block. To prevent flooding in the late May rains, which might wash radioactivity down the Pripyat River into the Kiev Reservoir, engineer units built five miles of earthen dams and barriers along the river and lined them with polyethylene sheeting. That spring, half a million cubic yards of mud and sand were dredged from the Pripyat riverbed and replaced with gravel to trap radioactive runoff.

Eight days after the accident, on Sunday, 4 May, Gorbachev had still not discussed Chernobyl publicly. "We sat in front of the television for days," a young woman who lived just outside the thirty-kilometer exclusion zone told Alexievich, "waiting for Gorbachev to speak. The authorities didn't say anything." *Pravda*, citing the U.S.S.R. Council of Ministers, continued to underplay the numbers of casualties. On 2 May it had admitted to eighteen people "in serious condition" and said there were "no foreign citizens among the victims." But secret protocols of the Politburo strategic group's meetings reveal much higher numbers. One of the few protocols made public, dated 4 May, reported that "1,882 people were treated in hospital [on that day]. The total number of people treated reached 38,000. Two hundred four people were discovered to have been affected to greater or lesser degrees by irradiation syndrome, of whom 64 were children. Eighteen are in serious condition."

Blix arrived in Moscow on Tuesday, 6 May, with two IAEA nuclear experts, an American and a Russian. The delegation, thoroughly briefed by Soviet officials and scientists, watched a film shot from one of the helicopters that surveyed the damaged reactor and heard from eyewitnesses who had reached the Chernobyl complex within a few hours of the explosions. But the vital question for Blix was whether or not he would be allowed to visit the accident site itself. "I know in retrospect," he says, "that the question went to the Politburo and that Mr. Gorbachev himself had argued that, yes, they should be invited, while others felt that the traditional policy of secrecy should be continued." Gorbachev won the argument, extending glasnost that much further; Blix and his team would fly to Kiev on Thursday.

Tuesday also saw the first official news conference devoted to the disaster, organized by the Soviet Ministry of Foreign Affairs. Shevardnadze sponsored such an unprecedented revelation, he writes, "so that the truth about Chernobyl would be known to the country and to the whole world." He adds that he "was not able to do much." At least Kiev was apprised that day—for the first time, ten days late—about the fallout risk. Tuesday's secret Politburo strategic group protocol reported that "the number of people treated in hospital [on 6 May] rose to 3,454; among these, 2,609 were admitted, of whom 471 were children. According to more precise figures, the number of people affected by irradiation syndrome is 367 people, of whom 19 are children. Of these, 34 are in a serious condition. One hundred and seventy-nine people have been admitted to six Moscow hospitals, of whom two are children." Gorbachev himself attended the Wednesday meeting of the strategic group and heard that "in one day, the list of people treated in hospital rose by 1,821. By . . . 7 May the number of people admitted to hospital had reached 4,301, of whom 1,351 were children. In 520 of these, irradiation syndrome was diagnosed, including people working for the Ministry of the Interior of the USSR [i.e., the KGB]. The number of people whose condition is serious is 34." He could not claim not to have been informed.

The IAEA team toured Kiev and then helicoptered north to the Chernobyl complex. "We circled the whole site," Blix told me, "and saw the black smoke coming up from the graphite, and then we had extensive briefings by the Russians about what had happened." Andranik Petrosyants, the head of the Soviet atomic energy program, who was traveling with Blix, remembered that "the helicopter made two rounds of the destroyed reactor building. We did not fly directly over the reactor itself, but circumvented it to avoid the high radioactivity. The reactor was smothered with debris, including lead, dropped from helicopters, and though smoke was still seeping from the burning wooden and other structures, it was clear the fire was over." Blix's dosimeter registered a hazardous 3.5 rem per hour, however, fire or no. "And then we went back to Moscow and we had a huge press conference there," Blix recalls. "We thought our main job was to inform the outside world by objective statements and understanding and we did. However, somewhat to my surprise I found that maybe our impressions were even more important in Russia, because the Russian population had not believed a word of what their own authorities said. But they believed outside people coming from an international organization. So it calmed the atmosphere, because they thought it was even worse than it was. It was bad enough."

In our conversation about Chernobyl, Blix emphasized twice that he had not gone to Moscow to "scream" at the Soviet leaders but to help them. Certainly the rest of the world was screaming by then, with minimal but measurable quantities of Chernobyl radionuclides falling out around the world and particularly on Western Europe; the Chernobyl fallout was roughly equivalent to the fallout from a twelve-megaton nuclear explosion (the explosions themselves had been equivalent to about thirty to forty tons of TNT). Blix's statements did help, and in exchange for them he extracted historic agreements from Gorbachev to make available timely information about the accident and its aftermath. "The Soviet authorities agreed," he said later, "to provide daily information on radiation levels from seven measurement stations, one close to Chernobyl and the other six along the Western border of the USSR." They agreed as well to participate in a post-accident review meeting and to increase cooperation in the field of nuclear safety. "It is sad, but a common experience," Blix concludes, "that only big accidents or other setbacks will provide the necessary impetus to move governments and authorities to act."

In this context, as in so many others, Chernobyl was exceptional. "It was the first time in Soviet history," Zhores Medvedev comments, "that an offer was made to put records of Soviet technology and details of an accident before the international scientific community for analysis and judgment."* Gorbachev judged the political effects of the accident to be mixed. On the one hand, it "shed light on many of the sicknesses of our system as a whole. Everything that had built up over the years converged in this drama: the concealing or hushing up of accidents and other bad news, irresponsibility and carelessness, slipshod work, wholesale drunkenness. This was one more convincing argument in favor of radical reforms." On the other hand, Chernobyl "severely affected our reforms by literally knocking the country off its tracks."

After their press conference on Friday, 9 May, Blix and his colleagues left Moscow to return to Vienna. And finally, on the following Wednesday, 14 May, eighteen days after the accident and one day after preparations had been announced to end school early for the 370,000 children of Kiev Province and send them south for the summer to work-and-recreation camps, a haggard Gorbachev appeared on Moscow evening television to deliver an unprecedented speech. "A misfortune has befallen us," he began,

* A conference for this purpose was held in Vienna under IAEA sponsorship in August 1986, where the physicist Valery Legasov spoke without notes and in unprecedented detail for almost five hours. Ultimately, however, the accident was blamed on the Reactor Number Four operators. Since it occurred in the course of an equipment test that should have been carried out before the reactor was certified for operation, and resulted from disconnecting the reactor's safety backup systems, the operators and plant management were certainly at fault, and were punished accordingly, with prison terms. But the reactor's flawed design, which made it unstable at low power and prone to running away to prompt criticality, should have indicted its designers and sponsors in the military-industrial complex as well. (See Yaroshinskaya, 1995, pp. 94–99.)

but with the old guard looking over his shoulder he went on to assert, falsely, that "this is the first time we have had to deal with a force as powerful as nuclear energy that has gone out of control." The secret Politburo protocol for 12 May had listed 10,198 people "admitted to hospital for observation or treatment, of whom 345 [including thirty-five children] show symptoms of radiation syndrome," but in his speech Gorbachev claimed that only 299 people had been hospitalized, "diagnosed as having radiation sickness at varying degrees of gravity." He praised the workers who were struggling "to eliminate the consequences of the accident" and the neighbors in the provinces outside the exclusion zone who received the evacuees into their homes. Implicitly he revealed the reason he had delayed so long before speaking publicly about the accident: to be able "to say today that the worst is over. The most serious consequences have been averted." He thanked Blix and the IAEA and "our friends in socialist countries" for their support.

Then, reverting again to old-style Cold War rhetoric, he warned the Soviet people that "certain NATO [North Atlantic Treaty Organization] countries, especially the USA," had launched "a wanton anti-Soviet campaign" that had piled up "a veritable mountain of lies—most brazen and malicious lies" about Chernobyl, such as "thousands of casualties," "mass graves of the dead" and "Kiev deserted." They were looking for a pretext, he said, that could be used "to try to defame the Soviet Union and its foreign policy, to lessen the impact of Soviet proposals on the termination of nuclear tests and on the elimination of nuclear weapons"—referring to the voluntary Soviet moratorium on weapons tests, begun in 1985, that the United States had pointedly not matched, and his bold January proposal to Ronald Reagan to eliminate all nuclear weapons before the end of the century.

Swinging back to his program of reform, Gorbachev then spoke with feeling of the impact of the Chernobyl nuclear accident on his understanding of the perils of nuclear war:

> For all this, it should not be forgotten that in our world, where everything is interrelated, problems with the military atom exist alongside those of the peaceful atom. . . . The accident at Chernobyl showed again what an abyss will open if nuclear war befalls mankind. The stockpiled nuclear arsenals are fraught with thousands upon thousands of disasters far more horrible than the one at Chernobyl.

Whereupon he announced that his government would extend its unilateral moratorium on nuclear tests until 6 August 1986, the forty-first anniversary of the U.S. atomic bombing of Hiroshima—a pointed reminder of the destructive force of even a small nuclear weapon, as the thirteen-kiloton bomb exploded over Hiroshima had come to seem.

THE STRUGGLE TO DEAL WITH THE fallout of radionuclides that had contaminated large areas of Soviet territory continued through the summer and fall and across the next winter. When the leaves fell from the chestnut trees that are the glory of Kiev, proud on its high bluff above the Dnieper River, they had to be raked up, all three hundred thousand tons of them, baled and buried outside the city as low-level nuclear waste. "Liquidators" by the hundreds of thousands, perhaps half a million in all—340,000 soldiers, many of them recently returned from service in Afghanistan, new draftees, minor government employees such as teachers and inspectors—were pressed into service and took their brief turn scraping away topsoil, paving over roads, spraying plastic coatings onto schoolyards and fallow fields, burying gardens, houses, equipment, wells. "We buried the forest," one of them told Alexievich. "We sawed the trees into meter-and-a-half pieces and packed them in cellophane and threw them into graves. . . . It was just your average Russian chaos. That's how we live." In November 1986, after a heroic effort, workers finished entombing Reactor Number Four within a sarcophagus made of half a million cubic yards of reinforced concrete, and only then did it cease releasing radiation into the environment.

"More than 500 residential communities, nearly 60,000 buildings and structures, and several tens of millions of square meters of exposed surfaces of technological equipment and internal surfaces at the [nuclear-power plant] itself have been decontaminated," Colonel-General Vladimir Pikalov of the U.S.S.R. Chemical Forces summarized a year later. "Tens of thousands of cubic meters of contaminated soil has been removed and the same amount brought in and several thousand insulating screens have been laid down. Dust has been suppressed on vast territories and several thousand samples have been taken for radioactive isotope analysis."

Shevardnadze came to call 26 April 1986 "Chernobyl Day." It "tore the blindfold from our eyes," he wrote later. It tore the blindfold as well from the eyes of hundreds of thousands of Soviet citizens living in the western Soviet Union. "Chernobyl happened," a Byelorussian biologist told Alexievich, "and suddenly you got this new feeling, we weren't used to it, that everyone has his separate life. Until then no one needed this life. But now you had to think: what are you eating, what are you feeding your kids? What's dangerous, what isn't? Should you move to another place, or should you stay? Everyone had to make her own decisions. And we were used to living—how? As an entire village, as a collective—a factory, a kolkhoz [i.e., a collective farm]. We were Soviet people, we were collectivized.... Then we changed. Everything changed."

Eastern Europe changed. The European Community banned imports of Soviet, Polish, Czechoslovakian, Hungarian, Romanian, and Bulgarian agricultural products worth $500 million annually as of 7 May 1986, inflicting great economic hardship on populations already restive in response to Gorbachev's relaxation of authoritarian control. Ironically, the purpose of recent Soviet nuclear-power development had been to increase electrical capacity available to Eastern Europe. "The decision to accelerate the nuclear-energy program had been taken in 1974," Zhores Medvedev explains, "when the international price of oil rose sharply and export demand increased. Oil became the main source of foreign exchange after 1974. Poor [Soviet] harvests meant that large imports of grain and food were necessary. As a result, the replacement of oil by nuclear energy became a priority." More than any other natural resource, oil propped up the stagnant Soviet economy, but the oil the Soviet Union supplied to Eastern Europe went at subsidized rates. Replacing most of that oil with nuclear electricity would free it up for foreign trade. The new Five-Year Plan that Gorbachev's government had introduced at the 27th Party Congress in February 1986 had called for doubling nuclear-generated electricity, primarily by building reactors in the Ukraine. Those plans were now in doubt.

Shevardnadze concluded that "Chernobyl was the first test of *glasnost,* and it failed." Certainly the disaster was never discussed publicly with the candor that Gorbachev and his advisers claimed. But as the affected population was changed by it, as Eastern Europe was changed, so also was Gorbachev changed. He had been "profoundly realistic" in his attitude toward nuclear proliferation even before Chernobyl, writes the Soviet historian Dmitri Volkogonov: "In April 1985 he had ordered that the North Korean leadership be told that a nuclear reactor being built with Soviet help must be under the control" of the IAEA. "In July of the same year he had informed Colonel Qaddafi that he would not agree to the Soviet-built nuclear research center in Libya being used for the production of heavy water, which could lead to Libya's acquiring nuclear weapons." In the months after Chernobyl, the American analyst William Potter reports, "senior Polish and Hungarian Communist Party officials who had contact with the Soviet political leadership" told him that the accident had a "profound impact . . . on Gorbachev's thinking about the consequences of nuclear war." Gorbachev had said as much in his speech to the Soviet people on 14 May, but the West had dismissed the statement as propaganda. It went much deeper than propaganda, deep as a wound. George Shultz, the secretary of state under the Reagan administration, saw its lasting effect on Gorbachev at a dinner in 1988 and noted it in a memo:

> I was struck by how deeply affected Gorbachev appeared to be by the Chernobyl accident. He commented that it was a great tragedy which cost the Soviet Union billions of rubles and had only been barely overcome through the tireless efforts of an enormous number of people. Gorbachev noted with seemingly genuine horror the devastation that would occur if nuclear power plants became targets in a conventional war much less a full nuclear exchange.

"His mind was undergoing a sweeping 'de-ideologization,'" Gorbachev's adviser Anatoly Chernyaev thought. The Soviet deputy foreign minister Alexander Bessmertnykh commented later that "Chernobyl . . . was something like one-third of the smallest nuclear explosive. And if it caused such great damage to almost half of Europe, what would happen if we should use all those arsenals we now have in our hands?" Gorbachev told a Politburo meeting in July 1986, "Global nuclear war can no longer be the continuation of rational politics, as it would bring the end of all life, and therefore of all politics." And thinking perhaps of Chernobyl, he added, "What happened in this country is that a rigid system was created and then life was herded into it."

TWO MOSCOW DOES NOT BELIEVE IN TEARS

MIKHAIL SERGEYEVICH GORBACHEV, a son of southern Russian farmers, was born in a time and place of neomedieval horror—corpses strewn along the roads and across the fields and starving families reduced to eating horse manure or the flesh of the dead. In medieval times such disastrous conditions would have measured an outbreak of the Black Death; in March 1931, in a western corner of the Stavropol steppe lands of the North Caucasus, over the mountains from Georgia, it measured Joseph Stalin's deliberate starvation of the independent farmers ("peasants," "middle peasants," "kulaks") who dared to resist giving up their hard-won land, animals, and machinery for the unrewarding serfdom of the collective farm. The name of the village where Gorbachev was born, on 2 March 1931, in a two-room wattle-and-daub house with a dirt floor, was Privolnoye, meaning "free and easy," but free and easy it had not been since the late 1920s, when forced collectivization began.

The Communist Party had first given what it was now taking away. "My [maternal] grandfather [Panteli Yefimovich Gopkalo] had been a poor peasant," Gorbachev says, "and beginning from a very early age, after the death of his father, had to be concerned about a family in which there were five children. During World War I my grandfather was on the Turkish front, and he returned from the war with a definitely radical outlook, which was typical of the soldiers at that time. Then after the revolution, when the family was given the land it worked on, my grandfather was won over completely to the side of the Soviet government. In the oral history of our family it was constantly repeated: *the revolution gave our family land.*" (Raisa Maksimovna Titorenko, whom Gorbachev would marry, heard a similar appreciation at home in western Siberia: "*Lenin gave my parents land*—that is what my mother always says. . . .")

Land or not, grandfather Gopkalo cast his lot with the Party from the beginning. The first version of collective farming that the Party endorsed, in the early 1920s, was the Association for the Joint Cultivation of Land, known by its Russian initials as a TOZ; the TOZ were "not really collective farms at all," the historian Robert Conquest notes, "but merely associations for joint tillage, ploughing, harvesting and sharing the proceeds." Gopkalo had signed on immediately, and Gorbachev's mother, Maria Panteleyevna, had worked on a TOZ as a young woman. In 1928, Gopkalo joined the Party. "He participated in organizing our *kolkhoz,* 'Khleborob,' " Gorbachev says of the collective farm his grandfather then helped to establish in Privolnoye, "and was its first chairman." He must have been an exceptional leader: Many if not most kolkhoz chairmen were Party members sent out from the city who couldn't tell a harrow from a plow. "Loyalty to the Party and to its policy in dealing with the farmers," writes a Ukrainian émigré who lived through this era, "were valid enough recommendations for this office." Kolkhoz chairmen were subservient in any case to resident Party leaders, whose veto authority paralleled that of political commissars in the Red Army. But Gopkalo knew farming, which gave him an advantage in trying to fulfill Moscow's increasingly draconian requisitions of grain; in the 1930s, when Gorbachev lived with his maternal grandparents, Gopkalo was promoted to the chairmanship of the larger Red October kolkhoz in a village twelve miles from Privolnoye.

Ironically, the campaign to decapitate the leadership of the rural communities of the Soviet Union, which Stalin called "the liquidation of the kulaks as a class," interfered with collectivization. (Kulaks were supposed to be "the capitalists of the village," but the net was cast wide. Conquest estimates the value of the average kulak's property at $150. "A typical kulak," he says, "would have something like 12 acres, a cow, a horse, 10 sheep, a hog and about 20 chickens, on a farm supporting four people." So-called middle peasants like Gorbachev's grandparents owned even less.) Early in 1930, some ten million small farms were forcibly collectivized in a matter of months, while millions of "kulaks" whose property had been expropriated— 40 percent of them children—were packed into railroad freight cars with little food or water, transported north of the Arctic Circle or into Siberia, and crowded together, starving, in churches, monasteries, and temporary barracks while the able-bodied among them struggled in the northern forests in deep snow and cold to build one of the first bitter islands of the Gulag archipelago. Dmitri Volkogonov, the Soviet historian, estimates that 8.5 to 9 million "men, women, old people and children . . . were affected by dekulakization, most of them torn root and branch from their native habitat. Many were shot for resisting, many died en route. In some places . . . the process also swept up many middle peasants. . . . One way or another something like 6 to 8 percent of peasant households were sucked into the vortex."

The farmers responded to forced collectivization—state appropriation of their property without compensation—and the threat of being designated kulaks and exiled by selling or slaughtering their animals; by March 1930, Conquest writes, "even by official figures, over 40 percent of the country's cattle and 65 percent of the sheep had gone" and "Stalin's policy lay in ruins." When the breaker of nations lifted away his hammer, more than half the farmers who had submitted to collectivization returned to independent farming. Stalin attacked again with orders to deport resisters beginning in February 1931, a month before Gorbachev was born. Conquest specifically mentions "the Stavropol area in the North Caucasus" as a place where farmers trying to escape "drove herds of oxen, dairy cows, horses and sheep from district to district," to no avail. "It is to an activist of this period," Conquest notes, "that the well-known saying is attributed: 'Moscow does not believe in tears.' "

Forcing families to give up their property, forcing them onto collective farms or into exile, was brutal business. If Gorbachev's grandfather Gopkalo participated in organizing and leading a collective farm, he could not have escaped complicity. Nor did collectivized farmers necessarily work willingly. One of Gorbachev's Moscow University roommates, the Czech political leader Zdenek Mlynar, remembers Gorbachev explaining to him "how insignificant farm legislation was in everyday life and how important, on the other hand, was brute force which alone secured working discipline on the collective farms."

"Up to the end of 1931," writes the Ukrainian émigré Miron Dolot, "the Communists fought their war against the farmers under the guise of fighting against 'the [kulaks] as a social class.' But by 1932, the situation had already changed: the so-called [kulaks] had already been physically liquidated, and collectivization had been completed except for a small number of farmers who were still clinging to their freedom. Thus, the battle now was fought between the Communist forces and the collective farmers; the Collectivization Campaign now changed into the Grain Collection Campaign."

In the 1930s, the new Soviet state pursued a program of rapid industrialization, primarily to prepare itself for the war against Fascism and capitalism that Marxist theory declared to be inevitable. "With collectivization" of agriculture, writes Martin Malia, ". . . economically the regime was guaranteed a food supply independent of the caprices of the market, a supply for which the regime therefore did not have to pay. With this assured, they could then advance on the second, and more important, front—the Promethean development of heavy industry. . . ." Stalin particularly feared the Japanese, who had invaded Manchuria in 1931 and were poised to invade China. Industrialization drew 8.5 million farm workers into the city among 12.5 million new industrial recruits in the Soviet Union between 1929 and 1932. "This increase in the urban population meant, among other things, that more food was needed to supply them," Conquest writes, adding that "26 million urban persons were provisioned by the State in 1930. In 1931, this had risen to 33.2 million, nearly 26 percent." Grain requisitions from the kolkhozy increased accordingly, more than doubling between 1929 and 1932, while production had in fact greatly declined—mostly because of the disruptive reorganization of agriculture, partly from the passive resistance of the kolkhozniks. As Nikita Khrushchev remembered, "All too frequently the peasants would have to turn everything over they produced—literally everything! Naturally, since they received no compensation whatsoever for their work, they lost interest in the collective farm and concentrated instead on their private plots to feed their families."

In retaliation, as of October 1931, a new law required the kolkhozy to meet their requisitions from the state before they met their own needs, and in July 1932, when Gorbachev was a sixteen-month-old toddler, Stalin set an impossibly high goal for the year's grain requisitions: nearly half the harvest. Since as much as 30 percent of the total harvest was routinely lost to inadequate collection, transportation, and storage, the 1932 requisitions programmed deliberate mass starvation. Famine had already broken out among the most vulnerable part of the population, Dolot writes:

> I remember the endless procession of beggars on roads and paths, going from house to house. They were in different stages of starvation, dirty and ragged. With outstretched hands, they begged for food, any food: a potato, a beet, or at least a kernel of corn. Those were the first victims of starvation: destitute men and women; poor widows and orphaned children who had no chance of surviving the terrible ordeal.

The final twist of the knife was an August 1932 decree that Stalin himself drafted. Dolot assesses its effect:

> One of the cruelest laws of all was enacted on August 7, 1932. This law decreed that all [kolkhoz] and cooperative property such as the crops in the fields, community surpluses and storehouses, livestock, warehouses, stores and so forth were hereupon to be considered as state owned. The protection of such prop-

erty from theft was to be enforced in every possible way. The penalties for theft were execution by firing squad and confiscation of all property of the guilty one. The alternative sentence was no less than ten years of penal servitude in a labor camp as well as confiscation of property. . . .

This law . . . was aimed at the starving farmers. No other interpretation is possible. Only those poor, hungry wretches in quest of food were driven and forced by hunger to steal from the communal, and now state-owned, property. . . . Not only petty thievery of a potato or a couple of heads of grain from the communal fields was considered a grave offense against the state: it was considered a great crime to even glean the already harvested fields, to fish in the rivers, or to pick up some dry branches in the forest for firewood. After the passage of this law, everything was considered socialist, state-owned property, and thus everything was protected by law.

Guard towers went up in the fields, manned by watchmen armed with shotguns. A further attack followed in December when a new decree imposed an internal passport system that the rural population was denied, preventing the starving from evacuating their villages for the city, where work and food might be found, a restriction more extreme than any that had prevailed for serfdom under the czars. A German agricultural attaché, Otto Schiller, traveled through the North Caucasus that spring and reported to Berlin in May 1933 on the appalling conditions he found there; the report, which included the Stavropol district, is worth quoting at length:

> The famine is not so much the result of last year's failure of crops as of the brutal campaign of State Grain Collection. Therefore even such localities as the Northern districts of North Caucasia in which the crops were quite satisfactory, did not escape. . . .
>
> In the villages I visited the number of deaths varied between 20–30 a day. Those still alive are enfeebled in the extreme through semi-starvation, and also by the eating of such unnatural food as grass, roots, charred bones, dead horses, etc. And the majority will doubtless die from malaria with the arrival of the warm weather, this disorder having prevailed to an unprecedented extent since last Autumn. The typhus which now appears sporadically will probably become an epidemic. . . .
>
> The villages stricken by famine give an impression of utter hopelessness. The abandoned homes are rapidly falling to ruin. . . . In the forsaken courtyards the present inventory is seen lying, perishing in disorder. . . . The kitchen gardens are for the most part unworked. . . . A dog or cat is extremely rarely met with—most of them had been eaten. . . .
>
> The present situation in Northern Caucasus may be summed up as follows:

In some of the villages the population is almost extinct. In other about half the population have died out. And there are still villages in which death from famine is not so frequent.

But famine reigns everywhere, at least in those regions which I have visited. . . .

People have become callous and indifferent to the fate of those near to them. One meets people with legs swollen from starvation who move with difficulty. Others have already become so weak that they lie about in the road waiting for death. Several days usually elapse before a chance passerby endeavors to help them.

One can therefore see bodies of those dead from famine not only on the highroads, but even in the streets of the towns. . . .

In Krasnodar a German living there told me that bodies from which pieces had been cut off to serve as human food had been found. Personally, however, I cannot vouch for this.

What strikes one in all the villages is the small percentage of men. They have evidently less power of resistance, and more easily fall victims to the famine. The women who have children die sooner than others, therefore single women predominate in the villages which have suffered most severely.

Gorbachev would acknowledge these events at various times, if briefly and impatiently. His paternal grandfather Andrei Moiseyevich Gorbachev, he said, had resisted collectivization, unlike Panteli Gopkalo, and had been denounced "for not fulfilling the sowing plan in 1933, a year when half the family died of hunger. They took him away to Irkutsk to a timber-producing camp, and the rest of the family was broken, half-destroyed in that year." Three of Andrei Moiseyevich's children starved to death, Gorbachev reveals in his memoirs. "The famine was terrible. A third, if not half, of the population of Privolnoye died of hunger. Entire families were dying, and the half-ruined ownerless huts would remain deserted for years." His father, Sergei, carried the burden of supporting his grandmother Stepanida and two aunts until grandfather Gorbachev returned from Irkutsk after serving only two years of a nine-year sentence, in 1935—"bearing two letters of appreciation for his work," Gorbachev notes, adding without irony that he "joined the *kolkhoz* immediately." Evidently Gorbachev lived with his maternal grandparents in his preschool years because the Gopkalos, unlike the Gorbachevs, had found a way not to starve.

Then in 1937, in the further brutal repression of the Great Terror, when executioners with axes were splitting skulls in prison basements all over the Soviet Union, when at least a million people were "purged" and murdered among more than five million arrested as Stalin consolidated his power, it was Gorbachev's grandfather Panteli Gopkalo's turn. Gorbachev calls his grandfather's arrest in the middle of the night when Gorbachev was only six years old his "first real trauma."

"After Grandfather's arrest," Gorbachev remembers, "our neighbors began shunning our house as if it were plague-stricken. Only at night would some close relative venture to drop by. Even the boys from the neighborhood avoided me. . . . All of this was a great shock to me and has remained engraved in my memory ever since."

Raisa's grandfather Petr Stepanovich Parada was arrested at about the same time as Gorbachev's grandfather, interrogated at about the same time, found guilty and executed. Gopkalo was luckier; the NKVD* itself was purged while his case was in process, "the head of our regional department committed suicide, and in December 1938 Grandfather was released from prison." Within a year the popular and resourceful Gopkalo was back running the kolkhoz.

He had suffered for his sins:

> I remember well the winter evening when Grandfather returned home. His closest relatives sat around the hand-planed rustic table and Panteli Yefimovich recounted all that had been done to him.
>
> Trying to get him to confess, the investigator blinded him with a glaring lamp, beat him unmercifully, broke his arms by squeezing them in the door. When these "standard" tortures proved futile, they invented a new one: they put a wet sheepskin coat on him and sat him on a hot stove. Panteli Yefimovich endured this too, as well as much else.

Gorbachev's grandfather never again spoke of his ordeal. And like many others of that era who were imprisoned and tortured, "he was convinced that Stalin did not know about the misdeeds of the NKVD and he never blamed the Soviet regime for his misfortunes." Shaken by the cognitive dissonance of having been tortured and imprisoned for crimes he did not commit by representatives of the ideology to which he had wholly dedicated himself, Gopkalo reduced the dissonance by dividing the Party and its leader off from its army of enforcers, blaming the enforcers for his mistreatment and idealizing the leadership. This early experience, Gorbachev's "first real trauma," is a point of origin for his similar mental separation of the Leninist ideal he believed in from the failing and corrupt bureaucracy he confronted when he

* The secret police, predecessor to the KGB.

came to power himself in 1985. As the writer David Remnick characterizes it, "The tragedy of the Stalin era and the farce of the Brezhnev period represented for Gorbachev not the failure of ideology, but rather its perversion."

Similar compartmentalization helped prepare Gorbachev to bury his doubts during the years of his rise to power and to conceal his radicalism from his Politburo colleagues even after they elected him general secretary. Dolot describes how the process worked on a Ukrainian kolkhoz:

> In the collective farm, our personal existence became completely dependent upon the dictates of the Communist Party, and on the whims of the local officials. Every detail of our life was supervised. Our daily routine was subject to the strictest regimentation. We had to obey orders without any protest, and without giving any thought as to their sense or purpose. A vast system of secret police, spies and *agents provocateurs* watched our every move.
>
> We were always suspected of treason. Even sadness or happiness were cause for suspicion. Sadness was thought of as an indication of dissatisfaction with our life, while happiness, regardless of how sporadic, spontaneous or fleeting, was considered to be a dangerous phenomenon that could destroy the devotion to the Communist cause. You had to be cautious about the display of feelings at all times, and in every place. We were all made to understand that we would be allowed to live only as long as we followed the Party line, both in our private and social lives.

But in Gorbachev's case, the local official whose "whims" he and his family depended upon was his grandfather, so that what was oppression for people like this Ukrainian émigré was opportunity for Gorbachev—and in any case, the only reality he knew. "Not only I," he reminisced once, "but the generation before me, took as an existing reality, as a given, everything that had taken place under Communist rule; we took it as a given that the system we lived under was socialism. . . . Thus we developed the outlook, in reference to the reality in which we were living, that no alternative was possible."

Conditions on the kolkhozy improved in the later 1930s, partly because the millions of executions in the years of the Great Terror had reduced the number of mouths to feed. "The shops had calico and [kerosene] to sell," Gorbachev remembers. "Grandfather Panteli replaced the thatched roof with tiles. Gramophones appeared in the shops. On rare occasions, 'silent' movies would be shown on portable film projectors. And the height of bliss for us children would be the ice cream brought into the village now and then." In those years, Gorbachev's quiet, hardworking father, Sergei, found a niche as a machine operator attached to a Machine Tractor Station, harvesting grain with a tractor-drawn combine, a new implement introduced into cereal farming in the 1930s that combined into one field operation the two previously separate functions of binding and threshing. Conquest calls the Machine Tractor Station—a centralized depot for farm machinery established by government decree in 1929—"the third great element of socialization in the countryside." (The other two elements were the collective and state farms.) Some 2,500 MTS's were operating by 1932, and since they controlled not only the schedule of farmwork on the kolkhozy but also the deliveries of grain and other crops from the kolkhozy to the Soviet government, they were quickly infested with Party officials and secret police. As such, they offered security and opportunity to farmers like Sergei Gorbachev who made themselves useful.

Nazi Germany invaded the Soviet Union on 22 June 1941. Having achieved complete surprise, the Wehrmacht troops rapidly swept eastward. "The village was drained of its inhabitants within weeks," Gorbachev remembers— "all the men had gone." For the rest of the war, the women and children worked the fields. "Gorbachev passed through the formative years of puberty working shoulder to shoulder with women," the writer Gail Sheehy points out, which was one source of his immense self-confidence. "He was a male child, a robust and energetic male child, and as such, prized beyond any possession. . . . One out of every three Soviet males between the ages of eighteen and twenty-one watered the ground of Russia with their dying blood" during the Second World War. "So it is easy to understand why mothers of that generation treated their living sons like gold." On the rare occasions when a batch of newspapers reached Privolnoye, Gorbachev read the news to the illiterate adults of his village, who even asked his advice about their problems. But he was young enough (twelve years old in 1943) that an evening among the women at someone's home, when fear for their lives and a reading of their husbands' letters started them weeping, left him feeling "unbearable terror."

The fighting front passed around Privolnoye in August 1942, close enough that Gorbachev saw a volley of the Red Army's Katyusha rockets for the first time, "fiery arrows crossing the skies with a frightening whistling sound." After the rockets, silence, and then on the third day the sound of German motorcycles approaching. The Wehrmacht troops crowded the village, uprooted its orchards for camouflage materials and soon passed on, pushing southeast along the Caucasus toward the Baku oil fields, leaving behind a sixty-man garrison. "Rumors of mass executions in the neighboring towns circulated," Gorbachev recalls, "and of machines that poisoned people with gas." Himmler's killing squads, the SS Einsatzgruppen, which followed behind the German Army murdering Jews, were just then changing their methods from shooting their victims into killing pits to poisoning them in mobile gas vans, but another Privolnoye resident, Grigory Gorlov, told Sheehy that some 370 Jewish families, both local and refugee, were shot to death into pits dug beside the river that edged the village. There were rumors that Communist families would be murdered as well; to protect their golden child, Gorbachev's mother and grandmother hid him on a farm outside Privolnoye until the village was liberated in late January 1943, after a five-month occupation.

The problem for the rest of the war was simple survival. The women grew hemp, processed it into thread, and wove cloth for clothing. (A shirt made from such rough thread, writes Gorbachev, "felt as if it was made of wood.") They spun wool for coats and made hides into shoes. Matches made of TNT from tank mines lit their fires; salt evaporated from a salt lake thirty miles away seasoned their food. Famine struck in the winter and spring of 1944; Gorbachev's mother organized an ox-cart mission to a distant district rumored to have a store of grain and sold a suit her husband had never worn and two new pairs of his boots for a hundred-pound sack of corn that saved their lives.

That summer, notice arrived from the front that Gorbachev's father had been killed in the Carpathians after surviving battles in Rostov, Kursk, Kiev, and Lvov. "The family cried for three days," Gorbachev writes. "Then a letter arrived from Father saying he was alive and well." The boy's response was typical: "I wrote to him to express my indignation at the death notice sent to us." Don't be so hard on us, his father responded: Anything can happen in a war. A shrapnel wound to the leg in Czechoslovakia sent Sergei Gorbachev to the hospital and then home not long before the German surrender in May 1945. During the war he had joined the Party.

Gorbachev's worst memory of the war, he says—he still had flashbacks in his sixties—was encountering the rotting remains of Soviet soldiers killed in battle in a forest near Privolnoye in 1943, when he was not quite twelve, his first unprotected look at the "unspeakable horror" of war: "decaying corpses, partly devoured by animals, skulls in rusted helmets, bleached bones, rifles protruding from the sleeves of the rotting jackets. . . . There they lay, in the thick mud of the trenches and craters, unburied, staring at us out of black, gaping eye-sockets." His generation, he adds, was "the generation of wartime children." The war had scorched them, "leaving its mark both on our characters and on our view of the world."

Like many of his peers, Gorbachev missed two years of school during the war. He studied all the harder afterward to make up for the loss, in a school knocked together from various village outbuildings, where students had to make their own ink and the horses kept for hauling firewood so nearly starved each winter that for weeks at a time they could not even stand. He joined the Communist Union of Youth, the Komsomol, as soon as he turned fourteen, in 1945, initiating his political career. The Komsomol was charged with "spreading the ideas of communism and involving worker and peasant youth in the active construction of Soviet Russia." Though it had become a mass movement by 1945, it still served as a Communist Party farm team. Gorbachev took it seriously, unlike many of his peers, already understanding that the Party was his only route to a future beyond Privolnoye. Could he have thought otherwise after what his father and grandfathers had survived?

At fifteen, in 1946, Gorbachev became an assistant at the Machine Tractor Station where his father worked. For the next four years and during university summer vacations, father and son labored together combining grain throughout the district from late June to late August, usually away from home. They slept with their machinery in the fields even when it rained, and when the weather was good they worked twenty hours a day—comfortable work in the cool of morning, hot, hard work in the blazing afternoon sun and then winding down to the buzz of cicadas in the cooling evening. Father and son could trade off at the controls without stopping the combine, and as all good farmers do, Gorbachev learned to judge the complicated machine's condition by listening to the sounds it made. But he was a teenage boy, not a grown man, and he suffered nosebleeds from the dusty dryness of the fields, sometimes fell asleep at the wheel, and lost at least ten pounds every summer.

In their downtime father and son talked about "a great variety of topics, work and life alike. Our simple father-son relationship . . . developed into a bond between two persons who shared a common cause and a common job. Father treated me with respect and we became true friends." From some-one—perhaps his father, perhaps the women who had surrounded him in his formative early adolescence during the war—Gorbachev learned to sub-stitute argument for violence. His high school girlfriend remembered him "correcting teachers in history class, and once he was so angry at one teacher he asked, 'Do you want to keep your teaching certificate?' He was the sort of man who felt he was right and could prove it to anyone, be it in the princi-pal's office or at a Komsomol meeting." An American journalist couple who followed him closely after he became general secretary confirm his old girlfriend's observation; they remark on Gorbachev's "dislike of violence and his reliance on words as his main political weapon." They explain:

> In difficult situations he was given to hectoring and lecturing; he believed that, if his conclusion was logical and based on good evidence, others should accept it automatically. For those who ignored or discounted his views, he was ready to explain them one more time, but his tone would suddenly acquire an authoritarian edge. . . . Among his most beguiling qualities were a self-deprecating humor and a sense of proportion, both of which he used to win people over. But he also showed himself unrelenting and profane when necessary, which, in the setting of his native province, was often. Classmates remembered him during his student days as being an extrovert southerner who relished the *ruski mat* (Russian mother), as the rich compendium of Russian obscenities is known generically.

Unlike so many of the men around him, particularly among the veterans and the secret police, Gorbachev was never violently socialized. He could swear like a southern farmer when need be, but he carried the *ruski mat* in his bag of tricks partly to avoid the "brute force" that he told Zdenek Mlynar was necessary to motivate work discipline on a kolkhoz. Obvious physical strength, quick intelligence, confident authority supported by good political connections, psychological astuteness, and a knack for the bold, colorful swearing that can be at the same time a form of bullying and an aesthetic performance that defuses potentially violent confrontations: these traits, a gift to the world from the women who raised him and the calm father who finished shaping his character in adolescence, substituted in Gorbachev's case for brutality.

Famine approached again in 1946 when drought limited the grain harvest to only 37 million tonnes, of which the state took 17 million—"very, very hungry and hard times here for eight more years," a villager told Sheehy. (For comparison, the grain harvest in the United States in 1946 totaled 120 million tonnes.) The country had a better harvest in 1947—70 million tonnes—but around Stavropol the yield was low. "We somehow managed to make it through the winter," Gorbachev recalls stoically. The next year looked to be as bad—dust storms in April, "the terrible companions of drought"—but warm rains followed and raised a bountiful harvest. In 1947, the Supreme Soviet had decreed that medals would be awarded to combine operators who set records for threshing: a Hero of Socialist Labor for a thousand tonnes threshed in a season, an Order of Lenin for eight hundred. In 1948, Sergei Gorbachev and his energetic son threshed 889 tonnes. Sergei received the Order of Lenin, Gorbachev himself the Order of the Red Banner of Labor, a handsome bronze medal hung on a red-and-white-striped ribbon with a red banner enameled over its bronze-on-white hammer and sickle. "I was seventeen then," Gorbachev writes, "and this has been the most cherished of all my awards." As well it should be: Along with the endorsement of his Komsomol and an outstanding school record, it qualified him for a free university education. He chose the best school in the country, Moscow University, and traveled to Moscow for the first time at nineteen, in the autumn of 1950, to claim his future.

MOSCOW WAS NOT YET A MODERN CITY, although by 1950 postwar reconstruction had finally begun. The Soviet Union had suffered terribly from the war; the civilian population continued to suffer for years afterward as billions of rubles were diverted to the military and to the crash program to build the atomic bomb and stockpile a nuclear arsenal. Mlynar, arriving from Czechoslovakia and about to become one of Gorbachev's roommates, claims not to have been shocked by his first sight of Moscow, but his description is brutal:

> The problem was not chiefly the fact that Moscow was a huge village of wooden cottages, that people scarcely had enough to eat, that the most typical dress, even then, five years after the war, was old military war-issue uniforms, that most families lived in one room, that instead of flush toilets there was only an opening leading to the drain pipe, that both in the student residences and on the street people blew their noses into their hands, that what you didn't hang onto tightly would be stolen from you in a crowd, that drunks lay unconscious in the streets and could be dead for all the passers-by knew or cared, and that there were dozens and dozens of similar phenomena. All these facts seemed somehow explicable by the past. We did not go to the Soviet Union expecting to find a consumers' paradise, and, in any case, such was not to be found anywhere in Europe five years after the war. On the contrary, we considered the poverty and wretchedness we saw in Russia as a direct consequence of the war and of the terrible backwardness of czarist Russia.

(The problem, Mlynar concludes, was the cynicism and hypocrisy of the Party officials, the "absence of values that the faith itself considered as primarily necessary to the future of communism.")

Gorbachev had hoped to study physics. The astrophysicist Roald Sagdeev, a contemporary of Gorbachev's at the university (and later one of his advisers), believes that the physics course was closed to him because admission required proof that a student could qualify for a security clearance: Physicists were likely to be recruited for nuclear-weapons work, as Andrei Sakharov had been while still a postdoc working with his mentor Igor Tamm. Gorbachev's residence in Privolnoye during its four and a half months of wartime German occupation was probably what disqualified him, Sagdeev speculates. If so, the implication that Gorbachev might have been turned by the Germans was absurd: He was only eleven at the time.

Barred from studying physics, Gorbachev chose law, a distinctly minority choice in a country run by an absolute dictator but a choice that Lenin had also made. "I had only a rather vague idea what jurisprudence and law were all about," Gorbachev writes. "But the position of a judge or prosecutor impressed me." Even before he left Privolnoye he had understood that whatever he would do with his life would have to be done through the Communist Party; he had applied for full membership as soon as Party rules allowed, when he turned nineteen.

A classmate characterizes the hayseed law student from Privolnoye as romantic and innocent; in his university years Gorbachev's entire wardrobe consisted of one suit jacket, a few shirts, and a pair or two of pants. Housed in an old czarist barracks, first-years like Gorbachev lived twenty-two to a room (down to eleven in their second year and six in their third). "The Soviet state had added two extra floors" to the old building, Mlynar recalls, "to make room for 10,000 students . . . and for the several hundred on each floor there was only one collective latrine with a washing area and a single common kitchen. For everyone in the building there was a single Russian *banya* (bathhouse) in the courtyard." But a cup of tea cost only a few kopeks in the student cafeteria, and there was always bread on the table. At the end of the month, when they waited, broke, for the next month's stipend, a one-ruble can of beans offered subsistence. For a provincial born in the midst of famine who had survived the Great Patriotic War, these were conditions of luxury, set among wonders. "Everything was new to me," Gorbachev reminisces—"Red Square, the Kremlin, the Bolshoi Theatre (my first opera, my first ballet), the Tretyakov Gallery, the Pushkin Museum of Fine Arts, my first boat trip on the Moskva River, excursions to the countryside around Moscow, my first October demonstration. . . . And every time, I was overwhelmed by an incomparable sensation of novelty." Most of all he was hungry to learn. "University studies captivated me from the start and they took up all my time. I studied eagerly and passionately."

He did not neglect the Party. If he studied much longer and later than his more sophisticated Muscovite classmates, he also made time to participate actively in the student Komsomol; alumni from his era remember that he could be shrill and dogmatic about even minor deviations from the

Party line. First he was chosen *komsorg* of his class—its Party monitor and organizer—and then, in 1952, the year he was admitted to full Party membership, *komsorg* of the entire law school student body. In his memoirs he calls the Party education he endured a "massive ideological brainwashing," which "was designed to prevent us from developing a critical mind." Yet he notes ironically that "the first authors who sowed the seeds of doubt about the unquestionable 'ultimate truth' presented to us were Karl Marx, Friedrich Engels and Vladimir Lenin." Their works contained "a detailed criticism of their opponents' theses, a system of counter-arguments and theoretically sustained conclusions" that contrasted sharply with Stalin's argument from authority or simply from ad hominem abuse. Farmers can be skeptical of abstract thought: They know how much the world depends on rain and weather. With Mlynar and his war-veteran roommates, Gorbachev debated what could be debated, what they dared debate even in the relative privacy of their room. "Before the university I was trapped in my belief system in the sense that I accepted a great deal as given, as assumptions not to be questioned. At the university I began to think and reflect and to look at things differently. But of course that was only the beginning of a prolonged process."

Stalin had been off-limits—even, perhaps, to thought. At the beginning of March 1953, in the hard cold of Russian winter, the breaker of nations suffered a cerebral hemorrhage that left him unconscious and partly paralyzed. With his drunken son Vasili storming around the room and the members of the Politburo helplessly wringing their hands, he died at 9:50 a.m. on Thursday, 5 March 1953. Word spread quickly. Gorbachev and Mlynar heard the news together in a university lecture hall. "The instructor came in," Gorbachev writes, "and informed us with a tragic voice, tears veiling his eyes, of Stalin's untimely death, in the seventy-fourth year of his life. Later, talking to Gorbachev, Mlynar recalled that, while they stood for the two minutes of silence the instructor had requested, he had whispered to his roommate, " 'Misha, what's going to happen to us now?' And you in a voice full of alarm and uneasiness, answered, 'I don't know.' " Like hundreds of thousands of others, they decided they must view the leader in his open coffin in the white-and-gold Hall of Columns, the grand ballroom of the House of Trade Unions on Okhotny Ryad, where Lenin had lain in state in 1924 with Stalin among his ceremonial guards. A huge crowd converged on central Moscow. "We advanced slowly," Gorbachev remembers, "all day, stopping for hours in one place." Mlynar takes up the tale:

> The density of the crowd became that of a streetcar full to bursting at rush hour. At the same time there was a continual influx of tens of thousands from

behind, in front were the horses and soldiers, and on each side the barrier of trucks and the buildings. It was cold and the slush was slippery underfoot; anyone who fell down had little hope of ever getting up again, and help was impossible. Naturally, no statistics have ever been released about the number of people trampled to death or wounded, and it is difficult to estimate the total toll. But that night I myself saw dozens of wounded and unconscious people, and some I saw were dead. The casualties were loaded into trucks and gradually taken away.

Gorbachev had never seen Stalin before. Now he saw him dead, "a stony, waxen face, devoid of any signs of life. I searched for traces of his greatness, but there was something disturbing in his appearance that created mixed feelings."

Of equal or greater importance to Mikhail Gorbachev's future evolution into the charismatic reformer he became was his discovery, among the ten thousand other students in his dormitory, of a beautiful young woman from western Siberia named Raisa Maksimovna Titorenko. Raisa—Raya to her friends—was a year younger than Gorbachev, but she had entered the university a year ahead of him, in 1949, among what she called "the generation of the seventeen-year-olds." She won her university education by graduating at the top of her class. Her childhood had been nearly as impoverished as Gorbachev's and as marked by political repression.

Her Ukrainian father, Maxim, was a railroad construction worker who moved with his work. Raisa remembered with some bitterness "the neverending moves the family had to make in the wake of my father the railwayman, the trouble that this caused, the various flats we found to live in—goodness knows how many such 'nests' we occupied, and huts and wooden-frame houses. . . . So can you imagine what our life was like?" In a conversational memoir published in 1991 she described in some detail the expulsion of her father's family from their land as kulaks "at the beginning of the 1930s." Somewhat later, she said, her maternal grandfather was arrested and executed, as a result of which her grandmother "died of grief and hunger as the wife of an 'enemy of the people.' " So traumatic was this experience to Raisa that she associated it in the memoir with the vicious gossip and scheming she and Gorbachev had encountered in the years of his leadership of the Soviet Union:

> I do not deny it: there are sometimes, it is true, bitter lessons to be learned. For example, if fate had not handed us the burden of *perestroika* I would probably never have known the many different shapes and forms human beings can

take. This is serious, you understand. For me this is one of the most difficult moral tests of *perestroika:* the specific way people behave, what they say and what they do. What they were yesterday and what they are today. What they are when they are with you, and what they are with other people. What they are when it is their advantage, and what they are when it is not. Sometimes I even see, or rather feel, that they are not faces but masks, but masks of the real world, not the fantastic world of fairy tales. And, do you know, the masks I see will suddenly disappear and I can see quite clearly the faces of the people who informed on my grandfather in the 1930s. And of those who destroyed him. And of those who, with their tails between their legs, would not approach a dying woman, just because she was from the family of an "enemy of the people."

But Raisa's father was transferred to Chernigov in the Ukraine, 1,800 miles from the two-year-old's maternal grandparents, in 1934, and his family moved with him, which means Raisa could not have seen "the faces of the people who informed on my grandfather," nor have experienced the mistreatment of her grandmother firsthand. Her grandfather was certainly purged and murdered. There is good reason to believe, however (though Raisa seems never publicly to have acknowledged the fact), that her father himself was purged in 1935, arrested and imprisoned for four years, leaving Raisa, her mother, and her two younger siblings to struggle for survival without support. That would explain the intensity of Raisa's feelings more than fifty years later about hypocrites who inform on innocent men and avoid the family of an "enemy of the people." It would also explain her mother's curious overresponse to what was supposedly her father's departure for "the front"—into Army service—in the following recollection:

I remember the scene when we accompanied my father off to the front. The overcrowded railway station—I really do recall from childhood so clearly and so sharply the railway stations with that unrepeatable sad atmosphere— women, children and tears. Many women even fainted. And I remember my mother, frozen in her grief. Her words were: "Who's going to support us? We must hold out."

A sad atmosphere is appropriate to a railroad station where young fathers are going off to war, but why would Raisa's mother be "frozen in her grief"? And since soldiers are required to assign pay allotments to their families, why would she be concerned about support? These inconsistencies immediately make sense if Maxim's departure was not to the front but to the Gulag, as a Trotskyite enemy of the people, and not in 1939 or 1941 but in 1935. He returned four years later, in 1939, in a railwayman's uniform because men who could construct railroads were suddenly in great demand as the Soviet Union made preparations to defend itself against Nazi Germany, itself gearing up toward war.

The Titorenkos suffered through the war, as everyone did. Raisa's school lunch was "a daily bowl of watery soup." Because they moved around so much she experienced "a sort of internal constraint, a feeling of diffidence, sometimes of isolation. . . . But the situation of being 'always the new girl' led me at the same time to develop contact with people. I simply had to become more social."

She arrived at the university a provincial, in a peasant blouse with her head wrapped in braids, but she adapted even more rapidly than Gorbachev, so that in a photograph from 1951 she already looks slim and sophisticated, with styled hair and a wristwatch. Classmates remember her coat, which seemed to announce her prosperity, but the effort of the coat was collective. "I received my first real overcoat as a present from my mother and father," she recalled, "when I was already a university student. It had a small fur collar—a 'Boston,' according to my mother. I wore it for a long time. The whole family remembers that coat. . . . It really was a milestone in the family history."

She studied philosophy as a way of studying sociology, then still marginalized as an aberration. "In our country," she would explain, "sociology practically ceased to exist as a science somewhere in the 1930s. It turned out . . . to be 'unwanted' and perhaps even 'dangerous' in conditions where a bureaucratic command system was being formed. Sociology is the embodiment of what we call 'feedback,' and for that reason alone a system of command is organically alien to it. Just as it is alien to the system." Like Gorbachev, then, and independently, she probed the system cautiously for an explanation of the suffering it had inflicted on her family and her country, splitting off the ideal from the real. Two handsome people, both intelligent, both provincial strivers, both with high ambitions, both with grievances: How could they not have found each other even in the crowd?

Gorbachev wanted her the first time he saw her. It took him three months to get her attention, at a student dance, but once they connected they were inseparable. They went to the theater, they read and discussed books, they took long walks together around the city, Raisa remembered:

Our relationship and our feeling were from the very outset perceived by us as a natural, inseparable part of our fate. We realized that our life would be unthinkable without each other. Our feelings were our very life itself. . . . We didn't know if our relationship would be lasting. . . . Whether our marriage would be harmonious. We didn't even think about it. It didn't worry us. Financial considerations didn't concern us: legacies, family connections, somebody's position, protectionism. No. There were no legacies and no family connections. All we had was ourselves. All we had was with us. *Omnia mea mecum porto*— "Everything I have I carry with me."

We were friends for a long time before we got married.

People who come from nowhere feel that way, that the world begins with them.

The first thing they bought together was her wedding dress—"a beautiful Italian crepe dress," Gorbachev writes, ". . . made for Raya at a dressmaker's shop on Kirovskaya Street. She simply looked gorgeous in it." He worked overtime in the summer of 1953 to raise the money. "You've got a new work incentive," his father kidded him. In her memoir Raisa quotes one of his letters:

> "I know, Rayechka, I haven't written to you. Our work team consists almost entirely of Gorbachevs. Papa is the combine operator, I do the steering and Semen Grigorievich Gorbachev is the tractor driver. There is a girl on the straw collector—Anna Mikhailovna Gorbachev, and the grain is transported from the combine in a truck by Vasili Alekseyevich Gorbachev. Our team is known as 'The Gorbachevs.' Papa, Semen and Vasili are cousins. . . . I must finish now. . . . Warmest greetings from the sphere of production to the sphere of the intellect."

Gorbachev and his father sold a thousand pounds of grain at the end of the summer; with his salary, Gorbachev took home nearly a thousand rubles. "I had never had so much money in my hands before." It bought the wedding dress, but Raisa had to borrow the white shoes. On 25 September 1953, twelve days after Nikita Khrushchev became first secretary of the Communist Party of the Soviet Union, Gorbachev and Raisa were married in a Moscow registry office.

THREE A HIERARCHY OF VASSALS AND CHIEFS

AFTER HIS GRADUATION FROM LAW SCHOOL in June 1955, Mikhail Gorbachev had hoped to work in Moscow, but he was not allowed that privilege. He was assigned instead to the Prokuratura—the public prosecutor's office—in Stavropol. Traveling out to the old city ahead of his wife, he found a room in a house occupied by two retired teachers and their children. The room was barely eleven by eleven feet, with an iron bed and a huge stove for heating, but its three windows looked out onto a luxuriant garden. The crate in which the Gorbachevs had shipped their belongings became a combination table and bookshelf; to round out the furnishings Gorbachev built a clothes rack and bought two chairs. The small room would be their home for the next two years. Their daughter and only child, Irina, would be born there on 6 January 1957, one day after her mother's twenty-fifth birthday. "Stavropol struck me by its greenery," Raisa recalled. The city had originated as an imperial fortress in 1777, and the old stone houses were overgrown with hops and grapevines, "a flood of green. It seemed as though the city had been decked out in luxurious green clothes. Lombardy poplars and such a lot of chestnuts. And willows and oaks and elms. And lilac. And flowers everywhere."

Gorbachev disliked the cold formality of the Prokuratura. A career there looked like a dead end. But Moscow had initiated an ambitious program of agricultural reforms in the fall of 1953 that had opened up promising positions within the district Party apparatus. Gorbachev talked his way out of the Prokuratura and into Komsomol work, winning appointment as deputy head of the Stavropol Department of Propaganda and Agitation. In practice that meant touring the countryside assessing conditions, solving problems, and promoting the Party; his first month's salary, 840 rubles, went for a pair of sturdy boots. He found no flood of green in the Stavropol outback but "sheer misery and complete devastation everywhere." Wading through the mud to a hilltop above one remote village he looked down on "low, smoke-belching huts [with] blackened dilapidated fences" stretched out twenty kilometers along both sides of a river:

> Down there, in those miserable dwellings, people led some kind of life. But the streets (if you could call them streets) were deserted. As if the plague had ravaged the entire village, no contacts or ties existed between these shanty-town microcosms, just the everlasting barking of the dogs. And I told myself that this was the reason why the young fled. . . . They fled from desolation and horror, from the terror of being buried alive. . . . People deserve a better life—that was always on my mind.

His birth village was only a little better off, he wrote Raisa during one of his tours:

> I don't know how many times I've been to Privolnoye hearing them talk of just twenty rubles—where were they going to find such a sum? Despite the fact that my father works day and night the whole year round. I am simply overwhelmed with shame. Honestly I can't keep back my tears. . . . There's a great deal yet to be done. Our parents and thousands like them really deserve a better life.

Khrushchev's reforms offered Gorbachev a first version of how the Soviet people might achieve the better life he believed they deserved. An early and important reform had been the abolition, in 1953, of the Special Board of the Ministry of Internal Affairs, which the American legal scholar Harold Berman calls "the chief instrument of [Soviet] terror." Since 1934, the secret three-man committee had dispatched hundreds of thousands of people to labor camps without legal representation, a hearing, or the right of appeal. Along with abolishing the Special Board, Khrushchev ordered all political convictions reviewed and many prisoners released; although the Gulag continued to function, large-scale amnesties followed in 1953 and again in 1957. A major liberalization of the Soviet legal system began in 1955 and continued throughout the rest of the decade, Berman notes, involving "hundreds, indeed thousands, of needed reforms," most of all the restoration of due process in political cases.

Renouncing wholesale domestic terror as a means of governing, Khrushchev and his followers worked to replace terror with law and with a degree of popular participation in political debate. Though Khrushchev's cultural gestures are better known—his approval of the publication of Aleksandr Solzhenitsyn's *One Day in the Life of Ivan Denisovich* in *Novy Mir* in November 1962, for example—his proto-glasnost effort to outmaneuver the Stalinist old guard by encouraging the Soviet people to support his reforms was more influential in the long run. Certainly it influenced Gorbachev. Berman reports "a substantial increase in the powers of the local municipal councils and a vast amount of activity of local government organizations, involving the participation of literally hundreds of thousands of Soviet citizens." Working through the Komsomol, Gorbachev facilitated that participation:

> The main thing for me at that time was the sense of hope being born. . . . I tried to function in such a way as to arouse people's interest and activism. I organized a discussion club for young people. There was a great deal of interest, and we had to rent larger and larger meeting rooms in order to fit everyone that wanted to attend. This success and the feeling that people were waking up, as though they were being released from shackles that had bound them and were beginning to lose the sense of fear and lack of self-confidence—I was completely inspired by such things at the time. . . . It was quite an extraordinary development.

Gorbachev felt something more wrenching than inspiration in the spring of 1956 when he read a transcript of Khrushchev's indictment of Stalin at the 20th Party Congress that February. Stalin "practiced brutal violence," Khrushchev charged; he authorized "barbaric tortures"; he originated the concept of an "enemy of the people," which "made possible the use of the most cruel repression . . . against anyone who disagreed with [him]." (But "Lenin had used the term," says Dmitri Volkogonov, "having borrowed it from the lexicon of the French Revolution.") "How were confessions extracted?" Khrushchev asked rhetorically. "Only one way, by beating, torture, deprivation of consciousness, deprivation of reason, deprivation of human dignity by means of physical violence and intimidation."

Khrushchev's speech "morally discredited totalitarianism," Gorbachev writes, "arousing hopes for a reform of the system." It staggered him. "I was shocked, bewildered and lost. It wasn't an analysis, just facts, deadly facts. Many of us simply could not believe that such things could be true. For me it was easier. My family had itself been one of the victims of the repression of the 1930s." The Komsomol sent him around to explain the speech to its local leadership. "I had no real idea of the true state of affairs up until the Khrushchev revelations," he said later. Such naïveté may seem unlikely, but his more sophisticated Czech friend Zdenek Mlynar was equally uninformed, acknowledging that "the concrete details of crimes committed by the Soviet security organs" that Khrushchev revealed, "of torture and forced confessions in political trials . . . had never crossed my mind."

The speech allowed Gorbachev for the first time "to understand the inner connection between what had happened to our country and what had happened to my family. My memories and associations from childhood became interwoven with the beginnings of an awareness of what Stalinism was." His grandfather Panteli Gopkalo had convinced himself that Stalin could not have known about the Terror famine and the purges (Stalin's apologists blamed the NKVD); such denial was no longer possible for Gorbachev. But young and ambitious as he was, he followed Khrushchev's lead in assigning responsibility narrowly to Stalin and the Stalinist system while exonerating Communism itself.

Yet he was no barren dogmatist. The Communist ideal connected him emotionally to his family and his family's struggles. "Am I supposed to turn my back on my grandfather, who was committed to the [socialist] idea?" he asked rhetorically in 1990. ". . . And I cannot go against my father, who defended Kursk, forded the Dnieper River knee-deep in blood, and was wounded in Czechoslovakia. When cleansing myself of Stalinism and all other filth, should I renounce my grandfather and my father and all they did?" Part of what they did was to embrace the Communist Party as a way past their mistreatment at its hands; and so now did Gorbachev: "I did not perceive [Khrushchev's speech] as a catastrophe or as the collapse of everything that had existed up until then. On the contrary, I perceived it as the beginning of something new, as providing tremendous new opportunities for the future."

GORBACHEV MOVED UP TO FIRST SECRETARY of the Stavropol city Komsomol committee in September 1956. At a session of the Komsomol Central Committee in Moscow he met a kindred spirit, his Georgian counterpart, Eduard Shevardnadze. "We had the same peasant roots," Shevardnadze says, explaining their instant friendship, "had worked on the land at a tender age, and had the same knowledge of folk life." Like Gorbachev, Shevardnadze had been "shaken . . . by the direct connection between the politics of terror and Stalin's activity. . . . It shattered my life and my faith." But Shevardnadze had experienced a more immediate trauma as well: the brutal suppression in March 1956 of protest demonstrations in the Georgian capital of Tbilisi, the beginning of what Shevardnadze calls "the East European upheavals of the 1950s and 1960s."

That summer, Soviet tanks massed on the Polish border in response to large-scale demonstrations by Polish workers demanding "bread and free-

dom." Khrushchev had barely finished negotiating an accommodation with
the new Polish Communist Party chief, Wladyslaw Gomulka, when student
demonstrations in Hungary enlarged into a full-scale anti-Soviet revolution.
Shevardnadze had been there before. "It is not true that the first time heavy
military vehicles were used against civilians was in Budapest in October
1956," he writes. "The tank was first deployed as an argument against dissent
in Tbilisi in March of that year." As a result, Shevardnadze adds significantly,
"My generation and I acquired a '1956 complex' for the rest of our lives—
rejecting force as both a method and a principle of politics." When, much
later, Gorbachev would refuse to use force to keep Eastern Europe within the
Soviet fold, it was partly the example of these early experiences that he and
his foreign minister, Shevardnadze, heeded.

Pressure on Khrushchev to order Soviet troops, tanks, and strafing and
bombing aircraft into Budapest to put down the Hungarian Revolution
came especially from the Soviet ambassador to Hungary at that time, Yuri
Andropov, a tough, smart Second World War partisan leader and Party func-
tionary who happened to have been born near Stavropol (in 1914). Dis-
tracted by Poland and the Suez Crisis, concerned to follow his new policy of
rallying popular support, Khrushchev was reluctant to use force to crush the
Hungarian uprising. Khrushchev's advisers, including Andropov, emphasized the importance of a show of force at a time when Britain, France, and
Israel were preparing to invade Egypt to wrest the Suez Canal back from
Gamal Abdel Nasser, the Egyptian leader, who had abruptly nationalized it.
Khrushchev seized on their argument to justify his abrupt reversal: "If we
depart from Hungary," he said, addressing a meeting of the Central Committee Presidium on 31 October, when Egypt was under active attack, "it will give
a great boost to the Americans, English and French—the imperialists. They
will perceive it as weakness on our part and will go onto the offensive. . . . To
Egypt they will then add Hungary." Andropov had been exiled to the Hungarian ambassadorship during the struggle for Politburo leadership that followed Stalin's death in 1953; after his work suppressing the Hungarian
Revolution, he was recalled to Moscow and renewed his rise to power.

By 1962, Gorbachev had found a mentor, Fedor Kulakov, the new first secretary of the Stavropol region (*krai*)—a position similar to governor of a
U.S. state, but appointed rather than elective. Kulakov encouraged Gorbachev to switch from Komsomol work to a newly created post as a Communist Party organizer responsible for managing production in three *krai*
agricultural districts. Young, highly intelligent, motivated, personable, seemingly committed to the Party system, Gorbachev appealed to the paternal

feelings of one powerful Soviet leader after another in the course of his advancement to leadership. Kulakov was the first; Andropov, whom Gorbachev would meet in 1969, was the most influential. The younger man gave good value:

> I was totally committed to my job. I spent days, and often nights, traveling around the districts, visiting farms and trying to develop new management structures. I was deeply convinced that we had embarked upon the right path and once the technocrats were free to do their job it would soon bear fruit. Being a candidate member of the [district] Party committee bureau, I had frequent dealings with Kulakov. . . . He would entrust me with all kinds of tasks and invite me on trips through the krai.

But if Gorbachev made use of the Mafia-like system that manipulated the formalisms of Communist Party rule, he did not necessarily approve of it. "Both the general secretary at the center and the various first secretaries in the regions repaid support with protection," he writes. "This hierarchy of vassals and chiefs of principalities was in fact the way the country was run. The democratic façade did not change the essence of the matter. It was a caste system based on mutual protection. To me this was a distortion of socialism and by no means a defect inherent in that system."

He and Raisa both felt the need for more education. Raisa was teaching philosophy, including sociology, at the Stavropol Agricultural Institute; her husband began studying agricultural economics in night school there, eventually writing a thesis on the economics of milk production. She pursued the equivalent of a Ph.D. in sociology. Her dissertation work gave both of them a deeper understanding of the conditions of rural life in the Soviet Union twenty years after the end of the immensely destructive war with Nazi Germany. It also, by its methodology, added to Gorbachev's understanding of democratic process.

Raisa chose to study "the peasant family, its material condition, daily life, cultural demands and the nature of relationships in the family." She used statistics, documents, and archives, but also—and significantly—questionnaires and interviews. "I personally collected about 3,000 questionnaires in those years. . . . On the collective farms I visited the farm workers' homes, the working brigades, the farms, schools, libraries, shops, medical centers, preschool nurseries and old people's homes." She interviewed "hundreds of people . . . on a whole variety of subjects. . . . I know what their daily life is like and what their problems are. I have traveled hundreds of kilometers along country roads, in a passing car, on a motorcycle or a cart, and sometimes on foot in rubber boots." It was from such meetings with real people, she believed, "and not from books or newspapers, not from plays or films, that I came to understand many of our [Soviet] misfortunes and the questionable nature of many undisputed assertions and established concepts." So did her husband. Contempt for ordinary people—for the difficulties of their lives and for their hopes—was the characteristic attitude of Party leadership at every level in the Soviet Union (Gorbachev writes critically of "the traditional concept of the peasant as a second-class citizen"). The Gorbachevs' personal histories and their extended encounter with rural life enabled them to avoid the narrowing corruption of such contempt.

NIKITA KHRUSHCHEV WAS OUSTED FROM POWER in October 1964 partly for the debacle of the Cuban Missile Crisis, when the United States and the Soviet Union came within hours of all-out nuclear war, but more immediately for his disastrous agricultural policies. Moscow no longer dared to impose food rationing when crops failed in the early 1960s; Khrushchev's attempt to ration meat and butter by raising their retail prices in 1962 provoked a riot in one Soviet city that the Red Army put down violently, leaving more than sixty dead. Instead of rationing, the Soviet government increased its imports of food grains from the West. "The leadership of the USSR in effect was challenged by its own 'revolution of rising expectations,' " writes an agricultural economist, "in which it could [no longer] 'run an industrial society on a diet of pickled cucumbers and black bread.' " To pay for grain imports in the previous decade, the government had drawn down its gold reserves, which declined, says Volkogonov, "from 13.1 million tonnes in 1954 to 6.3 million in 1963." It paid for the increased imports of the next two decades with oil revenues from new fields opened up in Siberia.

Kulakov moved to Moscow as the head of the Central Committee's agricultural department in October 1964, his reward for having connived with Leonid Brezhnev, Khrushchev's successor, to force Khrushchev's "retirement." In his place as Stavropol *krai* first secretary arrived a more sophisticated apparatchik, Leonid Yefremov, who was being banished to the provinces for the sin of having been an enthusiastic Khrushchev supporter. Yefremov spent two years brooding on his misfortune before he finally got down to work. Gorbachev, whose capacity for absorbing information was limitless, describes Yefremov ironically as "a refined product of the system" and judges "the years I spent working together with him [to have been] a most instructive experience for me."

In Volkogonov's view, Brezhnev was "a mild, indecisive man" whose favorite activity was big-game hunting. He allowed Khrushchev's programs of reform to be halted and eventually reversed. "We . . . did not [esteem] highly enough what Khrushchev had done," Gorbachev judges, "and what later on disappeared with him. With the advent of Brezhnev there gradually occurred a transfer of power to those who had an interest in restoring essentially the old order, although of course without the harshest methods of Stalinism."

Before the walls closed in, in 1966, the Gorbachevs made their first trip abroad together, part of a group of Soviet managers sponsored by a wealthy French businessman interested in promoting East-West relations. Three couples in three Renaults covered five thousand kilometers around Europe, and it is easy to believe that they were wide-eyed. The following year the Gorbachevs vacationed in Italy, living in Sicily for a time and then visiting Rome, Florence, and Turin. In the 1970s Gorbachev would travel officially or by invitation to Italy, France, Belgium, and East Germany. Travel also opened his eyes:

> My previous belief in the superiority of socialist democracy over the bourgeois system was shaken as I observed the functioning of civil society and the different political systems. Finally, the most significant conclusion drawn from the journeys abroad: people there lived in better conditions and were better off than in our country. The question haunted me: why was the standard of living in our country lower than in other developed countries?

With reform fading and Yefremov uncooperative, Gorbachev took a reduction in pay and became first secretary of the Party's Stavropol city committee, where he plunged into urban industrial development. He finished his agricultural economics study in 1967, the same year that Raisa earned her doctorate in philosophical sciences. The couple furnished a two-room flat and bought their first television set. Yefremov was further frustrated and angered when Moscow appointed Gorbachev second secretary of the Stavropol *krai* in August 1968—his immediate second in command—without consulting him, but the two men eventually contrived to work together.

The Prague Spring—Czechoslovakia's attempted liberalization in the spring and summer of 1968—came to its brutal conclusion on 21 August, only days after Gorbachev's appointment as second secretary. Zdenek Mlynar, his old roommate, had visited him in Stavropol the previous year and alerted him that Czechoslovakia was simmering. Mlynar himself was active in the movement toward liberalization and was eventually forced into exile in Austria. Gorbachev says the suppression of Czechoslovakia set him thinking critically about his government. He visited the country in 1969 and was shocked when workers in a defense plant he toured turned their backs on him. "I suddenly understood that despite all the global, strategic and ideological justifications, we had suppressed something that had grown up within our own society. From that time on I began to think more and more about our own situation and I came to rather unconsoling conclusions— that something wasn't right among us."

(According to the former Washington KGB station chief Oleg Kalugin, "the KGB stirred up fears . . . that Czechoslovakia could fall victim to NATO aggression or a coup" unless the Czech dissent was violently suppressed, one reason that the Brezhnev Politburo reacted so excessively. More ominously, Brezhnev may have put Soviet nuclear forces on full alert during the August invasion to warn off the West. The evidence that he did so—a declassified U.S. intelligence document—is provocative but not conclusive; a former Soviet general who was deputy commander of the invasion agrees that an alert was considered but denies that it was actually ordered. The Soviet government was extremely cautious about nuclear alerts during the Cold War, and stood down even during the Cuban Missile Crisis; an alert during its invasion of Czechoslovakia would have been a rare exception and a strong indication of Kremlin panic.)

The suppression of the Prague Spring, Gorbachev writes, "engendered a very harsh reaction in the Soviet Union, leading to a frontal assault against all forms of free thinking. . . . Soviet society . . . entered a stage of profound stagnation." Yuri Andropov, who became the chairman of the KGB in 1967, directed that frontal assault. Besides stifling dissent, Gorbachev adds, the Brezhnev reversal "practically put an end to all subsequent quests for ways and means to transform the existing system of economic management." Although Gorbachev was promoted to replace Yefremov as the Stavropol *krai*'s first secretary in 1970, he discovered "gradually, and more and more tangibly . . . that although I held positions of high authority, in fact there was little I could do, because I was bound hand and foot by orders from the center."

Gorbachev's concerns for the next ten years were largely agricultural: drought, crop failures, dust storms, irrigation projects, road building. His work brought him into regular contact with Moscow and frequent conflict with Kulakov, who by then was the Politburo member responsible for agriculture. Gorbachev saw the economy stagnate, saw regional initiatives rejected, saw "manipulators" become "the heroes of the day," and found himself increasingly disenchanted: "Should you come up with your own ideas—be prepared for trouble. You could even land in jail. It was actually impossible to do something sensible while complying with all the regulations and instructions. A popular adage hit the mark: 'All initiative is punishable.' "

GORBACHEV FIRST MET YURI ANDROPOV in the immediate aftermath of the Prague Spring invasion of 21 August 1968; supervising its brutalities had prevented the KGB chairman from taking his annual vacation. The North Caucasus region was famous for its mineral springs, and in April 1969 Andropov turned up at one of its spas, where Gorbachev was delegated to welcome him. Thereafter Gorbachev cultivated Andropov, not cynically but certainly realistically, understanding that the only way to power in his country was through alliances with its leaders, however black their souls. Gorbachev "was a great charmer," his biographers Dusko Doder and Louise Branson say of him at this period; "his extrovert personality and humor, bold ideas expressed in moderate language, and perpetual references to specific material achievements disarmed the old men of the Kremlin. . . . By then he was a totally political creature." As time passed and the friendship, or mentorship, deepened, the Andropovs and the Gorbachevs sometimes vacationed together. Gorbachev wrote:

> We made family excursions to the surroundings of Kislovodsk and went to the mountains. Sometimes we stayed late, cooked shashlik and sat around a bonfire. Like me, Andropov did not favor noisy parties. The southern night was magnificent, it was quiet and we talked openly. . . . Yet he never opened up completely, and his trust and frankness did not exceed the established framework. More than anyone else, Andropov knew what was going on [in the Soviet Union]. But I would think that he reasoned like many others: deal with the cadres, introduce tighter discipline, and the rest will be all right.

Mikhail Suslov, the Party's leading ideologist and effectively Brezhnev's second in command, was another important mentor. Suslov had been first secretary of the Stavropol *krai* during the Second World War and, like Andropov, often vacationed in the region. Andropov described Gorbachev to a colleague as one of "the entirely new people coming up . . . who can bear our hopes into the future," and on another occasion as "a brilliant man working in Stavropol."

Even Brezhnev seemed to like the young go-getter from Stavropol. David

Remnick cites the assessment of Anatoly Sobchak, a law professor and former mayor of Leningrad, on what might seem Gorbachev's sycophancy:

> Gorbachev could tell us much we do not know about how a man feels, doomed
> to daily renunciation of his own will in favor of that of his superiors, compelled
> to daily self-abasement for the sake of his career. . . . To me, the greatest mys-
> tery is how Gorbachev managed to retain his individuality, the ability to shape
> his own opinion and set it against the opinion of others. Evidently, it was to
> preserve his own self that he developed his almost impenetrable mask. He
> learned to conceal his disdain for those whom he must have despised, to speak
> with them in their own language.

Remnick adds: "Gorbachev appears to have few illusions about his double face. Years after coming to power, he told [the journalist] Vitaly
Korotich . . . 'In those days, we all licked Brezhnev's ass—all of us!' " Ass-
lickers are a staple of middle bureaucracies, of course, and are certainly not
unique to the former Soviet Union. The activist and strategic analyst Daniel
Ellsberg identifies the same pattern of behavior in American bureaucrats.
The U.S. government, he points out, "does not require true believers to run
it. . . . The system consciously runs by men who—in order to stay in the
game, to be close to the center of power, to have the hope that someday the
moment may come when their own true values will be served—will go on
for years serving values that are the opposite of what they privately believe."
Hence the frequent phenomenon of recantation from retirement.

Election to the Central Committee in 1971 opened other sources of information to Gorbachev. Foreign publications forbidden to officials of lower
rank were now made available to him in translation, including essays on the
Prague Spring and articles by the West German chancellor Willy Brandt and
the French Socialist Party leader and future president François Mitterrand.
His travels continued as well. "My trips abroad were of no small importance
to me," he recalls, "accompanied by numerous contacts, conversations
and discussions on the most varied themes." The scope of his interest and
concern enlarged beyond Stavropol as he talked through his ideas with
Andropov, with Shevardnadze, and, most of all, with Raisa. "I am very lucky
with Mikhail," she would say later. "We are really friends, or if you prefer, we
have great complicity." She noticed the change in her husband's focus in their
last years in Stavropol:

> I heard Mikhail Sergeyevich speak ever more frequently not only about the dif-
> ficulties involved in the social development of the villages and towns in the
> region, the provision of materials and technology, the lack of balance in the

terms of exchange of agricultural and industrial output, and the shortcomings in the system of payment for work done. He also talked about the need for profound changes in the country as a whole.

Finally, in July 1978, Fedor Kulakov, sixty years old, overdosed on vodka after major surgery and a position opened up for Gorbachev in Moscow. Not long after Kulakov's death, Georgi Arbatov, the director of the Institute for the United States and Canada, overheard Andropov complain in a telephone conversation, "those bastards don't want Gorbachev transferred to Moscow." Who "those bastards" were, Andropov did not say, but he found a way around them. On 19 September 1978, Gorbachev and Andropov, vacationing with their families at Mineral'nyye Vody, a historic spa in the foothills of the Caucasus, met a train carrying Leonid Brezhnev and his aide Konstantin Chernenko to Baku. "The train's departure was delayed for two hours," write Doder and Branson, "as the four men who would rule the country in succession—Brezhnev, Andropov, Chernenko and Gorbachev—met and talked on the narrow platform of the old tsarist railway station. . . . This was, in effect, Gorbachev's job interview, and it went well."

Gorbachev's appointment on 27 November 1978 as Central Committee secretary for agriculture was announced on the front page of *Pravda* the next day. Early in December, he and Raisa left Stavropol permanently for Moscow. (Their daughter, Irina, now twenty-one, and her new husband, Anatoly—the young couple had married the previous April—followed them at the end of the year.) On their last day in Stavropol, the Gorbachevs drove into the dense Russky Forest northwest of the city, where they had walked together in times past. "My character and my entire perception of the world were to a large extent shaped by nature," Gorbachev writes in his memoirs, recalling his childhood play in a mature orchard his grandfather Panteli had left to his parents. In that Eden of apple, apricot, cherry, plum, and pear trees, "there was always enough in the summer and the autumn," and he had improvised adventures in the jungle of elms and undergrowth that darkened beyond the fruit trees. Later, farther afield, he and his father had brought in the grain harvests together. The people in their poverty, the land, the cycle of the seasons, drought and flood and the precarious security of a full grain bin were not abstractions to him; they were real.

GORBACHEV'S FIRST GOAL AS secretary of agriculture was to try to understand why a country so rich in resources could not feed itself. The cost of food imports into the Soviet Union had increased from $700 million in

1970 to $7.2 billion in 1980, while gross domestic agricultural output had declined annually from about $26 billion in 1978 to about $24 billion in 1980. After a destabilizing wheat deal between the United States and the Soviet Union in 1972, when the Soviet purchase of $700 million worth of American wheat had helped push U.S. consumer food prices up by as much as 30 percent, the two countries had signed a Long-Term Grain Agreement in October 1975 that set a minimum for Soviet purchases of wheat and corn of 6 million metric tons per year. The Politburo met this drain on hard currency by selling oil, gas, and armaments ($20 billion in hard currency for armaments from Libya alone); in 1980, the Soviet Union led the world in the production of petroleum and natural gas, extracting 12 million barrels per day equivalent. (The United States followed at 10.8 million barrels per day equivalent, with Saudi Arabia next at 10.3.) And since the world price of oil tripled between 1973 and 1974 and again in 1979 through 1980, petrodollars staved off serious shortages—and serious reforms.

Gorbachev found ignorance, indifference, and neglect in Moscow's management of rural life and production. In Central Asia, he writes, "the careless expansion of cotton fields and the non-observance of crop rotation led to diseases of both the soil and the people." Farmers were treated as second-class citizens, with the rural population of 100 million people—38 percent of the total 1980 Soviet population of 266 million—receiving only 10 percent of national electrical production. Gorbachev cites many other examples as well:

> Despite the enormous growth in coal mining, the rural population was forced to use all sorts of devious ways to get fuel, because only one-third of their needs was met through official channels. I was shown a map of gas pipelines crisscrossing the country in every possible direction. A gas network was introduced in urban areas but the farmers were deprived of it, and there were no plans in prospect to make gas available to them. Rural areas were badly off for roads, schools, medical services, public utilities, newspaper and magazine supplies, cinemas and cultural entertainment.

Doder and Branson cite an official Soviet survey indicating that negligence and the lack of storage facilities led to the loss annually of "one-fifth of the grain harvest and one-third of the potato crop." More than half of the rural villages in the Soviet Union lacked paved roads. "Trucks broke down so frequently that four times as many men were engaged in repairing them as in making them." The half-million tractors produced annually were so poorly made that the total number of machines actually operating remained constant from year to year. Gorbachev summarizes: "Much more was siphoned off from agriculture than invested in it. And . . . the nation's economic development had been achieved largely at the expense of the countryside."

The chickens came home to roost in 1979, when the Soviet invasion of Afghanistan led the American president, Jimmy Carter, to embargo grain sales to the U.S.S.R. Limited sales of wheat and corn continued under the Long-Term Grain Agreement, but the immediate consequence of the embargo was a shortfall in 1980 of seventeen million tonnes. The Soviet government had to scramble to meet its needs with purchases from other grain-producing countries such as Canada and Argentina, and more petrodollars flew out the door. "The growing holes in the economy," writes Georgi Arbatov bitterly, "were being plugged by the barbaric plunder of our enormous, but not limitless, natural resources."

In January 1980, Gorbachev had his first taste of huddling with the men of the small inner circle who actually ran the country—in this case, Brezhnev, foreign minister Andrey Gromyko, and defense minister Dmitry Ustinov. "Gromyko and Ustinov began first," Gorbachev recalls, "by giving their optimistic view of the situation in Afghanistan. It was left to me to speak about the alarming grain shortage." He did, and was ordered to prepare various studies and documents, but then he raised a larger strategic question, "the problem of preparing a plan to free us from the necessity of importing grain." In Gorbachev's hands, that question led to the development of what came to be called the Food Program, which authorized changes in Soviet agricultural policy and practice that anticipated the changes of early perestroika: profit-like mechanisms that encouraged initiative, bonuses for increased output, increased production of consumer goods so that farmers might have something on which to spend their bonuses, prefabricated metal storage buildings to protect the expected bounty from rotting in the fields, and increased importation of advanced agricultural technology.

Exploring these possibilities, Gorbachev came up against the hard truth that the state had not a kopek to spare. Since increasing food prices led to riots (the Polish union Solidarity was born in Gdansk in September 1980 in demonstrations against meat-price increases), the only way the Soviet government could increase payments to farmers for their products was by subsidy. Agricultural subsidies already cost the state 40 billion rubles a year. "This problem dominated our debates," Gorbachev writes. "All agreed that the collective and state farms could no longer subsist on a starvation diet." The finance ministry was not moved. " 'The State has no money,' V. F. Garbuzov, the minister, repeated, countering all of my arguments. He knew the real state of the budget. Its mainstay was such sources of income as covert price increases, increases in the rate of vodka production, and, finally, petro-dollars. But even these could no longer make ends meet. The yawning deficit was covered by State Bank loans at the expense of citizens' savings."

It was in the course of this 1980 debate within the Soviet government that Gorbachev encountered for the first time the idea of cutting defense spending to free up resources for domestic programs. "N. K. Baibakov," he writes, "Chairman of the State Planning Committee of the Council of Ministers, was the first to hint to me at the possibility of cutting the defense budget. The growth in military expenditure was far ahead of the growth in national income. Yet no attempt had ever been made to analyze that budget rationally, with a view to an optimal redistribution of means and resources."

Neither Baibakov nor Gorbachev was yet prepared to question the defense budget, however. "We both knew perfectly well that even a mention of this subject would mean immediate dismissal. It was the General Secretary's turf." The day would come when Mikhail Gorbachev would occupy that turf. In the meantime, the idea of reviewing defense needs and priorities had been planted, well before Ronald Reagan became president. What originally spurred Mikhail Gorbachev to think hard about arms reduction was not Reagan administration pressure in the form of increased U.S. defense spending, but the pressure of Soviet domestic need. Gorbachev summarized this development succinctly in a 1996 symposium:

> With technological progress and the improvement of the educational and cultural level, the old system began to be rejected by people who saw that their initiative was suppressed, who saw they were not able to realize their potential.
>
> Therefore, the first impulses for reform were in the Soviet Union itself, in our society which could no longer tolerate the lack of freedom, where no one could speak out or choose their own party or select their own creed. In the eyes of the people, especially the educated, the totalitarian system had run its course morally and politically. People were waiting for reform. Russia was pregnant.

NOT ONLY SECOND-RANK OFFICIALS SUCH AS Baibakov and Gorbachev feared usurping Brezhnev's prerogatives where the military was concerned; so also did Gromyko and Andropov. One consequence of military influence over the Soviet leadership, ultimately devastating, was the 1979 decision to invade Afghanistan. Arbatov believes that "the military-industrial complex had grown to such proportions [by then] that it escaped political control." Brezhnev, Arbatov points out, had been the Central Committee's secretary of defense industries before he became the general secretary, and "treated the military as a very important power base." Ustinov, the minister of defense, "matched Brezhnev in his sycophancy toward the military." Brezhnev's failing health, exacerbated by an addiction to sleeping pills, added to the confusion.

Anatoly Chernyaev, an international analyst for the Central Committee who would become one of Gorbachev's most trusted advisers, points to Ustinov as the instigator of the December 1979 invasion:

> I learned that the intervention in Afghanistan was initiated by Ustinov. The project to present this "idea" to Brezhnev was organized by a group of four: Ustinov and Gromyko, plus Andropov and [the Central Committee secretary for international affairs Boris] Ponomarev. Andropov was reserved but didn't object, only noting certain "possible complications." Ponomarev also expressed some doubts, but then quickly joined in.

Both Arbatov and Chernyaev note that the senior military staff objected to the war, "arguing," says Chernyaev, "that it would be impossible and senseless," but according to Arbatov, the Ministry of Defense nevertheless promoted and even insisted upon the intervention, which he calls "a pretty typical escalation of military aid." With the United States covertly supporting the anti-Soviet Afghan mujahideen, Afghanistan in the 1980s became the Soviet Union's Vietnam.

An unintended consequence of military-industrial dominance of government policy was the piling up of Soviet arms during the 1970s, when both the Soviet Union and the United States were pursuing policies of détente. "As a result," Arbatov points out, "we reached absurdly high ceilings in many areas [including] such important components of conventional forces as the number of people under arms; tanks; artillery; tactical missiles; many types of aircraft; submarines; and many other weapons systems." In nuclear weapons "we surpassed the Americans in the number of delivery systems, megatonnage, and throw weight in strategic arms, and also in medium-range weapons"— as if more nuclear weapons meant more security.

The excesses of the Soviet military-industrial complex in the 1970s were as much the consequence of internal policy as they were of external threat. The complex was "something like a bull in a china shop" according to a former Soviet defense official named Vitaliy Katayev—"a sort of Soviet Texas." It "always demanded as much weaponry as possible." The decision to produce a new weapons system was usually made "not on the basis of military needs or technical merit . . . but rather on the basis of [the] authority of its sponsors" and their personal relationships with the political leadership. And since the complex was expected to increase its output by at least 3 percent annually, "production of many types of weapons was not stopped even after the army was saturated with them." The purpose of this overproduction, a former Soviet military economist explains, was "to keep the production base 'warm' "—to be ready to mobilize production in case war broke out. If mobilizing production—that is, preparing to fight a long war—looks like antiquated 1930s policy in a nuclear world, he adds, it was.

Massively overproducing arms, Arbatov concludes, "undermined Western trust toward us. Right-wingers and militarists in the United States and other NATO countries waged a successful campaign to create public mistrust of us. . . . More than that, our actions encouraged Americans to intensify the arms race."

By the early 1980s, the Soviet dissident Vladimir Bukovsky told a British journalist, "the regime was obviously in crisis. You can imagine that it was obvious to the Politburo sitting there and receiving all the reports about politics and economics. They knew the contempt for them of the entire country, they knew they were in trouble." The price of crude oil had begun declining as well, and by U.S. estimates every dollar per barrel the price declined cost the Soviets about $1 billion annually. "The creaky Politburo of Leonid Brezhnev began to panic," writes Thomas Reed, a former Reagan special assistant. "It demanded the immediate production of oil regardless of the long-term cost. It was this full-throttle, devil-take-the-hindmost approach to oil production that was a key indicator [of Soviet economic troubles] to us at the White House."

Mikhail Suslov died in January 1982. Yuri Andropov, then sixty-seven, moved from his position as the chairman of the KGB to replace Suslov as Central Committee secretary. The move was a necessary step if Andropov was to succeed Brezhnev, says Arbatov, since the election of a leader "straight from the . . . KGB would have been unprecedented and almost certainly would have been stopped by the apparat." When Brezhnev died, on 10 November 1982, Andropov immediately assumed the general secretaryship. As Andropov's protégé, Gorbachev saw his prospects improve accordingly. Even before Andropov's advanced kidney disease forced him into the hospital, limiting his ability to administer the country, he pushed Gorbachev to prepare himself for leadership:

> Andropov and I were drawn even closer together in our work during his early months as General Secretary. I sensed his trust in me and his support. At the very end of 1982 he suggested meaningfully: "You know what, Mikhail, don't limit your work to the agrarian sector. Try to look at other aspects."

He fell silent and then added: "In general terms, act as if you had to shoulder all the responsibility one day. I mean it."

Under Andropov's protection, Gorbachev reached out to what Chernyaev calls "leading reformist thinkers" for information and support. The agricultural economist Vladimir Tikhonov, the sociologist Tatyana Zaslavskaya, the physicist Yevgeny Velikhov, Arbatov, and others extended his knowledge of his country and its problems. It was a painful education. "The relations between town and country, the fate of the peasantry, the land and the people on the land, the preservation of nature—these ancient questions did not give me any rest," Gorbachev wrote. "The further I delved into them, the more I was overcome by alarm about the situation in the country, the more I began to doubt the wisdom of the economic policy being implemented in the country." He commissioned studies of necessary reforms and invited contributions; some 110 memoranda resulted, sent in by individuals as well as institutes and ministries. "Their analysis then became the basis for the documents of *perestroika*," Gorbachev notes.

In May 1983, invited to visit Canada by the Canadian secretary of agriculture, Gorbachev formed a crucial alliance with Alexander Yakovlev, a philosophic but outspoken Soviet apparatchik whose criticism in the early 1970s of a burgeoning Brezhnev personality cult had earned him a decade's exile as the Soviet ambassador to Canada. A small, balding man with a pronounced limp from severe war injuries, Yakovlev had begun losing faith in the Soviet system when he saw Soviet prisoners of war returning from Germany in 1945 hauled off to prison camps at Stalin's behest. He was "terribly ashamed," he said later; and further ashamed when he heard Khrushchev's speech on Stalin's crimes. A year studying at Columbia University in the Communist witch hunt days of the 1950s had left him unimpressed with American democracy, but ten years in Canada had given him time to study and reflect on Western values and Western prosperity. Like Gorbachev, he was a son of farmers—his father had been a kolkhoz chairman—which prepared him to admire the bounties of Canadian agriculture.

He and Gorbachev spent eight days touring the country, talking nonstop along the way. "We spoke very frankly about everything," Yakovlev said later. ". . . The main point was that society had to change, that it had to be constructed on different principles." They visited a state animal-husbandry research center, a dump-truck factory, a canning factory, family farms, a cattle ranch. "My Canadian travels served as a powerful impetus for thought," Gorbachev remembers. One of his thoughts was to return Yakovlev from exile. Within two months, Gorbachev's new ally was back in Moscow and installed as the director of the prestigious Institute of World Economy and International Relations.

Yuri Andropov died of complications of kidney failure in February 1984. Gorbachev in his memoirs expresses doubt that his mentor would have pursued serious reform had he not been ill, as some believe: "He realized the need for changes, yet Andropov always remained a man of his time. . . . Apparently the years spent in KGB work had left an imprint on his attitudes and perceptions, making him a suspicious man condemned to serve the system." Arbatov puts it more bluntly, listing among Andropov's negative traits "indecisiveness, faintheartedness and cowardice," which he speculates resulted from being "deeply traumatized, frightened for life," by his years working under Stalin, "like the majority of his generation."

Gorbachev's name was bruited for general secretary, but the elderly seniors of the Politburo considered him too young (he was fifty-three) and untested—and too independent—to promote to leadership; they chose Brezhnev's dull, ailing, seventy-two-year-old former aide Konstantin Chernenko instead, despite his advanced emphysema. Andropov's personal aide Arkady Volsky testified later to having overheard the defense minister, Dmitry Ustinov, tell another Politburo member, "Kostya [Chernenko] will be more amenable than Misha." "That," Volsky added bitterly, "is how the leader of our great country was chosen." Anatoly Chernyaev wrote in his journal at the time that he "looked at the members of the [Politburo] and thought I saw embarrassment in their faces, as if they were ashamed of dashing our hopes. Really, no matter who you talked to in those days, Gorbachev's name always came up. We didn't want to believe that it could be someone else."

Gorbachev himself had not felt ready to lead the country in 1984; he told a colleague, reports one of his biographers, Archie Brown, that he was "not psychologically prepared for the role of first person" after Andropov's death. He finished preparing himself in the inert thirteen months of Chernenko's lethargic reign, vigorously ("brilliantly," Gromyko would say) chairing meetings of the Politburo, deflecting efforts by the old guard to have him demoted, delivering what amounted to a campaign speech at a national conference on science and technology, visiting Britain and winning an endorsement from the British prime minister, Margaret Thatcher—"I like Mr. Gorbachev. We can do business together"—that brought him international attention. Behind the scenes, he talked through his ideas with Raisa and with Yakovlev. His old friend Eduard Shevardnadze assessed the situation bluntly when they met on vacation at a Black Sea resort in Georgia: " 'Everything's rotten. It has to be changed.' I really did say that to Gorbachev on a winter evening in 1984 at Pitsunda."

In his speech to the national conference on science and technology on 10 December 1984, "The People's Vital Creativity," Gorbachev called for carrying out "profound transformations in the economy and in the entire system of social relations." Sandwiched between the de rigueur boilerplate of tributes to Lenin and Chernenko and claims of a "crisis of capitalism" was a bold assertion of the necessity of reform:

> Life is setting before us a task of enormous political significance—to raise the economy to a qualitatively new scientific-technical and organizational-economic level and to achieve a decided improvement in the intensification of social production and an increase in its efficiency.
>
> The course aimed at intensification is dictated by objective conditions and by the entire course of the country's development. There is no alternative to it. Only an intensive economy developing on the basis of the latest scientific and technical achievements can serve as a dependable material base for improving the working people's well-being, ensure the strengthening of the country's positions in the international arena and allow it to worthily enter the new millennium as a great and prospering power.

Gorbachev introduced in this speech the words that would name his reforms and become known throughout the world. He spoke of "the *perestroika* of the forms and methods of economic management," using the Russian word for reconstruction or restructuring; he said that "*glasnost* is an integral aspect of socialist democracy and a norm of all public life," using the untranslatable Russian word that means both openness and publicity. "Extensive, timely and candid information," he continued, "is an indication of trust in people and of respect for their intelligence, feelings and ability to comprehend various events on their own." He spoke of a radical economics that would utilize "prices, profit [and] credit." He warned of "unfavorable trends in the economy" and threatened "implacability toward shortcomings."

The speech " 'was unambiguously perceived as a claim to political leadership,' " Archie Brown writes, quoting one of Chernenko's aides, and "both Gorbachev's 'champions and his opponents understood it that way.' " It was also, according to a Gorbachev ally, "regarded by quite a number of people as dangerous, as having gone too far." If Gorbachev put himself at risk in speaking out so publicly, he also practiced what he preached: glasnost, trust in people and respect for their intelligence.

Konstantin Chernenko died on Sunday evening, 10 March 1985, and this time Gorbachev was ready. Yevgeny Chazov, Chernenko's personal physician, called Gorbachev first to deliver the news. He in turn called Andrey Gromyko and two other members of the Politburo. He arranged to meet them at the Kremlin at eleven p.m., but contrived to see Gromyko privately before the meeting. Though they spoke in euphemisms, the message was clear: Gromyko, the old hard-liner, the Soviet foreign minister for twenty-eight years, would propose the young reformer at the Central Committee plenum to be called for five p.m. the next day. The meeting at the Kremlin ran on through the night; Gorbachev finally got home at four a.m. Raisa was waiting:

> Mikhail Sergeyevich returned home very late—we were then living in the country house near Moscow. We went out into the garden. There was something oppressive in the late-night air, still untouched by the spring. Three deaths in three years. The death of three General Secretaries, the country's top leaders, one after another. Mikhail Sergeyevich was very tired. At first he remained silent. Then he said: "Tomorrow there will be a full meeting of the Central Committee. The question may arise of my taking over the leadership of the party." . . .
>
> We strolled around the garden where the snow was still lying. My husband again remained silent. Then he appeared quietly to be thinking aloud. "I worked so many years in Stavropol. This is my seventh year in Moscow. But it is impossible to achieve anything substantial, anything on a large scale, the things the country is waiting for. It's like coming up against a wall. Yet life demands it and has done for a long time. No!" I heard him say. "We just can't go on like this."

That afternoon, says Chernyaev, when Gromyko pronounced Gorbachev's name, "the hall exploded with applause."

APES ON
A TREADMILL

It may be that we are jogging in tandem on a treadmill to nowhere.

PAUL WARNKE

FOUR "THE BOMBER WILL ALWAYS GET THROUGH" (I)

MIKHAIL GORBACHEV INHERITED A FORMIDABLE nuclear arsenal when he claimed the general secretaryship of the Communist Party of the Soviet Union (CPSU) on 11 March 1985. In that first year of the second term of Ronald Reagan's presidency, the Soviet Union faced an even more formidable nuclear arsenal arrayed against it by the United States, as well as the smaller but deadly arsenals of Britain, France, and Israel. Although no nuclear weapons had been exploded in anger since the Second World War, the total world stockpile had increased by the mid-1980s to about fifty thousand bombs and warheads with a combined explosive force of about 22,500 million tons of TNT equivalent (1.5 million Hiroshimas). "A few hundred of the fifty thousand," former secretary of defense Robert McNamara wrote in 1986, "could destroy not only the United States, the Soviet Union and their allies but, through atmospheric effects, a major part of the rest of the world as well." All mechanical systems risk failure, accident, criminal appropriation, or misuse; what fears and ambitions had justified such an apocalyptic accumulation?

NUCLEAR FISSION WAS DISCOVERED in Nazi Germany in December 1938, nine months before the beginning of the Second World War. News of the unexpected discovery of a physical reaction that liberated the enormous energy known to be latent in the nuclei of atoms quickly spread around the world. Physicists everywhere immediately understood that nuclear energy might now be harnessed to generate power or released explosively in bombs several million times more destructive, pound for pound, than ordinary high explosives. Such a weapon could assure victory in war or reverse an impending defeat.

It might also, paradoxically, protect against attack. "It must be realized," two physicists working in Britain advised the British government secretly in

1940, "that no shelters are available that would be effective [against a nuclear explosion] and could be used on a large scale. The most effective reply [to a threat of attack] would be a counter-threat with a similar weapon." Given these conditions, could any government that could afford nuclear weapons afford not to have them? Within three years of the discovery of nuclear fission, programs of research into the military potential of the reaction had begun in Germany, Britain, France, the United States, the Soviet Union, Canada, and Japan.

Only the Anglo-American program was successful before the end of the war, but the atomic bombings of Hiroshima and Nagasaki catalyzed the Soviet program and stimulated the initiation or renewal of bomb research in postwar Britain, France, Sweden, Norway, Switzerland, Yugoslavia, and Australia. The Soviet Union tested its first atomic bomb in August 1949. Britain followed in October 1952, France in February 1960, China in October 1964, India in May 1974, and Pakistan in May 1998. Every test was successful, and Israel and South Africa confidently built nuclear arsenals during the same period without testing at full yield. Yugoslavia, Sweden, Australia, Norway, Taiwan, South Korea, Indonesia, Turkey, Greece, Romania, Libya, Canada, Brazil, Argentina, and Switzerland interrupted weapons-development programs under diplomatic pressure from one or more of the nuclear powers or from the international community. South Africa dismantled its small nuclear arsenal of six uranium bombs at the end of the Cold War when the sizable and threatening army of Cuban forces stationed in nearby Angola went home.

Even before the end of the Second World War, the scientists in the Anglo-American program had begun investigating the development of thermonuclear weapons as well as fission bombs. Bombs that fused hydrogen to helium, releasing nuclear energy, would be orders of magnitude more destructive even than fission weapons, their fireballs measured in miles rather than feet, their yields measured in megatons (millions of tons of TNT equivalent) rather than kilotons (thousands of tons of TNT equivalent). The United States tested its first thermonuclear device—a bulky two-story experimental unit named Mike—in November 1952. It yielded 10.5 megatons (seven hundred Hiroshimas). A first Soviet thermonuclear test of a yield-limited but deliverable weapon (four hundred kilotons) followed in August 1953, and of a so-called true thermonuclear—a 1.5-megaton two-stage design like Mike of potentially unlimited yield—in November 1955. Britain tested a thermonuclear weapon in November 1957, China in June 1967, and France in August 1968. None of the smaller nuclear powers is known to have fielded

hydrogen bombs, but tritium, a radioactive isotope of hydrogen, is also com-
monly used in fission weapons to produce fusion reactions to boost fission
yields, and Israel at least is believed to have developed such boosted-fission
weapons.

In February 1963, McNamara prepared an estimate for President John F.
Kennedy of potential nuclear powers. McNamara's list included West and
East Germany, Belgium, the Netherlands, Canada, Sweden, Switzerland,
Japan, India, Israel, the United Arab Republic (Egypt), Brazil, Australia, Norway, China, Czechoslovakia, and Poland. McNamara also included Romania,
Bulgaria, and Hungary on a supplemental list as countries with "a scientific
community and industry to support nuclear programs." When Kennedy was
asked at a press conference on 21 March 1963, five months after the Cuban
Missile Crisis, if he was still hopeful of achieving a nuclear test ban, he
referred to the information in McNamara's estimate to justify continuing to
negotiate with a Soviet Union reluctant to allow U.S. inspections on its territory: "Personally, I am haunted by the feeling that by 1970, unless we are successful, there may be ten nuclear powers instead of four, and by 1975, fifteen
or twenty. . . . I see the possibility in the 1970s of the President of the United
States having to face a world in which fifteen or twenty or twenty-five
nations may have these weapons. I regard that as the greatest possible danger
and hazard."

Kennedy immediately stepped up efforts to limit nuclear-weapons testing
as one approach to limiting proliferation; without tests it would be difficult
if not impossible for nonnuclear powers or threshold nuclear powers to
develop the miniaturized, high-yield weapons required for delivery by ballistic missile. The Soviet Union had offered a first proposal to limit weapons
tests at the United Nations in 1955. President Dwight D. Eisenhower had tried
hard during his second term (1957–1961) to achieve a comprehensive nuclear-
test ban. In February 1960, after extensive negotiations among the United
States, Britain, and the Soviet Union had stalled because of Soviet resistance to intrusive inspections, Eisenhower had brought forward a proposal
banning tests in the atmosphere, the oceans, and outer space—which could
be policed from outside the Soviet Union—as well as "all nuclear weapons
tests beneath the surface of the earth which can be monitored." Nikita
Khrushchev had accepted Eisenhower's proposal, and the signing of a test-
ban treaty was expected to highlight a May 1960 summit conference in Paris.
But on 1 May, Soviet rocket forces shot down a CIA U-2 reconnaissance
plane conducting a secret flight over the Soviet Union in the final months
before the first U.S. spy satellites were scheduled to become operational.

(Eisenhower had only reluctantly agreed to the flight, the last in a series, trusting CIA assurances that the U-2 operated above the range of Soviet antiaircraft rockets and was rigged to be blown up if intercepted.) The pilot, Francis Gary Powers, choosing not to commit suicide, survived and confessed. Khrushchev walked out of the summit meeting in protest and the test-ban treaty went unsigned.

In June 1963, Kennedy proposed a more limited treaty banning weapons tests everywhere except underground. Eight years of prior discussions had cleared the way, and when the three powers met in mid-July they needed only ten days to negotiate an agreement. The Limited Test Ban Treaty entered into force on 10 October 1963. Since it allowed underground testing, it did little to limit the superpower nuclear arms race, but it contributed to slowing proliferation by making weapons tests much more expensive.

A more comprehensive international agreement addressing nuclear proliferation originated in a resolution that Ireland proposed to the United Nations General Assembly in 1961, which the General Assembly unanimously approved. It appealed to all nations to forego transferring or acquiring nuclear weapons. Negotiations to limit the transfer or acquisition of nuclear weapons went forward on several fronts in the years that followed. A major barrier was a program under development within NATO to field a multilateral nuclear force that would integrate U.S. nuclear weapons into NATO battalions in Europe; the Soviet Union considered such an arrangement equivalent to proliferation. The United States and the Soviet Union were able to agree on a draft treaty only in 1967, when the failure of the multilateral force concept allowed the United States to give assurances that it would retain final control of its nuclear arsenal in Europe.

Nonnuclear states had other concerns about the treaty draft. They wanted the nuclear industries of the five nuclear powers to be subject to International Atomic Energy Agency safeguards just as theirs would be, so that they would not be put at a commercial disadvantage. The United States agreed to such an arrangement in December 1967, as did Britain; over the next two decades, France, the Soviet Union, and China also complied. The nonnuclear states wanted guarantees that the nuclear powers would come to their aid if they were threatened with nuclear attack and would not attack them with nuclear weapons. The United States, Britain, and the Soviet Union offered the positive guarantee in 1968 and the negative guarantee a decade later. Finally, according to the arms-control expert and former U.S. ambassador Thomas Graham, Jr., the nonnuclear states wanted the nuclear powers to agree "to negotiate in good faith to achieve cessation of the nuclear arms race, nuclear disarmament, and general and complete disarmament. This, in effect, meant that the [treaty] included a basic bargain whereby the non-nuclear weapon states agreed to foreswear nuclear weapons in exchange for unfettered access to the peaceful benefits of nuclear energy and a pledge from the nuclear weapon states to eventually eliminate their nuclear arsenals."

The Nuclear Non-Proliferation Treaty (NPT) opened for signature on 1 July 1968 and entered into force on 5 March 1970. It provided that no nuclear-weapon state would transfer nuclear weapons to any other entity or assist any nonnuclear-weapon state in developing such weapons, while non-nuclear states pledged not to receive or try to develop nuclear weapons. It provided for safeguards of nuclear materials and verification of compliance. It specified that all the parties to the treaty had the right to develop nuclear energy for peaceful purposes, and that the parties would share knowledge of peaceful technologies to the fullest extent possible. It specified Graham's "basic bargain." But because states such as Sweden, West Germany, and Italy were skeptical that the nuclear powers would voluntarily disarm, the treaty also provided that a state could withdraw if it felt its "supreme interests" were being jeopardized, and that twenty-five years after the treaty entered into force—that is, in 1995—a conference would be convened to decide by major-ity vote, up and down, whether the treaty should continue in force indefi-nitely, or should only be extended for a fixed period or periods of time. In this regard it differed from all other multilateral arms-control treaties, which became permanent upon ratification.

The NPT curbed the nuclear proliferation that Kennedy had regarded in 1963 as "the greatest possible danger and hazard." It also put the five nuclear powers on notice that the rest of the world would not tolerate the presence of their menacing nuclear arsenals forever. In return for foregoing nuclear weapons, the nonnuclear states expected the nuclear powers to make good-faith efforts to limit, reduce, and finally eliminate those arsenals. They would not have to do so overnight; they would have a generous twenty-five years to work out their differences. If they were unable or unwilling to do so, the nonnuclear powers reserved the right to allow the treaty to lapse or to limit its extension.

Other international and bilateral efforts prior to the time Gorbachev took office in 1985 also sought to limit the proliferation of nuclear states and nuclear weapons and to reduce the risk of nuclear war: the Antarctic Treaty (1959); the hotline agreements (1963); the Outer Space Treaty (1967); the Seabed Arms Control Treaty (1971); the Anti-Ballistic Missile Treaty (1972); the Strategic Arms Limitation Talks (SALT I) Interim Agreement (1972); the

Threshold Test Ban Treaty (1974); and the first of several treaties establishing nuclear-weapon-free zones, the Treaty of Tlatelolco (1967), which demarcated Latin American and the Caribbean. But the Limited Test Ban Treaty and the Nuclear Non-Proliferation Treaty were the most effective in preventing rampant nuclear proliferation. Graham has called the NPT "the central document of world peace and security" after the United Nations Charter itself. "In a sense," he adds, "it is the club of civilization."

YET FOR ALL THEIR CONSIDERABLE VIRTUES, none of these agreements significantly limited the arms race between the two nuclear superpowers in the years before Gorbachev took office. That arms race began with the Anglo-American program itself—the Manhattan Project—because the United States and Britain had chosen not to share knowledge of the secret program (not of how to build atomic bombs—no one proposed to do that—but simply of the fact that the United States and Britain were developing them) with the Soviet Union even though it was an ally in the fight against Nazi Germany. Since the Soviets had recruited several high-level espionage agents within the Manhattan Project, they were fully aware that they were being excluded.

Stalin drew the logical conclusion that the Americans intended to use their unique weapon to intimidate him after the war. Once the evidence of Hiroshima and Nagasaki overcame his doubts about the authenticity of the bomb plans his spies had delivered, he made the full resources of the state available to the Soviet effort. By 1948, Soviet scientists under the charismatic physicist Igor Kurchatov had not only replicated the American plutonium implosion bomb ("Fat Man") but had also developed an improved design of half the weight and twice the yield. Lavrenty Beria, the brutal KGB chief whom Stalin had appointed to oversee the bomb program, was unwilling to risk the possible failure of an indigenous, untested design and ordered Kurchatov to copy the American design, which the atomic bombing of Nagasaki had proven would work. The Soviet copy, RDS-1 (Joe 1 in U.S. nomenclature), was tested on 29 August 1949 on a tower on the Kazak steppe lands at Semipalatinsk, yielding twenty-two kilotons, matching the yield of the Nagasaki bomb. A pilot series of five RDS-1 bombs inaugurated the Soviet nuclear arsenal in March 1950. Serial production of RDS-1s began in December 1951.

With its four-year lead, the United States was well ahead of the Soviet Union in nuclear-weapons development and production by the end of 1951.

Until 1948, the United States had stockpiled slightly improved Fat Man bombs and a few uranium bombs that were ruggedized for attacks on hardened targets such as submarine pens and command bunkers. In its first series of weapons-design tests, Operation Sandstone, which was conducted in the Marshall Islands in 1948, it had proved the principle of core levitation—suspending the nuclear core within its natural uranium tamper so that the tamper material had a gap across which to accelerate before imploding the core—and tested both a composite plutonium-uranium core and cores of highly enriched uranium (HEU) alone. These and other evolutionary improvements resulted in yields of up to forty-nine kilotons, effectively increasing the total yield of the U.S. stockpile by 75 percent. In 1951, that stockpile held 438 weapons; by then the Soviet Union had manufactured twenty-five.

Before 1949, the United States had considered its nuclear monopoly to be roughly the equivalent of the superior numbers of Soviet forces occupying the eastern half of Europe, a finding that had allowed President Harry S. Truman to bring U.S. troops home while cutting the defense budget drastically from its wartime highs. From Washington's point of view, adding atomic bombs to Soviet ground-force superiority deprived the United States of a unique capability and tilted the balance decisively in the Soviet Union's favor.

Truman responded in the autumn of 1949 by requesting advice from within his administration on whether or not to accelerate development of a thermonuclear or hydrogen fusion bomb, a new, unique weapon of potentially unlimited yield. The Hungarian-born theoretical physicist Edward Teller had been promoting a design for such a weapon, nicknamed the Super, that he had devised during and immediately after the war. Other Manhattan Project scientists who had studied the design and were now advisers to the U.S. Atomic Energy Commission were skeptical that the Super would work. They anticipated that it would require large quantities of tritium, but breeding tritium in the production reactors that bred plutonium for fission weapons would mean seriously slowing fission-bomb production with no guarantee that a workable thermonuclear weapon would emerge.

Since several fission bombs (which the United States knew how to make) would deliver damage equivalent to that of one thermonuclear bomb (which existed as yet as nothing more than an unproven design concept), the scientific advisory committee to the Atomic Energy Commission recommended in October 1949 that fission-weapon production, not hydrogen-bomb devel-

opment, be accelerated. Two physicists on the committee, I. I. Rabi and
Enrico Fermi, one a liberal and the other a conservative, both experienced in
weapons work and both Nobel laureates, added to the recommendation
their blunt judgment that "such a weapon goes far beyond any military
objective and enters the range of very great natural catastrophes. By its very
nature it cannot be confined to a military objective but becomes a weapon
which in practical effect is almost one of genocide. . . . It is necessarily an evil
thing considered in any light."

Robert Oppenheimer, the American theoretical physicist who had
directed the design and construction of the first atomic bombs at the secret
Manhattan Project laboratory at Los Alamos, New Mexico, and who was the
chairman of the advisory committee, explained the committee's strategic
reasoning in later testimony without moralizing:

> The notion that the thermonuclear arms race was something that was in the
> interests of this country to avoid if it could was very clear to us in 1949. We may
> have been wrong. We thought it was something to avoid even if we could jump
> the gun [on the Soviets] by a couple of years, or even if we could outproduce
> the enemy, because we were infinitely more vulnerable [because more of the
> U.S. population lives in large cities than does the Soviet population] and infi-
> nitely less likely to initiate the use of these weapons.

The U.S. military, which had not even heard of the idea of a thermonuclear weapon of potentially unlimited yield until the debate began in Washington in late 1949, had other ideas. The Joint Chiefs of Staff expressed them
in a memorandum to the secretary of defense that the secretary, Louis Johnson, passed on to Truman in January 1950. The Joint Chiefs judged that it
was "necessary to have within the arsenal of the United States a weapon of
the greatest capability, in this case the super bomb. Such a weapon would
improve our defense in its broadest sense, as a potential offensive weapon, a
possible deterrent to war, a potential retaliatory weapon, as well as a defensive weapon against enemy forces." The chiefs were sensitive to the charge
that a bomb with yields equivalent to millions of tons of high explosives
might be considered, as Rabi and Fermi had considered it, almost a weapon
of genocide. They demurred that they did "not intend to destroy large cities
per se [with hydrogen bombs]; rather, only to attack such targets as are necessary in war in order to impose the national objectives of the United States
upon the enemy." (The distinction between military and civilian targets had
already become a distinction without a difference in the Second World War.
In the 1930s and early 1940s, Japan and Germany had initiated terror bomb-

ing against cities such as Shanghai, Warsaw, and London, deliberately targeting civilians. When British and American attempts at precision bombing of
the German and Japanese war industries failed, the two allies had begun area
bombing and then firebombing German and Japanese cities in turn, and the
atomic bombings had overwhelmed all distinctions: Whether an individual
lived or died at Hiroshima or Nagasaki depended not on his status, military
or civilian, newborn infant or factory worker, but simply on his distance
from the bomb's hypocenter.) In conclusion, the Joint Chiefs ran off into
unsupported and somewhat hysterical speculation. Although fission bombs
were more than sufficient to destroy entire cities, as Hiroshima and Nagasaki
had demonstrated, and should therefore be an effective deterrent against
nuclear blackmail, the chiefs claimed that the nation would be put in "an
intolerable position" if "a possible enemy possessed the [hydrogen] bomb
and the United States did not." Worse, they argued, if the United States publicly renounced development of the hydrogen bomb, such renunciation
"might be interpreted as the first step in unilateral renunciation of the use of
all atomic weapons, a course which would inevitably be followed by major
international alignments to the disadvantage of the United States. Thus, the
peace of the world generally and, specifically, the security of the entire Western Hemisphere would be jeopardized."

No one within the U.S. government had suggested unilateral
renunciation—bomb production had actually been greatly expanded in the
autumn of 1949 on the advice of the scientific advisory committee—but the
Joint Chiefs, who had endorsed surprise attack as the necessary strategy of
the atomic age even before the first atomic bombings, had no intention of
giving up a powerful new weapon if such a weapon could be invented, even
if its advantages cut both ways. "Offense," they had written in 1947, "recognized in the past as the best means of defense, in atomic warfare will be the
only general means of defense." And if a first-strike policy—which is what
the Joint Chiefs were advocating—made sense with fission bombs, how
much more sense would it make with the thermonuclear?

The opinion of the Joint Chiefs was all that Truman needed. "What the
hell are we waiting for?" he asked his advisers. "Let's get on with it." On 31
January 1950, he announced that he was directing the AEC "to continue its
work on all forms of atomic weapons, including the so-called hydrogen or
super-bomb." Privately, the following month, Truman told his assistant press
secretary Eben Ayers of his decision to build the thermonuclear bomb that
"we had to do it" but that "no one wants to use it." We had to do it, he added,
"if only for bargaining purposes with the Russians." Thus the United States

announced to the world that it intended to make a potentially genocidal new weapon of mass destruction that it did not know how to make, did not want to use, but might need for political leverage in international negotiations. Even so, it took the Soviet Union, which had barely begun manufacturing atomic bombs, another full year to follow suit: Stalin formally approved a full-scale thermonuclear development program on 26 February 1951. By the late 1950s, more or less simultaneously, both sides were preparing to field deliverable megaton-yield weapons.

AMERICAN PLANNING FOR HOW TO USE its accumulating stockpile proceeded ad hoc during the years of the Truman administration (1945–1953). Truman had been shaken by the extent of civilian casualties at Hiroshima and Nagasaki. A third Fat Man had been ready for assembly and delivery in the final days before the Japanese surrender on 15 August 1945, but Truman had ordered atomic bombing stopped after the first two bombs were used. At a cabinet meeting, Henry Wallace, the secretary of commerce, recorded the president's reasoning: "He said the thought of wiping out another 100,000 people was too horrible. He didn't like the idea of killing, as he said, 'all those kids.' " After the war, Truman disguised his aversion to using nuclear weapons with public bluster, but his policies as well as private comments reveal his qualms. An artillery officer in the First World War, he hesitated to put atomic bombs into the hands of the military; he told James Forrestal, his first secretary of defense, that he did not propose "to have some dashing lieutenant colonel decide when would be the proper time to drop one." Through the Atomic Energy Act of 1946, the historian David Alan Rosenberg writes, Truman imposed "a system that made atomic weapons a separate part of the nation's arsenal, with the President of the United States the sole authority over their use. . . . His official policy initiatives through 1948 focused exclusively on the goals of establishing civilian control over American nuclear resources . . . and seeking international control of atomic energy in the United Nations. . . . International control remained the only official policy enunciated by the U.S. government relative to atomic weapons through the summer of 1948."

Truman changed his mind a year later when it became clear that international control of atomic energy was unacceptable to the Soviet Union so long as the United States alone knew how to build nuclear weapons. "Since we can't obtain international control," he decided, "we must be strongest in atomic weapons." The shock of the North Korean surprise attack on South

Korea on 25 June 1950 "led President Truman to take the lid off" nuclear-weapons production, a State Department official, Robert Bowie, remembers. The Atomic Energy Commission's eight sites and 55,000 employees in 1950 expanded to twenty sites and 142,000 employees by 1953, and the expansion continued. By the mid-1950s, the nuclear production complex consumed 6.7 percent of total U.S. electrical power and exceeded in capital investment the combined capitalization of Bethlehem Steel, U.S. Steel, Alcoa, DuPont, Goodyear, and General Motors. Between 1953 and 1955, the U.S. strategic stockpile doubled, from 878 weapons to 1,756, while its total yield increased almost forty times, from seventy-three megatons (4,867 Hiroshimas) to 2,880 megatons (192,000 Hiroshimas). Yet Truman wrote a critic during his last year in office, 1953, that the atomic bomb "is far worse than gas and biological warfare because it affects the civilian population and murders them by wholesale." In his farewell address, equally bluntly, he warned against trying to fight a war with nuclear weapons:

> The war of the future would be one in which man could extinguish millions of lives at one blow, demolish the great cities of the world, wipe out the cultural achievements of the past—and destroy the very structure of a civilization that has been slowly and painfully built up through hundreds of generations. Such a war is not a possible policy for rational men.

Truman assigned planning for the use of the new weapons to the Joint Chiefs of Staff, who turned over the preparation of target lists to the Air Force, the only service branch that could deliver the massive early-model bombs—the Mark 3 production model Fat Man, for example, was six feet in diameter and weighed ten thousand pounds. The target lists that the Air Force produced, David Alan Rosenberg notes, reflected the experience of planners who "were all veterans of the bombing campaigns against Germany and Japan," which is to say, they had experienced the failure of so-called precision bombing and the seeming success of mass bombings and firebombings using conventional explosives and incendiaries. A study presented to the National Security Council in 1950 estimated "that just sixteen atomic weapons, if properly targeted, could 'most seriously disrupt' the U.S. government." General Curtis LeMay, the commander in chief, as of October 1948, of the Strategic Air Command (SAC), who had overseen the firebombings of Japan and who would oversee the devastating but little-known strategic bombing of North Korea during the Korean War, was "firmly convinced that 30 days is long enough to conclude World War III."

Despite such vivid evidence that nuclear war would be completely different from conventional war, that it would be a destructive blitzkrieg providing no time to mobilize industry and workers for what had formerly been a long haul, Air Force and SAC planners nevertheless targeted cities, "with the primary objective," according to a classified Air Force history that Rosenberg cites, "of the annihilation of population, with industrial targets incidental." Thirty-day war or not, LeMay continued to believe that the right targets for atomic bombing were industrial complexes within urban areas, so that bombs that missed their aiming points would produce what he called "bonus damage," meaning massive destruction and civilian casualties. "What was a city," the planners asked each other, "besides a collection of industry?" Truman might have advised them that a city is also human beings, not to be "murdered . . . by wholesale" even if they were enemy subjects.

LeMay may have been ruthlessly rational in the tradition of Ulysses S. Grant, believing that it is better to wage total war from the first hour of a conflict than to allow it to drag on and consume more lives. His protégés were not necessarily so detached. Robert Gates, the director of the CIA under President George H. W. Bush, remembers an encounter at SAC with a general when Gates was a young Air Force officer and had the task of briefing commanders on the SAC targeting plan. Gates mentioned that most U.S. warheads were targeted on Soviet ICBMs (intercontinental ballistic missiles). "The general," he writes, "a LeMay 'wannabe' smoking a huge cigar, went ballistic. He jumped up and shouted that it was a 'goddamn outrage' to be targeting what would in war be empty missile silos. He demanded that I— a second lieutenant—change the targeting strategy, proclaiming that 'when the balloon goes up, I want to kill some fucking Russians, not dig up dirt.' "

But LeMay understood what his wannabes evidently did not: the impossibility of defending a nation against nuclear attack. Stanley Baldwin, the British prime minister in the years after the First World War, had formulated the essential dilemma of strategic bombing as long ago as 1932, telling the House of Commons, "The bomber will always get through." The only defense against an attack from the air is in offense, Baldwin argued, adding, in a phrase that shocked the country, "which means that you have to kill more women and children more quickly than the enemy if you want to save yourselves." He went on prophetically: "Fear is a very dangerous thing. It is quite true that it may act as a deterrent in people's minds against war, but it is much more likely to act to make them want to increase armaments to protect them against the terrors that they know may be launched against them." LeMay had paraphrased Baldwin's stark formula not long after he returned from Japan at the end of the Second World War: "No air attack," he told the Ohio Society of New York in November 1945, "once it is launched, can be completely stopped." He hoped that if the United States had a force in being that was prepared to retaliate, "it may never come. It is not immediately conceivable that any nation will dare to attack us if we are prepared."

He was whistling in the dark and he knew it. Even as he built SAC into the most devastating war machine in history, capable of visiting utter destruction upon any enemy anywhere in the world at the cost of millions upon millions of noncombatant lives, he knew that the bomber, the land-based missile, the submarine-launched missile, the low-flying cruise missile, would always get through, and now not merely carrying high explosives, which might destroy a block of houses, but carrying atomic or hydrogen bombs, which could destroy an entire city or region and take at least hundreds of thousands of lives. "In general," an Air Force evaluator briefed the Joint Chiefs of Staff in 1955 on the current nuclear targeting plan, "the destruction of Soviet aircraft and airfields has an important degrading effect on Soviet atomic capabilities, but even under the improbable assumption that only 5 percent of the aircraft survived, seventy-five [nuclear] weapons could [still] be lifted against the U.S." Not even preventive war could guarantee safety. Piling up armaments for massive preemption or retaliation might deter, but would invite disaster if deterrence failed.

Both sides took the point. McGeorge Bundy, the national security adviser to Presidents John F. Kennedy and Lyndon Johnson, stated it succinctly for the American side in an essay published in the journal *Foreign Affairs* in 1969:

> In light of the certain prospect of retaliation, there has been literally no chance at all that any sane political authority, in either the United States or the Soviet Union, would consciously choose to start a nuclear war. This proposition is true for the past, the present and the foreseeable future. . . . In the real world of real political leaders . . . a decision that would bring even one hydrogen bomb on one city of one's own country would be recognized in advance as a catastrophic blunder; ten bombs on ten cities would be a disaster beyond history; and a hundred bombs on a hundred cities are unthinkable.

On the Soviet side, Nikita Khrushchev recalled in retirement that his first nuclear-weapons briefing after he took power in 1953 had shaken him. "I couldn't sleep for several days," he said. "Then I became convinced that we could never possibly use these weapons, and when I realized that, I was able to sleep again." At least one member of the Soviet general staff, Vladimir Slipchenko, concurs. "The retaliatory strike of even one nuclear warhead," Slipchenko told a post–Cold War conference, "would cause unacceptable damage to a country."

Slipchenko's formulation notwithstanding, both military leaderships

thought in military terms, as their training and experience predisposed them
to do: A threat should be met with a more powerful counterthreat, and
nuclear war, if it came to that, could be won or lost. The experience of the
Second World War loomed large, not only for the military leaderships and
the target planners but also for the heads of state. Truman, with military
experience in the First World War, became president during the Second,
upon Franklin Roosevelt's death. Eisenhower had been supreme allied commander. Kennedy had been a young naval officer commanding a patrol boat
who saw action and was wounded in the Pacific. All the Soviet leaders
between Stalin and Gorbachev had fought in the war. Nikolai Detinov, a
lieutenant general who worked on arms control in the Soviet Ministry of
Defense, remembers his response to a speech given in Moscow in the 1960s
by the American arms strategist Herman Kahn:

> He said that the problem with the Soviet Union and the United States is that
> they are led by people who lived through the Second World War and are still
> thinking in the categories of World War II. And that explanation completely
> applied to the Soviet Union. If we think about Khrushchev or Brezhnev, these
> are people who went through all the hardships of World War II. They wit-
> nessed the early defeat of the Soviet army because we didn't have enough arms,
> they saw the cities and towns burning, they saw our divisions marching toward
> the east in retreat. And so they sought certain things, the promise of security.

That everything had changed with the advent of nuclear weapons was not
immediately apparent after the war, since the first bombs were not more
destructive in scale than the firebombings that had preceded them: The
ruins of Hiroshima and Nagasaki looked like the ruins of Dresden and
Tokyo, because all four cities had been burned out by mass fires, the primary
mechanism of destruction. "These weapons were simply looked upon as
larger conventional weapons," confirms Todd White, a SAC historian. No
one seems to have done the numbers, multiplied each bomber carrying a
single atomic bomb times the thousand bombers that it replaced and understood that the scale of war had changed, that bombing with even a single
nuclear weapon, as Rabi and Fermi had understood, went "far beyond any
military objective and [entered] the range of very great natural catastrophes," while a thousand bombers loaded with atomic and especially with
thermonuclear bombs—though evidently not unthinkable—would be at
least Bundy's "disaster beyond history."

With the memory of vast destruction and near-defeat at the hands of the
Nazis burned into the Russian soul, and the shock tearing at the American

spirit that the United States was for the first time vulnerable to such catastrophe delivered by Soviet bombers and, later, missiles, it hardly seemed possible to accumulate too many weapons, too many delivery systems, just as Baldwin had predicted. In an official oral history of U.S. strategic nuclear policy produced by Sandia National Laboratories, the historian Douglas Lawson of Sandia comments that "the large growth that we saw [in nuclear-weapons production] in the 1950s and 1960s was primarily driven by the capacity of the [production] complex and not truly by [military] requirements." A designer at Sandia, Leon Smith, notes that "it was our policy at that time not to wait for requirements from the military but to find out from the technologies that were available what the art of the possible would be." The former director of the Lawrence Livermore Laboratory, John S. Foster, Jr., adds, "We were making it up as we went along." So the bombs multiplied, while every national leader whispered to himself under his breath that he would never use them.

IN THE 1950S, U.S. PLANNERS FOR nuclear war with the Soviet Union and its Eastern European and Chinese allies defined three categories of targets: targets such as airfields directly involved in delivering nuclear weapons, which had to be "blunted"; targets such as roads and railroad yards that facilitated further military deployment, which had to be "retarded"; and targets such as industry and urban centers, which had to be "destroyed." Official SAC policy weighted targeting to reflect these categories, particularly blunting, but such distinctions, writes the historian David Alan Rosenberg, "all but disappeared at the operational level" because targets overlapped and the SAC commander Curtis LeMay intended to throw everything he had into the initial attack, which he called his "Sunday punch."

According to a Navy officer, Captain William B. Moore, who attended a briefing at SAC headquarters in Omaha in 1954, SAC had by then identified some 1,700 enemy designated ground zeros (DGZs), which included 409 airfields. At that time SAC had 2,400 ready flight crews, a mix of medium- and long-range bombers, including the huge B-36, with a range of eight thousand miles, the smaller but jet-powered and aerial-refueled B-47, and B-52s coming on line with an aerial-refueled range of nine thousand miles. Using these resources, Moore reported, SAC planned to

> lay down an attack . . . of 600–750 bombs by approaching Russia from many directions so as to hit their [radar] early warning screen simultaneously. It would require about 2 hours from this moment until bombs had been dropped by using the bomb-as-you-go system in which both [blunting] and [destruction] targets would be hit as they reached them [opening up corridors for the bombers that followed]. . . . The final impression was that virtually all of Russia would be nothing but a smoking, radiating ruin at the end of two hours.

As far as SAC was concerned, the more bombs the better. More bombs meant a more devastating first strike and a greater likelihood of effective retaliation if the United States was attacked by surprise and some of its strategic assets were destroyed. More bombs also meant more bombers to carry them and, not incidentally, a larger share of the defense budget for the Air Force. Between 1954 and 1957, for example, the Air Force's share of defense appropriations averaged 47 percent annually compared with the Navy's 29 percent and the Army's 22 percent.

The Soviet Union had produced two hundred bombs by 1955, most of them twenty-kiloton, ten-thousand-pound RDS-1s, but its bomber fleet was embryonic. The first Soviet postwar bomber, the Tu-4, was a copy of the U.S. B-29, with all of that Second World War aircraft's limitations. The round-trip from Moscow to New York to Moscow is fifteen thousand kilometers (ninety-four hundred miles); Moscow–London–Moscow is five thousand kilometers (three thousand miles). The Tu-4's three-thousand-mile maximum range thus made it suitable only for regional air strikes—on London at the outside—without refueling, while the real threat, U.S. strategic nuclear forces, remained based safely out of range.

A Soviet intercontinental bomber, the Bison A* turbojet, entered service in 1954, but its maximum range was only five thousand miles and it could only carry a 5,000-kilogram (11,000-pound) bomb load—that is, one RDS-1. An improved model, the Bison B, had a 7,500-mile range, and by 1960 about sixty Bison Bs had joined Soviet Long-Range Aviation. The larger Bear turboprop bomber entered service beginning in 1956. It could carry a heavier bomb load (nine thousand kilograms: 19,800 pounds) and had a range of more than eight thousand miles, but it was slow and vulnerable. Sixty Bears had reinforced the sixty Bison Bs in Long-Range Aviation by 1960, "deployed on airfields deep within the territory of the USSR and . . . on permanent alert" according to the best post–Cold War authority, the Stanford University scholar Pavel Podvig. The Soviets were working on aerial refueling by then (SAC had begun developing it a decade earlier). In the interim, they practiced refueling stops on ice airstrips in the Arctic. "Such action would greatly jeopardize their chance of surprising us," McNamara dryly concluded.

By 1960, the U.S. arsenal had increased to 18,638 bombs and warheads yielding 20,500 megatons (1.4 million Hiroshimas), of which 3,127 were strategic weapons deployed on B-47 and B-52 bombers, large first-generation Atlas and Titan liquid-fueled ballistic missiles and Polaris nuclear submarines. American megatonnage peaked in 1960. In those years, SAC favored massive ten- to twenty-five-megaton behemoths to maximize its delivery

---

* For simplicity I will use NATO nomenclature; for Soviet designations see Podvig (2001).

capacity and destroy multiple DGZs simultaneously, but as ballistic missiles came into prominence, the total yield of the U.S. stockpile declined to reflect the missiles' more critical weight requirements and greater accuracy. ("The rule of thumb," write the weapons historians Robert S. Norris and William Arkin, "is that making a weapon twice as accurate allows an eightfold reduction in yield while achieving the same level of destruction.")

Most Soviet nuclear weapons were tactical, designed for crushing NATO if a conflict arose with Warsaw Pact forces in Europe; the total Soviet arsenal in 1960 of seventeen hundred bombs and warheads included only about 350 strategic weapons. The small Soviet bomber force had been supplemented by late 1960 with only four intercontinental ballistic missiles and a limited and primitive force of submarines carrying short-range missiles. The Soviet bombers were slow and vulnerable; the KGB kept missile warheads separate from the missiles, which required up to twenty-four hours to assemble, warm up, and fuel; and the submarines, which were normally kept in port, would have to cross the Atlantic or Pacific to within about two hundred miles of North America and surface to launch their missiles. "The Soviets had paltry forces," comments the former secretary of defense James Schlesinger— "hardly enough to stage an attack on the United States."

Coordination of multiplying U.S. nuclear strike forces had become an obvious problem by the mid-1950s. "It became possible for fighter-bombers to carry megaton weapons," the chairman of the Joint Chiefs would explain. In consequence, the tactical air forces, the Navy, and the Army added nuclear weapons to their ordnance. SAC controlled about half the arsenal; commanders in Europe, the Atlantic, and the Pacific controlled the other half. Targets frequently overlapped, wasting weapons and threatening fratricide. The Joint Chiefs first tried to solve the problem by ordering annual World-Wide Coordination Conferences convened at the Pentagon where commanders could get together to swap and coordinate their targets and try to resolve what an official SAC history calls "the complex problems of generation, launch, mutual support and maximum bombing involved in preparing a single command's strike plan." But targeting duplications and triplications were not significantly reduced, the history notes. Exercises between 1958 and 1960 by the successors to these conferences, Joint Coordination Centers in Britain and Hawaii that were supposed to handle actual operational coordination, turned up more than two hundred "time over target" conflicts during which the aircraft or missiles delivering the weapons would probably inadvertently blow each other up.

The solution to the problem, the Joint Chiefs concluded in 1959 after

Government secrecy, risky design, and human error all contributed to the explosion and burnout of Reactor Number Four at Chernobyl, in northern Ukraine, on 26 April 1986. Millions of Soviet citizens learned that the state had lied to them and was powerless to protect them. Mikhail Gorbachev took away a deep sense of the unlimited destructiveness of nuclear war.

Intensely radioactive blocks of burning graphite blew out of the destroyed
Chernobyl reactor; to save the other reactors, firemen cleared their roofs
with wheelbarrows, shovels, and bare hands.

Left: Byelorussian physicist
Stanislav Shushkevich (here
with the author in 2005), later
the first Belarusian head of state
deplored Moscow's failure to
allow protective measures after
Chernobyl. *Above:* International
Atomic Energy Agency director-
general Hans Blix was the first
outsider allowed to visit the
burning reactor.

Mikhail Gorbachev, a farmer's son, was born in 1931, the time of terror famine in the U.S.S.R. when Stalin used mass starvation to force Soviet farmers onto collective farms. Gorbachev's own family suffered.

Left: Gorbachev as a small boy with his grandparents. In the mistreatment of his own family, Gorbachev learned early of the corruption of the Soviet state.

Above: Wedding portrait, 1953. Gorbachev met Raisa at Moscow University. Her childhood had also been scarred.

Above: Moscow University prepared Gorbachev for a government career. *Below:* In his native North Caucasus, Gorbachev struggled to improve Soviet agriculture.

Opposite, top to bottom: The brutal suppression of Czech liberalization during the 1968 Prague Spring intensified Gorbachev's doubts about the Soviet political system. Under Leonid Brezhnev (here with Jimmy Carter) the Soviet economy stagnated. In 1969 Gorbachev found a Politburo patron in Yuri Andropov, who called him "a brilliant man working in Stavropol." He would not move to Moscow for ten more years.

On 29 August 1949, Joe 1, the first Soviet atomic bomb test, ended the American atomic monopoly and set the stage for the nuclear arms race that followed.

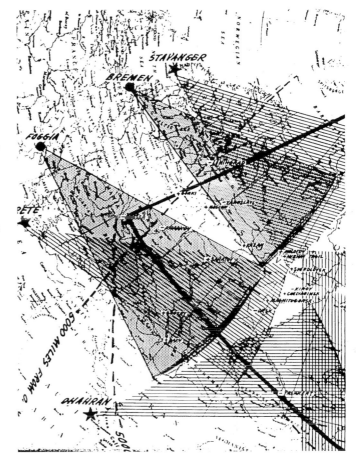

Right: Already in September 1945, the U.S. Air Force had plotted the ranges of its strategic bombers against a map of the U.S.S.R. to determine how many atomic bombs it would need. Even if 0% were duds, planners estimated, 466 20-kiloton bombs would destroy 66 Russian cities and obliterate its military and industry.

Below: Air Force chief of staff Curtis LeMay with John F. Kennedy. By 1960, the U.S. strategic nuclear arsenal exceeded 3,000 weapons and would ultimately number 16,000.

The B-52 bomber, first flown in 1954,
became the Strategic Air Command's workhorse.

In 1950 the State Department's Paul Nitze (*left*) and Secretary of State Dean Acheson (*center*)
deliberately exaggerated the Soviet threat in the founding document of the Cold War, NSC-68,
to boost defense spending. Dwight Eisenhower (*right*) pushed for moderation when
he became president in 1953. The Navy offered a less grandiose deterrent than bombers
and ICBMs, the ballistic missile nuclear submarine (*below*).

prodding from the secretary of defense, was that "atomic operations must be pre-planned for automatic execution to the maximum extent possible." Thus was inaugurated the Single Integrated Operational Plan (SIOP), developed initially under the direction of Air Force Lieutenant General Thomas Power, who succeeded Curtis LeMay as commander in chief of SAC from 1957 to 1964.

John F. Kennedy was briefed on the first plan, SIOP-62, by the chairman of the Joint Chiefs, General Lyman L. Lemnitzer, on 13 September 1961. SIOP-62, Lemnitzer told the president, was designed to work either preemptively or in retaliation for a Soviet nuclear strike on the United States. Like SAC's earlier plan, it targeted not only the Soviet Union but also the People's Republic of China and allies of the two countries in Eastern Europe and elsewhere, all to be hit at the outset of hostilities with a massive simultaneous attack from all sides at once, bomb as you go. The PRC and Eastern Europe would be hit even if they had not initiated hostilities. (When Kennedy's secretary of defense, Robert McNamara, learned of SAC's targeting priorities, he was appalled. "We essentially blasted our way through the Warsaw Pact countries in order to get to the Soviet Union," he told the Sandia oral-history project, "and I remember thinking, 'My God, what are we going to do to Poland?' ")

The number of U.S. strategic nuclear weapons available to be delivered had increased slightly by 1961 to 3,153, but megatonnage had declined by almost half with the phasing out of SAC's largest bombs. Four-fifths of the SIOP-62 designated ground zeros were military. Lemnitzer explained, however, that "because of fallout from attack of military targets and co-location of many military targets with urban-industrial targets, the casualties would be many millions in number. Thus, limiting attack to military targets has little practical meaning as a humanitarian measure." Contemporary estimates of the consequences of an all-out SIOP attack put the death toll at 285 million Soviet and Chinese citizens and millions more dead in Eastern Europe— more than twice the dead of all the wars of the twentieth century. The journalist Fred Kaplan reports that General David Shoup, the Marine Corps commandant, asked Thomas Power at a similar SIOP briefing in 1960 if the United States had any options to avoid bombing China if that country happened not to be involved in the conflict that had led to nuclear war. "Well, yeah, we *could* do that," Kaplan reports Power replying, "but I hope nobody thinks of it because it would really screw up the plan." Back in Washington, Kaplan writes, other U.S. military leaders endorsed SIOP-62 to the secretary of defense. "David Shoup stood and said, 'Sir, any plan that kills millions of

Chinese when it isn't even their war is not a good plan. This is not the American way.' "

As if such deliberate democide were not horrific enough, one SIOP reviewer after another discovered that its damage calculations were based only on the blast effects of nuclear weapons, when the primary mode of destruction of weapons with yields greater than one hundred kilotons— most U.S. strategic weapons—is fire. Admiral Harry Felt, the commander in chief of the Pacific fleet, cabled the Joint Chiefs in January 1961 after reviewing the SIOP, "ONLY BLAST EFFECTS WERE CONSIDERED. . . . OTHER EFFECTS SUCH AS HEAT, FIRE AND RADIATION SHOULD BE USED WHEN DRAWING UP DAMAGE CRITERIA FOR THE SIOP." A Ukrainian explosives expert and Manhattan Project veteran named George Kistiakowsky, President Eisenhower's astute science adviser, who was sent out to Omaha in late 1960 to review the work of the Joint Strategic Target Planning Staff, reported back, "The JSTPS used blast effect as the only criterion of damage and neglected thermal radiation, fires which will be caused by it, and fall-out. The question may be raised as to whether the resultant damage criteria are unnecessarily conservative, whether they result in overkill and will create unjustified additional 'force requirements.' "

Why should it matter whether people were killed by fire or blast? The answer began to emerge only in the 1980s, when a few independent scientists looked into the neglected subject of mass fires from nuclear weapons. As one of them, Theodore Postol, found, even a very limited attack on enemy industry "might actually result in about two to three times more fatalities than that predicted by the government for the [all-out] anti-population attack" if mass fires were included in casualty predictions. Two to three times the 285 million Soviet and Chinese dead that SIOP-62 predicted based on blast damage alone would raise that number close to 1 billion.

Until recently, the official explanation for why fire was left out of targeting calculations was that the extent of mass fire in an incendiary attack depends on weather conditions. Such had been true of the firebombings of the Second World War, but according to the preeminent expert on the subject today, the Stanford University scholar Lynn Eden, mass fires started by strategic nuclear weapons create their own environment:

> The extraordinarily high air temperatures and wind speeds characteristic of a mass fire are the inevitable physical consequence of many simultaneous ignitions occurring over a vast area. The vacuum created by buoyantly rising air follows from the basic physics of combustion and fluid flow. . . . As the area of

the fire increases, so does the volume of rising air over the fire zone, causing even more air to be sucked in from the periphery of the fire at increasingly higher speeds.

Using as an example a single three-hundred-kiloton airburst over the Pentagon, which by blast effects alone would hardly knock down buildings of heavy construction beyond Capitol Hill, Eden estimates that fire effects would generate "ground winds of hurricane force with average air temperatures well above the boiling point of water. . . . Within tens of minutes, the entire area, approximately 40 to 65 square miles—everything within 3.5 or 4.6 miles of the Pentagon—would be engulfed in a mass fire. The fire would extinguish all life and destroy almost everything else," south beyond Alexandria, Virginia, in one direction and north to Chevy Chase, Maryland, in the other. The intense light of a nuclear fireball, the equivalent at three miles of six hundred desert suns at noon, ignites fires simultaneously and instantly over a large area, with the fireball's shock wave, its blast, arriving long seconds later to break up, spread, and feed the flames. "A nuclear weapon could be considered the nearly ideal example of an incendiary weapon," Postol summarizes, because it delivers its entire yield in an instant—"about 300 trillion calories," Eden estimates, "within about a millionth of a second." Nor is one bomb over the Pentagon even remotely a realistic scenario. A former SAC commander told Eden, "We must have targeted Moscow with 400 weapons. . . . I would be comfortable saying that there would be several dozens of weapons aimed at D.C."

In her book *Whole World on Fire,* Eden finds organizational traditions and prejudices central to the neglect of mass fire in targeting calculations. Targeting planners and military leaders drew on their experiences in the Second World War to frame their priorities. At that time, strategic targeting had been focused on precision bombing—"tossing it right in the pickle barrel"—and only when that effort failed had the Air Force turned to area bombing and then firebombing. Though more successful, these practices were also a reminder of failure; the bureaucratic focus on precision bombing continued and renewed after the war. Precision bombing targeted specific structures that could be accumulated into target lists, so that destroying the structures would quantify destroying the enemy's capacity to make war. It also evoked a tradition of marksmanship with hand weapons that extends back through two centuries of American exploration and pioneering.

Targeting atomic and hydrogen bombs as if they were precision weapons is something like using a large meteor to drive a nail, and it depopulates the target zone. "The world of nuclear weapons damage," Eden writes, "is gener-ally an unpeopled one of physical objects—structures, installations, and equipment." Rendering invisible the people who occupy the structures and installations and operate the equipment being targeted has obvious benefits of emotional relief for the planners. Interviewing a recent vice director of the JSTPS, Navy Vice Admiral Michael Colley, Eden heard of larger benefits as well:

> We don't like hitting cities [Colley told her], we don't like killing people. So we have a philosophy of mass destruction, yes, but aimed at military targets. So it's politically comfortable and morally comforting for political leaders of our country to espouse "urban polygons" or "city withholds," so we can tell the world, hey, we don't hit cities. So I put this in the realm of political policy, not military effects. Because there are military targets all over the world that are in or near cities. . . . The emotion, the politics, is very, very important.

Eden comments:

> Admiral Colley had just taken me through the self-contradictory world of nuclear strategy and operations, a world in which potential horror, political nostrums, and mundane organizational problem solving are all mixed together. In Colley's words, "Nuclear war is irrational and unthinkable. *But,* if you're going to believe in deterrence, you have to have a war plan which makes sense, is executable—and devastating." The logic of nuclear strategy requires a fully executable and devastating plan, but politicians generally do not like to acknowledge the extent of the devastation. Thus, they espouse "limited" mass destruction in executable plans that would be irrational and unthinkable to carry out. What many comfortingly call the "paradox" of nuclear strategy is perhaps better understood as the "nonsense" of nuclear strategy—literally, that which does not make sense.

Nor was mass fire the only nuclear-weapons effect that targeting planners neglected. Among others, Eden lists radiation, smoke, ash, dust, noxious gases, fireball anomalies, electromagnetic pulse (EMP, which burns out elec-tronic circuits such as microchips and transformers), crater ejecta, and blast-driven debris. These would add their further lethalities to the results of a nuclear attack by either side, the United States or the Soviet Union—or both.

AS SAC ATE ITS WAY THROUGH the U.S. defense budget in the 1950s, the Navy, increasingly concerned that it would shrink to a vestigial service in a nuclear world, challenged and criticized the SAC program's obvious excesses while energetically looking for a strategic role of its own. It found that role— to become what it called the "ultimate national deterrent"—in the ballistic-missile nuclear submarine. The first SSBN,* the U.S.S. *George Washington,* was ordered hastily in December 1957, two months after the Soviet Union launched the world's first man-made earth-orbiting satellite, *Sputnik,* as the payload of its first intercontinental-range ballistic missile, the cryogenic liquid-fueled SS-6. Electric Boat, in Groton, Connecticut, built the top-priority *George Washington* by cutting apart a Skipjack fast-attack nuclear submarine already under construction and welding in a 130-foot compart-ment for sixteen missiles between the sub's navigation end and nuclear-reactor compartment. The *George Washington,* launched on patrol on 15 November 1960, carried Polaris A1 solid-fueled missiles with ranges of about thirteen hundred nautical miles, each carrying a Livermore-designed W47 thermonuclear warhead with a six-hundred-kiloton yield (forty Hiroshi-mas). Four more Polaris submarines entered service by March 1961, the five-boat fleet carrying a total of eighty missiles.

Around the ballistic-missile nuclear submarine the Navy elaborated an alternative concept of finite deterrence. A sea-based deterrent, Admiral Arleigh Burke told the Joint Chiefs in September 1959, hidden in the vastness and the depths of the world's oceans, would not invite preemption as land-based bombers and missiles did. And if the United States was attacked, a sea-based retaliatory capacity would remain viable and should therefore serve as a more robust deterrent than land-based systems that might be destroyed in a Soviet first strike. The first generations of submarine-launched bal-listic missiles (SLBMs) might be less accurate than land-based missiles or bombers, but accuracy would be of little importance in a retaliatory attack, when Soviet bombers and missiles would already have departed from their bases and their launchpads, leaving cities hostage. Following these assump-tions, David Alan Rosenberg reveals:

> The Navy projected that a fleet of 45 submarines, with 29 deployed at all times, could destroy 232 Soviet targets, "which was sufficient to destroy all of Russia. The total cost of such a program would be 7 to 8 billion dollars, and annual operating costs would be $350 million." This proposal, [Eisenhower adminis-tration] Budget Director Maurice Stans remarked, raised the obvious question as to why the U.S. needed "other IRBMs [intermediate-range ballistic missiles] or ICBMs, SAC aircraft, and overseas bases." Navy leaders agreed, but were in

---

* SSBN: "Submarine, submersible, ballistic-missile, nuclear-powered."

no position to propose the virtual elimination of SAC. That, they told Stans, "was somebody else's problem."

The Air Force fought back, of course, and won its argument to the extent at least that U.S. strategic nuclear forces came to be multiplied into a triad: ballistic-missile submarines, bombers, and land-based ICBMs. This triad, which has since been sanctified as a prudent redundancy vital to effective deterrence, was nothing of the kind; it was an artifact of interservice rivalries. The Navy's "finite deterrence" alone would have deterred the Soviet Union, unless one believes that the Soviet leadership would have been willing to accept, in return for gambling a first strike against the United States, the complete destruction of all its major cities and the violent death of most of its population.

Eisenhower didn't believe it, but his disillusion with massive retaliation came too late. By 1959, Rosenberg writes, Eisenhower judged "that military statements of nuclear weapons requirements were grossly inflated: 'They are trying to get themselves into an incredible position of having enough to destroy every conceivable target all over the world, plus a three-fold reserve.' " At a meeting of the National Security Council in November 1958, Eisenhower told the assembled Cabinet officers and military leaders (as the meeting notes paraphrase) "that in today's presentation of the U.S. retaliatory attack on the Soviet Union, the U.S. had as targets every city in the U.S.S.R. with a population of over 25,000 people. . . . Turning to General Twining and addressing him and other members of the Joint Chiefs of Staff, the President said that he could remember well when the military used to have no more than 70 targets in the Soviet Union and believed that destruction of these 70 targets would be sufficient."

Although the United States had little information about Soviet strategic assets before the advent of reconnaissance satellites and communications intelligence in 1960, Soviet strategic policy during this era revealed itself by its actions to have been cautious, conventional, and to some extent budget-driven. The only Soviet system capable of attacking the United States with nuclear weapons until the early 1960s was the small fleet of sixty Bison and one hundred Bear bombers. Since they were based deep within the Soviet Union, they would have to be staged forward before flying intercontinentally, which would give away their intention and make them vulnerable to preemptive attack.

Lacking access to bomber bases close to the United States, the Soviet military limited its inventory of bombers to concentrate more resources on ballistic-missile development. It focused on arming its forces in Europe first of all, developing intermediate-range "theater" nuclear missiles such as the SS-3, the first Soviet missile to carry a nuclear warhead, and the SS-4. Diesel-electric and nuclear-powered attack submarines armed with nuclear torpe-does, short-range missiles, and cruise missiles offered tactical and limited strategic force projection as well.

The Soviet Union began developing intercontinental ballistic and cruise missiles in 1954. The SS-6, the missile that carried *Sputnik* into orbit, was ready for flight testing in 1957, and the first two Soviet satellites were launched in November as part of those flight tests, the second with a dog aboard. The *Sputnik*s greatly impressed the Kremlin along with the rest of the world, Podvig writes, turning the Soviet leadership's attention to the missile-development program. The Strategic Rocket Forces emerged as a separate service in December 1959 to receive the new SS-6 ICBMs, but "the level of readiness of [the] missiles was extremely low," Podvig says—the cryogenic liquid-fueled missile required twenty-four hours to ready for launch—and "the high cost of launch complexes predetermined the very limited scale of their deployment."

At the time of the Cuban Missile Crisis, according to Podvig, the Soviet bomber fleet "could deliver about 270 nuclear weapons to U.S. territory." But fear of the SAC commander Thomas Power's bomber fleet, which he main-tained on airborne alert throughout the week of the crisis, flying orbits over the Mediterranean and northern Canada, landing only long enough to change crews, led the Soviets to keep their bombers grounded; the Soviet Union was nearly as defenseless against nuclear attack that week as Japan had been at the end of the Second World War, although Soviet submarines in the Caribbean could have launched their missiles against U.S. targets in retaliation. American nuclear assets consisted of several thousand bombs on 1,576 SAC bombers, 183 Atlas and Titan ICBMs, 144 Polaris missiles on nine nuclear submarines, and the first squadron of ten Minuteman I missiles car-rying W59 one-megaton warheads, brought to full alert for the first time at the height of the crisis on Friday, 26 October 1962.

The United States had discovered the vast discrepancy between U.S. and Soviet strategic forces when its first generation of Corona photographic reconnaissance satellites began returning film in August 1960. Kennedy had communicated the discovery to the Soviet leadership to call Khrushchev's bluff about barring the West from Berlin. American exposure of Soviet strategic weakness was one reason Khrushchev had attempted to install medium- and intermediate-range missiles—SS-4s and SS-5s—in Cuba. The weapons were intended primarily to protect Cuba from a U.S. invasion, but an additional purpose was certainly to boost Soviet deterrence capabilities through forward basing. The United States, after all, had Jupiter missiles with 1.4-megaton W49 warheads pointed at the Warsaw Pact countries and the Soviet Union from bases in Italy and Turkey.

While it is true, as Podvig writes, that "the U.S. superiority in capabilities and number of strategic nuclear weapons was one of the most decisive factors that shaped the evolution of the conflict and the positions taken by both countries during the crisis," it is also true that Kennedy and his advisers did everything possible to avoid provoking a Soviet attack—even if such an attack had culminated in no more than Bundy's "one . . . bomb on one city of one's own country." One bomb was always enough.

That the United States could force the leaders of the Soviet Union to remove their missiles from Cuba frightened and deeply humiliated them. "The results were very painful and they were taken very painfully by our leadership," the Soviet lieutenant general Nikolai Detinov remembers. "Because of the strategic [imbalance] between the United States and the Soviet Union, the Soviet Union had to accept everything that the United States dictated to it and this had a painful effect on our country and our government." As a result, says Detinov, "all our economic resources were mobilized [afterward] to solve this problem." The Soviet diplomat who negotiated the crisis settlement, Vasily Kuznetsov, had implicitly threatened such a response. "Well, Mr. McCloy," he challenged his American counterpart, John J. McCloy, "we will honor this agreement. But I want to tell you something. You will never do this to us again."

"Humiliation in Cuba," writes Robert Gates, "galvanized the Soviets into action. The USSR proceeded to undertake the largest military buildup in history over a twenty-five-year period, with profound consequences for the international balance of power, for the United States, and ultimately, and fatefully, for the Soviet economy and state." Detinov concurs:

> During the 1960s, the Soviet government mobilized the economy to the point that all industrial facilities were turned to military production. All factories were included. . . . The rate of growth of our national economy went down in all branches. While before the Caribbean crisis we had a very steady rate of production, after the Caribbean crisis all production in other areas started going down thanks to the fact that all factories were mobilized in the name of military technology. Turning the national economy around later on was very hard.

Work on what Podvig calls "a simple and relatively inexpensive missile that could be used to increase the number of missiles in the Soviet ICBM force and provide quantitative parity with that of the United States" was authorized in March 1963, just five months after the resolution of the Cuban Missile Crisis; the light SS-11 would carry a 1.1-megaton warhead to compensate for its inaccuracy. The following September, the Soviets tested a heavier missile already in development, the SS-9, with a 10-megaton warhead. SS-11 flight tests began in 1965, and by 1966 both missiles were being deployed. Soviet Yankee-class nuclear-missile submarines, each carrying sixteen missiles with 1-megaton warheads, began patrolling the coasts of the United States in 1967.

One casualty of the Soviet buildup of missile forces was the nation's program to put men on the moon. Soviet dreams of beating the United States to the moon "were quietly abandoned" in the late 1960s, writes the former Air Force secretary Thomas Reed, "in favor of a massive ICBM buildup."

Both sides were also investigating missile defense systems; the Soviets had built a primitive antiballistic-missile system (ABM) of sixty-four interceptors around Moscow beginning in 1962. To contribute to defeating a U.S. ABM system, Podvig reports, Soviet designers developed a fractional-orbital version of the SS-9 that could attack from any azimuth, a number of which were deployed in 1969.

"The Soviets increased the number of their ICBMs from fewer than a hundred to more than 850 by 1968 and to more than 1,500 by 1972," Gates writes, summarizing the Soviet buildup, "while the U.S. number remained constant at 1,054. They began a vast expansion of their submarine ballistic missile force and laid the foundations for qualitative improvements to their strategic forces . . . as well." Gates's enumeration omits the U.S. contribution to the doomsday contest. The American stockpile reached its historic high of about 32,200 bombs and warheads in 1966. The number of U.S. land-based missiles "remained constant at 1,054" because Kennedy and McNamara had decided in 1962 that a thousand Minuteman ICBMs were enough, added to the fifty-four Titan II ICBMs already in service. (The number reveals the political, as opposed to the strategic, basis of the decision. SAC had wanted ten thousand Minutemen. The Air Force leadership cut that request to three thousand. Kennedy and McNamara had come to favor a force of only six hundred, because the U.S. inventory already counted 656 Polaris missiles on forty-one nuclear submarines. But since Kennedy had made a supposed "missile gap" a major issue of his presidential campaign, a thousand Minutemen to fill the illusory gap was the least he thought he could order to save face.)

In addition, both sides began studying the possibility of MIRVing their missiles: clustering multiple warheads—as many as ten or more—on a platform called a "bus" that would carry them together into space, where they would then be sprung free on individual trajectories leading down to different targets; "MIRV" stood for "multiple independently targetable reentry vehicle." In 1969, when the two sides began the SALT I arms-control talks, the United States was five years ahead of the Soviet Union in mastering the destabilizing technology. Soviet missiles were larger and more powerful than their U.S. counterparts, however, primarily because they were designed to carry heavier and more powerful warheads to compensate for their inferior accuracy. When the Soviets mastered MIRVing, that greater "throw-weight"—effective payload—would be an advantage, but surprisingly few American experts challenged the wisdom of developing a force multiplier that could only benefit the Soviet Union when that nation caught up. Alfred Lieberman, a senior operations analyst at the Pentagon at that time, recalls demonstrating the consequences of MIRVing statistically using the large computer model of a Soviet–U.S. nuclear exchange that the Pentagon's Operations Analysis Office maintained to examine arms-control positions to make sure they were advantageous to the United States:

> One of the key issues was whether or not we should abolish the MIRVing of ballistic missiles. . . . The problem was that at the time we were way ahead of the Russians in MIRV technology. Some of our studies warned that they had larger missiles and some day might load more MIRVs on them than we had. We also showed that MIRVs created a destabilizing situation since one attacking missile could destroy several missile silos. It was however not possible at that time to convince the inter-agency that MIRVs should be limited because we were so far ahead of the Soviets. In the end the Soviets caught up and loaded many more MIRVs on their missiles than we did on ours.

"Other considerations," McGeorge Bundy comments on U.S. strategic nuclear decision making, "were always found more important at moments of choice." The Joint Chiefs wanted MIRVing because it would effectively (and cheaply) override McNamara's thousand-missile ceiling. McNamara himself, Bundy says, thought MIRVing "would be a powerful means of penetrating any Soviet ABM system." MIRVing eventually resulted in both U.S. and Soviet warhead numbers five to six times as high as they had been with single-warhead missiles. It also interfered with treaty verification, since identifying a MIRVed warhead from space was difficult. "The inadequacy of verification," wrote the Russian security analyst Alexei Arbatov, Georgi's son, "was used as an excuse to do what both sides intended to do anyway."

FROM THE BEGINNING, AND THROUGHOUT all the years of the Cold War, the United States led the Soviet Union in total numbers of strategic nuclear bombs and warheads. The bitter U.S. political debates of the 1970s and early 1980s about nuclear strategy, nuclear force levels, supposed Soviet first-strike capabilities, and strategic defense hinged on arguments as divorced from reality as the debates of medieval scholars about the characteristics of seraphim and cherubim.

To cite one example among far too many: Paul Nitze, the American arms-control negotiator, arguing in 1976 against the SALT II treaty then under discussion, which would set a limit of 2,400 launchers on each side's collection of ICBMs, SLBMs, and bombers, pointed to the superior throw-weight of Soviet launchers and a supposed Soviet "massive and meticulously planned civil defense effort" as reasons why the United States should be wary of limiting its arsenal to parity. Though he was well aware that the United States had concluded in the early 1960s, after thorough study, that it was better off with lighter but more accurate land-based missiles and fewer rather than more of those (since they would eventually be vulnerable to destruction by Soviet ICBMs), he nevertheless found it politically useful to argue that the Soviet march toward a greater number of missiles of greater throw-weight betokened an aim of establishing "a nuclear-war-winning capability on the Soviet side."

Jan M. Lodal, a deputy to Secretary of State Henry Kissinger, responded to Nitze's argument by pointing out what Nitze must have known that, "unless accuracies are better than about 0.2 nautical miles, no reasonable MIRV system can have much of a counterforce capability [that is, capability to destroy enemy missile silos]; once accuracies are better than 0.1 nautical miles, essentially any size missile, even those of relatively low throw-weight, can destroy silos." In the case of the new Trident I missile, then being developed for U.S. nuclear submarines, Lodal added, "the United States could have just as well increased the throw-weight, had it been thought important to do so. Nonetheless, our military planners—correctly in my opinion—chose to emphasize the survivability of our submarines, and thus to use the additional capability of the missile to extend its range [rather than increase its effective payload]; this extra range gives our submarines a much greater operating area and reduces dramatically any possibility that the Soviets could determine their location and attack them."

Of Soviet efforts at civil defense, Nitze cited the *Soviet Civil Defense Manual*, of all suspect authorities, as estimating "that implementation of the prescribed evacuation and civil defense procedures would limit the civilian casualties to five to eight percent of urban population or three to four per-

cent of the total population—even after a direct U.S. attack on Soviet cities."
Acknowledging that "the Soviets may well overestimate the effectiveness of
their civil defense program," Nitze argued that the *Manual* demonstrated
that they assumed "that nuclear war could happen, and that the Soviet
Union could survive." One of Nitze's early protégés, the Reagan-era deputy
secretary of defense Richard Perle, carried on this Soviet civil-defense argument for years. But Alfred Lieberman, the Pentagon's operations analysis
expert, remembers clearly his office's investigation of the Soviet civil-defense
program:

> We did a very large study which showed that the Russians' civil defense would
> not save them from disaster in a nuclear war. We got some data from the CIA;
> we also got a lot of data from the Defense Department and the [military] ser-
> vices. But the essence was that we ran our nuclear exchange model with many
> variables and showed what would occur under a variety of different conditions.
> Our studies showed what disasters would occur in case of nuclear war even
> with the most sophisticated civil defense. . . . Our offensive forces would create
> horrendous damage against even the most advanced civil defense program.

These two examples of one prominent nuclear strategist's threat inflation
are not in any way unique; on both sides, during the years of the high Cold
War, there was always political capital to be earned from exaggerating the
dangers or benefits of any particular nuclear strategy or weapons system. But
even for those within the two governments with the best of intentions, trying to find security among the shifting and partly obscured maps of both
sides' evolving force structures led to convoluted and sometimes absurd
conclusions.

Robert McNamara, for example, visited the Omaha offices of the Joint
Strategic Target Planning Staff for a briefing about the U.S. nuclear target list
in February 1961, shortly after he became secretary of defense. McNamara
was curious to compare the targeting-system criteria to a target known to
have been destroyed, Hiroshima, burned out by a mass fire after a fifteen-
kiloton bomb, Little Boy, exploded 1,900 feet above the city center on
6 August 1945. This dialogue ensued:

> Q.—McNamara—Have you applied your procedures to Hiroshima?
> A.—Smith—Yes. 3 DGZs of 80 KT each.

That is, were Hiroshima still a target, the JSTPS would have identified three
designated ground zeros within the city and would have assigned three

nuclear weapons, each equivalent to eighty kilotons of TNT, to destroy them. Such overkill gives meaning to Winston Churchill's notorious 1954 comment, "If you go on with this nuclear arms race, all you are going to do is make the rubble bounce." In the real world, one bomb of fifteen kilotons had been more than sufficient.

I asked McNamara, who has come to believe that nuclear weapons should be abolished, why the United States built so many more than it realistically needed during the Cold War. "Each individual decision along the way seemed rational at the time," he told me. "But the result was insane." His explanation echoed something he wrote in 1986, that "each of the decisions, taken by itself, appeared rational or inescapable. But the fact is that they were made without reference to any overall master plan or long-term objective. They have led to nuclear arsenals and nuclear war plans that few of the participants either anticipated or would, in retrospect, wish to support."

Among the reasons the decisions appeared rational or inescapable were difficult, threatening, and sometimes appalling political conflicts between the two sides which I have deliberately avoided discussing in this chapter and the last: from Soviet attempts to cut Berlin off from the West, to the Korean War, to brutal suppressions of dissent in Hungary, Czechoslovakia, and Poland, to the secret attempt to install missiles in Cuba and much more. Leaving these events out of the narrative must seem to some readers to severely bias my discussion of the progressive buildup of weapons on both sides, but none of these crises was resolved or resolvable with nuclear weapons.

However compromised the Soviet leadership felt afterward by the disparity between U.S. and Soviet strategic forces at the time of the Cuban Missile Crisis, for example, and contrary to Kennedy's public statements, there was never any question on the U.S. side of initiating a nuclear attack, McNamara reveals: "Despite an advantage of seventeen to one in our favor, President Kennedy and I were deterred from even considering a nuclear attack on the USSR by the knowledge that, although such a strike would destroy the Soviet Union, tens of their weapons would survive to be launched against the United States. These would kill millions of Americans. No responsible political leader would expose his nation to such a catastrophe." Kennedy's sanity was confirmed years later, after the end of the Cold War, and much to McNamara's surprise and shock, when Russian participants in the Cuban crisis revealed that no fewer than 162 nuclear weapons (warheads, submarine-launched missiles, and bombs) had already been deployed to the Caribbean and to Cuba before the crisis began. The missile warheads, McNamara learned, were "moved from their storage sites to positions closer to their delivery vehicles in anticipation of a U.S. invasion" at the height of the crisis on Friday, 26 October 1962. Khrushchev personally approved the move, which increased the risk, writes McNamara, that in the event of a U.S. invasion "the Soviet forces in Cuba would have decided to use their nuclear weapons rather than lose them. We need not speculate about what would have happened in that event. We can predict the results with certainty."

The conservative, seemingly prudent tendency on both sides was to pile destruction upon destruction with the hope that enough would eventually be enough. "We are piling up these armaments," Eisenhower said in 1956, "because we do not know what else to do to provide for our security." But the buildup itself added to the mutual fear, confirming to each side that the other must have nuclear-war-fighting plans, whatever its stated intentions. Worse, both sides' plans were regularly revised upward not to meet actual military needs but to justify the ongoing production of nuclear weapons. The operative concept in the United States was called the "greater than expected threat," which was based on the Soviet Union's potential weapons production capacity regardless of whether or not such production was actually budgeted. As a former assistant secretary of defense for systems analysis explained to two inquiring scholars, "We begin with the National Intelligence Estimate. We then use a planning and analytic device called the greater than expected threat. What we do is develop a substantially larger threat than the National Intelligence Estimate shows. This is developed by consulting various of the experts around the government . . . and approved by the Joint Chiefs of Staff." Since the threat is inflated, the two scholars point out, and the corresponding numbers of proposed weapons is therefore larger than the Joint Chiefs could have justified based on the National Intelligence Estimate alone, there is seldom any difficulty in winning their approval.

If actual needs were the basis of procurement, then the "assured destruction" criteria that McNamara's experts worked out at his request would have been sufficient. The Soviets would be deterred, McNamara advised President Lyndon Johnson in December 1963, if the United States possessed a survivable arsenal of four hundred one-megaton warheads, sufficient to kill 30 percent of the Soviet population, demolish 50 percent of Soviet industry, and destroy 150 Soviet cities.

Nuclear weapons were not simply larger conventional weapons. Their destructive force was orders of magnitude greater, producing mass fire and lethal fallout as well as blast damage. "We had maps of the United States," Alfred Lieberman recalls, "showing how a major Soviet attack would create fallout over most of the country. . . . In general, our study illustrated what would really happen in a major nuclear war. Not just the human casualties but also the massive destruction of the infrastructure of both the U.S. and the Soviet Union."

So much confusion, so much paranoia, so many good intentions, so much hard work, technical genius, cynicism, manipulation, buckpassing, buck-pocketing, argument, grandstanding, risk-taking, calculation, theorizing, goodwill and bad, rhetoric and hypocrisy, so much *desperation,* all point to something intractable behind the problem of how to deploy sufficient and appropriate nuclear arms to protect one's nation from a nuclear-armed opponent. There was such a beast. It was quite simply the fundamental phys-ical fact of nuclear energy: that such energy is relatively cheap to generate and essentially illimitable. Nuclear warheads cost the United States about $250,000 each: less than a fighter-bomber, less than a missile, less than a patrol boat, less than a tank. Each one can destroy a city and kill hundreds of thousands of people. "You can't have this kind of war," Eisenhower con-cluded. "There just aren't enough bulldozers to scrape the bodies off the streets." It followed, and follows, that there is no military solution to safety in the nuclear age: There are only political solutions. As the Danish physicist and philosopher Niels Bohr summarized the dilemma succinctly for a friend in 1948, "We are in an entirely new situation that cannot be resolved by war." The impossibility of resolving militarily the new situation that knowledge of how to release nuclear energy imposes on the world is the reason the efforts on both sides look so desperate and irrational: They are built on what philos-ophy calls a category mistake, an assumption that nuclear explosives are mil-itary weapons in any meaningful sense of the term, and that a sufficient quantity of such weapons can make us secure. They are not, and they cannot.

Mikhail Gorbachev came to that conclusion. But before he did so, one final, major crisis intervened. Unfortunately for the policy of détente that Richard Nixon and Henry Kissinger pursued during Nixon's years in the presidency (1969–1974), the desperate, all-out Soviet effort of the 1960s and 1970s to achieve nuclear parity with the United States looked to one group of American ideologues like an attempt to dominate the superpower competi-tion—or so its spokespersons argued. When one member of the group, a former professional actor and governor—Ronald Reagan—won election in 1980 as president of the United States, thirty-one other members moved into positions of federal authority and proceeded to act on their convictions.

SIX THE SORCERER'S APPRENTICES (I)

ACCURATE THREAT ASSESSMENT, ALWAYS AN IMPORTANT responsibility of government, became critical with the advent of nuclear weapons. Partly because the Soviet Union was a closed society, difficult to read, partly because measuring a threat requires judging intent as well as counting warheads, U.S. national-security studies were vulnerable to ideological bias. Since assessments often influenced policy decisions, those who wrote them and framed their conclusions could use them to ambush opponents and win bureaucratic battles.

No one was better at influencing policy by writing reports than Paul Nitze, a handsome, imperious patrician of German descent whose involvement in U.S. security strategy and arms diplomacy spanned five decades. Nitze's grandfather had been a banker, his father a professor of Romance languages at the University of Chicago, his mother an outspoken liberal and proto-feminist. Having made himself wealthy through marriage to a Standard Oil heiress and with Wall Street dealings during the Great Depression, Nitze had moved on to Washington as a dollar-a-year man managing wartime materials procurement. In 1944, he joined the fledgling U.S. Strategic Bombing Survey, an investigation critical to shaping his views of nuclear strategy. "I became interested in strategic concepts when I was with the USSBS," he acknowledged later. Interviewing captured Nazi leaders in Germany after its May 1945 surrender, he identified what he called "the essential requirement" for winning the air war in Europe: the necessity of first destroying the German air defense forces to open up the country to area bombing. Had the air defense forces not been destroyed first, too many Allied bombers would have been lost to sustain the campaign.

Moving on to Japan after its surrender in August 1945, Nitze made a thorough study of the atomic bombings, which impressed him perhaps less than they should have. He commented in 1989 that they "were not the most devastating air attacks that Japan had suffered," which was true but misleading.

The firebombings of Tokyo were more devastating, but by later standards Little Boy at fifteen kilotons and Fat Man at twenty-two kilotons were low-yield weapons. Nitze's judgment of the atomic bomb's significance, that it "compressed the explosive power of many conventional bombs into one," minimizes the potential impact of future bombs' more devastating fire and fallout effects and signals an early conviction that nuclear weapons not only could be used to fight wars but would not necessarily be decisive.

Nitze's "essential requirement" conclusion about the air war in Europe confirmed that conviction. If, as he believed, nuclear weapons simply improved the efficiency of strategic bombing, it followed that the conventional strategy of attacking military targets to clear the way for area bombing would be essential in an air war with nuclear weapons as well. "This experience and the concepts derived therefrom," he told a colleague in 1966, "go to the roots of the counterforce concept." That is, from the necessity of suppressing German air defenses to open the way to strategic bombing, Nitze extrapolated a strategy for fighting a nuclear war that involved attacking military targets first—called a "counterforce" strategy—rather than attacking industry and urban populations at the outset of a conflict—a "countervalue" strategy—as Curtis LeMay had programmed SAC to do.

Back home in 1946, Nitze worked as principal author with a small team of colleagues to write the Strategic Bombing Survey's final *Summary Report on the Pacific War.* He contributed importantly to the development and administration of the Marshall Plan, which underwrote the rebuilding of Europe. By 1949, he was deputy to George Kennan on the State Department Policy Planning Staff and then Kennan's successor when the originator of the U.S.'s Soviet-containment policy resigned at the end of the year.

President Truman announced his decision to proceed with the development of the hydrogen bomb on 31 January 1950. In his decision directive he asked his secretaries of state and defense, Dean Acheson and Louis Johnson, "to undertake a reexamination of our objectives in peace and war . . . in the light of the probable fission bomb capability and possible thermonuclear bomb capability of the Soviet Union." Acheson turned over the work of research and writing to Nitze.

Both men believed that Europe was vulnerable—two world wars had begun there—and that the Soviet leadership was fanatic beyond any possibility of negotiation. They also intended to prevent Germany from rearming. Acheson and Nitze were therefore committed to a major expansion of U.S. military forces and armaments to stabilize Europe, and the report that Nitze and his staff prepared between February and April 1950, "NSC-68: United

States Objectives and Programs for National Security," tendentiously constructed that case. "The purpose of NSC-68," Acheson would admit later, "was to so bludgeon the mass mind of 'top government' that not only could the President make a decision but that the decision could be carried out." Nitze, according to a scholar of the report who interviewed him on the subject, "wanted to sacrifice a degree of rationality in the analysis of NSC-68 in order to exaggerate the [Soviet] threat, with the hope that the reaction of opinion leaders would be commensurate with the threat." Which is to say, the bludgeon Nitze chose to use was threat inflation.

Although Nitze and his staff consulted no experts on the Soviet Union, and were neither experts themselves nor even fluent in Russian, NSC-68 is weighted with rhetorical absolutes. The Soviet Union, it claims, was "animated by a new fanatic faith, antithetical to our own, and seeks to impose its absolute authority over the rest of the world." Not only America but "civilization itself" confronted either "fulfillment or destruction" in the "endemic" conflict with the Soviet Union; and "every individual" faced "the ever-present possibility of annihilation" should the conflict enlarge to total war.

The United States had "purpose" in this Manichaean struggle; the Kremlin had "design":

> The design . . . calls for the complete subversion or forcible destruction of the machinery of government and structure of society in the countries of the non-Soviet world and their replacement by an apparatus and structure subservient to and controlled from the Kremlin. To that end Soviet efforts are now directed toward the domination of the Eurasian land mass. The United States, as the principal center of power in the non-Soviet world and the bulwark of opposition to Soviet expansion, is the principal enemy whose integrity and vitality must be subverted or destroyed by one means or another if the Kremlin is to achieve its fundamental design.
>
> . . . Thus unwillingly our free society finds itself mortally challenged by the Soviet system. No other value system is so wholly irreconcilable with ours, so implacable in its purpose to destroy ours, so capable of turning to its own uses the most dangerous and divisive trends in our own society, no other so skillfully and powerfully evokes the elements of irrationality in human nature everywhere, and no other has the support of a great and growing center of military power.

The "degree of reality" that Nitze sacrificed to this portrait of implacable evil was considerable. Just five years earlier, the Soviet Union had emerged from a brutal war to count its losses: at least twenty-five million people killed, one-tenth of its population; millions more invalided and twenty-five million made homeless; half its industry destroyed; coal production as of 1945 down 33 percent compared to 1941, oil production down 46 percent, steel 48 percent, meat 40 percent, dairy 55 percent, electricity 33 percent. Yet NSC-68 was asserting that the war-battered nation had recovered sufficiently five years later to muster the energy and resources for an implacable campaign to destroy the United States and rule the world.

The most egregious exaggeration of NSC-68 was its assessment of the Soviet Union's 1950 war-fighting capability. It was certainly true that Stalin had added two million more men to the three million kept under arms facing the West at the end of the war—his counterpoise to the American nuclear monopoly—and then had tested an atomic bomb as well. Nitze, however, citing the Joint Chiefs as his authority, claimed that if a major war should occur that year, 1950, the Soviet Union would be capable not only of immediately overrunning Western Europe, but also of "driv[ing] toward the oil-bearing areas of the Near and Middle East," consolidating "Communist gains" in the Far East, launching air attacks against Britain and air and sea attacks against the shipping lanes of both the Atlantic and the Pacific, and attacking "selected targets with atomic weapons, now including the likelihood of such attacks against targets in Alaska, Canada and the United States." (With only five atomic bombs in its arsenal that year, the Soviets would have had to be selective indeed in choosing targets.)

Further, Nitze judged that 1954 would be "a critical date for the United States," estimating (with CIA, military services, and Atomic Energy Commission concurrence) that by then the Soviets would have stockpiled about two hundred atomic bombs, enough to "seriously damage this country." The actual number in 1954 was about 150, so the estimate is not far off. But Nitze chose not to mention the rapidly enlarging U.S. stockpile: By 1954, the United States would have deployed more than fourteen hundred strategic nuclear weapons of a total yield of more than three hundred megatons, a powerful deterrent that would make any attempted attack by the Soviets suicidal and therefore highly unlikely. Nitze underplayed the American deterrent because he wanted his country not simply to deter a theoretical Soviet attack but also "to check and to roll back the Kremlin's drive for world domination." He, Acheson, and the military services thus called for "a rapid build-up of political, economic and military strength in the free world."

Truman, on the other hand, concerned about the federal budget, was skeptical of NSC-68 at first. Following the outbreak of the Korean War, which the president believed to be a Soviet feint into South Asia in preparation for war in Europe, he endorsed it. He had imposed a limit of $14.4 billion on the 1949 defense budget, and beginning in 1950 it was supposed to be cut further to $13 billion. After Truman endorsed NSC-68, he allowed the defense budget to increase almost fourfold; defense outlays in 1953 totaled more than $52 billion.

Even more significantly, NSC-68 began the historic uncoupling of the U.S. defense budget from fiscal policy. Truman and his predecessors had first determined a total budget number, based on available resources, and had then allotted part of that total to defense. Such prudence now became politically dangerous. Most administrations after Truman's determined the defense requirements first and then either allocated what was left to domestic needs or added to the deficit (or, more rarely, raised taxes) to sustain both guns and butter. Determining defense requirements first was the way it worked in the Soviet Union as well, with the significant difference that the far larger U.S. economy cushioned the impact of increasing diversions of federal income to the military. As the assistant secretary of the Army Karl R. Bendetsen summarized, "Once the President, upon recommendation of the National Security Council members, approved the recommendations" of NSC-68, "the foundation had then been laid for U.S. rearmament, for the reestablishment of an industrial mobilization base, for the generation of new, modern weapon systems and for NATO and the several follow-on mutual security pacts."

We have fear for things, Thomas Hobbes wrote in Leviathan, "not only which we know have hurt us, but also that we do not know whether they will hurt us or not." This latter "dimension of unknowable harm," writes the political scientist Corey Robin, "can make fear ripe for abuse. . . . Since the future is 'but a fiction of the mind' [in Hobbes's words], whoever defines the objects of our fear necessarily traffics in the realm of imagination. This makes the fear of unknowable harm a kind of rational fiction, a hypothetical speculation about the future, based upon experience and inference." Nitze's best-known hypothetical speculation about the future, NSC-68, characterized the United States as vulnerable to as few as one hundred Soviet atomic bombs but the Soviet Union as implacable despite America's thousands. On what experiences and inferences did he base this "rational fiction," if rational it was?

Nitze was specific about the basis for his argument. NSC-68, he wrote in his memoirs, "addressed what I have considered throughout my career to be the fundamental question of national security: How do we get from where we are to where we want to be without being struck by disaster along the way?" Even the title of his memoirs, *From Hiroshima to Glasnost,* reflected his sense that life is a dangerous journey. Curiously, of the very few incidents from his childhood that Nitze mentioned in his memoirs and in interviews, the two that stand out as formative concern dangerous journeys. The first, to which he attributed his interest in influencing world affairs, began in the Austrian Alps in 1914:

> At the beginning of the war I was seven and we were in Austria, climbing mountains in 1914, when the Austrian archduke was murdered at Sarajevo. And that is what set off the powder chain that led to the outbreak of World War I. We saw it happen, we saw the mountaineers in Austria being mobilized for war. My father decided it had become dangerous in Austria, decided to go to a safe country. So he took us all off to Germany, and we arrived in Munich on the day that Germany declared war on Russia. Bombs were thrown in the railroad station. Then we lived through the early days of the war when the Germans were marching to the Western Front. Most of them were eventually killed in that war. We saw the wounded come back, so the horror of that war—I had a second cousin who was killed on the Eastern Front by the Russians at the battle of Königsberg, where the Russians were defeated. He lost his life in that. We finally got out through Holland and came back to the United States, but that memory of what happened during World War I stuck with me. It still sticks with me. It's one of the most moving, dreadful events that I lived through.

His second dangerous journey, a little later in childhood, Nitze also associated with his diplomatic career, calling it his "first lesson in power politics":

> We lived on Fifty-sixth Street [in Chicago]. On Fifty-fifth, just one block away, lived and operated some of South Side Chicago's toughest gangs. My mother insisted on dressing me in a Buster Brown outfit, complete with flowing tie. In this attire, I walked the gauntlet to and from school every day.
>
> I soon received my first lesson in power politics. The gang on the block bounded by Fifty-fifth Street, Woodlawn and Kimbark avenues, would waylay and soundly beat me up every day on my way home from school. For protection, I joined the Scotti brothers' gang on the neighboring block run by the sons of an Italian family. The eldest brother was a charismatic leader, a blue-eyed, blond Italian, full of courage and paternal kindness to his gang. He inspired great loyalty in me; I did whatever he asked, without concern for the fine distinction between legal and illegal activities.
>
> Of course, a good part of this admiration came from intense gratitude, for from the moment I joined the gang, they defended me. Thereafter I was able to live in relative peace in that part of Chicago's jungle.

Among the activities the charismatic leader asked of Nitze was theft: "One time he gave me a directive to rob the construction site across the way from our house, where a whole row of houses were being built, and liberate the work tools for the use of the gang. And I liberated them, and turned them over to the gang."

So Nitze's memorable lesson in power politics, still recalled near the end of his life, was that the way to get from where you are to where you want to be without being struck by disaster is to surround yourself with overwhelming force. "To have the advantage at the utmost level of violence helps at every lesser level," he argued chillingly in 1978, calling the point "a copybook principle in strategy." (It has been a fundamental principle of U.S. nuclear strategy across more than six decades.) What Nitze only barely acknowledges in his story—in the phrase "relative peace"—is the protected ten-year-old's concomitant fearfulness, caught as he is between two rival violent gangs over which he has no control. The man the ten-year-old became spent most of his life exaggerating the Soviet threat and scolding his countrymen for what he believed to be their feeble and naïvely insufficient commitment to maintaining "the utmost level of violence." A free society is vulnerable, he wrote oddly in NSC-68, "in that it is easy for people to lapse into excesses—the excesses of a permanently open mind wishfully waiting for evidence that evil design may become noble purpose, the excess of faith becoming prejudice, the excess of tolerance degenerating into indulgence of conspiracy." In his own lapse into "excess," Nitze transformed the crude and deeply insecure men in the Kremlin into masters of evil—a small boy's view of a menacing gang.

NITZE'S NEXT IMPORTANT OPPORTUNITY to influence defense policy came in 1957, when President Eisenhower appointed a large panel of private citizens headed by the former Ford Foundation president H. Rowan Gaither, Jr., to assess a Civil Defense Administration proposal to build a $40 billion system of fallout shelters to protect the U.S. population in the event of nuclear war. Unknown to Eisenhower, the Gaither panel went rogue, enlarging its mandate to include the same range of policy issues that NSC-68 had covered. Nitze's name is buried in the back of the Gaither report—because he was a Democrat helping out a Republican administration, he said—but McGeorge Bundy confirms that he was "a principal draftsman."

By 1957, a series of events and confrontations had raised the specter of Communism on the march. Herbert York, a physicist and the first director of the Lawrence Livermore Laboratory, was a consultant to the Gaither panel, and remembers being concerned. "You have to recall that in 1948 there was the Berlin Blockade," he told an interviewer, "in 1948 there was the coup in Czechoslovakia, and the expansion that these things represented seemed quite real. And then there was the fall of China, as we put it, to the Communists [in 1949,] the creation of the Sino-Soviet Bloc, the Korean War in the early fifties. So looking back from the late fifties, what we saw was a lot of successes or what seemed to be successes on the part of the Russians, including territorial expansion." In retrospect, York adds ruefully, "that was the high-water mark, but we didn't know it at the time."

But whether or not the advances of Sino-Soviet Communism were real or only apparent by 1957, Nitze and his colleagues on the Gaither panel chose to exaggerate the dimensions of the threat. Nineteen-fifty-four had been NSC-68's year of maximum danger. That year having passed without attack, the Gaither report moved the threat forward to 1959, much as frustrated prophets revise their estimates of the end of the world. By 1959, it seemed, "the USSR may be able to launch an attack with ICBMs carrying megaton warheads, against which SAC will be almost completely vulnerable under present programs." Although the Gaither report itself mentions no specific number of Soviet ICBMs, Eisenhower's science adviser George Kistiakowsky wrote later that the Gaither panel "predicted a catastrophic 'missile gap'— claiming that by 1959 as many as 150 Soviet ICBMs would be aimed at the U.S." The columnist and Washington insider Joseph Alsop confirmed having heard the number in private briefings, adding that U.S. strategic forces presented "no more than about 50 targets" according to the Gaither panel, and therefore "the Soviets were expected to be able to wipe out American strategic striking power by 1961." (In fact, the Soviets had deployed no operational ICBMs at all by 1959.)

If such a preemption were successful, the report continued, "manned bombers could then deliver a decisive attack against the U.S." (The Soviet Union had fielded a total of 115 strategic bombers by 1959, carrying 210 strategic weapons. Few would be likely to penetrate U.S. defenses, especially if no Soviet ICBM blunting attack had prepared the way.) Already, according to the report, the Soviets had developed "a spectrum of A- and H-bombs and produced fissionable material sufficient for at least 1500 nuclear weapons." (If so, they were behind in production, because the actual number of nuclear weapons in the Soviet arsenal in 1959 was about 1,050, of which only 283 were strategic weapons. They had built three thousand short-range jet bombers, the report claimed, "and probably surpassed us in ICBM development."

To counter these dangers, the Gaither report proposed increasing U.S.

intermediate-range ballistic-missile numbers "from 60 to 240" and Atlas and Titan ICBM numbers "from 80 to 600." It proposed augmenting the alert status of SAC bombers and developing "a nationwide fallout shelter program to protect the civilian population."

Eisenhower was not impressed, nor did he believe the panel's inflated threats. Given the president's years of military experience, McGeorge Bundy notes, "he knew . . . that in essence the gloomier predictions were based mainly on what estimators believed about what the Soviets would decide to do and not on activities of which anyone had significant direct experience." The U-2 overflights Eisenhower authorized, while not covering the entire Soviet Union, gave him information about "the most likely [missile] sites," Bundy says, which were "along railroad lines . . . and to a man with a long experience of estimating the enemy, the absence of any positive confirmation was significant." Impressed or not, Eisenhower and his vice president, Richard Nixon, had to challenge John F. Kennedy's assertions of a "missile gap" during the 1960 Nixon-Kennedy presidential campaign, and in the end, by the smallest of margins, Kennedy won the presidency. Threat inflation—appealing to fear for political advantage—worked.

IF NITZE'S PENCHANT FOR threat inflation was driven by his own deep-seated fears as well as his ambitions, it also followed from his conviction that the American people and too many of their leaders lacked what he called "moral fiber" and needed to be frightened into action. Eisenhower did not embrace the conclusions of the Gaither report, Nitze alleged in his memoirs, not because the former supreme allied commander thought they were aberrant but because "he was anxious to maintain his image as a man of peace" and "fell into that broad category of people who believed that nuclear war was 'unthinkable,' and therefore the effort to achieve a reliable deterrent capability was not urgent." Similarly, Nitze believed that those who judged that "defense against nuclear war was futile" were not judging on technical grounds but cravenly endorsing "what can only be described as a policy of preemptive surrender." In the late 1960s, amid the political turmoil generated by the Vietnam War, Nitze cast resistance to the development of an ABM system—which was strong among experts who doubted the technical feasibility and strategic benefit of such a system—as the response of "prominent members of the scientific-academic community who had become disgruntled with defense policy in general and Vietnam in particular."

To counter this anti-ABM campaign, Nitze decided to set up a committee to lobby in favor of the ABM. In doing so, he unleashed a team of sorcerer's apprentices whose trail of wreckage extends well into the present century. In 1969 he, Dean Acheson, and a University of Chicago professor and nuclear strategist with the RAND Corporation named Albert Wohlstetter formed the Committee to Maintain a Prudent Defense Policy; "lacking funds to hire a full-time staff for research and writing, we recruited three young but exceptionally talented graduate students who agreed to work for expenses—Peter Wilson, Paul Wolfowitz and Richard Perle." Wilson went on to serve in the Carter State Department. Wolfowitz, born in 1943, a graduate student of Wohlstetter's at the University of Chicago, returned there after his CMPDP summer to finish his Ph.D., went on to teach at Yale, and then moved permanently to Washington in 1973 to work at the Arms Control and Disarmament Agency under the conservative former RAND analyst Fred Iklé.

Perle, a night owl with characteristic dark circles around his eyes even as a young man, was an informal Wohlstetter protégé. Born in 1941, the son of a self-made textile merchant of Russian Jewish ancestry, he had dated Wohlstetter's daughter Joanie in high school in Hollywood, where he grew up, and seems to have modeled himself on her prominent father while moving through his later education: college at the University of Southern California, graduate study at the London School of Economics, and then work toward a Ph.D. at Princeton. "Wohlstetter was flamboyant and eccentric, worldly and suave," an admiring Perle biographer writes, "and spoke as easily about food and wine as he did [about] the threat of Russian bombers and missiles." Perle came to share Wohlstetter's style, if not his substance. Returning to graduate school to finish his doctorate looked pallid after a summer working for a former secretary of state, a leading strategist, and a legendary Cold Warrior; instead, Perle won a position on the congressional staff of Democratic senator Henry "Scoop" Jackson of Washington, whose specialty was defense. Perle—bright and bashful, a young man on the make—learned the game of defense politics from Jackson himself and from Jackson's hawkish staff director for the Senate Permanent Subcommittee on Investigations, Dorothy Fosdick, a daughter of the Reverend Harry Emerson Fosdick who also happened to be Adlai Stevenson's mistress. Congressional staff members siphon authority from their high-octane bosses. Perle discovered a gift for bureaucratic infighting and rapidly accrued power.

Nixon and his national security adviser, Henry Kissinger, moved toward détente with the Soviet Union at the beginning of the 1970s with the expectation that the Soviets in return would help the United States extricate itself from Vietnam. Simultaneously they normalized relations with the People's

Republic of China, hoping to take advantage of the increasing conflict between the two Communist powers. (By 1977, Robert Gates writes, Leonid Brezhnev was telling people that China was now "the number one enemy.' ")

Nixon and Brezhnev signed an ABM treaty in Moscow on 26 May 1972 as well as an Interim Agreement (SALT I) temporarily capping the numbers of strategic arms. The Interim Agreement was limited to a life span of five years to allow for further negotiation of unresolved issues. Because it recognized the United States's preponderance of heavy bombers (the United States, with an estimated 450, had 300 percent more than the U.S.S.R. with 150) it allowed the Soviet Union about 50 percent more ICBMs and 30 percent more SLBMs, sensibly decoupling warhead parity from parity in delivery systems. (In fact, since the United States was five years ahead of the Soviet Union in MIRVing its missiles, the United States's total delivery capability was superior to the Soviets' especially since bombers could carry more than one bomb each.)

Scoop Jackson was outraged at the agreement's appearance of ballistic-missile inequality. "A longtime anti-Communist," writes the defense analyst Anne Cahn, "supporter of Israel, and defender of the defense industry ('the senator from Boeing' some said derisively), Jackson, whom John F. Kennedy passed over as his choice for vice-president in 1960, still harbored serious presidential ambitions. By identifying himself with the attack on détente, Jackson hoped to broaden his political base and to tap into the wide ideological diversity present in the strange bedfellows' coalition." When SALT I came up for Senate ratification, Jackson introduced an amendment to the resolution of ratification asking the president "to seek a future treaty that, *inter alia* [i.e., among other things], would not limit the United States to levels of intercontinental strategic forces inferior to the limits provided for the Soviet Union."

Even among those like Jackson who demanded it, strategic equality answered to perceptions rather than reality, as the clinical psychologist Steven Kull discovered when he interviewed a range of defense policymakers for a study of how they coped with the counterintuitives of nuclear strategy. Kull's sample of eighty-one men and three women included two former secretaries of defense, two Joint Chiefs, two senators, two representatives, five high-level current and former members of the State Department, five presidential advisers, six "key nuclear strategists from the 1950s and 1960s," and fourteen current and former RAND Corporation employees as well other influentials. When traditional rationales drawn from conventional strategy failed under Kull's polite but relentless questioning, the men and women he was interviewing typically invoked the perceptions of third parties (such as Japan and Germany) and of the American people themselves to justify the nuclear-arms race. One respondent had this to say:

> The game between the United States and the Soviet Union tended to be two frogs in a pond, each one of them blowing one's self up larger than the other and wanting to be more impressive. And the impression that was made was not only on the other frog but on third audiences—particularly so in the case of the United States because we had acquired, one way or another, the responsibility of holding a nuclear umbrella over the heads of other people.

A RAND analyst attributed the need to maintain numerical equality with the Soviets to political pressure:

> If you had a strong president, a strong secretary of defense, they could temporarily, if you will, go to Congress and say, "We're only going to build what we need, and we're not going to spend a penny more on it, we're going to cancel this, we're going to cancel that, and if the Russians build twice as many, tough!" . . . But I personally think that that kind of situation is unstable politically, and that five years hence—maybe less—there would be a political scandal. . . . And it's therefore better for our own domestic stability, as well as international perceptions . . . to insist that we remain good competitors, even if the objective significance of the competition is—uh—dubious.

A "prominent strategic analyst" concurred:

> Strategic weapons are political artifacts first. And when they cease to be political artifacts, then they're entirely irrelevant, entirely without a purpose. . . . The only existence that these weapons have that has any meaning is in political terms. And perceptions is the only relevant category.

Another strategic analyst—from the context, possibly Nitze or Wohlstetter—told Kull with uncharacteristic candor, "Let's put it this way, in more understandable terms. All roads in the strategic equation lead to MAD"—that is, mutual assured destruction, McNamara's four hundred megatons. "All the other ones . . . are games, are window dressings, and they are window dressings for upmanship. . . . But when you take away all these layers of cloth, at the bottom of the thing, basically, is MAD, and no one likes it."

Leaders may default to perception in nuclear matters because they lack direct experience with weapons effects, find confronting the brutalities of war disconcerting, or are accustomed to manipulating political issues for their advantage, to list only a few of many possible reasons. The veteran journalist Robert Scheer, who followed Jackson around for *Esquire* in 1975, when the senator was exploring the possibility of running for president, noticed Jackson's proprietorship in this area:

> He pushes MIRVs and Polarises and atomic bombs with the detachment of a delicatessen owner summarizing his collection of cold cuts. He has never witnessed war except from a guided tour and thinks of it more in terms of points to be scored against the Russians, or even the Secretary of State, than of pain to be suffered by people. His concern is an abstraction called national security, a science that he feels he has mastered.

Jackson's butcher shop was Richard Perle's postgraduate school. Whatever Perle's fundamental convictions, he learned from mentors like Nitze, Wohlstetter, and Jackson that politics, even the politics of mass destruction, was sausage-making. Gates reports his similar enlightenment while serving as a CIA representative to the SALT talks:

> Participation in SALT both in Washington and overseas was a real education for me. I saw that the internal negotiations in both our government and the Soviets' were probably tougher and dirtier than between the two countries. The more complicated the issues became, the more senior officials—especially Presidents—found themselves deferring to the experts. Four of the five Presidents I worked for were bored to tears by the details of arms control.*

"Because fear is a pliable emotion," Corey Robin paraphrases Thomas Hobbes, "shaped and reshaped by moral instruction and ideology, the sovereign has great power to define its objects. No sovereign automatically possesses such power; indeed, he often competes with 'private' men attempting to persuade people to fear objects he has not authorized them to fear." When presidents, from distraction or distaste, avoid thinking about arms control in any detail, they leave unclaimed a space of power where other politicians such as Jackson, bureaucrats such as Nitze or Perle, or ideology-driven groups of private citizens can battle for dominance.

AN OPPORTUNITY FOR SUCH A COMPETITION opened up in the mid-1970s when Americans, impressed with détente, had begun to feel more favorable toward the Soviet Union even as the Soviets, continuing their post–Cuban Missile Crisis buildup, started MIRVing their missiles while

---

* Gates doesn't say which president was exceptional—probably Jimmy Carter.

introducing several new models as well. "Most threatening of all," writes Thomas Graham, Jr., "was the replacement of the SS-9 with the very large SS-18 ICBM with ten MIRVs, each containing a warhead of around half a megaton. Now Minuteman was really threatened—the 308 SS-18s alone could lay over 3,000 large warheads on the [1,000-Minuteman] U.S. ICBM force, 50 percent more than would be needed to destroy the force." Graham understood that the United States had ample retaliatory capacity in the other legs of its triad, but also understood that "private men" are eager to persuade people to fear if such fear can be turned to political advantage: "Whether a first strike on Minuteman could ever realistically be considered anything other than an act of complete madness—with the SLBM force out there, not to mention the bomber force—is beside the point. After 1975, the theoretical capability existed to threaten Minuteman and this had significant political repercussions."

The ongoing SALT talks were a key battleground and Henry Kissinger a primary target. At a press conference in Moscow in July 1974, confronted about giving away nuclear superiority after the talks had stalled, Kissinger had responded in exasperation, " 'One of the questions which we have to ask ourselves as a country is what in the name of God is strategic superiority? What is the significance of it, politically, militarily, operationally, at these levels of numbers? What do you do with it?' " Revealing in public what Kull's nuclear policymakers would acknowledge at length in private—the uselessness of overkill—made the secretary of state few friends among the policy elite, Cahn writes. One of them told her, "Those were remarks that he would always regret." Telling the truth about the cynicism of the nuclear arms race was politically dangerous.

"The critics of détente," Cahn notes, "were certain that the Cold War was far from over and were determined that American hegemony should not disappear." On the evening before a conference on strategic doctrine in Beverly Hills in June 1974, some of them, including Wohlstetter and Nitze, assembled for dinner and discussion at a private home in Santa Monica. Forty more joined the conference the next day to hear Wohlstetter present a long paper that was about to appear in the journal Foreign Policy: "Is There a Strategic Arms Race?" Drawing on newly declassified data, Wohlstetter argued that the Department of Defense had consistently underestimated the buildup of Soviet strategic nuclear forces. At the same time, Wohlstetter asserted, U.S. strategic forces and the budgets to sustain them were decreasing, not increasing, and thus "the United States had not been running a quantitative strategic race" at all. By implication, inadequate methods of intelligence estimating had played into the hands of those such as Henry Kissinger who believed the Soviets could be trusted to keep the bargains they had made in the name of détente. The ideology that underlay Wohlstetter's argument was the same Manichaean division between the two nuclear superpowers that Nitze had been preaching since the late 1940s.

At least one conference participant was not taken in by Wohlstetter's numerical razzle-dazzle. Sidney Drell, a Stanford physicist and government adviser, told Cahn that Wohlstetter's "conclusions were the result of his choosing the right year for starting his comparisons." The graph of U.S. warhead deployments that Wohlstetter displayed, Cahn explains, "stopped with 1972, but a substantial number of warheads were coming into the American force in 1974, and Wohlstetter and many in the audience had known that for several years. The Soviet inventory of intercontinental ballistic missiles reached its peak of 1,600 in 1975 and dipped to 1,400 by 1979. Their submarine fleet declined from 370 to 257 during the decade as they retired many of their diesel subs."

A year after the Beverly Hills conference, an expert at Harvard, Michael Nacht, published a rebuttal to Wohlstetter's article. By 1974, Nacht pointed out, the United States had 6,318 total ballistic missile warheads compared to the Soviet Union's 2,319. And although the Soviets led the United States in total megatonnage, 3,618 to 2,144, "for the vast majority of targets, any warhead in the strategic arsenal is capable of producing untold damage and destruction. . . . High-yield warheads are militarily significant only against hardened targets [such as missile silos], and even against these targets they are substantially less important than high accuracy and the number of deliverable warheads." Wohlstetter's work, Nacht concluded damningly, had "not lived up to his own previously established high standards. . . . When advocacy is portrayed as analysis . . . no one's cause is served."

Drell told me something similar when I asked him about Paul Nitze. "His problem was that he believed in numbers," Drell said, "way beyond their actual value or reliability. He thought he was smarter than everyone else." Apparently the same was true of Wohlstetter, and, like Nitze, he was not above manipulating the numbers to political advantage. "Wohlstetter's charges," Cahn concludes, "were the opening salvo of a movement determined to destroy détente and to steer U.S. foreign policy back to a more militant stance vis-à-vis the Soviet Union."

Ironically, the anti-détente campaign was launched just as détente was succeeding, and serving as political cover for a U.S. military buildup as well. Nixon and Kissinger, Robert Gates points out, used it "to defend a number of strategic-weapons programs from the budget knife on the Hill—from ABM to Trident [missile submarines], cruise missiles, and the B-1 bomber." The new generation of weapons systems that Jimmy Carter stalled in 1976 and then restarted in 1979 and that Ronald Reagan greatly expanded in the 1980s "amid applause from conservatives," says Gates, "could not have been started or sustained politically in the Nixon years without détente. During the 1970s, on defense programs, the conservatives were never able to put congressional votes where their mouths were." Meanwhile, the growth in Soviet military spending, Cahn adds, "declined sharply" in 1975, "from 4–5 to 2 percent, and procurement of weapons was flat."

The conservatives responsible for this burgeoning exercise in threat inflation, many of them Democrats allied with Scoop Jackson, fought détente through the inglorious conclusion of the Nixon administration—the humiliated president resigning his office and flying home to California in August 1974, and a new president, Gerald Ford, taking the reins. These conservatives discerned a nation in decline, reeling from a war lost in Vietnam, dangerously misled by détente—and themselves ignored and out of power. "Soviet policy never changes," the former undersecretary of state Eugene Rostow, one of the most outspoken, scolded Henry Kissinger at the time. Kissinger responded sharply that "a balance of mutual interest" was a better guide to policy than "ideological dogma." But "the Democratic Party didn't want to hear us," Rostow complained, "and we weren't getting any general publicity" because Americans were sick of domino theories and war-derived domestic conflict.

SEVEN **THE SORCERER'S APPRENTICES (II)**

ORGANIZING HIS PRESIDENCY IN AUGUST 1974, Gerald Ford called in Richard Nixon's forty-three-year-old ambassador to NATO and former presidential counselor, Donald Rumsfeld, to serve as his White House chief of staff. Rumsfeld brought along his longtime protégé and factotum, thirty-four-year-old Richard B. Cheney, to be his second-in-command. Ford's senior speechwriter and trusted adviser Robert Hartmann worked with Rumsfeld and Cheney and observed them closely throughout the brief Ford administration; his portrait of the pair, published in 1980, is uncontaminated by post-2000 events:

> Cheney was a serious student of political power and derived both his employment and his enjoyment from it. Whenever his private ideology was exposed, he appeared somewhat to the right of Ford, Rumsfeld or, for that matter, Genghis Khan.
> Rumsfeld and Cheney were a rare match. Their differences reinforced the team. Rummy was darkly handsome, like Tyrone Power. Cheney was a presentable young man who could easily be lost in a gaggle of Jaycee executives. His most distinguishing features were snake-cold eyes, like a Cheyenne gambler's. Rummy was expansive and, when it suited him, all smiles; Cheney's demeanor was low-key and even dour. He was tough, tireless, book-smart, with a touch of sarcasm occasionally overcoming studied subordination. Rumsfeld was more secure, more sensitive to others' feelings, more sophisticated and, when crossed, more passionate. But Don had some class; he was ruthless within the rules.

Rumsfeld had been on Ford's list of candidates to appoint as vice president. Ford thought Nelson Rockefeller better qualified and chose him instead. Rumsfeld harbored presidential ambitions in those days, however, and when pressure from the Ronald Reagan end of the Republican Party made Rockefeller a liability, Rumsfeld and Cheney helped convince Ford to dump him from the 1976 presidential election ticket. At a private meeting with Ford on 28 October 1975, Rockefeller agreed to announce his withdrawal from candidacy whenever the president asked him to, which turned out to be 3 November, in the wake of a 31 October reorganization of Ford's cabinet so extensive that the press came to call it the Halloween Massacre. Besides dumping Rockefeller from the ticket (he continued as vice president until the end of the term), Ford relieved Kissinger of his White House position as national security adviser, replacing him with Brent Scowcroft but leaving him as secretary of state; removed William Colby as director of the CIA, replacing him with George H. W. Bush; removed James Schlesinger as secretary of defense, replacing him with Rumsfeld; and appointed Cheney as White House chief of staff.

"Rumsfeld and Cheney were the right wing of the Ford administration," writes the journalist Sidney Blumenthal, "opposed to the policy of détente with the Soviet Union, and they operated by stealthy internal maneuver." Once Rumsfeld became secretary of defense, he attempted to sabotage Kissinger's SALT II negotiations. An important reason for Colby's replacement with the more pliable George H. W. Bush, Blumenthal says, was the CIA's unwillingness to cooperate with the Rumsfeld-Cheney effort. "Instead of producing intelligence reports simply showing an urgent Soviet military buildup, the CIA issued complex analyses that were filled with qualifications. Its National Intelligence Estimate on the Soviet threat contained numerous caveats, dissents and contradictory opinions. From the conservative point of view, the CIA was guilty of groupthink, unwilling to challenge its own premises and hostile to conservative ideas."

The nuclear-weapons establishment fed into this moil of manipulation in the person of John S. Foster, Jr., a lean, wary California physicist and nuclear-weapons designer who had been the director of the Lawrence Livermore Laboratory from 1961 to 1965 and then for the next eight years director of the Pentagon's Department of Defense Research and Engineering, DDR&E. In that capacity, in 1969, Foster had promoted the view that the Soviet heavy SS-9 ICBM, which in one configuration carried three two-megaton warheads, was a MIRV. He did so, it seems, to promote the Nixon administration's Safeguard ABM system then under fire in Congress: "If the public and Congress could be made to see the SS-9 missiles as threatening Minuteman silos," Anne Cahn explains, "it would be easier to sell the ABM system" to protect them. A single MIRVed SS-9 might threaten three Minuteman silos, while an SS-9 with three un-MIRVed warheads would only indicate that the missile needed to shotgun three large warheads on each Minuteman silo simply to compensate for its poor accuracy—and in fact its maximum error was no less than five kilometers.

The CIA disagreed with Foster's and the Nixon administration's assessment of the SS-9's capability. Nor did CIA analysts believe, as Foster did, that the Soviets were building toward a first-strike capability. The agency underlined its arguments in an update of one of its 1968 National Intelligence Estimates and held its ground against not only Foster and the defense secretary, Melvin Laird, but also against Henry Kissinger. Foster never forgot. In 1973, now out of government, he joined the President's Foreign Intelligence Advisory Board (PFIAB*), an elephant's graveyard of influentials including such fellow conservatives as Edward Teller; the future director of Central Intelligence (DCI) under Reagan, William Casey; Polaroid's founder, Edwin Land; a former governor of Texas, John Connally; the former army secretary Gordon Gray; George Shultz; and Clare Boothe Luce. Finding that their suspicions of Soviet intentions and fears of Soviet dominance matched his, Foster began organizing a revolt. He consulted with Teller and the influential RAND and Livermore physicist Richard Latter. Latter told Cahn he suggested to Foster "that what was needed was a second CIA, an alternative source of information." Though Teller had used that approach to institutionalize his disagreements with Los Alamos, lobbying successfully for a second weapons lab established on an old Air Force base in Livermore, California—the Lawrence Livermore National Laboratory—he balked at the idea of a second CIA. "Foster . . . liked the concept but thought it would be too difficult bureaucratically, and came up with a less grandiose notion—a small group of outside experts should perform an alternative threat assessment. Teller agreed with this plan."

After Foster convinced the chairman of PFIAB of his idea, Cahn writes,

Teller quickly prepared a draft "alternative NIE" and gave it to State Department counselor Helmut Sonnenfeldt to pass on to Secretary of State Kissinger. Teller explained to Sonnenfeldt that current NIEs didn't deal with worst-case scenarios but his draft did. Teller introduced three propositions: Soviet missile accuracies might be better than estimated [by the CIA] and would continue to improve [thus threatening U.S. missile silos and ICBMs]; U.S. submarines would become increasingly vulnerable due to breakthroughs in Soviet antisubmarine warfare; and U.S. bombers might be destroyed before reaching the Soviet Union [by improved Soviet air defenses]. Sonnenfeldt effectively discounted Teller's NIE by commenting, "Teller's technique is to take propositions that can neither be proved nor disproved at this time. Nevertheless, his consis-

_____
* Pronounced "piffy-ab."

tent suggestion that every proposition will unfold in a worst case situation for the U.S. undermines the overall credibility of his 'alternative' NIE."

Stonewalled at the State Department, Teller and Foster next took their worst-case scenarios to the CIA, which not surprisingly found them unconvincing, since they were unsupported by evidence. By November 1975, the CIA's director, William Colby, had won the endorsement of the U.S. Intelligence Board (the formal body of the U.S. intelligence community) of a letter to President Ford that opposed setting up an outside team. "It is hard for me to envisage," Colby wrote, "how an ad hoc 'independent' group of government and non-government analysts could prepare a more thorough, comprehensive assessment of Soviet strategic capabilities . . . than the Intelligence Community can prepare."

Colby was a lame duck by then, however; he was only able to send the letter because he had remained as CIA director until George H. W. Bush could be confirmed, early in 1976. The two Livermore physicists continued to agitate. "Foster and Teller believe intelligence officers should deliberately try to shape policy," a Bush deputy wrote the new director, "by calling attention to the worst things the Soviets could do in order to stimulate appropriate countermeasure responses by the U.S. Government. This, they believe, is the path of prudence; but is not the view of intelligence held by your predecessors." The Foster-Teller worst-case approach recalls Acheson and Nitze's bludgeon approach to NSC-68. The physicists and their fellow PFIAB members soon renewed the issue formally with Bush. "Bush was more compliant in the political winds than his predecessor," Blumenthal comments. Bush agreed to experiment with intelligence assessment by appointing three outside panels, "B teams" that would review the data and conclusions of the "A teams" within the CIA that were preparing the 1976 NIE, after which a panel of senior military and civilian "consumers" would critique the results.

One B team examined Soviet air defenses, a second examined the accuracy of Soviet ICBMs. The third—the one that concerns us here—examined the larger question of Soviet strategic objectives. The Team B project benefited from White House Chief of Staff Cheney's instrumental support, Blumenthal writes. This aid was the origin of Cheney's alliance with the loose association of blusterous Manichaean Democratic and Republican radicals who came to be called the neoconservatives. Rumsfeld put up Paul Wolfowitz to represent his interests, Blumenthal adds; the young special assistant to the Arms Control and Disarmament Agency would coauthor the team's final report.

The Team B Strategic Objectives Panel was led by a Polish-born, waspish

Harvard historian named Richard Pipes. A Richard Perle discovery, Pipes was a former director of the Harvard Russian Research Center, "imported to Washington" originally, according to Blumenthal, "as a consultant to [Scoop] Jackson." Other Team B members and advisers included Lieutenant General Daniel Graham, the chief of defense intelligence who would soon become the main proponent within the Pentagon of strategic missile defense; Nitze; and, informally, Teller, Foster, and Albert Wohlstetter, whose *Foreign Policy* essays served as a starting point for deliberations. Although their bias was a fundamental basis for their appointment—"Members of Team 'B,' " their report would explain, "were deliberately selected from among experienced political and military analysts of Soviet affairs known to take a more somber view of the Soviet strategic threat than that accepted as the intelligence community consensus"—they were given unprecedented access to the nation's intelligence secrets. No comparable "Team C" from the liberal political community contributed balance; as Team B saw it, the CIA professionals represented that community.

In Pipe's paranoid formulation, revealed in a *Commentary* essay a decade later, the vast U.S. intelligence community was merely the handmaiden of a naïve and arrogant body of natural and social scientists who had "acquired a dominant voice in the formulation of U.S. nuclear strategy" under Dwight Eisenhower and had "used this voice to lead U.S. strategy away from traditional ways of military thinking and toward arms-control negotiations." They scorned history, claimed this conventional historian:

> So persuaded are many scientists of the incontrovertible and universal validity of their [scientific] method that in their public capacity they readily succumb to a fanaticism that is quite impervious to both argument and experience. They are no more prepared to take seriously the proposition that nuclear weapons might be effective instruments of warfare than to waste time proving that the earth is not flat.

The "fanaticism" Pipes had in mind, as he went on to explain, was McNamara's Mutual Assured Destruction, which he labeled sarcastically "the only scientifically sound strategy." The public at large, he wrote, "was not initiated into the complexities of Mutual Assured Destruction," implying a cover-up by the fanatical scientists and their intelligence-community devotees. "It was told simply that there was 'overkill,' that nuclear build-ups beyond the figures set by McNamara constituted 'madness,' and that henceforth security lay not in unilaterally arming but in mutually disarming." Such logic was anathema to Pipes, whose argument recalls Edward Teller's timorous, unremitting insistence across his long career that there was no such thing as enough nuclear weapons when it came to dissuading an implacable Kremlin from attack. Pipes credits Teller (a scientist, but one with "a great deal of civic courage") with leadership of the group that advocated "deterrence through strength," contrasting it with scientists such as Hans Bethe, a Manhattan Project veteran and Nobel laureate in physics who supposedly advocated "deterrence through agreement" and who "believed that nuclear weapons were so destructive that they could deter at a low level."

Were they, and could they? Jerome Wiesner, science adviser to President Kennedy and president of MIT, argued the case in a speech at Stanford in 1984:

> I will give you a simple piece of calculus. For most cities it is reasonable to equate one bomb and one city. It would take a bigger bomb for Los Angeles or New York. If you are a weapons expert you know you should probably use several, "pepper 'em down"; you would get a better effect. In any event, it does not take many. And if you ask yourself: "Where would you put 300 large nuclear weapons to be most destructive?" you run out of vital cities and towns and railroad junctions and power plants before you get to 300. The same thing is true in the United States and the Soviet Union. If I was not trying to be conservative I would say 50 bombs, properly placed, would probably put a society out of business, and 300 in each of the two countries leading the arms race would destroy their civilizations. That is a pretty clear-cut fact.

However clear-cut, it was not a fact that Pipes, Teller, Perle, Wolfowitz, Rumsfeld, Cheney, Nitze, Wohlstetter, and their comrades-in-arms, each perhaps for his own reasons, were prepared to accept. In their own eyes tougher and more realistic, they shared that disagreement with experts on the Soviet side, as Pipes wrote nastily, who "simply ignored the doctrine of Mutual Assured Destruction which Soviet disinformation agents were ladling out at their convivial encounters to science professors from Harvard, MIT and Stanford." (Pipes had been excluded from the prestigious Pugwash and Dartmouth Conferences organized between Western and Soviet scientists and resented it.) The Team B report accuses the CIA's experts of "mirror-imaging," which Pipes defines as attributing to others—in this case the Soviet leadership—"one's own motives and intentions on the unspoken assumption that these alone are 'normal' or 'rational.' " According to Pipes, the CIA analysts and the fanatic scientists he believed to be behind them assumed that the Soviets thought the same way about the perils of nuclear weapons as they did: believed in MAD, believed in détente, believed a nuclear war must be too destructive to fight. But in aligning themselves with purported "Soviet experts" as hard-eyed realists, it was Pipes, Wolfowitz, and their team who were mirror-imaging; their argument was with the American arms-control community, not with the Soviets. The Soviets had demonstrated by their caution and their desperate race to catch up with a technologically and economically superior adversary that they would follow our lead wherever we led them, evidently believing we knew where we were going. They had even sacrificed their cherished goal of putting men on the moon to turn their science and industry to missile building in the years after the Cuban Missile Crisis. The "scientific" view that Pipes despised, based as it was on the fundamental physical reality that nuclear weapons were devastating instruments of terror and mass fire, so destructive that one or two per city would deliver chaos and suffering enough to terminate any war, needed no one's insight or approval. Pipes told the American physicist and government adviser Richard Garwin that his argument was based on "his deep knowledge of the Russian soul." But nuclear reality was never a matter of opinion, however soulful. It was a matter of fact, as political leaders facing the brink seem repeatedly to have understood.

Once again, as with Nitze's earlier policy papers, the Team B report suffered from its authors' underestimate of the destructiveness of the weapons they were manipulating. The political scientist Hans Morgenthau identified the problem in an essay published that same year, 1976:

> We have a disjunction between the conventional ways we think and act about nuclear weapons and the objective conditions under which the availability of nuclear weapons forces us to live. . . . We have tried . . . instead of adapting our modes of thought and action to the objective conditions of the nuclear age, to conventionalize nuclear war. . . . The idea that a nuclear war should necessarily end in a stalemate or in the mutual destruction of the belligerents is simply unacceptable to people who have made it their business to prepare for victorious wars.

Team B, reflecting the conventionalized consensus about nuclear war that united nuclear conservatives like Nitze and Pipes with neoconservatives like Paul Wolfowitz and Richard Perle, gave its beliefs urgency and authority by discovering them to be Soviet policy. Mirror-imaging with a vengeance, it found that the CIA's national intelligence estimates "ignore the possibility that the Russians seriously believe that if, for whatever reason, deterrence were to fail, they could resort to the use of nuclear weapons to fight and win a war." The NIEs misunderstood Russian history, the Team B report

argued—here Pipes inserted a long Harvardian disquisition—and it emphasized in italics that the NIEs lacked "*a realistic overall conception of Soviet
motives and intentions.*" They "*consistently underestimate the significance of
the Soviet strategic effort.*" The Soviets were building more bombs, more
bombers, more missiles, more submarines. If they had devoted "a substantial
portion of [their] strategic defensive budget" to anti-submarine-warfare
research but seemed to have nothing to show for it, "the implication could be
that the Soviets have, in fact, deployed some operational non-acoustic systems and will deploy more in the next few years." That is, it's probably out
there, but it's so good it's invisible. ("Yes, that's important," Pipes would tell
an interviewer mysteriously. "If something is not there, that's significant. But
the CIA was not aware of that.") Nitze's signature threat, of a menacing window of vulnerability a few years down the road, turns up once again in the
Team B report, perfunctorily, like a bone thrown to an old dog; the report
proposes "the possibility of a relatively short term threat cresting, say, in 1980
to 1983, as well as the more obvious long range threat."

The conclusion of the Team B report pulled out all the stops:

> An intensified military effort has been under way designed to provide the
> Soviet Union with *nuclear as well as conventional superiority both in strategic
> forces for intercontinental conflict and theater or regional forces.* While hoping to
> crush the "capitalist" realm by other than military means, *the Soviet Union is
> nevertheless preparing for a Third World War as if it were unavoidable.* The pace
> of the Soviet armament effort in all fields is staggering; *it certainly exceeds any
> requirement for mutual deterrence. . . .* So does the high proportion of the
> national budget devoted to direct military expenditures. The intensity and
> scope of the current Soviet military effort in peacetime is without parallel in
> twentieth century history, its only counterpart being Nazi remilitarization of
> the 1930's. . . .
>
> *In Soviet perceptions the gap between long-term aspirations and short-term
> objectives is closing.* This probably means that the Soviet leaders believe that
> their ultimate objectives are closer to realization today than they have ever been
> before. *Within the ten year period of the National Estimate the Soviets may well
> expect to achieve a degree of military superiority which would permit a dramati-
> cally more aggressive pursuit of their hegemonial objectives,* including direct mil-
> itary challenges to Western vital interests, in the belief that such superior
> military force can pressure the West to acquiesce or, if not, can be used to win a
> military contest at any level.

"All of it was fantasy," Anne Cahn said later. "They looked at a facility at
the nuclear test range in Semipalatinsk and said, This is a facility for tests of

nuclear-powered laser beam weapons, when in fact it was nothing of the sort—it was used to test nuclear-powered rocket engines [for space flight]. They even took a Russian military manual, the correct translation of which is *The Art of Winning,* and translated it as *The Art of Conquest.* If you go through most of Team B's specific allegations about weapons systems and you just examine them one by one, they were *all* wrong. All of them."

IF THE SOVIET MILITARY wasn't preparing for World War III in building up its forces to match and sometimes to exceed (at least in numbers) the forces of the United States, what was it preparing for? The clinical psychologist Steven Kull, wishing to know if Soviet defense policymakers struggled with the same cognitive dissonance about nuclear weapons as U.S. policymakers, managed to interview a small number of such men in the early 1980s. "Several [Soviet] respondents used the term *inferiority complex* to describe the Soviet psychology," he writes. "This stemmed from the traumatic experience of being in a unilaterally vulnerable position [compared to the United States], particularly in the 1950s. Several respondents became very emotional as they explained how frightful this period was, and seemed to be imploring me to be more understanding of Soviet policies that may have come out of an effort to 'compensate.' "

No doubt nuclear conservatives such as Richard Pipes would dismiss Kull's respondents (without evidence) as deliberate plants, sent by the KGB to disinform a naïve American. The same can hardly be said of Andrei Sakharov, however, who reported in his memoirs similar motives for working on atomic and thermonuclear weapons:

What was most important for me at the time, and also, I believe, for [Igor] Tamm and the other members of the group, was the conviction that our work was *essential.*

I understood, of course, the terrifying, inhuman nature of the weapons we were building. But the recent [Second World] war had also been an exercise in barbarity; and although I hadn't fought in that conflict, I regarded myself as a soldier in this new scientific war. . . .

Our initial zeal . . . was inspired more by emotion than by intellect. The monstrous destructive force, the scale of our enterprise and the price paid for it by our poor, hungry, war-torn country, the casualties resulting from the neglect of safety standards and the use of forced labor . . . all these things inflamed our sense of drama and inspired us to make a maximum effort so that the sacrifices—which we accepted as inevitable—would not be in vain. We were possessed by a true war psychology, which became still more overpowering after our transfer to the Installation.

In Soviet and other journals as well, Kull found an explanation for what American analysts such as Pipes took to be an effort to develop a war-fighting capability. A Soviet colonel, Viktor Girshfeld, an analyst at a Soviet institute, sought to explain that effort in an anonymous interview with the magazine *Détente,* for example:

> *Col. X:* All of us, more or less, know that nuclear war would be the end. All our theoreticians say that there is no way of preventing nuclear war from escalating to the global level, that you cannot win a nuclear war. That is our *general theoretical* position.
>
> But from a *professional military* point of view, such a position is impossible. Can a professional military man say that nuclear war is inconceivable? No, because some fool of an American president may really start a nuclear war. A professional military man must consider what to do in that event.
>
> *D: What difference does it make what you do in that event?*
>
> *Col. X:* Ah, *you* can say that. Mr. General cannot say that.
>
> *D: I am still confused.*
>
> *Col. X:* Consider the point of view of another professional, the doctor who knows that his patient is suffering from an incurable disease. He cannot for that reason abandon further efforts. . . . To make no plans for [a nuclear war] . . . would be openly to proclaim our helplessness. It would be *psychologically* wrong.

So this Soviet analyst, at least, attributed to the arms race the sole value of disguising from the Soviet people their utter helplessness in the face of nuclear attack, just as Kull had found American policymakers did when he pushed them into a logical corner. The difference for the Soviets was that they felt they had come from an even more terrifying place—far behind the United States—and were finally, at the end of the 1970s, catching up, which changed the nature of the confrontation. "There was an expressed optimism," Kull summarizes, "that the Soviets were gaining more confidence and would soon be less preoccupied with the balance. One respondent explained, 'It is easier to arrive at a more sophisticated understanding when we are strong. . . . Now we're more secure.' "

Lieutenant General Nikolai Detinov spoke more bluntly at the 1998 conference at Brown University of the terrifying place where the Soviets had found themselves during the Cold War. "There was not a year and not a moment," he told his fellow American and Russian panelists impatiently, "when the Soviet Union, in the actual number of nuclear warheads that delivery vehicles could deliver, exceeded the United States. Quite the contrary, the United States was always ahead by 20, 30 percent. . . . In other words, the Soviet Union was always catching up with the United States on strategic arms. Therefore, accusing Russia of perpetuating the arms race and of having certain advantages is absolutely and totally incorrect." Detinov added perspicaciously, "We always viewed these kinds of statements by U.S. leaders as an attempt to knock some extra money out of their own Congress for their own military programs." The American ambassador Jack Matlock, Jr., responded to Detinov's assessment by explaining why U.S. hardliners had believed that their nation was lagging behind: "We did not believe that either bombers or submarine-launched ballistic missiles would ever be considered credible first-strike weapons. Obviously the picture looks different depending on how you define it, but I think that perception on our part was quite genuine." Since the Soviets would be on the receiving end of those bombs and SLBMs, the picture did indeed look different to them.

What the Team B analysts and their supporters never seemed to grasp, or chose not to take into account, was how surrounded the leaders of the Soviet Union felt. Though they had achieved what they considered to be parity with the United States by around 1970, they were far from finished protecting themselves from their increasing numbers of enemies, according to a former deputy chief of the Soviet general staff, A. A. Danilevich:

There is another factor which explains why we created such a huge quantity of weapons. We perceived our main opponent to be the United States, and the second one to be the European NATO countries, in particular [West] Germany. As a result of our political mistakes we began also to be in conflict with China. This was a serious threat. If one considers Brezhnev and [defense chief] Andrei Grechko, then in the 1970s they were not so much afraid of the United States as of China. Our strongest conventional forces were stationed in the east. We considered that Western politicians and military leaders were more sober and rational than was the case in China. With China anything was possible.

In the 1960s and 1970s, twenty-three countries were categorized as our potential enemies. Among our main allies, we counted the six countries of the Warsaw Pact and seven other countries. Forty countries were considered basically neutral, but their orientation, especially in case of war, was uncertain. It is often said that the USSR squandered its resources by helping all these countries, including extending them military aid. However, just consider the global balance of power—we had to do something about this lopsided situation. If the forty countries regarded as neutral joined the enemy, we would have to face sixty-three rather than twenty-three countries. So we had to try to convince these countries, or at least some of them, to come on our side. . . .

Some threats were simply concocted by our short-sighted policy. These alleged threats were grounded in pure ideology, fueled by the simplistic logic of global confrontation, the quest for an "iron shield" around our borders. . . . I recall a 1987 meeting of the Defense Council at which our military doctrine was discussed. [General Sergei] Akhromeyev spoke about the likely scenario in case of global military conflict. His attitude enraged Shevardnadze, who said: "Is this the basis for our defense strategy? You want to fight practically the entire world!"

The most authoritative statement of the Soviet mentality during the later years of the Cold War comes from Anatoly Chernyaev, one of Mikhail Gorbachev's two most intimate advisers (other than Raisa), also speaking at the Brown conference:

There were two layers in our political life: ideology and real politics—*realpolitikom*. You mentioned [Soviet support of] Angola and Cuba. Those were ideological issues. We had to maintain our image as an ideological superpower. This was important to us. However, it did not mean that we were planning to organize or begin a nuclear war. Among our elders [i.e., the aging members of the Politburo], there was not a single person who believed that one day we were going to take over the United States or that we could defeat the United States, or that we were seriously preparing for a nuclear war with the United States. No one, as far as I know, had this absurd notion.

I listened to their speeches. I was present at every one of the Politburo meetings beginning with the time when I became the assistant to the General Secretary. Look at détente, look at the situation in the 1970s with Nixon, and Brezhnev who hugged Nixon in Washington, and everything that happened as a result of détente. You cannot think that this was just Pharisaical and hypocritical games—acting, role-playing to fog up the vision of the United States, to get out of the current moment and then to become more and more aggressive and build up more and more muscles and defense. No, détente was a sincere policy. We wanted détente, we wanted peace, we craved it. . . .

Look at [Central Committee Secretary Yegor] Ligachev, he was a conservative, right? A reactionary, even, and yet he . . . would stand up, right in front of Gorbachev, and he would scream, "How long will our military-industrial complex keep devouring our economy, our agriculture and our consumer goods? How long are we going to take this ogre, how long are we going to throw into its mouth the food of our children?" Even [the Soviet premier Nikolai] Ryzhkov,

[and] all who were located on the conservative side, everybody was against the arms race. They were against the fact that the military-industrial complex was depressing not only the whole economy but also the psychology. We did not want to feel like a fortress under siege. We needed to unchain and liberate our brains from this military-psychological setup which, you are right, does come from the Great Patriotic War, from World War II, where we lost 27 million [people].

"Apes on a treadmill," the American arms negotiator Paul Warnke famously characterized both sides in a 1975 essay in *Foreign Policy* responding to Albert Wohlstetter's question if the United States could even be said to be racing the Soviet Union for advantage in strategic arms. "We couldn't ignore the Soviet Union as an international power," Warnke wrote, "in the many years when we dwarfed its strategic nuclear forces. Today both countries know, and the rest of the world knows too, that we dare not fight one another. The respective strategic nuclear forces serve only as offsets [i.e., they cancel each other out], not as exploitable resources. They are not translatable into sound political currency." What was needed, Warnke believed, was "not a conceptual breakthrough but a decision to take advantage of the stability of the present strategic balance. It's futile to buy things we don't need in the hope that this will make the Soviet Union more amenable. The Soviets are far more apt to emulate than to capitulate. We should, instead, try a policy of restraint, while calling for matching restraint from the Soviet Union."

AT FIRST THE TEAM B REPORT seemed to go nowhere. It was secret, and CIA Director George H. W. Bush, who believed in loyalty, agonized over what to do with it, since it criticized the shop of which he had just become proprietor. Someone on Team B leaked its story to the *Boston Globe* on 20 October 1976, before the report was even finished (it was completed in December), but the national press failed to take it up. The *New York Times* had noticed, however, gained CIA access by promising not to go public until the report was approved and finally ran an account the day after Christmas. The *Washington Post* followed up a week later, describing "one source on the Pipes panel" as gloating, " 'We just licked [the CIA analysts] on a great number of points.' " Ray Cline, a former CIA deputy director, offered the *Post* a more accurate assessment. "It means, Cline said, that the process of making national security estimates 'has been subverted,' by employing 'a kangaroo court of outside critics all picked from one point of view.' " Shortly before leaving office, early in 1977, Henry Kissinger dismissed Team B as a scheme to "sabotage SALT II." No American president, he told the National Press Club, "would ever allow the Soviet Union to gain superiority over the United States."

Writing a decade before Vice President Richard Cheney, Secretary of Defense Donald Rumsfeld, and their associates in the administration of George W. Bush pushed the CIA to inflate the threat of Iraqi weapons of mass destruction to make a case for war, a Nitze biographer, David Callahan, identified a similar modus operandi in the Team B episode:

> To critics in Congress, the Team B episode was a blatant attempt to undermine the objectivity of intelligence and twist CIA estimates to fit an ideological agenda. Nor did the timing of [George H. W.] Bush's undertaking—during the last months of the Ford administration—seem coincidental. Democrats suspected that Team B was aimed at saddling any incoming administration with a preordained, anti-Soviet pessimism. Three congressional committees began investigations into the affair. Summing up the sentiments of many who looked into the matter, Senator Gary Hart would write that " 'competitive analysis' and use of selected outside experts was little more than a camouflage for a political effort to force the National Intelligence Estimate to take a more bleak view of the Soviet threat."

(The deeper flaws in the report, which were common to the A team analysis as well, awaited later reexamination. Arthur Macy Cox, who had been an assistant to George Kennan at the State Department and a CIA officer, identified one important misunderstanding: The A team's realization that Soviet defense spending as a percentage of Soviet GNP was twice as high as the CIA had previously estimated meant not that Soviet spending had dramatically increased, as the Team B report alleged, but, to the contrary, "that Soviet defense production, in fact, was not very efficient. . . . Soviet defense industries . . . all experts now agree, produce weapons at a much higher cost than ours." And a thorough 1993 CIA-sponsored reexamination by a team of outside reviewers noted, "If the objective is to provide the best evidence regarding the military threat . . . the most appropriate subjects of comparison should have been NATO and the Warsaw Pact," not the United States and the U.S.S.R. alone. "The main reason is that, in our strategy for meeting the Soviet military threat, it was not U.S. military forces alone on which we counted but also the substantial forces of our NATO allies. . . . In seeking to understand Soviet strategy, the U.S.S.R. should have been seen as facing not only U.S. military forces but those of Germany, Britain, and the other allies, including France in most circumstances. . . . Had greater attention been directed toward NATO-Warsaw Pact comparisons, the magnitude of the Soviet military threat would not have appeared as large as it appeared from the U.S.S.R.-U.S. comparisons alone.")

A newly elected Jimmy Carter summarily rejected the Team B report and abolished PFIAB for good measure, which might have quelled the debate, but by then the nuclear conservatives' threat-inflation project had found a new home. Former undersecretary of state Eugene Rostow, his effort to influence Kissinger in the autumn of 1974 having been rejected out of hand, had cast about for the next year for an effective vehicle to block détente and influence domestic politics. He settled on the idea of a bipartisan citizens' committee—a lobby—to communicate the conservative defense perspective to the American public and the world, discussed his idea at length with Defense Secretary James Schlesinger, and recruited Paul Nitze, who reached out in turn to his wide circle of influential friends. Schlesinger's recent dismissal by Gerald Ford, and "a couple of bloody Marys before lunch" on Thanksgiving Day 1975, inspired Rostow, he said, to propose to Nitze and another colleague, "by God, why don't we just do it?"

The organization that resulted borrowed a name out of the Cold War past: the Committee on the Present Danger. The first CPD, long defunct, had been formed by James Bryant Conant, a Harvard president and Manhattan Project overseer, at the time of the Korean War to promote a beefier defense program and universal conscription; Nitze had been a member. It had taken its name from Supreme Court Justice Oliver Wendell Holmes's famous 1919 opinion that "the most stringent protection of free speech would not protect a man in falsely shouting fire in a theater and causing a panic." Ironically, the phrase "a clear and present danger" appears in the Holmes opinion in the context of just such a false act: "The question in every case is whether the words used are used in such circumstances and are of such a nature as to create a clear and present danger that they will bring about the substantive evils that Congress has a right to prevent." The Committee on the Present Danger, the old one and the new, did indeed shout fire and cause panic erroneously, if not falsely, and to the great detriment of the very cause—the security and prosperity of the American people—that each committee believed itself to be patriotically defending.

The new CPD attracted a large membership from both political parties, including Rostow; Nitze; Pipes; Hewlett-Packard's cofounder David Packard; the AFL-CIO treasurer Lane Kirkland; the former secretary of state Dean Rusk; the former chief of naval operations Elmo Zumwalt, Jr.; the future

Reagan administration national security adviser Richard Allen; Reagan's campaign manager and a future DCI William Casey; the former DCI William Colby; Eisenhower's aides Gordon Gray and Andrew Goodpaster; a scholar and future U.N. ambassador under Reagan, Jeane Kirkpatrick; Clare Boothe Luce; Richard Perle; the neoconservative journalists Norman Podhoretz and Midge Decter; the civil-rights leader Bayard Rustin; the right-wing Republican billionaire Richard Scaife; Edward Teller; and even the writer Saul Bellow. Ronald Reagan joined the organization in the spring of 1976, before its formation was announced publicly. "He needed credentials," his campaign manager explained.

When the CPD went public, on 11 November 1976 (nine days after Jimmy Carter's election), before a large audience of journalists at the National Press Club, it used the occasion to release its first policy statement, a Pipes creation titled "Common Sense and Common Danger." Three CPD founders read it aloud, purporting to find "the principal threat to our nation" to be "the Soviet drive for dominance based upon an unparalleled military build-up." The solution was "higher [American] levels of defense spending"; otherwise, "we shall become second best to the Soviet Union in overall military strength . . . isolated in a hostile world, facing the unremitting pressures of Soviet policy backed by an overwhelming preponderance of power."

Despite the large Press Club audience and the new CPD's grand ambitions, none of the national media bothered to announce its founding. Of fifty-three CPD members recommended for positions in the Carter administration, the new president chose not one, not even Nitze, who had offended Carter the previous July by trying to bully him at a defense policy seminar the Democratic candidate had organized at his home in Plains, Georgia. "Nitze was typically know-it-all," Carter said later. "He was arrogant and inflexible. His own ideas were sacred to him. He didn't seem to listen to others, and he had a doomsday approach." When eight CPD members met with Carter at the White House early in 1977, Rostow recalled, "we were stunned, just stunned. The notion that that fellow was president was just frightening."

What frightened the CPD was Carter's initial program, as he described it later, "to try to put forward to the Soviet Union a much more dramatic reduction in the total quantity and effectiveness of the nuclear weapons in our arsenals, and to bring about a comprehensive test ban to eliminate the explosion of any nuclear devices, either underground or in the air." By March, Carter had dispatched his secretary of state, Cyrus Vance, to Moscow "with what I thought was a very good proposal for dramatic cuts [in the two sides' nuclear arsenals]," Carter said. At that point the CPD declared all-out war, opposing Carter and his "frightening" notions of nuclear sufficiency with a full arsenal of op-eds, talk-show appearances, position papers, and congressional testimony. CPD resistance was all the more odd since the proposal had been drafted by Zbigniew Brzezinski, Carter's anti-Soviet national security adviser, with substantial input from Richard Perle, and was designed to be unacceptable to the Soviet Union.

In the meantime, Albert Wohlstetter had organized a low-profile alliance of U.S. and NATO defense strategists, the European-American Workshop. German participants in the workshop counseled the West German chancellor, Helmut Schmidt, no friend of Carter's in any case, that he should pursue adding cruise missiles to the NATO nuclear arsenal to counter the Soviet deployment within the Soviet Union, facing Europe, of a sophisticated new intermediate-range, solid-fueled, mobile ballistic missile, the SS-20 (Pioneer). The missile had a five-thousand-kilometer (thirty-one-hundred-mile) range, sufficient to reach Europe, Britain, the Middle East, and parts of Asia, and carried three MIRVed 150-kiloton warheads that it could deliver within three hundred meters of its intended targets. "Owing to their limited range," Schmidt would write, "the SS-20s are directed not at the United States but practically only at countries which cannot reach the Soviet Union with similar weapons." Even though the SS-20s were clearly being installed to replace an earlier generation of Soviet liquid-fueled missiles that required hours to launch and were therefore useful only for a first strike, Schmidt's advisers convinced him, he wrote, that "the Soviet Union has upset the military balance in Europe."

Since Carter appeared to be more concerned with intercontinental strategic assets than European-theater assets, Schmidt agitated for a NATO response, and, in a 1977 speech, invoked for the first time a requirement of parity between Warsaw Pact and NATO strategic weapons. NATO had more than enough nuclear weapons aimed at the Soviet Union to cover any contingency: four hundred Poseidon 50-kiloton warheads on U.S. Polaris nuclear submarines allotted to European defense and 164 U.S. F-111 long-range fighter-bombers based in Britain carrying B-61 bombs with variable yields up to 340 kilotons, as well as thousands of tactical weapons. Several hundred British and French warheads and bombs added to Europe's defenses as well. Schmidt, however, worried that Carter might give some of the NATO arsenal away in the SALT II negotiations.

Carter eventually responded to European pressure for a more politically visible land-based deterrent, and in 1979 NATO announced that it would pursue a two-track strategy: "Arms control would be attempted for four years," Thomas Graham, Jr., summarizes, "to try to remove or contain the threat of the SS-20s. If after four years, in 1983, satisfactory results had not been achieved on the arms-control track, then NATO would proceed with the planned deployments" of 108 Pershing 2 medium-range ballistic missiles, each with a single maneuverable W85 fifty-kiloton warhead, and 464 Tomahawk ground-launched cruise missiles with W84 fifty-kiloton warheads. The seemingly precise numbers of these weapons followed not from any special deterrent requirements, the scholar Raymond Garthoff points out, but from a general decision to deploy a mix "in the range of 200–600 missiles. . . . More, it was deemed, would seem provocative; less, too weak." The 108 Pershing 2s would replace the U.S. Army's 108 Pershing 1As. The Tomahawks came in squadrons of sixteen, and "units of 48 were the minimum logical units per major deployment area. The Tomahawk total was set at 464 [i.e., 29 times 16] as the next to highest multiple of 16 keeping the . . . total (including the 108 Pershing 2s) under the 600 ceiling. . . . That level also was designed to allow some negotiating room for talks with the Soviet Union as well."

The new Euromissiles were not only a surprise to the Soviet leadership; they were also a grave new danger. The Pershing 1A's five-hundred-mile range had made it a tactical weapon. Moscow, one thousand miles from Berlin, was outside its perimeter. But the Pershing 2 had been reengineered with a Kevlar body and more powerful rockets to extend its range to beyond one thousand miles, which meant, given its forward position in Germany, that it was a strategic, first-strike weapon that could reach Moscow in less than ten minutes after launch. Tomahawks were slower—with turbofan engines, they flew close to the ground at subsonic speed, comparing the terrain to a stored digital map—but their maximum range was fifteen hundred miles with an accuracy of eighty feet. If the Soviets had introduced the SS-20 as a challenge and a provocation, they could have expected such an escalation, but in fact, writes Garthoff, they had thought the SS-20 deployment "was a normal modernization program. . . . There is no evidence to support the idea that the Soviet leaders saw a political option flowing from their decision on the SS-20 or that they even considered such a political purpose in making the decision. . . . They did not see this action as creating any gap [in theater nuclear forces] in their favor."

The event that finished off détente, even for Carter, was the Soviet invasion of Afghanistan in December 1979. He and Brezhnev had signed the SALT II treaty in Vienna on 18 June limiting strategic delivery vehicles; Carter had submitted the treaty to the U.S. Senate for ratification four days later. The CPD had then fanned out across the country agitating against its ratification. Scoop Jackson, speaking words Richard Perle had crafted for him, proposed that even Neville Chamberlain had been more realistic in 1938 once his "policy of appeasement lay in ruins." Carter, however, believes that the Soviet invasion, which came as a complete surprise, not the CPD assault, was the reason SALT II ratification stalled. "The Congress never did ratify this treaty," he told an interviewer, "... because that winter ... the Soviet Union invaded Afghanistan, and at that time it would have been almost impossible to get the Congress and the American public to approve anything that related to commonality with the Soviet Union." What Carter failed to tell the interviewer was that he himself pulled the treaty from Senate consideration within days of the Soviet invasion.

Afghanistan seemed at first to reveal the Soviets on the march. "I could see that the Soviet movement into Afghanistan was not an end in itself," Carter recalled. "The intelligence that I had from various sources, including within the Soviet Union, was that the Soviets' long-term goal was to penetrate into access to warm-water oceans from Afghanistan, either through Iran or through Pakistan. I saw this as a direct threat to global stability and to the security of my own nation." (Despite Carter's contemporary intelligence sources, the primary reason for the invasion, besides quelling a growing anti-Soviet insurgency, has turned out to be concern that the Afghan prime minister, Hafizullah Amin, who had recently had his predecessor murdered, was planning to defect from his country's alliance with the Soviet Union and align with the United States.)

Carter, who believed he and Brezhnev had gotten along well and felt personally betrayed, responded forcefully by threatening military action, not excluding nuclear weapons, should the Soviets invade either Pakistan or Iran. Besides that threat, Gorbachev wrote, "the USA and other nations took a number of measures against us. The Americans, in particular, stopped shipping even those consignments of grain that they had already contracted to send. The embargo resulted in our not receiving about 17 million tonnes" of grain, a shortage Gorbachev called "alarming." The White House and the State Department worked up a long list of possible sanctions, most of which were adopted. In his State of the Union address on 23 January 1980, Carter extended U.S. military protection (and implicit hegemony) over the Persian Gulf and proposed increasing the U.S. defense budget by 5 percent, which would amount to $20 billion in real growth in 1981 and 1982 (about $102 billion in 2006 dollars). "By the 1980 presidential election," Anne Cahn summarizes, "the choice in foreign and defense policy was between that of the Carter administration, which favored the [MIRVed, ten-warhead] MX missile, the Trident submarine, a Rapid Deployment Force, a 'stealth' bomber, cruise missiles, counterforce targeting leading to a first-strike capability, and a 5 percent increase in defense spending, and that of the Republicans under Ronald Reagan, who favored all of these *plus* the neutron bomb, antiballistic missiles, the B-1 bomber, civil defense, and an 8 percent increase in defense spending."

The official Soviet response to the Carter reversal was to reaffirm détente. Privately, however, Yuri Andropov, then still head of the KGB, began to suspect that the United States was preparing for nuclear war.

EIGHT **DECAPITATION**

FOR MANY AMERICANS, THE SOVIET INVASION of Afghanistan on 25 December 1979 confirmed the conclusions about the expansion of Soviet power that the Committee on the Present Danger had been proclaiming across the land. During the 1980 presidential election campaign, Ronald Reagan made the CPD agenda his own, even comparing Jimmy Carter directly to Neville Chamberlain (as Scoop Jackson had done as well). "Reagan openly disdained arms control in favor of an arms race with the Soviets," Sidney Blumenthal summarized. "America would seize the initiative, and Russia would be pushed into collapse."

Reagan at least understood that the Soviet system was vulnerable—he called it "some bizarre chapter in human history whose last pages are even now being written"—which is more than can be said of the CPD. Nitze, Perle, Rumsfeld, Wolfowitz, Pipes, and their associates believed their own exaggerations, or acted as if they did. "By virtue of the billboard effect of publicizing their views that the Soviet Union was stronger than the United States and getting stronger all the time," Anne Cahn concludes, "that it meant to achieve world domination, that it was the fount and origin of all radical movements around the world, that détente and arms control negotiations were a snare and a delusion, Team B and the CPD prevented the intelligence community and the public from correctly interpreting the many signs of the coming demise of the Soviet Union. That is the real legacy of Team B."

Were there such signs? Could the dissolution of the Soviet Union have been predicted? Would knowing it was failing have made a difference?

Cahn found evidence of public discussion of Soviet economic problems from as early as 1966, when "a study prepared for the Congressional Joint Economic Committee reported that 'both official Soviet data and Western estimates show a marked decline in the rate of growth of industrial production in the U.S.S.R.' " The same committee learned in the late 1960s that the rate of Soviet oil production was declining, resulting in fuel shortages, and that population demographics were worsening. This information went to the President's Foreign Intelligence Advisory Board (PFIAB), Cahn notes, and therefore was available to Nitze and other board members and thus to Team B. The near-collapse of Soviet agriculture was obvious to the whole world, of course, exposed by the Soviet Union's massive grain purchases. Cahn cites Melvin Laird, the secretary of defense during Nixon's first term— "surely no dovish liberal," she comments—enumerating Soviet economic problems in 1974:

> By any assessment the Soviet economy is in trouble. The growth rate of Soviet productivity has been declining. Her technological industries, so vital in today's world, have shown a marked incapacity to come up with economical, efficient and innovative products. The loss of the "moon race," which was felt very acutely by the Soviets, is but one indicator of this. The wheat deal . . . was forged to save the Soviets from the results of a disastrous agricultural program. The availability of consumer goods in the Soviet Union is still among the lowest of developing nations.

Andrei Sakharov diagnosed the real predicament of Soviet industry and society in the second of three celebrated memoranda that he sent to Leonid Brezhnev between 1968 and 1972. The first and best-known was his appeal for superpower cooperation, "Reflections on Progress, Peaceful Coexistence, and Intellectual Freedom," which was published in the *New York Times* in July 1968. In the second memorandum, sent to Brezhnev in 1970 after having circulated in *samizdat* and published in the United States in 1973, Sakharov wrote:

> The more novel and revolutionary the aspect of the economy, the wider becomes the rift between the USA and ourselves. We are ahead of the USA in the production of coal but behind them in the production of oil, gas, and electric power, ten times behind in chemistry and immeasurably behind in computer technology. The latter is especially essential, for the introduction of electronic computers into the national economy is of decisive importance which could radically change the face of the system of production and culture in general. This phenomenon has rightly been called "the second industrial revolution." Meanwhile the total capacity of our computers is hundreds of times less than in the USA, and as for the use of electronic computers in the national economy, here the rift is so enormous that it is impossible to measure. We are simply living in a different era.

These problems, Sakharov added, "cannot be resolved by one or two persons in positions of power and who claim to know everything. They demand the creative participation of millions of people at all levels of the economic system. They require a broad exchange of information and ideas." Otherwise, the Soviet Union could "gradually revert to the status of a second-rate provincial power."

Sakharov went further in a postscript to his third memorandum, which he gave to Western journalists in 1972, correctly diagnosing the basic Soviet economic problem as runaway militarization of the economy:

> In socialist countries it is also essential to reduce the militarization of the economy and the role of a messianic ideology. . . . Militarization of the economy leaves a deep imprint on international and domestic policy. . . . The role of the military-industrial complex in US policy has been thoroughly studied. The analogous role played by the same factors in the USSR and other socialist countries is less well known. It is, however, necessary to point out that in no country does the share of military expenditure with relation to national income reach such proportions as in the USSR (over 40 percent).

The boldest prediction of impending Soviet collapse during this period, however, was the work of a young and previously unknown French historical demographer named Emmanuel Todd, reported in a book titled *The Final Fall*, published in France in 1976 and in translation in the United States in 1979. (Demography is the branch of anthropology that concerns statistics of health and disease, birth and death; historical demography uses demographic tools to study the past—or, in Todd's case, to investigate a closed society that deliberately obfuscated its demographics.) Todd had written his remarkable book while still a graduate student. It was reviewed in English primarily in journals of Russian studies, exactly where it needed to be noticed to alert the community of experts on which the U.S. government relied for information about Soviet trends. Unfortunately, almost without exception, professional Sovietologists—Richard Pipes was a typical specimen—were the last to recognize the decline and fall of the political system on whose leviathan enigmas they had built their careers. The reviewers praised Todd's innovative approach, but his prediction of impending Soviet collapse was dismissed as a "penchant for dramatic prophesying."

"Internal pressures are pushing the Soviet system to the breaking point," Todd dramatically—but also accurately—prophesied on the opening page of his book. "In ten, twenty, or thirty years, an astonished world will be witness to the dissolution or the collapse of this, the first of the Communist systems." To explain how he came to such a radical conclusion in an era when the Committee on the Present Danger was claiming that the Soviet Union was growing in strength and malevolence, he demonstrated that Soviet statistics, otherwise "shabby and false," could still be mined for valuable information on the state of society. Even censored statistics, such as rates of birth and death missing from the charts for the Terror famine years 1931 to 1935, "indicate the abuses of Stalinism, especially when they succeed a period marked by a relatively large volume of data." Age pyramids, he pointed out—graphs in which stacked horizontal bars represent the percentage of the population in each age group—"have fixed for everyone to see the errors of Stalinism, Maoism, or any other totalitarian alternative which declares war upon a human community. . . . Rather belatedly, it is apparent that 30 to 60 million inhabitants in the USSR are missing. In 1975, it was clear that about 150 million were missing in China. Given population, the proportions are nearly the same."

Todd noted and moved past the zero growth of the Soviet economy, from which he predicted "there will be no recovery." The "sluggishness" of the centralized Soviet economy, he remarked, "appears to be natural, obvious, and inevitable. . . . The lack of common sense on the part of Stalinist economists remains a curious historical phenomenon. How is it possible for a central organization to coordinate the activity of 250 million Soviet inhabitants, distributed over 22 million square kilometers, by arbitrarily fixing prices and wages?" In fact, Todd argued, "the degree of polarization and level of economic development in the USSR today is most clearly reminiscent of the West in the 1860s. . . . In Communist countries the working class is frequently fired upon, as they were in Western Europe during the nineteenth century. They have personally witnessed what is a set piece of *Marxist* art and literature. . . . Real Communism has all the legendary vices of the capitalism condemned by Marx: misery, class conflict and alienation."

Soviet defense spending, Todd realized, was not simply a consequence of the Soviet Union trying to steal a march on the United States, as the neoconservatives believed. Had it been, the Soviets could have alleviated their economic problems merely by switching to minimal deterrence such as the Chinese have practiced since they first developed nuclear weapons. (As late as 2006, the People's Republic of China had fielded only about twenty ICBMs capable of reaching the United States.) As I hope I have demonstrated by now, there has never been a realistic military justification for accumulating large, expensive stockpiles of nuclear arms. In the United States the pressures to do so, seldom acknowledged publicly, have been primarily political, bureaucratic, economic, and palliative. In the Soviet Union, Todd discerned, the pressure to do so was dictated in part "by the logic of the economic system, which depends on central planning (i.e., strict control) and thus must only produce goods which are *held in common and impossible to consume individually.* Armaments is not the only dynamic sector of Soviet industry. All individually *nonconsumable* goods are given priority. This includes such things as ores and petroleum, of which there are *surpluses* that can be exploited."

Why only nonconsumable goods? The Soviet economy was a double system, Todd pointed out, half official and half black market or "free sector." The free sector, decentralized and robust, clandestinely produced some of the consumer goods that the official sector disdained:

> Consider that every advance in the production of consumable goods in the USSR encourages the parallel or free black market sector. *The Soviet system cannot take the path of a consumer society because this would automatically encourage the growth of the free sector at the expense of the centralized sector....* Increasing decentralization would, in and of itself, lead to political awareness. Consumer culture develops from the market and is completely incompatible with a totalitarian system.... A highly developed consumer society is more and more individualized; *everyone does his own thing.* We readily perceive that this saying is more compatible with a "developed liberal society" than with the "dictatorship of the proletariat," a totalitarian system under the sway of a single party. Why limit the choice to a single party, if there is freedom to choose among different life-styles?

"In 1976," Todd added, "an enormous portion of national revenue was still devoted to arms production and the armed forces. This very high percentage is *necessary to prevent the transfer of productive forces to the consumer sector. Arms expenses* serve, among other things, *to maintain the preeminence of the centralized sector of the economy.*" (Todd was describing the Soviet Union, but of course the description also applied, and still applies, to the United States.)

Locating the origins of liberty in the heart of the marketplace may have made some of Todd's more socially conscious Western readers wince. Paralleling his mercantile model with an analogous model frequently invoked in those years—the "marketplace of ideas"—clarifies his point. The Soviet leadership tried to centralize control over thought directly as well as by centralizing economic power. It restrained its citizens' movements and communication and restricted and even criminalized discussion of unofficial (particularly liberal democratic) ideas; simultaneously it forced approved speech—official Marxist-Leninist speech—into a worn, cast-iron mold of orthodoxy. Todd took note of this phenomenon as well, although he did not draw its parallel with the Soviet economic system: "To transform Marxism into an empty, meaningless litany is absolutely crucial for the regime. The Soviets must speak, but not think, like 'Marxists.' The official ideology must transform Marx's texts into a collection of high-sounding but irrelevant rhetoric. If the Communist masses understood the true meaning of terms like 'exploitation,' 'alienation' and 'oppression,' the system that dominates them could not survive."

Arms production, Todd concluded, "is the chief element which keeps the Soviet economy functioning. These nonconsumable goods pose no threat to centralization." But since Soviet workers knew "that every increase in [their] productivity will eventually be absorbed by armaments expenditures," they had no reason to work harder; "they are a dispirited group whose only incentive is to lower productivity." No one who visited the Soviet Union at any time in its last twenty years missed hearing the disillusioned mantra of Soviet labor: "They pretend to pay us and we pretend to work."

For the Soviet system to function at all, the bureaucracy had to be bought off; thus the emergence of the *nomenclatura* class with access to higher-quality food and consumer goods at special stores, to better apartments, dachas, and medical services, to travel outside the country, and even to Western journals and books.

The most fundamental measure Todd found of the deep malaise affecting Soviet society was an increasing infant-mortality rate, which he believed marked "the beginning of a large-scale regressive cycle." The Soviet Union's worsening demographics, already revealing themselves a decade and a half *before* its dissolution in 1991, offer further evidence that the Communist society was imploding domestically before the Carter and Reagan arms buildup that Reagan partisans in particular have claimed to be the cause of the Soviet collapse. "No one dares even imagine," Todd commented, "the real extent of their problems. The relaxation of [totalitarian] pressure, accompanied by the simultaneous lowering of administrative and industrial productivity (not to mention the agricultural deficits) as a result of centralization is bringing about the *absolute regression* of the national wealth."

Yet the perspicacious young Frenchman doubted that the Soviet regime would "suffer a violent upheaval." Its organization protected it from mass uprisings, and the West was intervening with grain sales to protect it from famine. Astonishingly, he thought "the successive or simultaneous breaking away of the [East European] satellites should soon be accepted by the Kremlin without too much fuss." His imagination failed him where Afghanistan was concerned, however; he "could not imagine the Red Army in a situation like Viet Nam." As it happened, even the Soviet Union's war with Afghanistan did not detonate revolution. "Change in the USSR," Todd concluded, "might take the form of what happened in Czechoslovakia, when intellectual reformers took control of the state apparatus. . . . Soviet reform would have to be intelligently executed. The situation in which the USSR finds itself is so implausible and tangled that it would require perfect mastery on the part of a solidly established ruling class. The way elites are recruited assures that mediocrity will reign in precarious positions of power. This is because elites are selected by their peers and not by free elections. Let's pray for a uniformly intelligent Politburo in the years to come."

It mattered greatly whether the U.S. government believed the Soviet Union to be an expanding or a declining power. The Soviet government's decision to replace its first-generation missiles in Europe with threatening new SS-20s had already strained détente, as did the United States and NATO's decision in response to deploy Pershing 2s and Tomahawks in Europe late in 1983 if negotiations to remove the SS-20s failed. Carter and Brezhnev still signed the SALT II treaty in Vienna on 18 June 1979, limiting strategic nuclear-delivery vehicles, but Carter soon found himself forced to endorse a larger U.S. defense budget to improve the treaty's chances for Senate ratification. Then the Soviets invaded Afghanistan. Carter responded by increasing the defense budget even further, asking Congress in January 1980 for 5 percent real growth.

As early as November 1978, addressing Warsaw Pact leaders in Moscow, Leonid Brezhnev expressed serious concern about U.S. and NATO intentions. "Even the tentative parity in armaments and armed forces [between NATO and the Warsaw Pact]," he said, "is perceived quite nervously in the ruling imperialist circles. In those circles—especially in the USA and in the ruling leadership of NATO—they obviously do not want to let go of the hope of achieving some kind of breakthrough, of overturning the existing correlation of forces, and of gaining an opportunity to impose their will [and] their ways on the rest of the world." Washington's defense budget that year was $130 billion, Brezhnev pointed out. "They are working on new systems of weapons of mass destruction—we know this very well—in closed American engineering and construction offices." At the same time, he complained, the Americans were "pushing their allies toward the path of unrestrained growth of military expenditures. . . . In this atmosphere, one could anticipate a massive attack against détente, against the policies of the socialist states." Similarly, a German scholar notes that in secret discussions among Warsaw Pact defense ministers during this period, "the threat of a nuclear surprise attack appears as a constant theme in [their] threat perceptions."

Yuri Andropov confessed his concerns to Markus Wolf, the head of East German intelligence, during a meeting in February 1980. Wolf reports:

> [The KGB chief and I] began discussing the East-West conflict. I had never before seen Andropov so somber and dejected. He described a gloomy scenario in which a nuclear war might be a real threat. His sober analysis came to the conclusion that the US government was striving by all available means to establish nuclear superiority over the Soviet Union. He cited statements of President Carter, his adviser Zbigniew Brzezinski, and of Pentagon spokesmen, all of which included the assertion that under certain circumstances a nuclear first strike against the Soviet Union and its allies would be justified.

"When Carter announced a record defense budget of $157 billion," Wolf adds, ". . . the reaction in Moscow was one of barely controlled panic. 'We cannot fight them with funds,' a leading Soviet nuclear strategist confided to me. 'Thank God we are good at other things.'" Wolf tactfully chose not to speculate about what those "other things" might be.

The increasing misapprehension between the nuclear-armed superpowers produced its share of near disasters in 1980. "On at least three occasions" that year, writes Robert Gates, "there had been failures of the U.S. early warning computer system leading to combat alerts of U.S. strategic forces. CIA later learned that during the first half of June 1980, the KGB had sent a message to all of their residencies reporting these failures and saying that they were not the result of errors but were deliberately initiated by the Defense Department for training." Gates dismisses the KGB's response as "paranoid," and perhaps it was, but in the context of the Carter defense buildup and the proposed NATO deployments it might also be interpreted as an attempt by Andropov, a chess player, to think more than one move ahead. "The KGB circular," Gates concludes, "stated that the Soviet government believed that the United States was attempting to give the Soviet Union a false sense of security by giving the impression that such errors were possible, and thereby diminish Soviet concerns over future alerts—thus providing a cover for possible surprise attack."

Nor was the KGB the only entity that took the computer errors seriously, Gates reports:

> As he recounted to me, [Carter's national security adviser Zbigniew] Brzezinski was awakened at three in the morning by [his military assistant, William] Odom, who told him that some 220 Soviet missiles had been launched against the United States. Brzezinski knew that the President's decision time to order retaliation was from three to seven minutes after a Soviet launch. Thus he told

Odom he would stand by for a further call to confirm a Soviet launch and the intended targets before calling the President. Brzezinski was convinced we had to hit back and told Odom to confirm that the Strategic Air Command was launching its planes. When Odom called back, he reported that he had further confirmation, but that 2,200 missiles had been launched—it was an all-out attack. One minute before Brzezinski intended to telephone the President, Odom called a third time to say that other warning systems were not reporting Soviet launches. Sitting alone in the middle of the night, Brzezinski had not awakened his wife, reckoning that everyone would be dead in half an hour. It had been a false alarm. Someone had mistakenly put military exercise tapes into the computer system. When it was over, Zbig just went back to bed. I doubt he slept much, though.

Defense experts in the Soviet Union debated the question of the likelihood of war vigorously in 1979 and 1980, writes the CIA staff historian Benjamin Fischer, "and by June 1980 a CPSU Central Committee Plenum resolution expressed the official view that 'adventuristic actions of the United States and its accomplices have increased the danger of war.'"

On 25 July 1980, Carter added further to Soviet fears by promulgating a new presidential directive, PD-59, that included an argument for fighting extended nuclear wars rather than attacking at the outset with everything in the arsenal, the early LeMay strategy that was still enshrined in the SIOP. "If deterrence fails initially," PD-59 argued, "we must be capable of fighting successfully so that the adversary would not achieve his war aims and would suffer costs that are unacceptable, or in any event greater than his gains, from having initiated an attack." The Republican National Convention that had just nominated Ronald Reagan as its candidate for the presidency had also endorsed preparing to fight prolonged nuclear wars. The Republican platform and PD-59 together presented the Soviet Union with a solid front in favor of a new and more threatening U.S. nuclear posture.

To fight an extended nuclear war meant holding Soviet cities hostage by not attacking them first. Instead, PD-59 proposed attacking the Soviet leadership itself, a strategy that would soon win the grisly name "decapitation." Two conservative defense strategists, Colin Gray and Keith Payne, described the strategy in an essay published that summer under the provocative title "Victory Is Possible." "The most frightening threat to the Soviet Union," Gray and Payne wrote, "would be the destruction or serious impairment of its political system. Thus, the United States should be able to destroy key leadership cadres, their means of communication, and some of the instruments of domestic control. The USSR, with its gross overcentralization of authority, epitomized by its vast bureaucracy in Moscow, should be highly vulnerable to such an attack. The Soviet Union might cease to function if its security agency, the KGB, were severely crippled. If the Moscow bureaucracy could be eliminated, damaged, or isolated, the USSR might disintegrate into anarchy."

I remember hearing statements in those years that the United States would soon be capable of targeting the individual offices, apartments, and dachas of Politburo members—of delivering nuclear warheads through office windows on opposite corners of an intersection, a capacity that seemed incredible at the time, not to mention redundant, though it would find dramatic demonstration a decade later in the conventionally armed cruise-missile attacks on Baghdad at the beginning of the first Gulf War. And already in December 1980, in an early field test, a Tomahawk cruise missile flew six hundred miles out to sea and returned to impact within sixteen feet of its target; twelve hundred miles was a range more than adequate to deliver Tomahawks from West Germany to Moscow.

Specified among PD-59's targets were seven hundred so-called leadership relocation sites, meaning fortified underground bunkers, and fourteen hundred ICBM silos hardened against U.S. missile attacks. To that end, the U.S. Air Force's Minuteman II ICBMs and the U.S. Navy's Trident C4 SLBMs received higher-yield warheads and new terminal guidance systems that greatly improved their accuracy, which increased their kill probability to about 99 percent even against superhardened Soviet ICBM silos. The new Pershing 2s scheduled for European deployment in 1983 looked even more dangerous and destabilizing to the Soviet leadership: In their forward location they would be positioned outside the range of Soviet launch-detection satellites and early-warning radar, their flight time was ten minutes or less, and they were accurate to within one hundred feet. In their original configuration, intended to carry an earth-penetrating 340-kiloton W86 warhead, they had been planned for bunker-busting, but in September 1980, two months after PD-59 was announced, they were reconfigured with a lighter, 0.3- to 45-kiloton dial-a-yield W85 warhead that extended their range, allowing them to be targeted against Soviet mobile missiles or for low-yield precision decapitation strikes in central Moscow with limited collateral damage.

RONALD REAGAN WAS INAUGURATED as the fortieth president of the United States on 20 January 1981. Besides the president himself, no fewer than thirty-one appointees to his administration would be members of the Committee on the Present Danger, including the national security adviser,

Richard Allen; the CIA director, William Casey; the U.N. ambassador, Jeane
Kirkpatrick; the Navy secretary, John Lehman; the Arms Control and Disarmament Agency (ACDA) director, Eugene Rostow; the ACDA adviser
William Van Cleave; the undersecretary of defense Fred Iklé; the assistant
secretary of defense Richard Perle; the National Security Council adviser
Richard Pipes; and the arms negotiators Max Kampelman and Paul Nitze.
Casey was sworn in on 28 January; two days later, at the first meeting of the
new administration's National Security Principals Committee, he proposed
mounting a covert program of deliberate intimidation against the Soviet
Union by assaulting it from every side with military probes, feints, and surprises. The goal of the program, according to Peter Schweizer, an enthusiastic chronicler of the Reagan administration, was to make the Soviet
leadership "less prone to take risks":

> "It was very sensitive," recalls former Undersecretary of Defense Fred Iklé.
> "Nothing was written down about it, so there would be no paper trail."
>   "Sometimes we would send bombers over the North Pole, and [Soviet]
> radars would click on," recalls Gen. Jack Chain, the former Strategic Air Com-
> mand commander. "Other times fighter-bombers would probe their Asian or
> European periphery." During peak times, the operation would include several
> maneuvers in a week. They would come at irregular intervals to make the effect
> all the more unsettling. Then, as quickly as the unannounced flights began,
> they would stop, only to begin again a few weeks later.
>   "It really got to them," recalls Dr. William Schneider, undersecretary of state
> for military assistance and technology. . . . "They didn't know what it all meant.
> A squadron would fly straight at Soviet airspace and their radars would light up
> and units would go on alert. Then at the last minute the squadron would peel
> off and return home."

Why such threat displays would make a nuclear superpower known for its
insecurity "less prone to take risks" is a question only Casey and his colleagues might have answered; the actual Soviet response was to judge the
new American leadership to be dangerous and reckless and probably intent
on starting a nuclear war. The probes began quickly, in mid-February, by
which time the administration had gone public with its intention to greatly
enlarge the already large increase in defense spending that Carter had
authorized.

   Carter's 5 percent increase in defense spending had been borrowed from a
Reagan campaign proposal; Reagan's budget director, David Stockman,
describes Carter's preemption of that figure as "a parting 'up yours' gesture at

the new administration." Secretary of Defense Caspar Weinberger wanted an 8 or 9 percent increase for the Reagan defense budget. At a hasty meeting on 31 January, Stockman proposed a compromise interim real-growth increase of 7 percent and Weinberger signed on. Only later, going over the numbers several weeks after the meeting, did Stockman discover that by starting their calculations from 1982 forward, a point where Carter's increase and a preliminary Reagan increase had already been factored in, they had not added 2 percent more but had unintentionally doubled Carter's parting gesture. "We had taken an already-raised defense budget and raised that by 7 percent. Instead of starting from a defense budget of $142 billion, we'd started with one of $222 billion. And by raising that by 7 percent—and compounding it over five years—we had ended up increasing the real growth rate of the United States defense budget by *10 percent* per year between 1980 and 1986." Stockman "nearly had a heart attack. We'd laid out a plan for a five-year defense budget of *1.46 trillion dollars!*" But by then, he concludes, "the February 18 budget was out and they were squealing with delight throughout the military-industrial complex."

Never a detail man, Reagan seems not to have been disturbed by the magnitude of the defense buildup budgeted in his name, nor to have questioned budget numbers derived from such a late-night crap game. Few backroom episodes demonstrate so clearly the disconsonance between national-security politics and military necessity.

Reagan ended up spending almost as much on defense in the first five years of his presidency as had Ford, Nixon, and Carter combined, more than the cost of both the Korean and Vietnam wars—the largest peacetime buildup in American history. One purpose of the Reagan defense buildup, of course, was to starve the beast of government domestic spending, part of the conservative Republican agenda. As the political scientist Daniel Wirls notes, "for fiscal 1982, Reagan negotiated with Congress for about $35 billion in cuts in hundreds of domestic programs. . . . In budgetary terms, this change is . . . striking: from [fiscal year] 1981 to 1987 discretionary spending on domestic programs *decreased* by 21 percent in real terms while defense outlays *increased* by 45 percent." Reagan himself, however, was primarily interested in the United State's relationship with the Soviet Union—the CPD's bogus "window of vulnerability." His administration's "extraordinary surge in defense spending," Wirls writes, "was devoted to the modernization and expansion of the gamut of military programs, conventional and nuclear, but first and foremost to the nuclear weapons rearmament program."

"In all of their writings on foreign policy," the journalist Frances Fitzger-

ald writes, assessing what she calls the "warrior intellectuals" of the CPD and
the Reagan administration, "they offer not one single constructive suggestion as to what the United States might do to, say, prevent widespread
famine, stop the crazy lurches of the economic system, prevent ecological
disaster or simply keep the peace and lessen the risk of nuclear war. The solution they have to all problems is confrontation and the threat, or use, of military force. Nowhere do they attempt to count the cost of keeping the Third
World down by force, and nowhere do they consider in any serious fashion
what risks this policy may pose to the physical security of the United States."

The Reagan rearmament program included more than $20 billion to
improve and protect the most vulnerable part of the U.S. nuclear deterrent,
its far-flung command, control, communications, and intelligence (C3I) systems, which had been given short shrift for years by contending military
services more interested in buying new weapons systems than in hardening
radars, satellites, and telecommunications systems. C3I was the greatest
vulnerability of both the superpowers, writes the strategic analyst John D.
Steinbruner, susceptible to destructive disconnection by "fewer than 100
judiciously targeted nuclear weapons. . . . Even 50 nuclear weapons are probably sufficient to eliminate the ability to direct U.S. [or Soviet] strategic
forces to coherent purposes." But $20 billion was not nearly enough. The
military services, across Democratic and Republican administrations alike,
had chosen not to modernize the key systems that controlled the vast U.S.
nuclear arsenal that was supposed to protect the nation, the better to limit
the politicians' options to the only option the services ever believed to be
realistic, which was firing first and preempting. "Command vulnerability,"
Steinbruner confirms, "has produced powerful incentives within the U.S.
military planning system to conduct full-scale strategic operations at the
outset of any serious nuclear engagement. This bias is very likely strong
enough and deeply enough entrenched to defeat any attempt to utilize
strategic forces in limited engagements of significant size." So one purpose of
the Reagan C3I allocation was to push the U.S. military toward acceptance of
its schemes of limited nuclear war.

If the massive Reagan administration arms buildup threatened what the
Soviet leadership perceived to be rough nuclear parity between the two
nations, the administration's decision to spend a significant share of its
enlarged budget on C3I improvements sent an even more threatening message, Steinbruner concludes: "As seen from current Soviet perspective, an
extensive U.S. program to prepare the command structure to support a
nuclear campaign will be understood as a sign of increased willingness to
initiate war."

And taken together with Reagan's hostile rhetoric and his arms buildup, it was. Yuri Andropov shocked a major KGB conference in Moscow in May 1981 with the news that the Reagan administration was preparing for a surprise nuclear first strike against the Soviet Union. In consequence, he instructed, both the KGB and its military intelligence counterpart, the GRU, for the first time in Soviet history, would combine their efforts in the largest intelligence-gathering program the Soviet services had ever mounted in peacetime, to be code-named Project RYAN, an acronym derived from the Russian words for a surprise missile attack, *raketno-yadernoye napadenie.* "Those in the KGB familiar with the United States," Gates writes, "thought this was 'alarmist' and suggested that Andropov's 'apocalyptic vision' origi- nated with the Soviet military high command and, specifically, Andropov's close associate Defense Minister [Dmitri] Ustinov."

Donald Maclean thought so as well. The former British diplomat, who had been a Soviet spy in his own country and in Washington during and after the Second World War until he defected to the Soviet Union in 1951, had made himself useful in Moscow as an expert on British and U.S. foreign and domestic policy. As a committed Communist, he judged the Brezhnev regime to be biased toward military strategies, writing in a private memo- randum in 1981: "What appears to have happened during the last five years is that at certain crucial turning points in policy-making the views of the mili- tary authorities with their natural professional interest in maximizing the armed strength of the country, have, with the support of the top leadership, prevailed over the views of those who are called upon to assess the overall influence of military policy upon the international interest of the country." Maclean was particularly concerned with the Soviet introduction of SS-20s into Europe, which he suspected the leadership had not understood would prompt a NATO response. "The next result . . . will be, unless the Soviet Union changes its policy, a rise in the level of nuclear confrontation in Europe with no compensating advantage to itself, indeed quite the reverse." Ustinov should not have been surprised at the NATO response, since he con- ceived his own SS-20s to be war-fighting weapons, writing secretly in Sep- tember 1981 that the strategic goals for the system were "participation in the first and subsequent nuclear strikes by the strategic offensive forces of the Soviet Union . . . on the territory of all European NATO states and adjacent seas. . . . Currently, and in the coming years, the United States and other NATO states do not have a comparable missile system ready." (The SS-20s could not, of course, reach the United States.)

But if KGB residencies in the West thought Andropov was being alarmist, they were not prepared to challenge him. "RYAN," writes the Cambridge

University historian Christopher Andrew, "thus created a vicious circle of intelligence collection and assessment. Residencies were, in effect, ordered to search out alarming information. The Center was duly alarmed by what they supplied and demanded more."

RYAN was the KGB's top priority in 1982, and Andropov's elevation to general secretary on 10 November, Gates writes, "only added to the priority given RYAN." Reagan had seemed to confirm Soviet fears in his speech to the British Houses of Parliament assembled at Westminster on 8 June 1982, when he characterized the Soviet Union as a country "that runs against the tide of history by denying human freedom and human dignity to its citizens" and one that was also "in deep economic difficulty." He had pledged "to foster democratic change" in Eastern Europe and in the Soviet Union itself, to offer "open assistance to fraternal, political, and social institutions to bring about peaceful and democratic progress." According to Thomas Reed, who worked on Soviet policy in the White House at the time, Reagan's Westminster speech was a public version of National Security Decision Directive 32 (NSDD-32), which Reed says called for nothing less than seeking "the dissolution of the Soviet empire." The Cold War "was no longer to be viewed as some permanent condition. . . . We were not just going to *talk* about freedom anymore. One side in this Cold War was going to win and one was going to lose." Reagan's "open assistance" would also "include covert action," Reed noted: Neither the public speech nor the secret decision directive would have come as any surprise to Andropov.

"The president has publicly blamed the Soviet Union for all events abroad adverse to U.S. interests," Charles William Maynes, the longtime editor of *Foreign Policy,* wrote that year. "He has asserted that Soviet leaders will resort to any tactics to achieve their revolutionary goals. A senior national security council adviser [i.e., Richard Pipes] has stated that unless the Soviet internal system changes, war is inevitable." Today, Maynes went on, "some Soviet officials contend privately that the United States is increasing arms expenditures at the worst possible moment. They argue that having achieved nuclear parity, the Soviet Union was ready to level off its strategic programs but that the Reagan administration is now reopening the arms race with its massive defense programs. If so, the Soviets must ask themselves how any American administration can understand or believe in the benign intent of plans so buried in secrecy that they are never relayed until it is too late."

Defense Minister Ustinov's response to American threats, Benjamin Fischer reports, was "a spectacular Soviet military exercise on 18 June 1982 that simulated an all-out first strike against the US and Western Europe. The

Soviets dubbed it the 'seven-hour nuclear war' that demonstrated the 'might of the Soviet Space Troops to the West.' " The exercise opened with a submarine ballistic-missile launch. "Next, two ground-based SS-11 ICBMs and an SS-20 intermediate-range ballistic missile (IRBM) were fired off and then destroyed in flight by Soviet ABM-X-3 antiballistic missile interceptors. The simulated attack included the launch of a Kosmos-1379, a low-orbit 'combat' satellite; a practice 'destruction' of US reconnaissance satellites 'whose role was played by Kosmos-1379 and Kosmos-1375'; and the launch of two missiles carrying photo-reconnaissance and navigational satellites as a 'prompt replacement' for Soviet spacecraft 'destroyed by the enemy.' " Ustinov's deputy marshal Nikolai Ogarkov, who was also the Soviet chief of staff, underlined the Soviet military's mood three months later in a speech to Warsaw Pact chiefs of staff in Minsk. He compared the American challenge to the situation on the verge of the outbreak of the Second World War: "The Reagan administration has inaugurated open preparations for war. This can be seen every day in the political, economic, diplomatic and military fields. . . . The United States has, in effect, already declared war on us, the Soviet Union and some other states of the Warsaw Treaty. In several fields, the battle is already going on. . . . In the present stage, the risk of war is as high as ever before."

NINE

REHEARSING ARMAGEDDON

TO THE SOVIET GOVERNMENT, NOW NEWLY INVIGORATED by Yuri Andropov's leadership, the approaching year, 1983, appeared to mark a turning point. The American Pershing 2s were scheduled to be deployed in Europe beginning in late November if no agreement stood them down. For negotiating terms, Reagan had offered his zero option, a Richard Perle contrivance designed to look to the millions of Europeans and Americans in the burgeoning Nuclear Freeze movement like a reasonable bargain. It required the Soviet Union to give up all its intermediate-range ballistic missiles in Europe, including its new SS-20s, while the United States pledged merely to retire some older theater missiles it had planned to retire anyway and not to deploy the new Pershings and Tomahawks. Nor would British or French nuclear assets be reduced.

According to the diplomatic correspondent Strobe Talbott, the idea of such a *Null-Lösung*, a "zero solution," had originated with the West German Social Democratic Party. The Reagan administration national security adviser, Richard Allen, had rejected it as "illusory" until Perle resurrected it. Perle "intended [it] to be unacceptable," Thomas Graham, Jr., writes, an assertion supported by Douglas MacEachin, a Soviet specialist with the CIA: "I do know from firsthand knowledge that some of the people who designed our zero solution . . . designed it believing they had come up with a proposal which would not get a yes, which would therefore make it possible to deploy the missiles, and we could still say we're not being aggressive." Talbott also characterized Perle as someone opposed to arms control, "at least as it had traditionally been practiced. . . . Many Europeans were calling for the zero solution. So why not give it to them? Then, when it failed, they would be party to the failure, just as they had been party to what Perle saw as the folly of the December 1979 decision"—to negotiate withdrawal of the SS-20s, if possible, before deploying the Pershings and Tomahawks.

Perle himself evidently considered the zero option a cynical masterstroke.

Not long after he left government at the end of the Reagan years he published a novel, *Hard Line,* about a sophisticated, espresso-sipping assistant secretary of defense very much like Richard Perle, "compact and reserved"; ever at bureaucratic war with a State Department counterpart modeled on Perle's perennial adversary in the Reagan administration, Assistant Secretary of State Richard Burt, "convinced that only a hard line would produce a Western victory in the Cold War." With no help from the German Social Democrats, "Michael Waterman," Perle's fictional alter ego, invents a zero option, noting as he does so that it was "unlikely the Soviets will agree":

> Zero. That was it. Zero. Zero for both sides.
> *Get rid of all of them—SS-20s, Pershing IIs, ground-launched cruise missiles, the whole lot.*
> We will abandon our deployment if the Soviets give up theirs. Oh, it was perfect. It was fair. Balanced. Simple. Elegant. Obvious. Clean. Tidy. Neatly wrapped.
> How could they say no? How could *anyone* fail to say yes? Who would criticize it—and how? With what argument? The simple flawlessness of it. It was exquisite. It was fastidious. It was sublime. It was . . . *inevitable.*
> His fingers flew like Bach's at the harpsichord. The words were music to his ears.

"Urbane guerrillas in dark suits," Perle characterizes his sturdy breed of heroes, "they fought not with AK-47s but with memos, position papers, talking points, and news leaks." (A reviewer, Robin Winks, a Yale historian, came to a different conclusion. "What is intriguing," he wrote of Perle's novel, "is the sense of how bureaucrats deal with one another in Washington, how they devote inordinate time to silly activities, how they speak in a special kind of wise-guy jargon, and how they let their ambitions overcome their good sense. Waterman is not an attractive person. . . . He loves the perks of office, the limousines, the flights to Paris, the chance to eat in the best restaurants. He is unwilling to learn; he undermines colleagues; he is intent on the triumph of his will, his ideas, his solutions. In the end we are led to believe that this is a good thing, though some readers may simply stand aghast at the pettiness of so much of this activity.")

Perle's zero option did not inspire Andropov with the music of a Bach fugue. The new general secretary took missile threats seriously, and the approaching deployment of Pershing 2s was beginning to look to him like another Cuban Missile Crisis, with Reagan in the Khrushchev role. Speaking to the Warsaw Pact's Political Consultative Committee in January 1983,

Andropov was shockingly candid. "What has caused the sharp turn in U.S. and NATO policy, which produced the current flare-up of tensions, and how long will this aggravation last?" he asked. The Soviet achievement of "military-strategic parity with the West" was one cause, he asserted; so was its "dynamic policy of détente." But the United States and NATO had found opportunity as well "in the difficulties we have all been facing to one extent or another in our economic development. I have in mind the growth of foreign debts, the food situation, our technological lag in certain areas and a series of other bottlenecks. Internal political complications in some socialist countries have been appraised in a similar vein."

"Especially dangerous," Andropov continued, "is the military challenge thrown at us. . . . The new round of the arms race, imposed by the USA, has major, qualitative differences. Whereas before, the Americans, in speaking about their nuclear weaponry, preferred to accentuate the fact that it was above all a means of 'intimidation' and 'deterrence,' now, in creating modified missile systems, they do not hide the fact that they are really intended for a future war. From here spring the doctrines of 'rational' and 'limited' nuclear war; from here spring the statements about the possibility of surviving and winning a protracted nuclear conflict. It is hard to say what is blackmail and what is genuine readiness to take the fatal step."

A month later, following up Andropov's cautions, the KGB sent its residents in the capitals of Europe and North America imperative further instructions on Project RYAN. The first of two directives spoke of the "growing urgency of the task to uncover NATO preparations for a nuclear missile attack on the USSR" and suggested watching for activity at "the places where government officials and members of their families are evacuated," identifying "the location of specially equipped civil defense shelters," assessing "increased purchase of blood from donors and the prices paid for it," counting cars at defense offices in the day and in the evening, noting changes in the police administration system, and reporting regularly. A second directive explained that determining the launching of a missile from the United States "leaves roughly 20 minutes reaction time. This period will be considerably curtailed after deployment of the 'Pershing-2' missile in [West Germany], for which the flying time to reach long-range targets in the Soviet Union is calculated at 4–6 minutes." Since the United States had pledged to its NATO allies that it would not launch nuclear weapons against the Soviet Union without first consulting with them, the second KGB directive emphasized that the "most important problem for the information-gathering apparatus of Soviet intelligence" was "to ascertain in good time the moment when nuclear consultations begin inside NATO."

Reagan, not yet aware of the developing Soviet war scare, ratcheted his rhetoric higher in a March 1983 speech to the annual convention of the National Association of Evangelicals in Orlando, Florida. There he named the Soviet Union "the focus of evil in the modern world" and, famously, "an evil empire." The speech, built in part from paragraphs cut by more cautious advisers from his speech at Westminster, was meant to win the support of fundamentalist Christians against the Nuclear Freeze movement. It won the support as well of Vladimir Slipchenko, a member of the Soviet general staff:

> The military, the armed forces . . . used this [speech] as a reason to begin a very intense preparation inside the military for a state of war. . . . We started to run huge strategic exercises. . . . These were the first military exercises in which we really tested our mobilization. We didn't just exercise the ground forces but also the strategic [nuclear] arms. . . . For the military, the period when we were called the evil empire was actually very good and useful, because we achieved a very high military readiness. . . . We also rehearsed the situation when a non-nuclear war might turn into a nuclear war.

EVEN AS SOVIET FORCES WERE PREPARING their exercises, the U.S. Pacific Fleet began three weeks of maneuvers in the North Pacific. Doughty little John Lehman, Perle's former business partner, who was now Reagan's truculent secretary of the Navy, intended the maneuvers to demonstrate his "forward strategy" policy of dominating "high-threat" areas near the Soviet Union—in this case, the Kurile Islands, which the Soviet Union had wrested from the Japanese in the last days of the Second World War and, farther north, the vulnerable intelligence-collecting centers on the Kamchatka Peninsula. Making sure that Soviet intelligence was aware of the U.S. presence, the journalist Seymour Hersh writes, "was one of the basic purposes of such exercises . . . to show the Soviets who is boss." Reagan had just authorized U.S. warships to sail closer to Soviet borders, Hersh notes. Now "three aircraft carrier battle groups, part of a forty-ship armada accompanied by Air Force B-52 bombers . . . sailed defiantly in the icy waters off Alaska's Aleutian Islands, 450 miles from . . . Kamchatka. . . . American attack submarines and antisubmarine aircraft began operating for the first time inside the normal patrol area of the Soviet submarine fleet. In all, 23,000 American military men took part. . . . As one expert later said, 'They know we're there.' "

In the midst of these aggressive exercises, on 23 March 1983, Reagan announced to the world his unvetted, pristine new program to render nuclear weapons "impotent and obsolete," the program that would shortly be named the Strategic Defense Initiative (SDI) by the administration and Star Wars—from George Lucas's 1977 film of the same name—by the public:

> Let me share with you a vision of the future which offers hope. It is that we embark on a program to counter the awesome Soviet missile threat with measures that are defensive. Let us turn to the very strengths in technology that spawned our great industrial base and that have given us the quality of life we enjoy today.
>
> What if free people could live secure in the knowledge that their security did not rest upon the threat of instant U.S. retaliation to deter a Soviet attack, that we could intercept and destroy strategic ballistic missiles before they reached our own soil or that of our allies?
>
> I know this is a formidable technical task, one that may not be accomplished before the end of this century. . . . There will be failures and setbacks, just as there will be successes and breakthroughs. And as we proceed, we must remain constant in preserving the nuclear deterrent and maintaining a solid capability for flexible response. But isn't it worth every investment necessary to free the world from the threat of nuclear war? We know it is. . . .
>
> Tonight . . . I'm taking an important first step. I am directing a comprehensive and intensive effort to define a long-term research and development program to begin to achieve our ultimate goal of eliminating the threat posed by strategic nuclear missiles. This could pave the way for arms control measures to eliminate the weapons themselves.

Senator Barry Goldwater wrote Reagan the next day, "That was the best statement I have ever heard come from any President."

SDI was seemingly the last piece in a puzzle that Reagan had been trying for several years to solve, the puzzle of how to eliminate nuclear weapons from the world when one's main adversary, as Reagan had said at his first presidential press conference, reserved unto itself "the right to commit any crime, to lie, to cheat, in order to attain [world revolution]." The SDI proposal would lead to major debate and maneuvering between the two superpowers as well as debates within each government, but its immediate effect was more ominous.

A KGB spy working at the Soviet Embassy in Washington, Yuri Shvets, remembers with delight his relief from his onerous RYAN duties, which "took prodigious amounts of time and energy with negligible effect. And here President Reagan comes with the SDI! As far as the leaders of the KGB intelligence service were concerned, this program jibed beautifully with the RYAN concept, and could not have come at a more opportune time. There was no longer any need to peek into windows, count cars and cut facts out of whole cloth."

Though SDI was as yet only a twinkle in the president's eye, Christopher Andrew and the former KGB colonel Oleg Gordievsky note that "the rhetoric and television advertising with which the project was unveiled were interpreted by the Center as further evidence of the US administration's attempts to prepare its citizens for nuclear war." The British novelist James Buchan, at that time the Bonn correspondent for the *Financial Times,* recalls that he "paid a visit to Moscow in the summer of that year. . . . And every Soviet official one met was running around like a chicken without a head—sometimes talking in conciliatory terms and sometimes talking in the most ghastly and dire terms of real hot war—of fighting war, of nuclear war." Thomas Powers explains why: "Civilians debated whether anybody could afford such a system [as SDI] or whether it could ever work, but defense theorists all knew that space-based defenses were well-suited only to one job—mopping up the ragged retaliatory missiles that would be fired by strategic forces devastated by a first strike. The tough talk in Washington was actually aimed at rallying Congress to support politically difficult cuts in domestic spending to free up funds for Star Wars; but the Soviets did not appreciate such nuances." Andropov confirmed the point at a Moscow press conference on 26 March. He said SDI was meant to leave his military "unable to deal a retaliatory strike" and was thus "a bid to disarm the Soviet Union in the face of the U.S. nuclear threat."

APRIL BROUGHT FURTHER PROVOCATIONS as the U.S. Navy continued its maneuvers close to Soviet waters in the North Pacific. Seymour Hersh:

> One night in early April, the *Midway,* after cutting off all electronic equipment whose emissions could be monitored by the Soviets, slipped away from the flotilla and steamed south toward the Kuriles. The Soviets did not track it. "When he [the *Midway*] popped up southeast of Kamchatka [by turning its electronics back on]," one Navy intelligence officer recalled, "they were clearly surprised." The *Midway*'s next act surprised not only the Soviets but also the senior commanders of the U.S. Pacific Fleet. On April 4, a group of at least six Navy planes from the *Midway* and the *Enterprise* violated Soviet borders by overflying the island of Zeleny in the Kurile archipelago. . . .
>
> The incident inevitably was viewed by the Kremlin as highly provocative and an explicit challenge to Soviet sovereignty over the heavily fortified Kurile Islands. . . . Within twenty-four hours, Soviet aircraft responded with a direct overflight of American territory in the Aleutian Islands; there was no doubt in the U.S. government that the Soviet overflights were, as one State Department official put it, "clear retaliation." . . .

Within hours of the overflight, the Soviet Air Defense Forces in the Far East were put on alert. They would stay that way through much of the spring and summer. The stakes, already high, had become higher.

Andropov responded to the April 4 Zeleny overflight by ordering more than simply a Soviet retaliatory overflight of the Aleutians. According to the investigative journalist Murray Sayle, he also ordered a new law added to the Soviet Air Code, Article 53, to complement Article 36 of the Law on the State Border of the U.S.S.R. that had been promulgated the previous November. "Read together," Sayle writes, "these two laws closed the whole of Soviet airspace to 'intruder' aircraft, and 'in instances in which the violation cannot be stopped or the violator detained by any other means,' Article 36 *instructed* the 'frontier guard troops and air-defense forces . . . to use weapons and combat equipment' . . . to shoot the intruder down."

Andropov warned the Central Committee in late June, Andrew and Gordievsky report, of an "unprecedented sharpening of the struggle" between the United States and the Soviet Union; he said "the threat of nuclear war [was] hanging over mankind." Another telegram went out to Soviet NATO residencies urging close attention to RYAN. Ironically, now that SDI was in release Reagan was contemplating not nuclear war but nuclear abolition, much to the dismay of his advisers. In a letter responding to one from Andropov that Reagan drafted by hand in mid-July, he wrote, "If we can agree on mutual, verifiable reductions in the number of nuclear weapons we both hold, could this not be a first step toward the elimination of all such weapons? What a blessing this would be for the people we both represent. You and I have the ability to bring this about through our negotiators in the arms reduction talks. . . . ~~that could lead to the total elimination of all such weap~~ [ons]" [*sic*]. Impatiently, on the advice of his second national security adviser, William Clark, the president agreed to delete the paragraph, including the line he had struck through himself, from the rewritten copy he sent to Andropov.

AN HOUR BEFORE DAWN ON THE MORNING of 1 September 1983, beyond the Kuriles above Sakhalin Island in the Sea of Okhotsk, a Soviet Sukhoi-15 fighter jet prepared to shoot down a Boeing 747 civilian airliner, Korean Airlines flight KE007, off course en route to Seoul from a refueling stop in Anchorage. KE007, which originated in New York, carried 269 passengers, sixty-one of whom were U.S. citizens, including Rep. Larry P. McDonald of Georgia, the national chairman of the far-right-wing John Birch Society. The airliner was 360 miles off course because its overworked captain, Chun Byung-in, had set the automatic pilot to fly on its magnetic compass rather than its more accurate inertial guidance system. It had already overflown the southern tip of the Kamchatka Peninsula; it would have been intercepted there had the Soviet fighters scrambling to intercept it not run short of fuel. Their tanks were deliberately kept only lightly filled to prevent their pilots from defecting, as one had done in 1976.

KE007 had crossed flight paths with a U.S. Air Force RC-135 reconnaissance aircraft, a Boeing 707, east of Kamchatka. The RC-135 had been sent out, legally, to monitor a Soviet missile test. The test had been scrubbed and the military aircraft was returning home. The appearance of the airliner, far off course, had sufficiently confused Soviet radar monitors on Kamchatka when the two planes crossed paths that they had assigned it the RC-135's track number, 6065. They told Sakhalin command center when they handed it off that it had been "provisionally identified as an RC-135."

Sakhalin sent up the Sukhoi-15, radio identifier 805, and a trailing MiG-23. Eight zero five located KE007, tracked it, observed its lights. (Eight zero five to ground station *Deputat:* "The air navigation lights are burning. The light is flashing.") Orders to close on it came from *Deputat.* The 805 pilot began to do so, and swore when he discovered his missiles were prematurely live and locked on. Turning off lock-on, he approached the target.

After KE007 crashed into the Sea of Okhotsk, the Soviets secretly recovered the downed plane and played back its flight recorders. The recordings revealed that the sleepy Korean Airlines pilots had been unaware that they had drifted over forbidden Soviet territory. The Soviets had taped their own communications as well. Andropov received transcriptions of the several recordings on 18 November 1983; thereafter they were hidden away in the GRU archives in Moscow. A decade later, Boris Yeltsin handed them over to the U.N.'s International Civil Aviation Organization. Murray Sayle quoted them in his comprehensive 1993 account of the incident:

> The Soviet tapes confirm that a hurried, half-hearted attempt was indeed made to intercept the straying airliner, and, at the same time, the tapes show that the Soviet air defense never made up its collective mind what the "target" was. The fighter pilot broke his electronic lock on KE007, approached the airliner from the right side . . . and fired a warning burst of cannon shells, which were invisible to the airliner. By now, KE007 is a few seconds from safety [it was nearing neutral waters], and [ground control] General Kornukov has made a decision:
> "Has he fired the warning burst?"

"Affirmative, he has."

"Destroy the target."

"Task received. Destroy Target Six-oh-six-five with missile fire."

As the fighter positions itself to fire, Kornukov worries that KE007 may escape. "Oh, fuck. He is already getting out into neutral waters. Engage afterburner immediately. Bring in the MIG-23 as well. While you are wasting time, it will fly right out."

"He has launched. He fired both missiles."

In three quick transmissions just seconds apart, 805 radioed to *Deputat*, "I have executed the launch. . . . The target is destroyed. . . . I am breaking off attack." When KE007, its tail damaged and one wing destroyed, slammed into the Sea of Okhotsk twelve minutes later at 600 miles per hour, all 269 people aboard were killed instantly. Sayle argues that the deaths "were mandated by Andropov's pitiless laws sealing the Soviet air borders, which must share much of the blame. . . . The laws had no requirement for intruders to be identified, or for them to be guilty of anything at all, beyond mere intrusion." Since the laws, however cruel, had responded to John Lehman's belligerent policies of naval threat display, of showing the Soviets who was boss, some share of blame for the loss of innocent life surely belongs as well to the Reagan administration.

Reagan called the destruction of KE007 "an act of barbarism" and a "crime against nature." He was still speaking months later of "the murder of 269 innocent people in a defenseless airliner." Secretary of State George Shultz, scheduled to hold private talks with Andrey Gromyko during a meeting of the Conference on Security and Cooperation in Europe in Madrid on 8 September 1983, kept his appointment but used the occasion to deride the Soviet government coldly for shooting down the plane and blaming the incursion on the United States. Gromyko's responding statement "was astonishingly brutal," Schultz wrote in his memoirs, adding, "The meeting became so outrageous and pointless that we just ended it."

The national security lesson Andropov learned from the airliner incursion was the vulnerability of his borders, now evident to the world, which may explain the belligerence of his response. "The 747 had been in Soviet airspace for over two hours before Soviet air defense forces were able to approach the aircraft," writes the University of Toronto scholar Beth Fischer. "Even more disturbing, eight of the eleven Soviet tracking stations on the Kamchatka Peninsula and Sakhalin Island had failed to detect the plane." Beleaguered, with advanced diabetes, his kidneys failing, his life sustained by dialysis, Andropov issued a statement from his hospital bed on 28 September

1983 that George Kennan described as the kind of invective that would once have been a prelude to war.

The mortally ill general secretary said that the United States was on "a militarist course which poses a grave threat to peace." He spoke of "the unprecedented build-up of U.S. military potential, the large-scale programs of manufacturing weapons of all types—nuclear, chemical and conventional," adding, "Now it is planned to project the unrestricted arms race into outer space as well." For the sake of its "imperial ambitions," he cautioned severely, "[the American] Administration goes to such lengths that one begins to doubt whether Washington has any brakes at all to prevent it from crossing the line before which any sober-minded person must stop." Not yet knowing what the flight recorders would reveal, he accused the United States of an "insidious provocation involving a South Korean plane engineered by U.S. special services," a conspiracy that was "also an example of extreme adventurism in politics." He said the United States was "a country where an outrageous militarist psychosis is being implanted" and warned Europe away.

October 1983 brought more conflict and suffering. On 23 October, a suicide bomber driving a yellow Mercedes delivery truck loaded with six tons of explosives barreled into a U.S. Marine barracks at Beirut International Airport in Lebanon and detonated his load. The building shattered and collapsed and 241 American service personnel were killed. A parallel attack seconds later at a French barracks in West Beirut killed fifty-eight French paratroopers. The Iranian-funded Lebanese terrorist group Hezbollah was eventually charged with the attacks. Two days later, coincidentally, Reagan ordered the invasion of Grenada, the small, formerly British island in the eastern Caribbean where Cuban forces and workers had been building a large airport and advising a new Revolutionary Military Council that had installed itself after a coup. In the back of Reagan's mind and of George Shultz's was concern that a thousand American students attending medical school on the island might be taken hostage as Americans had been taken in Tehran during the revolution there in 1979—an event that had sunk Jimmy Carter's chances for reelection. The marines who liberated Grenada—diverted from their transport by sea to Beirut to replace those killed there in the terror bombing at the airport—captured Soviet advisers as well as Cuban.

The culminating and most dangerous misunderstanding in that year of misunderstandings involved a nine-day NATO military exercise designated ABLE ARCHER 83, scheduled for 2 through 11 November 1983. NATO annually conducted multinational exercises called AUTUMN FORGE from its northern to its southern flank, mobilizing aircraft and moving tanks, troops, and artillery across rivers and through mud in realistic battle simulations. In some years AUTUMN FORGE ended with a command-post exercise, ABLE ARCHER, that practiced the coordinated consultations among NATO national leaderships necessary to authorize the use of nuclear weapons, just the procedure that the KGB's Project RYAN directives of the previous February had instructed its residencies to be particularly alert for—"to ascertain in good time the moment when nuclear consultations begin inside NATO." ABLE ARCHER 83 differed from previous command-post exercises in involving the actual participation of senior U.S. and NATO leaders who would have had to approve such nuclear releases. Reagan himself had been expected to participate as well as Vice President George H. W. Bush, Caspar Weinberger, and the chairman of the Joint Chiefs. "I had serious misgivings about approving the drill as originally planned," Reagan's third national security adviser, Robert McFarlane, told the scholar Beth Fischer. "There were concerns that superpower relations were too tense. There was a concern with how Moscow would perceive such a realistic drill." McFarlane scrubbed participation by the highest-level U.S. leaders, but British prime minister Margaret Thatcher and German chancellor Helmut Kohl both took part. Even McFarlane's caution was subject to misinterpretation in the fog of cold war. "The sudden disappearance of such figures," the British correspondent Martin Walker noted, "the disruption of usual schedules and the swift movement of the military high command around Washington were precisely the signs the Soviet intelligence had been told to look for under RYAN."

James Buchan had reported seeing Moscow officials the previous summer running around like chickens without heads. "They were extremely frightened of some kind of large military exercise by NATO in the autumn of '83," he recalled, "after the Bundestag [the parliament of the Federal Republic of Germany] had approved the [Pershing] missile deployments." By late 1983, the CIA's Ben Fischer writes, "the entire [Soviet Union] was in a frenzy, stimulated by peace rallies, civil defense drills and classified briefings for the party *aktiv* on the war danger. (Photographs from this period show students practicing air-raid and gas-mask drills.) A foreign ministry official returning to Moscow in November 1983 described the atmosphere as 'pre-war.' " Melvin Goodman, a senior analyst at the CIA at the time, recalls seeing "some clandestine reports that suggested great alarm in Moscow. But frankly they weren't taken very seriously by anyone but the analysts." Angelo Codevilla, a conservative analyst for the Senate Select Committee on Intelligence in 1983, told Beth Fischer, "When the report surfaced that the KGB was worried about an American first strike, there was a great deal of incredulity: How could anyone be this ignorant of America?" The KGB was mirror-imaging, as Richard Pipes might have put it: The Soviet war plan proposed disguising a move toward nuclear war within a seemingly routine military exercise. The Soviet leadership had every reason, including knowledge gained from spying, to believe that a NATO attack would begin the same way. And indeed, starting a war from within an exercise was NATO's strategy as well.

Robert Gates came to be convinced that the Soviet scare over ABLE ARCHER 83 was far more serious than the CIA judged it to be at the time. According to the KGB defector Oleg Gordievsky, Gates writes, "the exercise especially alarmed Moscow because (1) the procedures and message formats used in the transition from conventional to nuclear war were different from those used before, and (2) in this exercise the NATO forces went through all of the alert phases from normal readiness to general alert. Further, he says that alarmist KGB reporting persuaded 'the Center' that there was a real alert involving real troops. Also, surveillance around U.S. bases in Europe reported changed patterns of officer movement. Thus 'the KGB concluded that American forces had been placed on alert—and might even have begun the countdown to nuclear war.' " The former CIA director describes a pattern of Warsaw Pact alerting:

> Between November 2 and 11, there had been considerable activity by Soviet and other Warsaw Pact forces in the Baltic Military District as well as by East German, Polish and Czechoslovak forces in response to preparations for the exercise and the exercise itself. Elements of the air forces of the Group of Soviet Forces Germany had gone on heightened alert because, according to the commander, of the increase in the threat of possible aggression against the USSR and its Warsaw Pact allies during the exercise. Soviet military meteorological broadcasts were taken off the air during the exercise. Units of the Soviet Fourth Air Army had gone to increased readiness and all combat flight operations were suspended from November 4 to 10.

The director of the Australian Defense Intelligence Organization at that time, Paul Dibb, adds a further detail to Gates's account. "The Group of Soviet Air Forces in East Germany was forward-loading tactical nuclear weapons onto Sukhoi-17 long-range strike aircraft to strike West Germany," he reports. "They were tactical nuclear weapons to bomb military and other targets just across the border from East Germany in West Germany."

All this evidence points to the same conclusion: that the United States and the Soviet Union, apes on a treadmill, inadvertently blundered close to nuclear war in November 1983. That, and not the decline and fall of the Soviet Union, was the return on the neoconservatives' long, cynical, and radically partisan investment in threat inflation and arms-race escalation.

During the Cuban confrontation, when American nuclear weapons were ready to launch or already aloft and moving toward their Soviet targets on hundreds of SAC bombers, both sides were at least aware of the danger and working intensely to resolve the dispute. During ABLE ARCHER 83, in contrast, an American renewal of high Cold War rhetoric, aggressive and perilous threat displays, and naïve incredulity were combined with Soviet arms-race and surprise-attack insecurities and heavy-handed war-scare propaganda in a nearly lethal mix. Gates reviews the episode from a post–Cold War perspective, to the same conclusion:

> Information about the peculiar and remarkably skewed frame of mind of the Soviet leaders during those times that has emerged since the collapse of the Soviet Union makes me think there is a good chance—with all of the other events in 1983—that they really felt a NATO attack was at least possible and that they took a number of measures to enhance their military readiness short of mobilization. After going through the experience at the time, then through the postmortems, and now through the documents, I don't think the Soviets were crying wolf. They may not have believed a NATO attack was imminent in November 1983, but they did seem to believe that the situation was very dangerous. And U.S. intelligence had failed to grasp the true extent of their anxiety. A reexamination of the whole episode by the President's Foreign Intelligence Advisory Board in 1990 concluded that the intelligence community's confidence that this all had been Soviet posturing for political effect was misplaced.

As if ABLE ARCHER 83 were not enough, the first sixteen Tomahawks arrived at England's Greenham Common Air Force Base, west of London near Newbury, on 14 November. Eight days later the United States began deploying the first Pershing 2 missiles in West Germany and the Soviet delegation walked out of the Intermediate Nuclear Forces talks in Geneva. Ustinov, the Soviet defense minister, announced at a meeting of Warsaw Pact defense ministers on 6 December that the Soviet Union was "lifting its voluntary moratorium on the deployment of intermediate-range Soviet nuclear weapons in the European part of the country. These weapons will now also be deployed at locations from which they could reach the territories of the relevant West European countries." On 8 December the Soviets suspended the Strategic Arms Reduction Talks (START) as well—the Reagan administration's answer to Jimmy Carter's SALT II negotiations—which in any case had been deliberately held to a glacial pace for months by the administration's self-important negotiator Edward Rowny, a retired Army general. "Never, perhaps, in the postwar decades," Gorbachev would summarize later, "has the situation in the world been as explosive . . . as in the first half of the eighties."

Reagan was surprised and shocked that the Soviets had taken his years of militant rhetoric and his massive arms buildup seriously. He belittled their concerns in his diary on 14 November: "I feel the Soviets are so defense minded, so paranoid about being attacked that without being in any way soft on them, we ought to tell them no one here has any intention of doing anything like that. What have they got that anyone would want?" A few weeks later William Casey returned from meeting with British intelligence in London and briefed Reagan further on RYAN and ABLE ARCHER 83. "Do you suppose they really believe that?" the president of the United States asked McFarlane less defensively afterward, the truth finally dawning. "I don't see how they could believe that—but it's something to think about."

THE PIVOTAL YEAR 1983 WAS CROWDED with experiences that gave Ronald Reagan, as he said, "something to think about." Besides the hostile Soviet reaction to Reagan's announcement of his Strategic Defense Initiative, the suicide bombing of the U.S. Marine barracks in Beirut, the destruction of Korean Airlines flight KE007, and the Soviet war scare around ABLE ARCHER 83, several more personal experiences also influenced the president to rethink his approach to superpower relations.

"Columbus Day," Reagan began a diary entry on Monday, 10 October 1983. "In the morning at Camp David I ran the tape of the movie ABC is running on Nov. 20. It's called 'The Day After' in which Lawrence, Kansas, is wiped out in a nuclear war with Russia. It is powerfully done, all $7 million worth. It is very effective and left me greatly depressed. So far they haven't sold any of the 25 ads scheduled and I can see why. . . . My own reaction: we have to do all we can . . . to see that there is never a nuclear war." *The Day After*, a television film that Nicholas Meyer directed for the ABC network, graphically depicted the effects of a nuclear war between the United States and the Soviet Union on the people and buildings of Lawrence, Kansas, a quiet university town in the hilly eastern part of the state, and on Kansas City, Missouri, and its rural surroundings. Jason Robards played a country doctor overwhelmed with wounded and dying victims, JoBeth Williams a compassionate nurse, John Lithgow a college professor, and Steve Guttenberg and Amy Madigan two young people caught up in the disaster.

In 1983 I was in the midst of writing *The Making of the Atomic Bomb*; I lived in Kansas City at the time and remember well the shock of seeing simulated mushroom clouds rising over the city where I grew up and Minutemen launched in reprisal from the missile silos that punctuated the abundant farmlands to the east. I had lived in Lawrence as well and used the University of Kansas library there for research. Having visited Hiroshima and Nagasaki by then, having interviewed survivors, walked the ground,

and studied photographs and film of the aftermath of the atomic bombings, I understood that the ABC production underplayed the destruction it
depicted, a point the popular astrophysicist Carl Sagan made in an interview
after the broadcast when he discussed the possibility of nuclear winter—a
possibility that he and other scientists had only just proposed in a controver-
sial paper in *Science* that year. But if it pulled its punches, *The Day After* was
nevertheless sufficiently realistic to stir national angst and extensive debate,
some of it partisan, even before the production's late-November airing. Liberals worried that such a universal disaster might be a real possibility given
Reagan's hostile anti-Soviet rhetoric and trillion-dollar rearmament program. Conservatives suspected that the production was part of a liberal plot
to scare the country into arms negotiations. Educators feared that it would
give children nightmares, and no doubt it did.

As a former movie actor, Reagan was famously responsive to stories told
on film. "I knew from Sacramento days that he liked celluloid," the national
security adviser and former California Supreme Court Justice William Clark
told Reagan's biographer Lou Cannon. Film became a way to educate a president who had come to the White House notoriously ill-informed about
foreign affairs, Cannon writes:

> When Bill Clark became Reagan's second national security adviser at the
> beginning of 1982, he found that the president knew next to nothing about
> what was going on in many corners of the globe. . . . Clark . . . realized from his
> first day at the White House that the gaps in the president's knowledge were
> potentially dangerous ones that needed to be filled. His technique for doing
> this demonstrated an understanding of Reagan's mental processes and work
> habits that was unmatched in the White House. Clark knew that the president
> responded to visual aids and reasoned that he would be most receptive of all to
> films. So he took Reagan to the movies. Clark obtained Defense Department
> movies on "the Soviet threat," the problems of the Middle East and other issues
> and showed them to Reagan in the White House theater. [He] asked the CIA to
> provide a "profile movie documentary" on world leaders Reagan was scheduled
> to meet. "And the agency started producing some great stuff that was enjoyable
> for all of us," Clark said. "[It was] far more interesting to see a movie on Mrs.
> [Indira] Gandhi covering her life than sitting down with the usual tome the
> agency would produce."

To the point, Edmund Morris, another Reagan biographer, commented
that Reagan's diary entry about *The Day After* was "the first and only admission I have been able to find in his papers that he was 'greatly depressed.' "

For a president who shied from personal conflict and stopped his ears against bad news, viewing *The Day After* was an unsettling experience.

The experience in turn affected Reagan's reaction to an extensive briefing on the SIOP (the Single Integrated Operational Plan) that he received in preparation for ABLE ARCHER 83. By 1983, the SIOP had been distended to an attack on five thousand decapitation targets among a preposterous total of fifty thousand targets of military, industrial, or economic significance. Beth Fischer interviewed several officials who attended the late October briefing. They reported, she writes, that the president "was 'chastened' by what he witnessed and became withdrawn. Weinberger has attested that the president found the briefing to be a terribly disturbing experience. 'He had a very deep revulsion to the whole idea of nuclear weapons,' the defense secretary explained. 'These war games brought home to anybody the fantastically horrible events that would surround such a scenario.' " Afterward, Reagan wrote in his diary: "A most sobering experience with Cap W [i.e., Weinberger] and Gen. Vessy [*sic*: JCS chairman Gen. John W. Vessey, Jr.] in the Situation room, a briefing on our complete plan in the event of a nuclear attack. . . . In several ways, the sequence of events described in the briefings paralleled those in the ABC movie. Yet there were still some people at the Pentagon who claimed a nuclear war was 'winnable.' I thought they were crazy."

How Reagan's mind worked was a subject of considerable discussion during the years of his presidency and among his biographers afterward. Most discussants came to similar conclusions, although their estimates of the quality of Reagan's thinking depended on whether they were promoters or detractors of his goals. In a word, Reagan thought "anecdotally, not analytically," as the journalist and former assistant secretary of state Leslie Gelb put it. The president organized events and ideas on a Procrustean bed of personal experiences and rigid beliefs. Taxes stifled enterprise because in the 1950s a top federal income tax rate of 91 percent on earned income had led him and other movie stars to limit their acting work to four films a year. Communists were cynical, brutal, cold-blooded, and completely lacking in morality because the Communists he believed he had fought for control of the Screen Actors Guild when he was its president had seemed to him to be such people. "Firsthand discoveries are the ones that matter to Reagan," Cannon confirms. "When he expressed his view of Communist morality at his first presidential news conference, he believed he was talking from experience."

Cannon found that "most of his aides thought of him as intelligent, but many also considered him intellectually lazy." In fact, they laughed at him behind his back. He was Joe Six-pack, they told each other, his opinions and judgments exactly those guileless truisms you would expect to find among patrons of a neighborhood bar. "The sad, shared secret of the Reagan White House," Cannon writes, "was that no one in the presidential entourage had confidence in the judgment or capacities of the president. Often, they took advantage of Reagan's niceness and naïveté to indulge competing concepts of the presidency and advance their own ambitions. Pragmatists and conservatives alike treated Reagan as if he were a child monarch in need of constant protection. They paid homage to him, but gave him no respect." A book in his hand was more likely to be a Tom Clancy novel than a Henry Kissinger memoir—though the same could be said for many Americans. "Not one of the friends and aides" Leslie Gelb interviewed "suggested that the President was, in any conventional sense, analytical, intellectually curious or well-informed—even though it would have been easy and natural for them to say so. They clearly did not think it necessary. Time and again, they painted a picture of a man who had serious intellectual shortcomings but was a political heavyweight, a leader whose instincts and intuition were right more often than their own analyses. His mind, they said, is shaped almost entirely by his own personal history, not by pondering on history books." For George Shultz, in Cannon's paraphrase, "Reagan's seemingly irrelevant anecdotes were tools that the president used to comprehend the world. 'He often reduced his thinking to a joke,' Shultz said. 'That doesn't mean it didn't have a heavy element to it.' " Cannon counters that Reagan "sometimes used humor to avoid facing issues he ought to have faced, particularly the reality that it was impossible to increase military spending, reduce taxes and balance the budget simultaneously." Reagan's difficulty with governing went deeper, Cannon insists:

> His biggest problem was that he didn't know enough about public policy to participate fully in his presidency—and often didn't realize how much he didn't know. Reagan's legal advisers learned that he knew little about the law, his national security advisers found that he was devoid of knowledge on the capabilities of most U.S. and Soviet weapons systems and his economists discovered that he was poorly informed on economics, even though he sometimes reminded them that he had majored in economics and sociology at Eureka College.

("Playing it safe," the cultural historian Garry Wills writes, explaining Reagan's economic lacunae, "he majored in economics—[economics professor] Archibald Gray was the most notoriously easy grader on the campus.")

Less politely, the political scientist Richard M. Pious, reviewing Cannon's biography and other studies of the president, reduced their findings to three parallel axioms: "Reagan could only understand things if they were presented as a story; he could only explain something if he narrated it; he could only think about principles if they involved metaphor and analogy." For Sidney Blumenthal, who contrasts Reagan's triumphant promotion of political conservatism with Barry Goldwater's failure, the president's storytelling was the secret of his success:

> With him, facts don't determine the case; they don't make his beliefs true. Rather, his beliefs give life to the facts, which are tailored to have a moral. Reagan doesn't use stories the way experts use statistics. They seek mathematical certainty, whereas he has moral certainty. He asks listeners to trust the tale, not necessarily the detail. If the facts belie his premises, then the facts are at fault, and he can shift ground without making any fundamental change in his beliefs. His policies might be contradictory and counterproductive, but his mythology remains appealing. . . . His life experience vindicates his nostalgic approach to the future; he feels what he says, and that gives it authenticity and force.

Such a mode of thought, far from being baffling or unique, is characteristic of religious, and particularly of fundamentalist, thinking, an archaic mode in which facts are allegorized into parables or reinterpreted to match doctrine. If the Bible says the world was created in seven days and humankind is a separate creation, then evolution must be an unsupportable theory and fossils simply traps God has set to confound unbelievers. If homosexuality is proscribed in Genesis and Leviticus, then it must be a lifestyle choice, not a biologically determined orientation. If religious belief is necessary to morality, then Communists—atheists by definition—must be amoral.

Reagan's fundamentalist mentation encouraged him to find the supernatural as credible as the natural. He had been convinced since at least his days as governor of California that the end of the world was approaching. He believed that the Bible predicted the future. "Everything is in place for the battle of Armageddon and the second coming of Christ," he told a surprised California state senator one day in 1971, citing as a sign his understanding that Libya had gone Communist. The founding of Israel in 1948, the Jews thus reclaiming their homeland, was another sign Reagan credited as meaning that a great final battle between good and evil would soon be fought on the plain of Armageddon. The atomic bombings of Hiroshima and Nagasaki, he believed, fulfilled the prediction in Revelation of an army out of Asia of "twice ten thousand times ten thousand" routed by plagues of "fire and smoke and sulfur." He added Chernobyl to his list when he learned that the name of the old town was the Byelorussian word for wormwood, fulfill-ing the prophecy of "a great star [that] fell from heaven, blazing like a torch, and it fell on a third of the rivers and on the fountains of water. The name of the star is Wormwood."

  Cannon describes an occasion in 1970 when the singer Pat Boone and two radio evangelists visited Ronald and Nancy Reagan at their residence in Sacramento; while the five were holding hands and praying together, the evangelist George Otis "was seized by what he took to be a visitation of the Holy Spirit [when] he prophesied that Reagan would become president." Otis's hands were shaking, Cannon reports, and so were Reagan's. The visit "stirred Reagan's interest in Armageddon," a story that "appealed to Reagan's adventurous imagination and met his requirement of a happy ending. As Reagan understood the story, Russia would be defeated by an acclaimed leader of the West who would [then] be revealed as the Antichrist. He, too, would fall, and Jesus Christ would triumph."

  Robert McFarlane concluded that Reagan's commitment to strategic defense derived primarily from his belief that Armageddon was approach-ing. "From the time he adopted the Armageddon thesis," the national secu-rity adviser told Cannon, "he saw it as a nuclear catastrophe. Well, what do you do about that? Reagan's answer was that you build a tent or a bubble and protect your country. This was one of the intellectual contradictions in Rea-gan's thinking. He sees himself as a romantic, heroic figure who believes in the power of a hero to overcome even Armageddon. I think it may come from Hollywood. Wherever it came from, he believes that the power of a per-son and an idea could change the outcome of something even as terrible as Armageddon. This was the greatest challenge of all. . . . He didn't see himself as God, but he saw himself as a heroic figure on earth." Frank Carlucci, deputy secretary of defense under Caspar Weinberger and subsequently one of Reagan's five national security advisers, confirmed that Reagan connected Armageddon with nuclear war. "He would say to me that nuclear weapons are inherently evil," Carlucci told Cannon. When Carlucci argued the case for nuclear deterrence, Cannon paraphrases, "he did not convince Reagan, who responded to the argument by telling Carlucci about Armageddon."

  If Reagan actually believed he might be the "acclaimed leader of the West" who might beat Russia, the evil empire, then he must also have considered the possibility that he himself might be the Antichrist, Christ's opposite, the disguised embodiment of evil. Better to rewrite the script to give it a happy ending, to prevent the "hail and fire, mixed with blood," falling on the earth, the burning up of "a third of the earth . . . a third of the trees . . . and all green grass." Better to prevent a nuclear war. Evidently the president didn't dwell on the unintended consequences of his rewrite, that saving the world from Armageddon would also delay the second coming of Christ.

Beliefs are often not logical, though they are anchored in the inner logic of profound personal experience. The inner logic of Reagan's life, as he himself testified, posited that "God has a plan for everyone," an idea that came to him originally from his devout Disciple of Christ mother, Nelle. He practiced the plan that God had for him, he wrote in his autobiography, in "seven summers [as] a lifeguard at Lowell Park" on the Rock River, which ran through Dixon, Illinois, a hundred miles from Chicago. Dixon was where he moved with his father, mother, and older brother, Neil, when he was nine and where he lived, he wrote, "the life that . . . shaped my body and mind for all the years to come after":

> Lifeguarding provides one of the best vantage points in the world to learn about people. During my career at this park, I saved seventy-seven people. I guarantee you they needed saving—no lifeguard gets wet without good reason. In my case it really took an emergency because my job was seven days a week, and from morning until they got tired of swimming at night. A wet suit was a real hardship and I was too money-conscious to have a spare. Not many thanked me, much less gave me a reward, and being a little money-hungry I'd done a little daydreaming about this. They felt insulted. . . .
>
> I got to recognize that people hate to be saved: almost every one of them later sought me out and angrily denounced me for dragging them to shore. "I would have been fine if you'd let me alone," was their theme. "You made a fool out of me trying to make a hero out of yourself."

The ingratitude of the rescued may have been the basis for a platitude Reagan adopted as his own and often quoted to his advisers; as William Clark rather stiffly recalled it: "We can accomplish almost anything together, if we do not concern ourselves with the question of who might receive the credit." Curiously, and noted as such by those who worked with him, Reagan insisted that the Strategic Defense Initiative was his idea and his alone. "The SDI program was very much driven by Ronald Reagan," Shultz would recall. "It was personal." At a press conference two days after his announcement, Reagan told reporters, "I've been having this idea, and it's been kicking around in my mind for some time here. I brought this up one day in a meeting [at] which the Chiefs of Staff were present and others, and we talked about it and discussed it and then discussed it some more." Several years later he told a reporter, more impatiently, "It kind of amuses me that everybody is so sure I must have heard about it, that I never thought of it myself. The truth is, I did." Reagan didn't mean that he originated the idea of ballistic missile defenses, of course; research and even deployment of various versions of such defenses, none of them effective, had been under way since the 1950s in both the United States and the Soviet Union. He meant he originated his own grandiose version of strategic defense (which he described, in his original announcement of the initiative on 23 March 1983, as having the "ultimate goal of eliminating the threat posed by strategic nuclear missiles") as providing "the means of rendering these nuclear weapons impotent and obsolete." In later speeches he would describe his goal even more specifically as a system "that might one day enable us to put in space a shield that missiles could not penetrate, a shield that could protect us from nuclear missiles just as a roof protects a family from rain."

"Lifeguards are solitary objects of adoration," Cannon writes, "who intervene in moments of crisis and perform heroic acts without becoming involved in the lives of those they rescue." Cannon's description might apply as well to the kind of movie star Reagan became, one who played the role of genial hero in movies that invariably ended happily. Next he scaled the role up to politics, becoming a two-term governor of California and then running for president once unsuccessfully before finally winning—twice—that most powerful of all roles.

He wanted to be president to accomplish a great rescue, he told his campaign manager, Stuart Spencer. "The sum total of him is simply this," Spencer recalled in an oral history interview: "Here's a man who had a basic belief, who thought America was a wonderful, great country. . . . This guy came from an alcoholic family, no money, no nothing. He was a kid who was a dreamer. He dreamed dreams and dreamed big dreams and went out to fulfill those dreams with his life and he did it. . . . [And] he had real concerns about all this leaving us because of communism. . . . It was the only thing that he really thought about in depth, intellectualized, thought about what you can do, what you can't do, how you can do it." Spencer told the future secretary of the Air Force Thomas Reed of a conversation he had with Reagan on the flight from Los Angeles to Detroit to join the 1980 Republican National Convention, where Reagan would be nominated as the party's presidential candidate:

> In the afternoon the conversation turned philosophical. Spencer asked the question all political pros learn to ask their candidates early on. "Why are you doing this, Ron? Why do you want to be President?"

Without a moment's hesitation Reagan answered, "To end the Cold War."

Spencer: "How do you plan to do that?"

Reagan: "I'm not sure, but there has got to be a way."

Reagan went on at length about the weakness of the Soviet system, about his horror at the thought of nuclear war, and about his annoyance with the accommodating, détente-oriented posture of the incumbent and preceding Presidents. Reagan was not a hawk. He did not want to "beat" the Soviets. He simply felt that it would be in the best interests of both countries, or at least of their general citizenry, to "end this thing." If the United States was strong enough, it could capitalize on the Soviet weaknesses that Reagan knew were there.

"There has to be a way, and it's time."

Michael Deaver, who became Reagan's deputy chief of staff, understood him similarly. "Reagan thought that he had to run for president," Deaver told the historian Paul Lettow. "He was the guy that could get the Soviets to the table and end nuclear war. . . . This was a guy who believed in predestination, who believed that there was a purpose for everybody's life and we had to fulfill it. And that was his purpose. . . . He was running for president because he believed he was destined to do away with nuclear weapons."

A sense of destiny muscled Reagan's dream of doing away with nuclear weapons, but its driving force was visceral dread, much as Curtis LeMay's had been when he came home to green Ohio after masterminding the devastating firebombing of Japan. LeMay's answer was preventive war before the Soviets acquired enough bombs to retaliate, or, failing that, early crisis preemption. Reagan, for all his totalistic anti-communism, sought a less dangerous solution. "One of the first statistics I saw as president," he recalled in his 1990 memoir, *An American Life,* "was one of the most sober and startling I've ever heard. I'll never forget it: The Pentagon said at least 150 million American lives would be lost in a nuclear war with the Soviet Union—even if we 'won.' For Americans who survived such a war, I couldn't imagine what life would be like. The planet would be so poisoned the 'survivors' would have no place to live. Even if nuclear war did not mean the extinction of mankind, it would certainly mean the end of civilization as we knew it. No one could 'win' a nuclear war." As Spencer saw him, "He was willing to roll those dice, because he absolutely had an utter fear of the consequences of nuclear warfare." Richard Pipes told Lettow smugly, "Reagan, for all his toughness, was terribly afraid of nuclear war."

In the spring of 1981, after Reagan was shot by John Hinckley, Jr., in an assassination attempt, and nearly died of blood loss, he wrote in his diary, "Whatever happens now, I owe my life to God and will try to serve him every way I can." Having come so close to death, he recalled in his memoir, "made me feel I should do whatever I could in the years God had given me to reduce the threat of nuclear war." The career diplomat Jack Matlock, Jr., who served as Reagan's principal adviser on Soviet affairs from 1983 to 1987 and then as ambassador to the Soviet Union, confirmed Reagan's horror of nuclear war in an interview with Lettow:

> Matlock . . . suspected Reagan would not retaliate in the event of a nuclear attack: "I think deep down he doubted that, even if the United States was struck, that he could bring himself to strike another country with [nuclear weapons]. He could never hint, but I sort of sensed [that]." Matlock believed that Reagan's unwillingness to retaliate against a nuclear attack contributed further to his desire for a missile defense. Matlock paraphrased Reagan's thoughts as: "How can you tell me, the president of the United States, that the only way I can defend my people is by threatening other people and maybe civilization itself? That is unacceptable."

Pipes's phrase "for all his toughness" in his comment on Reagan's fear of nuclear war implies that such fear was a weakness, a common attitude among nuclear strategists inside and outside the government. Shultz caught a glimpse of the strategists' protective alienation from the destruction they were contemplating during a briefing he received from Paul Nitze: "I listened as Nitze described these horrible, cataclysmic weapons of mass destruction in his genteel, bland manner, as if he were talking about baby farm animals." And easy enough for Pipes to say; the self-important academic never had to be responsible for the terrible decision that would face a president (or a general secretary) if deterrence failed and his country absorbed the devastation of a successful first strike: whether or not to respond with what was left of his nuclear arsenal, potentially killing millions more human beings for no other purpose than revenge. Far from being signs of weakness, Reagan's fear of nuclear war and his determination to reduce its risks measured his maturity as a human being—but also the extent to which he was and remained an outsider to the government over which he presided. At least twice during the first two years of his presidency, the diplomatic correspondent John Newhouse reports, "Reagan asked the bureaucracy to give him a plan to eliminate nuclear weapons. The bureaucracy did not respond." Nor did the problem go away.

Negotiation had been a traditional approach to limiting nuclear arms. The United States had negotiated nuclear issues with the Soviet Union and with other countries since shortly after the Second World War, when it offered the Baruch Plan for international control of atomic energy to the United Nations in 1946 (a negotiation that failed, a fact that Reagan sometimes lamented). The Limited Test Ban Treaty, the Outer Space Treaty, several Nuclear-Weapon-Free-Zone Treaties, the Nuclear Non-Proliferation Treaty, the Seabed Arms Control Treaty, the Anti-ballistic Missile Treaty, and the Threshold Test Ban Treaty, as well as the several SALT agreements, had all been designed to limit the development, deployment, and use of nuclear weapons. A president determined to "do away with nuclear weapons" might well be able to negotiate dramatic nuclear reductions or even nuclear abolition, especially one as popular and otherwise conservative as Reagan, who was elected to a second term by an overwhelming majority, carrying every state in the Union except Minnesota, his opponent's home state, and winning nearly 60 percent of the popular vote. He could hardly endorse such changes without intrusive programs of verification, of course, but those would be matters of negotiation as well.

Unfortunately for the world, one dimension of Reagan's Procrustean bed of fixed opinions prevented him from trusting negotiation as a path to ending the nuclear arms race. He discussed it at a West Point commencement on 27 May 1981. "Already," he told the graduating class, "the Congress has . . . mightily increased the spending for the military. The argument, if there is any, will be over which weapons, not whether we should forsake weaponry for treaties and agreements." Then he mentioned a book by a former Screen Actors Guild attorney that had settled his opinion about treaties and agreements, a book he called "the best book written on defense": "My good friend Laurence Beilenson authored a book a few years ago called *The Treaty Trap*. It was the result of years of research, and it makes plain that no nation that placed its faith in parchment or paper, while at the same time it gave up its protective hardware, ever lasted long enough to write many pages in history. Now this is not to say that we shouldn't seek treaties and understandings and even mutual reduction of strategic weapons. The search for peace must go on, but we have a better chance of finding it if we maintain our strength while we're searching." (Later in the address, the president referred obliquely to the Soviet Union, if not indeed to the Antichrist. "Today," he told the graduates, "you are that chain holding back an evil force that would extinguish the light we've been tending for 6,000 years.")

But if deterrence doesn't work, and treaties fail, and your opponent is prepared to lie, cheat, and steal to have his way, what's left? That would seem to be the question Reagan pondered once he decided that his personal destiny was to prevent Armageddon; he "thought about what you can do," as

Stuart Spencer understood Reagan's engagement with the challenge, "what you can't do, how you can do it." Edward Teller pointed him down the garden path of strategic defense when he visited Teller's Lawrence Livermore National Laboratory in 1967 as governor of California, introducing him to what Teller presented as defensive systems but what in later congressional testimony the Hungarian-born physicist would characterize as a "third generation of nuclear weapons." (The first generation of nuclear weapons were fission weapons, the second thermonuclear. The third generation that Teller had in mind would focus and transform the enormous energy of a nuclear explosion to drive directed-energy devices such as lasers, particle accelerators, or microwave beams—rifles, as it were, rather than firecrackers.) Lettow found "no documentary evidence that Reagan wrote or spoke of missile defense before 1967," which points to the governor's visit to Livermore as his earliest exposure to the idea.

"He took fifteen years to make up his mind" about strategic defense, Teller would say. Along the way he was encouraged by a self-appointed group of millionaire friends banded together into an organization they called High Frontier, founded by a founding member of the Committee on the Present Danger, Karl R. Bendetsen, who had the distinction of having directed the confinement of more than 100,000 Japanese-Americans in internment camps during the Second World War. Others who joined High Frontier included Joseph Coors, the right-wing Colorado brewer; an oilman, William Wilson; Jacquelin Hume, a friend of White House counselor Edwin Meese through the Bohemian Club, a men's club in San Francisco, and thus a direct link to Reagan; and Teller, the only scientist among them but one with a reputation for exaggeration and partisanship. Bendetsen recruited retired lieutenant general Daniel Graham, of the CPD and Team B, to run the organization. Unlike most military technologies, in other words, strategic defense as its proponents conceived it did not emerge from new developments in science and technology; it was instead a political concept, technologically barefoot, something that the United States could buy that would obviate any need to negotiate with the Soviets and that might restore the lost U.S. capability to destroy the Communist world in an overwhelming first strike.

SDI in Reagan's mind was never about any specific technology, however, not Teller's oversold and unproven X-ray laser nor Graham's off-the-shelf battle stations in space. Strategic defense was a dream, a fantasy, an uninformed, winner-take-all bet that American technology could make miracles happen if only a sufficiently committed leader stepped forward to offer sup-

port and run interference. It was a fond wish, as Reagan said in the speech
when he announced it, "that the human spirit must be capable of rising
above dealing with other nations and human beings by threatening their
existence." Unlike Teller and the Bohemian Club Edisons of High Frontier,
the president linked it quite specifically, then and later, to nuclear abolition.
"I would hope that if such a weapon proves practical," he said in 1985, "that
we can realistically eliminate these horrible offensive weapons, nuclear
weapons, entirely."

But the warheads will always get through, political scientist Kerry L.
Hunter reminds us:

> The truth is, SDI could have never provided a way out of the world of mutual
> assured destruction. Though MAD may feel morally bankrupt, there is no
> escaping the vulnerability caused by nuclear weapons. . . .
>
> The power of Reagan's Star Wars vision . . . lay in its utopian characteristics.
> It did not matter that Star Wars ignored reality. In fact, it was for this reason
> that the ideal was so appealing. The Star Wars dream allowed Americans to
> avoid a very stark truth that was practically intolerable to face: there was noth-
> ing they could do to protect themselves from nuclear annihilation outside of
> cooperating with the Soviets. Reagan seemed to sense this. Accordingly, he
> never did participate in discussion over the difficult questions the actual SDI
> program created. Even when the goals of the program were limited to seeking
> measures for protecting missiles, Reagan continued to believe in and espouse
> the vision of population defense—a total security from nuclear weapons, not
> security by having them. . . . The world his Star Wars dream promised was
> symbolic of how things ought to be, of what American presidents ought to be
> dreaming of.

And if wishes were horses, beggars would ride.

WHETHER REAGAN BELIEVED SDI WAS POSSIBLE, or only hoped it
would be, he knew when he learned of the Soviet war scare in the midst of
ABLE ARCHER 83 that weapons were armed and ready and no defenses had
yet come to hand. Surprised, angered, chagrined that his hot rhetoric could
be so coldly misunderstood, he moved quickly to send a message to the
Soviet leadership that he was not preparing to attack. "President Reagan was
not able to discount the Soviets' alarm as readily as his advisers did," writes
Beth Fischer. "According to McFarlane, the president responded with 'genuine anxiety' to the news of the Soviet panic. Reagan was visibly shaken by

the Soviets' misinterpretation of the NATO drill. The president had never believed that his war of words would lead to an armed conflict with the Soviet Union. More ominously, he had always felt that, in the face of an impending nuclear exchange, reason would not prevail. As he saw it, both sides 'had many contingency plans for responding to a nuclear attack. But everything would happen so fast that I wondered how much planning or reason could be applied in such a crisis.' "

On the last day of ABLE ARCHER 83, 11 November, Reagan spoke to the Soviet alarm—appropriately, in a speech before the Japanese Diet in Tokyo, in the only nation where atomic bombs had ever been used in war. He (or his speechwriters) could not resist continuing his attacks on the Soviet system, aligning the United States with Japan as nations that "do not build walls to keep our people in. We do not have armies of secret police to keep them quiet. We do not throw dissidents into so-called mental hospitals. And we would never cold-bloodedly shoot a defenseless airliner out of the sky." With the boilerplate delivered, he then reemphasized a conviction he had expressed before, at the United Nations and during one of his radio addresses. "I believe there can be only one policy for preserving our precious civilization in this modern age," he told the Japanese legislators. "*A nuclear war can never be won and must never be fought.* The only value in possessing nuclear weapons is to make sure they can't be used, ever. I know I speak for people everywhere when I say our dream is to see the day when nuclear weapons will be banished from the face of the Earth."

Several weeks later Reagan followed up his Diet signal with a further initiative, Shultz recalls: "When I met with the president on Saturday, December 17, he said he wanted to make a major Soviet speech and include in it his readiness to get rid of nuclear weapons. He told me he had noticed that Soviet Defense Minister Ustinov, in a speech two days previously, had proposed a ban on all nuclear weapons. By Monday, December 19, we had a good draft speech in the president's hands." That speech, which Reagan delivered from the White House on 16 January 1984, the morning before the first meeting of the Conference on Security and Cooperation in Europe (CSCE) in Stockholm—a "European disarmament conference" in Reagan's formulation—repeated the usual boilerplate, but in muted voice.

In the last ten years, Reagan said, the Soviets had "produced six times as many ICBM's, four times as many tanks, twice as many combat aircraft" as well as its SS-20s. He chose not to mention that the United States during the same period had deployed fifty-five hundred new warheads, five hundred more than the Soviets. He did say that his arms buildup had "halted America's decline." That made deterrence more credible, he added, but it might also be "the reason that we've been hearing such strident rhetoric from the Kremlin recently." He made clear that he was alluding to the war scare of the previous months: "These harsh words have led some to speak of heightened uncertainty and an increased danger of conflict. This is understandable but profoundly mistaken." Restored deterrence had made the world safer, but nuclear arsenals were still "far too high, and our working relationship with the Soviet Union is not what it must be." What he wanted it to be—the speech's central message to the Kremlin—was buried deep in the text:

> In our approach to negotiations, reducing the risk of war, and especially nuclear war, is priority number one. A nuclear conflict could well be mankind's last. And that is why I proposed over 2 years ago the zero option for intermediate-range missiles. Our aim was and continues to be to eliminate an entire class of nuclear arms. Indeed, I support a zero option for all nuclear arms. As I've said before, my dream is to see the day when nuclear weapons will be banished from the face of the earth.
>
> Last month the Soviet Defense Minister stated that his country would do everything to avert the threat of war. Well, these are encouraging words, but now is the time to move from words to deed. The opportunity for progress in arms control exists. The Soviet leaders should take advantage of it.

He might as well have been talking to a wall. Andropov, now mortally ill, had already dismissed the Reagan administration as beyond the pale. A "hackneyed ploy," Andrey Gromyko said, condemning the speech. When Andropov died, in early February 1984, Reagan pointedly chose not to attend his funeral, sending George H. W. Bush and Senate Majority Leader Howard Baker to Moscow instead. Reagan and Andropov's successor, the emphysemic seventy-three-year-old Konstantin Chernenko, exchanged letters— five were sent and answered between February and May—but made little progress. The Soviets were prepared to talk only if the United States first renounced SDI; as Chernenko put it, "What is needed is not the negotiations on what such systems might be, but a resolute and unequivocal renunciation of the very idea of creating such systems." In May, Tass compared Reagan to Hitler and called one of his speeches "a shameless lie from beginning to end." In July 1984, the Soviet Union boycotted the Los Angeles Olympics in retaliation for Jimmy Carter's boycott four years before.

By now Nancy Reagan, worried about her husband's place in history, had weighed in on the side of negotiations. According to Shultz, "hints came in" during August "that Gromyko might be looking for a chance to meet the president." Though he was nearly at the end of his first term, Reagan had not

Top: Humiliated during the Cuban Missile Crisis, the Soviet Union in 1963 began an all-out effort to match the U.S. nuclear arsenal.

Center: Kennedy *(back to camera)* and Secretary of Defense Robert McNamara *(right)* tried to limit nuclear proliferation. Flanking Kennedy to his left and right, McGeorge Bundy, Paul Nitze, and Gen. Maxwell Taylor.

Bottom: Dick Cheney and Donald Rumsfeld, a durable team, first emerged into prominence in the administration of Gerald Ford.

Left: Sen. Henry "Scoop" Jackson and staffer Dorothy Fosdick with Richard Perle, who used Jackson's authority to attack U.S.-Soviet détente. Richard Pipes (*center left*), Paul Wolfowitz (*center*), Edward Teller and John S. Foster, Jr., (*bottom*) inflated CIA estimates of Soviet intentions as advisers to "Team B"; Wolfowitz coauthored the Team B report. *Center right:* Nuclear strategist Albert Wohlstetter was a Perle and Wolfowitz mentor.

Opposite page, top: The Soviet invasion of Afghanistan in late 1979 soured U.S.-Soviet relations; Carter sharply increased defense spending.

Center: Ronald Reagan used his overwhelming 1980 electoral mandate to justify a trillion-dollar armaments program, including new missiles and bombers, and a more belligerently anti-Soviet policy.

Bottom: CIA director William Casey invented provocations, including a Saudi oil price cut that cost the U.S.S.R. billions of dollars.

Above: Bellicose Navy secretary John Lehman invented more provocations, including overflights of the Soviet Far East and aggressive naval exercises that set the stage for the Soviet shootdown of Korean Airlines flight KE007 in September 1983.

Left: Secretary of State George P. Shultz, who favored diplomacy, and Secretary of Defense Caspar Weinberger, who took his cues from Richard Perle, battled for Reagan's soul.

A massive new U.S. "Peacekeeper" missile with ten warheads fueled Soviet suspicions of U.S. war preparations. Reagan, as a young lifeguard who saved 77 lives, secretly dreamed of eliminating nuclear weapons and ending the Cold War.

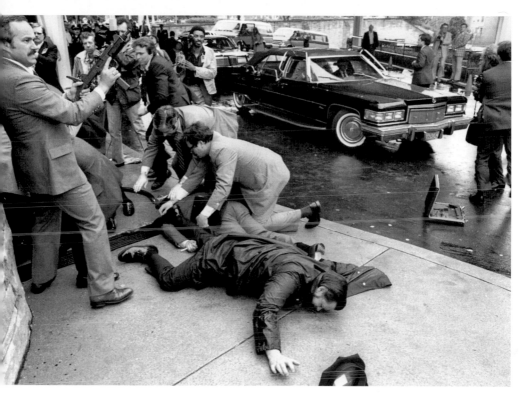

Above: Reagan nearly bled to death after his attempted assassination; he concluded God had spared him for the great purpose of negotiating peace between the superpowers.
Below: Reagan thought strategic defense—space-based antimissile systems—would protect the U.S. from hold-outs and "madmen." Though Edward Teller promoted it, SDI was a political concept with no technological base.

Above: When the Soviets upgraded an old medium-range missile deployed in Eastern Europe with a solid-fueled mobile SS-20, the U.S. responded in late 1983 by threatening to deploy Pershing 2s (*below*) which could reach Moscow in 10 minutes or less. *Opposite, top:* Deployment went ahead despite Reagan's increasing uneasiness, fueled by grisly war-plan briefings and a television movie, *The Day After,* about nuclear war. *Bottom:* NATO exercises in November 1983 nearly led to a Soviet first strike.

Right: Bobbies arrested anti-U.S. demonstrators at Greenham Common, west of London, in November 1983.

Old warhorse Andrei Gromyko, the Soviet foreign minister,
nominated Gorbachev to lead the U.S.S.R. on 11 March 1985.

Gorbachev, here with Defense Minister Sergei Sokolov and Nikolai Tikhonov
on the Lenin Mausoleum, was a new kind of Soviet leader,
eager for reform and chary of using violence.

Gorbachev soon replaced Gromyko with Eduard Shevardnadze *(left)*
as foreign minister; shrewd Anatoly Chernyaev became a close adviser.
Both counseled ending the Cold War.

yet actually talked to a member of the Politburo. He did so, finally, in late September. "The president later told me," Shultz writes, "that in their private conversation he had been struck by Gromyko's description of the two super-powers sitting on top of ever-rising stockpiles of nuclear weapons and by Gromyko's statement that the Soviet Union wished to reduce the size of those piles. 'My dream,' Reagan had told him, 'is for a world where there are no nuclear weapons.' "

Once Reagan was reelected, in November 1984, the Politburo had little choice but to deal with him. Preparations went forward on both sides for a meeting between Gromyko and Shultz in Geneva in January 1985 to plan three independent, concurrent negotiations on strategic weapons, intermediate-range weapons, and defensive systems. With Chernenko still officially in charge, Gorbachev made his debut in London in December and Margaret Thatcher hallmarked him. In a speech before Parliament he took a cue from Willy Brandt and spoke of a common European heritage: "Whatever is dividing us, we live on the same planet and Europe is our common home—a home, not a theater of military operations." Reagan, dreaming his dream, noticed in a news report a pledge Gorbachev had made during a luncheon speech: "The Soviet Union is prepared . . . to advance towards the complete prohibition and eventual elimination of nuclear weapons." Thatcher joined Reagan at Camp David three days before Christmas to report on her conversations with Gorbachev and dropped the other shoe; as the official memorandum of conversation has it, "Gorbachev had told her 'tell your friend President Reagan not to go ahead with space weapons.' He suggested if you develop SDI the Russians would either develop their own, or more probably, develop new offensive systems superior to SDI."

Shultz fought off the assaults of the Weinberger-Perle faction to organize his meetings with Gromyko, noting as others have noted that "the toughest negotiations take place within your own team, on your own side of the table." His toughest negotiation may have been with Reagan himself:

> Ronald Reagan's views were definite: all nuclear weapons should be eliminated, and strategic defense should take over the role of deterrence. He was annoyed with me for expressing reservations. I pointed out that offensive weapons were needed and that even the most far-reaching version of his dream of strategic defense was incomplete. What about defense against bombers, stealth aircraft, sea-launched cruise missiles? SDI wouldn't cover them. The Soviets didn't need to be convinced about the importance of strategic defense; they had always valued it. It was the United States that had deprived itself intellectually and actually of such defenses. SDI was essential, I agreed, but it was not everything. The president listened, but he didn't give any ground.

In Geneva, Gromyko played bait-and-switch games with the agreed text that the two sides put together on Monday and Tuesday, 7 and 8 January 1985. Monday night, at the inevitable reception, Shultz was amused "to see hard-line cavemen with their muscle-bound approach to the Kremlin sporting big but uncertain smiles on their faces, elbowing each other to get close enough to be photographed with Gromyko." The agreement that the foreign minister and the secretary of state finally forged, at eleven p.m. on Tuesday evening, included an allusion to abolition: "The sides believe that ultimately the forthcoming negotiations, just as efforts in general to limit and reduce arms, should lead to the complete elimination of nuclear arms everywhere."

There was more infighting in Washington afterward to pick the chief negotiator who would oversee the three deliberations. Shultz had been studying nuclear strategy with Paul Nitze and would have chosen him but for the illness of Nitze's wife, which precluded his moving to Geneva. Weinberger suggested Edward Teller, of all people, on the grounds, says Shultz, that "no one else could be trusted to be totally committed to SDI." All sides finally agreed on Max Kampelman, a soft-spoken lawyer and ambassadorial diplomat. Negotiations were set to begin on 12 March 1985. They did, but in the immediate days before and after that beginning, Reagan was diagnosed with colon cancer and underwent surgery, Chernenko died, and Gorbachev assumed the leadership of the Soviet Union. Shultz and Bush met Gorbachev for the first time in the Kremlin late on the evening of 13 March 1985, the day of Chernenko's funeral. "The USSR has never intended to fight the United States," Gorbachev told the two U.S. leaders candidly, "and does not have such intentions now. There have never been such madmen within the Soviet leadership, and there are none now." Shultz registered the impression Gorbachev made on the many leaders he spoke with that day; "the result was a certain Gorbachev euphoria in the air." The fifty-three-year-old former minister of agriculture was totally different from any Soviet leader he'd ever met, the secretary of state concluded. By late March, Gorbachev had written Reagan proposing that they hold "a personal meeting . . . to search for mutual understanding."

Shultz, normally so deliberately impassive that one observer compared him to a Toby jug, seems to have smiled at the shift in policy he had managed to organize for his strange but agreeable president: "We were smack in the middle of what was ever more clearly shaping up to be the endgame of the cold war."

PART THREE

COMMON SECURITY

Security can now only be achieved in common. No longer against each other but only with each other shall we be secure.

EGON BAHR

ELEVEN GOING AROUND IN CIRCLES

MIKHAIL GORBACHEV AND RONALD REAGAN MET for the first time on 19 November 1985, a cold, gray Tuesday, near Geneva, the substantial Swiss guildhall of international diplomacy mortared around the lower end of Western Europe's largest lake. The United States had rented the Château Fleur d'Eau on the western shore of Lake Leman for the summit meeting; Reagan, the host of the first morning's tête-à-tête, thrilled his staff by emerging hatless and coatless from the château's glassed-in atrium as the Soviet limousines arrived and bounding down the steps to greet a Gorbachev carefully bundled against the cold. The trivial upstaging had been the last-minute inspiration of a White House advance man, but such was the freight of public attention to the first U.S.-Soviet summit in more than six years—some thirty-five hundred journalists had been granted credentials to read the tea leaves—that Gorbachev needled Reagan thereafter at the end of each session, "The next time we meet, will it be coats on or coats off?"

Leaders who make history are often provincials: Provincials attempt what sophisticates consider naïve. The two current candidates for world leadership were both country boys, a state park lifeguard and a champion harvester, each an outsider to the inner elites of the government he headed, each in his own way an idealist determined to push beyond the status quo. Reagan had been tailored in Hollywood, but the sophistries of Washington's nuclear mandarins had failed to complicate his apocalyptic Dixon, Illinois, worldview. Gorbachev's southern Russian accent and hillbilly grammar offended the ears of the suave Moscow bureaucracy he outmanipulated a dozen times on any ordinary day.

Their handlers had scheduled only fifteen minutes for their first morning meeting, the two of them alone with their translators. They took an hour. The official photographers left, the doors closed, the general secretary said they could really talk now, and the president held forth. Both he and Gorbachev had come from similarly modest beginnings, he said, and now the two of them held the fate of the world in their hands. Their countries were superpowers, the only countries that could start World War III but also the only countries that could bring peace to the world. They would talk about many things in the plenary sessions to come; perhaps now, at the beginning, they should try to eliminate their suspicions of each other. And then a Reagan truism, repeated in speeches and private conversations for decades: Countries don't mistrust each other because of armaments; they build up their armaments because they mistrust each other. (While his aides believed the maxim was a Reagan coinage, he had in fact borrowed it without attribution from the writings of the Spanish historian and diplomat Salvador de Madariaga, who had headed the League of Nations disarmament section for six years in the 1930s and written a bittersweet memoir about the experience—although a likelier source of the Madariaga maxim was Reagan's friend Lawrence Beilenson's disquisition on treaties.)

Gorbachev thanked the president for receiving him. He had prepared for their meeting for months, he said, studying all the president's statements. His main conclusion was that he and the president could not ignore each other. He was convinced that they could begin to change their relations for the better. He'd reviewed his conclusion a thousand times, wondering if it was too simplistic with two countries so tremendously different. Certainly they were different, but they had a long history of cooperation.

They had disagreed, Gorbachev went on. There had been squalls, some of them extreme. But the Soviet people and the Soviet leadership recognized the role of the United States in the world and wished it no harm. They realized that international relations could not be built on a desire to harm American interests.

A rich history lay behind Gorbachev's opening argument, his first statement at Geneva of a theme central to what he and the reformers who advised him called their "new thinking": the idea of common security. Framed as a negative ("international relations could not be built . . . to harm"), it may have sounded to Reagan like boilerplate. The record does not indicate that he acknowledged it, and later in this first conversation he told Gorbachev that the Soviet belief "that the Marxist system should prevail" was one reason the United States distrusted the Soviet Union. Yet by assigning common security a higher value than class conflict, Gorbachev was repudiating both Marxist theory and long-standing Soviet practice.

The idea of common security had come to Gorbachev from the social democrats of Europe, in particular Olof Palme of Sweden and Willy Brandt of the Federal Republic of Germany. Brandt's adviser and Bundestag member Egon Bahr had formulated the concept succinctly in May 1981: "Security can now only be achieved in common. No longer against each other but only with each other shall we be secure." The venue of Bahr's formulation was a high-level international commission, the Independent Commission on Disarmament and Security Issues, convened in 1980 to prepare a report for the Second United Nations Special Session on Disarmament, scheduled for June 1982. A previous commission that Brandt had chaired considered conventional military forces; the new commission focused on nuclear forces. Palme, the prime minister of Sweden, was its chairman. Its membership included Bahr, the former British foreign secretary David Owen, the French parliamentarian Jean-Marie Daillet, the Norwegian parliamentarian Gro Harlem Brundtland, the former secretary of state Cyrus Vance, representatives of India, Japan, Indonesia, Mexico, Canada, Tanzania, and several other countries, and, most significantly, Georgi Arbatov, the director of the Soviet Institute for the U.S.A. and Canada, who later served as Gorbachev's principal adviser on foreign affairs prior to Eduard Shevardnadze's appointment as foreign minister in July 1985. ("We met many times," Arbatov said later of his work with the general secretary, "usually at his invitation, and I sent him scores of memos.") Gorbachev had read the Palme Commission report, *Common Security: A Blueprint for Survival,* had reviewed its ideas with Arbatov as well as with Brandt, Bahr, and Palme himself, and had seized on common security as a more realistic national-security policy than those of his predecessors for dealing with the hard realities of the nuclear age.

Before Gorbachev, even during the years of détente, the Soviet military had operated on the assumption (however unrealistic) that it should plan to win a nuclear war should one be fought—a strategy built on the Soviet experience of fighting Germany during the Second World War. Partly because a massive surprise attack had initiated that nearly fatal conflict, the Soviet military had been and still was deeply skeptical of relying on deterrence to prevent an enemy attack. For different reasons, so were the proponents of common security. Brandt, who followed the Palme Commission's deliberations closely, wrote that he "shared the conclusions [the commission] came to: collective security as an essential political task in the nuclear age, and partnership in security as a military concept to take over gradually from the strategy of nuclear deterrence; [because] deterrence threatens to destroy what it is supposed to be defending, and thereby increasingly loses credibility."

One explanation bruited today for Gorbachev's decision to change official Soviet policy from war-fighting, with its essentially limitless demand for resources, to common security is that he needed to reduce his defense budgets to save the Soviet Union from imminent economic collapse. According to this triumphalist argument, the United States drove the Soviet Union to rein in its imperial ambitions by outspending it. But the evidence does not support this self-congratulatory claim. The Soviet arms buildup of the 1970s was largely complete by the time Reagan became president in 1981, and in any case Soviet defense budgets gradually increased, not decreased, through 1988.

Neither George Shultz nor even Caspar Weinberger credited the triumphalist theory of Cold War victory. "I never really bought that," Shultz told an interviewer. "The idea of building up our military capability was not to outspend them but to provide ourselves with adequate defenses." Weinberger commented similarly in 2002, "There were some people who said that the whole thing was just an attempt to run the Soviet Union into bankruptcy," not acknowledging that he had once been one of them. He went on: "Actually it was not, in my view. What [the president] needed, what we needed—and we were in full agreement on it—was to restore our military deterrent capability—to get a capability that would make it quite clear to the Soviets that they couldn't win a war against us—in such black and white terms as that."

Jack Matlock, Jr., Reagan's adviser on Soviet affairs on the National Security Council, and former Soviet ambassador Anatoly Dobrynin both concur. "None of the key players were operating from the assumption that we were going to do the Soviet Union in," Matlock said in 1998, "or that the purpose of the pressure was to bring them down. . . . Our goal was always to give the Soviets incentives to bring the Cold War to an end." And as Dobrynin points out in his memoirs, "Reagan's second term coincided with the appearance of a new Soviet leader, Mikhail Gorbachev. Without Gorbachev, there is no way that the Cold War would have ended. But if Reagan had also been farsighted enough to divine the Soviet Union's true motives and agree to the disarmament treaties that were already on the table, that would have ended the Cold War without the crushing military expenditures he laid on the backs of the American people." Dobrynin adds:

> Throughout the Reagan presidency, the rising Soviet defense effort contributed to [the Soviet Union's] economic decline, but only marginally as it had in previous years. The troubles in our economy were the result of our own internal contradictions of autarky [i.e., economic self-sufficiency], low investment and lack of innovation, as even Western economic specialists at the World Bank and elsewhere now believe. . . .

If the president had not abandoned his hostile stance toward the Soviet Union for a more constructive one during his second term, Gorbachev would not have been able to launch his reforms and his "new thinking." Quite the contrary, Gorbachev would have been forced to continue the conservative foreign and domestic policies of his predecessors in defense of the nation against America. And who knows how the world would have developed?

Certainly Gorbachev saw the Soviet defense budget as a sump from which he might siphon funds for modernizing and upgrading Soviet industry. "Although the Defense Ministry was well aware of the price the arms race extracted from the country," he writes sardonically, "in all the years of my work in Moscow they never made any suggestions for cuts in defense spending." His suggestions were blunt: "What are you doing?" he would ask anyone who presumed to lay claim to state funds for new weapons systems. "Still preparing to fight a nuclear war? Well, I'm not." Anatoly Chernyaev adds: "Since there was no real threat of an attack from the United States against the Soviet Union, and Gorbachev felt so, he assumed the need for an arms reduction process, and this was what underlay his thinking from the start."

Common security for Gorbachev was first of all a response to the dangers implicit in the vast nuclear arsenals of the two superpowers, dangers he had come to understand in searching conversations with Soviet scientists as well as European political leaders. He paid special attention to the conclusions of the assembly of presidents of scientific academies and other prominent scientists convened by Pope John Paul II in the summer of 1982. The declaration the assembly presented to the pope that September predicted the immediate deaths of "many hundreds of millions of people" in the aftermath of a major nuclear war, denied the prospect of "making defenses sufficiently effective to protect cities, since even a single penetrating nuclear weapon can cause massive destruction," and appealed to national leaders "to take the initiative in seeking steps to reduce the risk of nuclear war . . . and to eschew military conflict as a means of resolving disputes." The declaration evoked a "common responsibility" to avoid war and defined an "ultimate goal of complete nuclear disarmament."

The physicist Yevgeni Velikhov, the sturdy, ruddy vice president of the Soviet Academy of Sciences, had represented the Soviet Union among the sixty-four scientists at the assembly. Velikhov worked for reform within the Soviet system during the Brezhnev era and would become Gorbachev's chief scientific adviser. In Rome he had met the Austrian-born American theoretical physicist Victor Weisskopf, one of the most principled alumni of the United States's atomic bomb program during the Second World War.

Weisskopf, Velikhov said later, "made a great impression on me by his commitment to abolishing nuclear weapons. It's one thing when preachers say
this must be done, but Weisskopf had worked on the Manhattan Project
and lived through all of atomic history. He and I worked together on [the]
declaration. . . . If you read it you'll see some of the ideas we now call the new
thinking—the need for a nuclear-free world, the impossibility of nuclear
superiority or of a defense against nuclear weapons. I won't say that the declaration influenced Gorbachev, but I know that he read it and reached his
own conclusions." Velikhov, along with the astrophysicist Roald Sagdeev, a
Tatar who was the director of the Soviet space program, and the historian
and engineer Andrei Kokoshin of Arbatov's institute also participated in
semiofficial back-channel talks with American scientists interested in arms
control during the early 1980s. These included Jerome Wiesner, a former
president of MIT; the IBM physicist Richard Garwin, a protégé of Italian
physicist Enrico Fermi who had worked on the design of the first U.S. hydrogen bomb; the Stanford physicist Sidney Drell; and Carl Sagan.

"The task of insuring security," Gorbachev would tell the 27th Party Congress a few months after the Geneva summit, "is more and more taking the
form of a political task and can be resolved only by political means." In that
statement he echoed, perhaps unknowingly, Niels Bohr's formulation of the
central paradox of the introduction of nuclear weapons into the world: "We
are in an entirely new situation that cannot be resolved by war." Nor could
the situation be resolved by deterrence, which, as Brandt said, risked destroying, if it failed, what it was meant to protect. "In our time," Gorbachev continued, "genuine equal security is guaranteed not by the highest possible, but
by the lowest possible level of strategic balance, from which it is essential to
exclude entirely nuclear and other types of weapons of mass destruction."

Ironically, one important source of the idea of common security was the
program Willy Brandt had championed with Egon Bahr in West Germany in
the 1960s and 1970s, a program they called *Ostpolitik*—"East policy." As early
as 1963, Brandt writes, "I criticized the official attitude in Bonn that we were
engaged in a race, and that we must 'always be swift and firm in rejecting any
suggestion from the East just because it comes from the East. . . . Progress
with the problems of Germany, I said, was unthinkable without détente. . . .
There was no mistaking the fact that '*no solution to the German question can
be found in opposition to the Soviet Union, only with it.* We cannot give up our
rights, but . . . to realize them we need a new relation between East and West,
and with it a new relation between Germany and the Soviet Union.' " Central
to *Ostpolitik,* Bahr adds, was making "renunciation of force the guiding principle in relations between ourselves and Eastern Europe."

This bilateral version of common security led West Germany to sign a treaty with Moscow acknowledging the sovereignty of its Communist East German counterpart, the German Democratic Republic. From there the West Germans moved to "raise our principle of renunciation of force to a European level." They succeeded, Bahr goes on, "insofar as the wording of the Moscow Treaty was also used in the Helsinki Final Act" of 1975. The Helsinki Final Act, signed by thirty-five countries including the United States, the Soviet Union, and all the states of Europe, acknowledged the existing borders of the nations of Europe, both Eastern and Western, and renounced the use of force in changing them—seemingly a triumph for the Soviet Union and its control of its Eastern European satellites, but in fact the beginning of the end of that control. This larger success underlay the work of the Palme Commission and its formulation: "The principle of common security asserts that countries can only find security in cooperation with their competitors, not against them." In meetings in Moscow between Gorbachev and Brandt in which Bahr personally participated, Bahr heard Gorbachev "make reference to the reports of the Brandt and Palme Commissions" in discussing "global problems." In rethinking the superpower arms race and the sources of superpower conflict, Gorbachev took his most valuable lessons not from the Reagan administration's hostile rhetoric and reassertion of trillion-dollar military power but from the ideas and experiences of the European community, with which he identified his country strongly as part of a "common European home."

HOWEVER WELL BRIEFED REAGAN might have been at Geneva, he could hardly have known that all this background lay behind Gorbachev's opening remarks in that first morning tête-à-tête. In fact, Gorbachev had led off with his central argument for changing the direction of U.S.-Soviet relations. Having done so, he suggested that the president speak, reserving time later to talk about the current international situation.

Reagan responded with one of the nuggets he always carried in his possibles pouch: There was no question, he said, that the Soviet and American peoples, if they learned more about each other, would find that they had many things in common and that friendship between them would grow. It wasn't people who created armaments, he said, but governments. A wave of good wishes for this meeting had come from the people of the United States, primarily hopes for peace. He knew the Soviet Union had suffered greatly during the Second World War and knew it was concerned about war. People don't like war. Americans hate war.

Reagan had been reading from a pocket set of cue cards he carried. He produced another nugget: People don't get into trouble when they talk *to* each other, he said, but rather when they talk *about* each other. There had been too much of that kind of talk from both sides. When he and the general secretary met in plenary session with their advisers—they should go in to that meeting soon—they could discuss such mistrust and make a start at moving beyond it.

Gorbachev spoke up again, impatient with the president's clichés and determined to put his points on the table before the two leaders joined the plenary. (He was appalled at Reagan's cue cards and his initial unwillingness to engage Gorbachev directly, recalling "the blank, uncomprehending eyes of the president, who mumbled banalities from a piece of paper.") A new policy was needed, Gorbachev said, one that would be adequate to the present international situation. It ought to be aimed at resolving the central issue of the age, which was the question of war and peace. If they could reach a substantive agreement in Geneva it would be a great accomplishment. (Eight months earlier, on the day Gorbachev took office, he had asked his principal adviser, Alexander Yakovlev, to assess Reagan's motives for proposing a meeting, as Reagan had done in a letter delivered that day. "He would like to solve a number of problems," Yakovlev had responded, "in the context of his dream about [being] a 'great peacemaker President.' " So Gorbachev was baiting his hook with Reagan's presumed ambition when he talked about "a great accomplishment.") Young people were worried about whether they would live or die. So was the older generation, which had already endured so much suffering. They needed to get things moving or there would be great disappointment. People would say that they were irresponsible. They shouldn't subject themselves to such a fate.

There were many problems in the world, Gorbachev continued—problems between capitalist and socialist countries, problems in the Third World as well. There was hunger, illiteracy, and disease. These problems demanded their attention. They required solutions based on cooperation rather than confrontation. He was speaking sincerely, he insisted. The Soviet Union wasn't playing a game with the United States. It wasn't being duplicitous. If it were, if it harbored secret intentions, then the relationship couldn't be improved.

(Outside the room, White House Chief of Staff Donald Regan and National Security Adviser Robert McFarlane worried about the schedule—or, more likely, about what their maverick president might be giving away. They pushed the president's assistant, Jim Kuhn, the coat-switch specialist, to break into the meeting before it ran any longer. Knowing better than to interrupt the president of the United States at his deliberations, Kuhn proposed asking George Shultz, who was meeting in another room with Shevardnadze. "Bud and Don are concerned about the Reagan-Gorbachev meeting," Kuhn remembers whispering to Shultz. Shultz responded full-voice: "Are you out of your mind? This is what it's about. The longer they talk, the better it is." Kuhn retreated to the anteroom and told Regan and McFarlane that Shultz had just "ripped my neck off in front of Shevardnadze." They left the president and the general secretary alone, facing each other in their fireside chairs.)

Reagan said he wanted to make a brief reply, after which he thought it would be best for them to join the rest of the group. The two countries could mutually help the developing countries, he agreed, but the U.S.S.R. created mistrust with its Marxist idea of helping socialist "revolutions" throughout the world and—Reagan repeated—its belief that the Marxist system should prevail. The United States felt to the contrary that what was most important to a country was its right to self-determination. The Soviet Union tried to use force to shape the developing countries to the Soviets' own pattern, and too often such force was used only by a minority.

Reagan tried again to herd his guest into the plenary session. When they moved on to the plenary, he told the general secretary, they would each greet the members of the opposite delegation, then they would have a photo opportunity beside the fireplace before they joined the others at the table.

Gorbachev had no intention of leaving the tête-à-tête with Reagan's last accusation hanging in the air. People had believed that the American Revolution should be crushed, he challenged the president—and the French and Soviet Revolutions as well. Millions of people had engaged in similar struggles in India, in Indonesia, in Algeria, where 1.5 million people had died in their struggle for freedom. The Soviet Union didn't believe a way of life could be imposed on a society if the society wasn't ready for it. These revolutions had their national roots. Moscow wasn't omnipotent. Gorbachev didn't wake up every morning thinking which country should have a revolution today.

THAT MUCH HAVING BEEN SAID, the two leaders moved over to the first plenary session—"wreathed in smiles," according to Jim Kuhn. Gorbachev joined Shevardnadze, Dobrynin, Yakovlev, Deputy Foreign Minister Georgi Kornienko, and other Soviet advisers on one side of the table; Reagan joined

Shultz, McFarlane, Nitze, Matlock, Donald Regan, and other American advisers on the other side. The president offered Gorbachev the floor and the general secretary reiterated what he had told the president in their private session. If they couldn't deal with the critical, pivotal issue of peace and war, he repeated, they would devalue the whole process. The situation was so acute that if they returned to their home countries without saying anything about arms control, people would say the meeting had given birth to a mouse.

Gorbachev said he knew what American think tanks such as the Heritage Foundation were advising. They advised that the United States should use the arms race to frustrate his plans, to weaken the Soviet Union. But history taught that such a program of intimidation hadn't been possible even earlier, when the Soviet Union wasn't as strong as now. Such a program was a delusion.

He saw a basis for movement on the issues between them, Gorbachev concluded. The president had said recently that there should be no nuclear war. (So Gorbachev had noted Reagan's deliberate repetition of the phrase "a nuclear war can never be won and must never be fought.") Gorbachev agreed. The president had said that they should proceed as equals. Gorbachev agreed. The president had said that he was in favor of exchanges among our peoples. The Soviet side agreed with that as well, Gorbachev said, provided such exchanges took place within a framework of respect for sovereignty and each society's values. (This proviso was Gorbachev's response to U.S. demands for Jewish and other emigration, demands responding to Soviet persecution of dissidents and refuseniks that Gorbachev deeply resented.) But the central question, Gorbachev concluded forcefully, was how to halt the arms race and disarm. The two countries could only live in the world together, so both had to think how to put their relations on a new track.

Reagan took up his version of the history of the arms race, which quickly resolved itself into his standard anti-Communist stump speech. Why did the United States distrust the Soviet Union? he asked rhetorically. After all, the two countries had fought together in two wars. Americans who had delivered supplies to help the Soviet Union during the Second World War were buried near the Soviet port of Murmansk. When that war ended, the United States was the only country whose industry had not been bombed and which had not sustained great losses. It was the only country as well to have built atomic bombs. It could have used them on the Soviet Union if it had chosen to. It didn't. Instead it reduced its armed forces from 12.5 to 1.5 million men, its navy from a thousand ships to fewer than half that number. It began proposing to do away with nuclear weapons and share nuclear technology with the world. Eighteen times before this meeting, said Reagan, the United States had proposed such meetings to deal with the divisions between the two countries, and on twelve of those occasions the United States had nuclear superiority. His country had been willing to give up that superiority, but most of the time Gorbachev's predecessors had refused to cooperate.

The eighteen meetings before this one had only addressed regulating the increase in nuclear weapons, Reagan contradicted himself. Now for the first time the United States was seeking with the Soviet Union actually to reduce the mountain of weapons. But the Soviet government talked about a one-world Communist state. It had inspired revolutions around the world. The United States was fully aware of the Soviet military buildup, including in nuclear weapons, which continued even after dozens of American arms-control proposals had been put on the table. The United States had fewer nuclear weapons now than in 1969 (which was true, but with MIRVing, more of them were targeted on the Soviet homeland). The Soviet Union had the largest military in history, with 5.4 million men in arms compared to the United States's 2.4 million. The United States had a Soviet satellite state, Cuba, just ninety miles off its shores. There had been problems in Cuba with nuclear missiles, but those had been settled. Now the Soviets were involved in Afghanistan, Ethiopia, Angola, and Yemen, with thirty-five thousand Cubans in Angola, for example. Reagan explained that he mentioned all these things because they were reasons for America's concern and distrust.

Warming to his subject, Reagan proceeded to relieve Gorbachev of any illusions about the burden of military spending on the U.S. economy. The United States spends more for its elderly, its handicapped, and for other social needs than it does for the military, he informed the general secretary. Two-thirds of U.S. military spending paid for manpower; only a very small percentage of the American gross national product (GNP) was spent on weapons. (Two weeks earlier, when Gorbachev had first heard these figures from Shultz and Robert McFarlane—McFarlane had specified defense spending at 6 percent of U.S. GNP—he had been "astonished," McFarlane says.) But spending none at all would be even better, the president said; the United States had no interest in carrying on an arms race.

Maybe the Soviets didn't want war, Reagan challenged, but they seemed to want to have their way. There had been violations of arms-control agreements already signed. (This assertion was a neocon theme and a Richard Perle favorite, by which, writes the arms-control analyst Michael Krepon,

Perle had "succeeded in transforming modest compliance flaps into serious violations, while blocking any diplomatic resolution of these problems.") The United States was ready to try to meet Soviet concerns if they were ready to reciprocate. It would take more than words. The two sides needed to get on to deeds.

After summarizing the general argument he had offered Gorbachev in their tête-à-tête—theirs were the only nations that could cause a world war, the United States had no hostile designs and hadn't taken advantage when it had been in a position to do so—Reagan said he wanted to bring up one specific question. It concerned SDI. He said Gorbachev had claimed the United States was pursuing strategic defense, a shield against missiles, because it wanted to achieve a first-strike capability. Well, he didn't know if a shield would be possible; the United States had a research program and the Soviet Union had a similar program. But if both sides continued their research and if one or both came up with a system, then they should sit down and make it available to everyone so that no one would have a fear of a nuclear strike. A madman might turn up with a nuclear weapon. If the United States and the U.S.S.R. could develop a shield and share it, then nobody would worry about a madman. Reagan said he didn't even want to call SDI a weapon; it was a defensive system.

Gorbachev, eager to challenge Reagan's arguments, asked if there was any time left. Should they stick to their schedule? Reagan joked that they should stick to their schedule because the next item on the schedule was lunch. Gorbachev reserved the right to open the next session with his response to the president's remarks. He said he hoped they would get to more specific discussion in the afternoon. Reagan agreed, and the two delegations left the large table (hauled all the way from New York on an Air Force cargo plane) and went their separate ways.

Both men had been anxious about their first encounter. They were relieved to have taken each other's measure but frustrated to be—as they saw it—misunderstood. The Gorbachevs were staying at the Soviet Embassy on the Avenue de la Paix in Geneva, and Gorbachev and his party now drove there for lunch. "I returned at the break to meet my colleagues," Gorbachev recalled. "They asked, 'What's your impression?' I said 'I have met a caveman—a dinosaur!'"

Reagan's party returned to the Maison de Saussure, an eighteenth-century residence where the Reagans were guests of the Aga Khan. Kenneth Adelman, the brash associate director of the U.S. Arms Control and Disarmament Agency, remembered the president arriving to be scolded by his son

Ronald Reagan, Jr., who had been granted credentials for the summit as a journalist writing for *Playboy:*

> The first words I heard were Ronnie's, saying, "Dad, you know you're late, we've been waiting for you to have lunch." Reagan says, "It's those interpreters." The translations that morning reminded the ex-actor of foreign films wherein someone on screen talks endlessly while a one-sentence subtitle—like "That's fine"—flashes on the bottom of the screen.
>
> Reagan said, "Excuse me," and headed for the men's room. . . . So we all stood at the [dining] table waiting for Reagan. . . .
>
> When he came out, Reagan stood at his place and had a grin like a cat who had just swallowed a canary. He was just so beaming. Then one by one all of us realized that one of his arms was in his suit coat [but] the other [sleeve] was just hanging down [empty]. . . . Then the whole room started laughing. I was one of the last to catch on. Finally someone next to me [asked], "Where's your arm?" And Reagan burst out [laughing] and said, "Well, it was here before I met Gorbachev. I don't where it is now." He just got the biggest kick out of it, all of us laughed. It . . . really put all of us at ease.

AT THE BEGINNING OF THE AFTERNOON plenary session, Gorbachev tried to avoid what he called "a big debate" over Reagan's accusations at the plenary that morning. He felt the need to defend himself nevertheless. He reminded Reagan that the Soviet leadership wasn't "primitive," meaning unsophisticated. Soviet policy, he said, wasn't based on some global plan for supremacy, on empire-building. He agreed that there were hotbeds of conflict that caused problems with the relationship between the superpowers, but he couldn't agree that Soviet "expansionism" was responsible—that idea was either a misunderstanding or a deliberate distortion, and if the United States based its policy on such a view it would be hard to find a way to move forward.

Reagan overemphasized the power of the Soviet Union, Gorbachev scolded him; it had no secret plans for world domination. It was unreal anyway to think that a small group of people could dominate the world with all its millions. Turning to Afghanistan, where the Soviet Union had been at war since 1979, Gorbachev offered a significant concession: He would support a political settlement in Afghanistan, he said, a political settlement under the United Nations. The United States could help. But while it claimed it wanted his country to withdraw its troops, it actually wanted them engaged there, and the longer the better. (Implicit in Gorbachev's accusation was his understanding that the war, as he would say frequently in the years to come, was a "bleeding wound," and that the United States was happy to see the flow of Soviet blood, treasure, and credibility left unstanched.) His country had no plan to use the war to gain access to a warm-water port or to the Persian Gulf, or to infringe on U.S. interests in any way; no such plan existed.

Having thus briefly responded to Reagan's conviction that the Soviet Union ran an evil empire and schemed to dominate the world, Gorbachev returned to the subject of armaments, his primary focus at the Geneva summit. Reagan had said that the Soviet Union built and the United States lagged behind. The president had claimed they were committed to an arms race. He'd charged that while the United States was showing restraint, the Soviet Union was building up its military potential. But twenty years ago there was no strategic balance. The United States had deployed four times as many strategic delivery systems as the U.S.S.R. and forward-based systems as well. The Soviet leadership had needed to offset the American advantage, just as the United States would have done, to avoid being manipulated. But since 1960, the United States had tripled the number of its warheads, and even now it had more nuclear weapons than the Soviet Union. The U.S.S.R. didn't want to lag behind, but neither was it trying to get ahead. Superiority didn't lead to normal relations, so it wasn't productive, even if the imbalance had been in the Soviet Union's favor. All the institutes that studied the problem, including the IISS* in London and Reagan's own Joint Chiefs of Staff, had concluded that their two countries had strategic parity. The forces were different, but they supported different strategies.

Now, Gorbachev continued, they needed to reduce parity to lower levels. He was all in favor of equal security at lower levels of force. That's why he came to Geneva. If they were to reduce strategic weapons, they needed to meet each other halfway. Of course America could meet any challenge from the Soviet Union—and the Soviet Union could meet any challenge from America. It was time for them to muster the realism and the political will to stop trying to outsmart or overrun each other.

The key disagreement on Gorbachev's mind was SDI, against which he now marshaled every argument he had. The Soviet Union, he said, believed that SDI could lead to an arms race in space, not simply a defensive arms race but an offensive arms race with space weapons. Space weapons would be harder to verify and would feed suspicions and mistrust. Why not take the obvious next step?

* The International Institute for Strategic Studies.

His scientists told him that any shield could be pierced, Gorbachev said. If SDI couldn't save America, why create it? It only made sense if its purpose was to cope with a weakened Soviet retaliatory strike after a U.S. first strike. Reagan's own defense secretary, Caspar Weinberger, had said that it would be bad for the world if the U.S.S.R. achieved such a defensive system first. What would the West think, Gorbachev asked sharply, if the Soviet Union were developing these weapons? It would react with horror. (Someone on Gorbachev's staff read *The Wall Street Journal*, which on 7 December 1983 had quoted Weinberger seemingly giving away the game: "I can't imagine a more destabilizing factor for the world than if the Soviets should acquire a thoroughly reliable defense against these missiles before we did." Weinberger, however, like Reagan and others in the Reagan administration, claimed to believe that an antimissile system in U.S. hands ought to threaten no one, since the United States had pledged to use it only for defense and in the context of reductions in offensive missiles.)

Gorbachev said he knew that the president was attached to the program, and because of his endorsement, Soviet scientists had studied it seriously. The conclusion they came to was that it would lead to an arms race on earth and in space. The Soviet Union would not cooperate in a plan intended to achieve superiority. It seemed that the United States had military aims in space that would violate the ABM Treaty—a treaty of fundamental importance. Testing, he said, was also inconsistent with the treaty, which could only exacerbate mistrust.

If the United States embarked on its Strategic Defense Initiative, Gorbachev predicted, two things would happen: One, there would be no reduction in offensive weapons; and, two, the Soviet Union would respond. "We will build up in order to smash your shield," Jack Matlock, who was there, says Gorbachev "thundered." Their response would not be a mirror of the American program, Gorbachev added, but a simpler, more effective system. What would happen if the United States put up "seven layers" of defenses in space? It would just destabilize the situation, generate mistrust, and waste resources. All of the American SDI schemes were based on using computers to monitor thousands of targets. They would all be holed up in bunkers, Gorbachev predicted, with the computers making the decisions. The world could end because a meteor passed by. Reagan hadn't thought it through, he scolded the president. It would be a waste of money and it would cause more distrust and more weapons. America didn't need SDI to avoid a madman with a bomb. Both countries had mounted sufficient retaliatory capability to deal with that problem for many years. And if they both began to disarm, other states would join them and aid in verification. The Soviet Union was prepared for full verification.

Concluding his argument, Gorbachev offered a carrot and a stick. If America agreed to ban space weapons, he told the president and the secretary of state, then the two nations could negotiate on their respective proposals for offensive weapons reduction. He was ready to compromise, he added earnestly. If space weapons were banned, it would create a new attitude on the Soviet side. The result would be very different if Reagan and Gorbachev left Geneva without any agreements. Then, Gorbachev threatened, the Soviet Union would have to rethink its offers.

Matlock, a seasoned negotiator, was not impressed with Gorbachev's negotiating skills at Geneva. "I observed him from across the table with growing disbelief," he writes. "Here was a man reputed to be a formidable debater. . . . But now he was leading with his chin" by denying the obvious and painting himself into a corner by reacting so strongly against SDI.

THE SOVIET SCIENTISTS WHO HAD studied SDI included Yevgeni Velikhov and Roald Sagdeev as well as engineer and historian Andrei Kokoshin and young Alexi Arbatov, Georgi's son, a political scientist. "Velikhov and I were in Washington just prior to Reagan's Star Wars speech," Sagdeev told me. "We learned of it from the newspapers on the plane out of Washington. Nothing could have predicted such an unexpected speech. We had been talking to our back-channel contacts at the National Academy of Sciences, scientific people such as Richard Garwin, and we learned later that they were just as surprised as we were. We saw that investigating Reagan's proposal was the first thing we had to do coming back to Russia. You know what the major argument was for investigating? What we were most afraid of? We were afraid that the industrialists in our military-industrial complex would say, 'Great, we should do the same thing.' "

Sagdeev laughs when he tells that story, but it almost came true. At a meeting sometime after Geneva in Gorbachev's office in the Kremlin, Sagdeev wrote in a memoir, the head of commercial services for the Soviet space program, noticing "Gorbachev's genuine involvement in strategic thinking," wheedled, " 'Dear Mikhail Sergeyevich, I completely understand your concerns. Trust me. We are losing time while doing nothing to build our own counterpart to the American SDI program.' " Sagdeev writes that he "almost died from suppressing my laughter," but adds soberly, "this brief episode gives at least a clue as to why we Russians were, as many in the West thought, overescalating the anti-SDI rhetoric. In my own frame of reference, I always had in mind the potential danger that could arise if . . . influential members of the military and industrial sectors in our own country were to involve us in a nonstop escalation of an SDI budget at that time, at the expense of the deteriorating strategic stability and our economy."

The scientists' investigation, which took the form of an extended meeting in April 1983 at the Soviet Academy of Sciences and culminated in a book, benefited from what Velikhov calls the Soviet government's previous "vaccinations" against strategic defense systems. The Soviet military had begun discussing strategic defenses in the late 1960s, Velikhov writes, when "the idea emerged of using lasers or charged-particle beams to hit warheads as they approached their targets." The scientists, led by Lev Artsimovich, quickly pointed out the futility of the scheme, however: "Compact reentry vehicles, specially designed to withstand the high temperatures of reentry from space, are hard to locate and lock on to for enough time to administer fatal doses of energy." Nor would such beams easily pass through the atmosphere. Yuli Khariton, the director of the Soviet Union's primary weapons-design laboratory, Arzamas-16, since the beginning of the Soviet nuclear-weapons program in 1946, insisted that "an honest and principled critique" be written and given to the government, "which decided to stop the program around the time the antiballistic-missile treaty was concluded in 1972."

The second vaccination came in 1980, when a Soviet engineer who designed booster rockets managed to slip a proposal to Leonid Brezhnev to create "a space-based defense using interceptor missiles"—a proposal similar to Daniel Graham's High Frontier program for battle stations in space. "Owing to the principled stand of a number of scientists and military experts," Velikhov writes with relief, "the heated debate resulted in a correct decision: The proposal was turned down."

Armed with these experiences, Velikhov and his group prepared an extended report on strategic defense in 1983 that Velikhov, Sagdeev, and Kokoshin edited and published in 1986 as a book, *Weaponry in Space: The Dilemma of Security.* The report reviewed the history and science of strategic defenses, but its essence was a careful analysis of the destabilizing consequences of an ABM-system buildup for strategic balance and of relatively inexpensive countermeasures that could foil any anticipated strategic defense. "The 'balance of terror,' " the report argued, "is a precarious balance. A really secure and peaceful world is only possible when both sides (and any other nations) have no nuclear arms. The world would be much safer if it were free of nuclear weapons and respective delivery vehicles, if all conflicts were tack-

led by negotiations, if economic, scientific and cultural international cooperation were improved and expanded." Nuclear abolition was a brave and radical argument to make in the Soviet Union of Yuri Andropov in 1983, the year of
the Soviet war scare and ABLE ARCHER 83.

The "simpler, more effective system" that Gorbachev threatened to build
to penetrate Reagan's defensive shield incorporated several of the countermeasures described in *Weaponry in Space*. "Our response to SDI will be
effective," Gorbachev told Chernyaev. "The United States expects us to create
analogous systems, they hope to outrun us technologically. . . . But . . . for
only 10 percent of its cost we can produce a countersystem capable of nulli-
fying SDI." Among the countersystems Gorbachev had in mind was an
advanced version of a three-stage, solid-fueled mobile ICBM, the Topol-M
(SS-27), with a 550-kiloton warhead with a maximum error of nine hundred
meters across a range of eleven thousand kilometers (6,900 miles). The
Topol-M's short engine burn time, flat ballistic trajectory that minimizes its
time in space, maneuverable reentry vehicle, and advanced penetration aids,
all discussed in the scientists' report, were intended to avoid or defeat
antimissile attacks. Design of the advanced Topol system began in 1985, and
development survived the dissolution of the Soviet Union. The Topol (silo-
based) and Topol-M (mobile) missile is Russia's designated primary ICBM
today; by 2006, 312 had been deployed.

But if Gorbachev had a system already under design that could nullify SDI
(if indeed a comprehensive system of strategic defense could ever be made to
work in the first place, which is highly unlikely), why was he so determined
to convince Reagan to abandon it? Or as the American physics Nobel laureate Steven Weinberg would ask later, "How could Gorbachev have been worried about something so silly?"

The answer seems to lie primarily with the Soviet military, and behind the
military with the large and powerful bureaucracy of the Soviet military-
industrial complex—the nine ministries overseen by the Military Industrial
Commission (known by its Russian initials as the VPK) and the eight additional ministries that supported them. "Experts at the Soviet Academy of
Sciences," writes the foreign correspondent Don Oberdorfer, "argued that
the Star Wars program was impractical and that any partial success it might
achieve could be nullified by modest countermeasures. But despite such
advice and doubts about its practicality, the Soviet leaders 'could not ignore
such a position' as that outlined by Reagan on March 23, [1983,] especially
since it was soon to be backed up by many billions of dollars, according
to Andropov's foreign policy assistant, Andrei Aleksandrov-Agentov. 'So

whether it was a practical idea or not, they had to account for the reality—the real factor in the policy of the United States.' " And if the Soviet military worried about the danger that a multibillion-dollar U.S. research program into strategic defense could turn up new offensive weapons along the way, the VPK might well, as Sagdeev feared, take the opportunity to press Gorbachev for a larger share of the Soviet budget to carry on parallel research and development to forestall an American breakout. William Odom, the lieutenant general who directed the National Security Agency during Reagan's second term, judges Gorbachev's primary opposition on the question of reform within the Soviet government to have been the VPK:

> A surprisingly broad consensus existed among most of the Soviet elite that the Soviet economy was in serious trouble and that the burden of military expenditures was much to blame. To reduce it, Gorbachev turned to disarmament through arms control. That was impossible, he realized, without a fundamental change in the Soviet Union's relationship with the world, both the capitalist world and foreign communist parties.
>
> To set a new course in military policy, therefore, Gorbachev quite logically began by changing Soviet foreign policy. His breakthrough in personal relations with Western political leaders convinced most of them that he was serious. Soviet negotiators returned to Geneva and Vienna, and under Shevardnadze's determined guidance, they surprised Western leaders with major changes in traditional Soviet positions.

"Disarmament through arms control"—seemingly the key to relieving the Soviet economy and improving the quality of life for the Soviet people—meant major reductions in the Soviet military. "Cutting military forces," Odom continues, "could free manpower for the civilian economy's workforce, but it would not save significant military expenditures because military pay was abysmally low—five or six rubles per month for conscripts. A very large part of the military budget went to the VPK for constant modernization of weaponry." (Which was how, for example, the Soviet Union came to replace its old first-generation liquid-fueled missiles in Europe with more modern solid-fueled SS-20s, and why it had produced so many more ICBM models than the United States.) "The key point," Odom writes, "is that Gorbachev confronted more than the uniformed military in this cat-and-mouse game. Somewhere between 20 and 40 percent of the state economy was tied up in military production. The issue of military reform, therefore, set Gorbachev and his allies against this large and privileged sector of the economy as well as against the conservative elements of the uniformed military leadership." He might win their grudging agreement to some degree of arms reduction, but they expected him in return to smother SDI in its crib.

REAGAN'S RESPONSE TO GORBACHEV'S CHALLENGES surprised some of his own advisers. He said the general secretary's presentation illustrated the lack of trust between their two governments. He proceeded to read through a list of twelve U.S. nuclear initiatives, beginning all the way back in 1946. He counted up the warheads the Soviets had added since SALT II and denied that the two nations' arsenals were presently equal. "With righteous indignation," Gorbachev writes sarcastically, "President Reagan tore apart the American policy of deterrence, which had triggered the arms race and led mankind to the brink of destruction." Reagan claimed proudly that SDI was his idea. There had never been a weapon without a defense, he said. He was talking about a shield. No one knew yet if it was possible. But if such a weapon could be produced, it shouldn't be added to present offensive forces. The two sides should sit down and get rid of nuclear weapons, and with them the threat of war. And defenses should be shared—they should be made available to all.

Sharing a high-tech weapons system that would have cost the United States many billions of dollars to invent was the proposal that surprised some of Reagan's advisers. "We had no idea where the idea had come from," Kenneth Adelman recalled, "none of us. We thought it was wacko." Evidently Adelman had been asleep at the switch. Reagan had discussed sharing strategic defenses during his second debate with the Democratic presidential candidate Walter Mondale in Kansas City in 1984. Since Adelman, like many others in the Reagan administration, found themselves unable to take their president seriously on questions of arms control, his lapse of memory probably reflects his contempt for the idea. Mondale took Reagan seriously. He rejoined that he "sharply disagree[d] with the President on sharing the most advanced, the most dangerous, the most important technology in America with the Soviet Union."

Reagan in Geneva talked for a while about Third-World conflicts, but soon returned to SDI. Gorbachev, trying a different tack, interrupted to ask what directions they should give to their negotiators. Reagan proposed that Shevardnadze, Shultz, and their advisers work on the structures of forces that would allow the two superpowers to reduce their nuclear arsenals by 50 percent. Gorbachev reminded the president that their foreign ministers (Shultz and Gromyko) had agreed in January 1985 that there should be no arms race in space. ("If the USA agreed to negotiate a total prohibition of offensive space weapons," Gorbachev had declared at a secret Warsaw Treaty summit in Moscow in April, "the road to radical reductions in the number of strategic assault weapons would be opened" and both sides could "reciprocally rid Europe of both intermediate-range and tactical nuclear weapons altogether." He had also announced the unilateral suspension of deployment of SS-20s and other missiles "until November 1985.") What about that goal? he asked Reagan, his voice rising.

Reagan said a defensive shield wouldn't be an arms race in space. It would be a way to eliminate weapons. He told a story. "Our U.N. ambassador, Vernon Walters, was asked what happens when a man with a spear that can penetrate anything meets a man with a shield that's impenetrable. Walters said he didn't know, but he did know what happens when a man with no shield meets a man who has a spear." Neither of us wants to be in that situation, Reagan told Gorbachev. If the technology is developed, he said again, it should be shared.

"Ronald Reagan's advocacy of the Strategic Defense Initiative struck me as bizarre," Gorbachev wrote of this debate. "Was it science fiction, a trick to make the Soviet Union more forthcoming, or merely a crude attempt to lull us in order to carry out the mad enterprise—the creation of a shield which would allow a first strike without fear of retaliation?" It was all those things, though not for Reagan. For Reagan it was a hubristic dream, a hope, a fantasy that American technological ingenuity could finesse a dangerous dilemma without resort to negotiation or compromise. Like the nuclear-arms race itself, it derived from a fundamental misunderstanding of the new knowledge that science had revealed to the world, knowledge of how to release energies millions of times greater than those released in chemical explosions.

" 'It looks like a dead end,' " Gorbachev remembers saying then. "An uneasy silence fell upon the room," he wrote. "The pause was becoming oppressive.

" 'How about taking a walk?' " the American president suddenly asked.

" 'That seems like a good idea to me,' " Gorbachev replied.

THE BREAK AND THE WALK had been planned; the two leaders, accompanied by their interpreters, were supposed to walk from the main château across a courtyard to the Fleur d'Eau pool house, where a small side room with a fireplace had been prepared where they could hold another tête-à-tête. Rather than try to negotiate as they walked, they talked about Reagan's

movies. At a press conference earlier in the summit, a journalist had asked
Georgi Arbatov if Gorbachev had seen any of the films the president had
made. Arbatov had said he didn't know, adding gratuitously, "and
besides . . . those were B movies." On their walk to the pool house Reagan
asked Gorbachev to enlighten his foreign policy adviser; he had made not
only B movies but also a few good ones. Gorbachev diplomatically volunteered the information that he had recently watched *Kings' Row* and had
liked it very much. *Kings' Row* was based on a lurid novel drawn from turn-
of-the-century life in Fulton, Missouri, where Winston Churchill would later
deliver his "Iron Curtain" address—small world. Reagan plays a genial rake
who is bruised in an encounter with a train, after which a sadistic Kings' Row
doctor who disapproves of his behavior saws off both his legs. When "Drake
McHugh" wakes from the anesthesia and discovers his amputations he cries
out to his girlfriend, Ann Sheridan, "Where's the *rest* of me?" Curiously, Reagan would choose the line for the title of his 1965 as-told-to autobiography, a
book that served to announce his entry into politics.

"The walk," Gorbachev remembers, "the change of scene, the crackling of
burning wood—all these helped to alleviate the tension. But as soon as we
sat down, Reagan rushed back to his old tactics. Seemingly anxious that I
might take up SDI again—this time 'one on one'—he decided to anticipate
my move by taking out a list of arms control proposals and handing them to
me." There were nine proposals on Reagan's list, which he presented to Gorbachev in both English and Russian versions. The general secretary took the
time to read through the list before responding, qualified his responses as
preliminary, pointed to the first proposal for 50 percent reductions in strategic offensive weapons, and noted that Shultz and Gromyko's agreement in
January to find a way to avoid an arms race in space—linked to that reduction—seemed to have evaporated.

So they would debate SDI that afternoon regardless. SDI was a defensive
system, Reagan reiterated, and anyway, the two sides would share it. But why
do you need it? Gorbachev countered. The Soviet Union had declared for all
the world to hear that it would not be the first to use nuclear weapons, he
said. Shouldn't that be enough? But it seemed the United States did not
believe him. Then why should he believe the president's statement about
sharing the results of research into strategic defense? Why should he believe
that the United States would not take advantage of having deployed such a
defense?

They could negotiate and sign an agreement, Reagan countered, forget-
ting or choosing not to mention his belief that treaties were a trap. Gor-

bachev responded passionately, with an intensity that even comes through the formality of the translator's notes:

> With some emotion Gorbachev appealed to the President as follows: if the two sides were indeed searching for a way to halt the arms race and to begin to deal seriously with disarmament, then what would be the purpose of deploying a weapon that is as yet unknown and unpredictable? Where was the logic of starting an arms race in a new sphere? It must clearly be understood that verification of such weapons would be totally unreliable because of their maneuverability and mobility even if they were classified as defensive. People would not be in a position to determine what it was that would be placed into space and would surely regard it as an additional threat, thereby creating crisis situations. If the goal was to get rid of nuclear weapons, why start an arms race in another sphere?

But these weren't weapons that would kill people or destroy cities, Reagan replied stubbornly. These were weapons that would destroy nuclear missiles. And then a significant concession, never to be heard of again: If they could agree that there would be no need for nuclear missiles, the president offered, then there might also be no need for defenses against them. Why did Gorbachev keep on speaking of space weapons, the president asked. He certainly had no intention of putting something into space that would threaten people on Earth. In 1925 in this city, Geneva, he said, all the countries that had participated in the First World War had met and agreed not to use poison gas again in war. But they had all kept their gas masks. What he was saying now was that they should go forward to rid the world of the threat of nuclear weapons, but at the same time retain something like that gas mask—a shield that would protect their countries should there be an unforeseeable return to nuclear missiles. They were not alone in the world. There were others such as Gadhafi and people of that kind who were not at all against dropping a nuclear bomb on the White House. Both their countries should conduct the relevant research and both should share the results; if one country produced a defensive shield before the other, it would make it available to all.

They should rejoin the plenary session, Reagan said, but before they did so, he had to tell Gorbachev that the people overwhelmingly wanted this defense. They look at the sky and think what might happen if missiles suddenly appear and blow up everything in our country. We believe that the idea of having a defense against nuclear missiles involved a great deal of faith and belief. And when he said we, he meant most of mankind.

Exasperated, Gorbachev pointed out that missiles were not yet flying, and whether or not they would fly would depend on how he and the president conducted their respective policies. But he calmed down enough to appeal to Reagan to recognize that the Soviet Union did indeed wish to establish a new relationship with the United States and to deliver their two nations from the increasing fear of nuclear weapons. He hoped, he said, that Reagan would not regard this wish as a sign of weakness on his part or on the part of the Soviet leadership.

"We were going around in circles," Gorbachev writes. "The fire was burning and the room was warm and cozy, but the conversation had not improved the general mood. We went outside again and I suddenly felt very cold—maybe in contrast to the warmth by the fireside or to our heated discussion. At that point, the President unexpectedly invited me to visit the United States, and I reciprocated by inviting him to Moscow." Thus, effortlessly, Reagan had accomplished his advisers' primary goal for the summit, which was to open the way to further meetings down the road.

They went around in circles again the next day, meeting at the Soviet Embassy, repeating the same arguments. Yet gradually the two men connected. "The day was difficult," Gorbachev told Chernyaev afterward, "but something very important happened in both of us. I think two factors were at work: responsibility and intuition, which as it turns out, Reagan possesses to a very high degree. Imperceptibly the human factor began to work. Some sense told each of us to continue talking and somewhere in the depth of our minds the hope was born to come to an understanding." An even deeper change came to Gorbachev, Chernyaev saw, a shrugging off of the accumulated weight of dogma: "For a Soviet leader, for Gorbachev, for the first time he got the sense that there is something deeply wrong in our general evaluation of the American administration and American life, that our class analysis is failing and does not give us an answer that would provide a good basis for any kind of realistic politics."

Reagan's evident sincerity influenced Gorbachev's change of heart. Shultz noticed: "We had a dramatic session . . . with Gorbachev on the second day. . . . Gorbachev out of the clear blue sky started this attack on SDI. When he got through, Reagan just gave a deep, well-thought-out but very emotional [response]. . . . Gorbachev finally said, 'Well, Mr. President, I don't agree with you, but I can see that you really mean it.'" Most of all, Gorbachev apparently realized that Reagan no more intended to use nuclear weapons than he did. Both men, each in his own way, were scouting a path out of the Minotaur's lair.

It took their advisers until two in the morning to put together a joint communiqué, and even then the two leaders had to knock heads to finish the work. Gorbachev rightly calls the communiqué a "truly historic document," because it incorporated Reagan's mantra about nuclear war:

> The sides, having discussed key security issues, and conscious of the special responsibility of the U.S.S.R. and the U.S. for maintaining peace, have agreed that a nuclear war cannot be won and must never be fought. Recognizing that any conflict between the U.S.S.R. and the U.S. could have catastrophic consequences, they emphasized the importance of preventing any war between them, whether nuclear or conventional. They will not seek to achieve military superiority.
>
> The President and the General Secretary discussed the negotiations on nuclear and space arms [then under way separately in Geneva].
>
> They agreed to accelerate the work at these negotiations, with a view to accomplishing the tasks set down in the Joint U.S.-Soviet Agreement of January 8, 1985, namely to prevent an arms race in space and terminate it on earth, to limit and reduce nuclear arms and enhance strategic stability.

However expectantly the two leaders left the old Swiss city by the lake, SDI still divided them. During the shouting match on the second day of the summit, Gorbachev had a glimpse of how deeply Reagan cherished his dream of spreading his arms to protect the world from its own encapsulated violence. He didn't know, Reagan had said, whether or not the general secretary believed in reincarnation, but for himself, he wondered if perhaps, in a previous life, he had been the inventor of the shield.

MIKHAIL GORBACHEV RETURNED TO MOSCOW from Geneva with mixed feelings about Ronald Reagan. When Gorbachev told his colleagues he had met "a caveman—a dinosaur," he was referring to Reagan's "primitive" anti-Communism, the president's pedantic conviction that Soviet leaders were slaves to Marxist dogma. (Accordingly, Reagan had been surprised at Geneva to find that "not once during our private sessions or at the plenary meetings did [Gorbachev] express support for the old Marxist-Leninist goal of a one-world Communist state," and intrigued with Gorbachev's frequent references to God.) According to the historian Vladislav Zubok, a Geneva participant noticed that "Gorbachev . . . was bothered by a huge chasm between the United States and Soviet positions, perceptions and logic. He said in a narrow circle: 'What is this President doing? He would be a good *dacha* neighbor, but as a political partner he leaves a dismal impression.' "

Despite Reagan's seeming limitations, Gorbachev concluded that the American president was someone he could work with. When the two of them concurred publicly that "nuclear war cannot be won and must never be fought," the Soviet leader writes, it "made meaningless the arms race and the stockpiling and modernizing of nuclear weapons." Gorbachev "decided that Reagan meant what he said at Geneva," concluded Arthur Hartman, the U.S. ambassador to the Soviet Union: Reagan "did want to rid the world of nuclear weapons, and he was deadly serious about SDI." Gorbachev's idea thereafter, Hartman speculated, "was to persuade Reagan to take the one without the other. He seems to have decided at Geneva that he could bring it off."

Reagan, for his part, wrote Gorbachev in late November confirming his mutual feeling that the two of them had been serious about eliminating nuclear weapons. "Obviously there are many things on which we disagree," Reagan wrote, "and we disagree very fundamentally. But if I understand you correctly, you, too, are determined to take steps to see that our nations manage their relationship in a peaceful fashion. If this is the case, then this is one point on which we are in total agreement—and it is after all the most fundamental one of all." A few days later, on 5 December 1985, a letter arrived from Gorbachev that had crossed in the mail, as it were, proposing that the United States join the Soviet Union in the voluntary moratorium on nuclear weapons tests it had introduced on 6 August of that year, which was due to expire at the end of the year unless the United States also canceled testing. Gorbachev's invitation was not without guile: If the United States gave up nuclear testing, then it would also forego developing space weapons powered by nuclear explosions, because any such new designs would have to be tested. On the other hand, if Reagan was serious about nuclear abolition, why would he need further nuclear weapons tests? (Gorbachev's letter and later appeals went unanswered, and after extending his self-imposed moratorium twice in the first six months of 1986, he reluctantly allowed Soviet nuclear weapons tests to resume.) At Christmastime Gorbachev responded at length to Reagan's late November letter, once again arguing that SDI would lead to the development of first-strike and space weapons, a new and less stable arms race in space. By then Yevgeny Velikhov and Roald Sagdeev had joined his circle of advisers; it was they who particularly encouraged him to continue the voluntary testing moratorium.

Despite these disagreements, Gorbachev resolved to move as rapidly as possible toward breakthrough arms negotiations, Nikolai Detinov remembers. "Gorbachev told the Ministry of Defense and all other ministries to start preparing a proposal about solving the issues that remained unresolved." Anatoly Chernyaev noted in his contemporary diary his "impression that [Gorbachev had] really decided to end the arms race no matter what. He is taking this 'risk' because as he understands it, it's no risk at all, because nobody would attack us even if we disarmed completely. And in order to get the country out on solid ground, we have to relieve it of the burden of the arms race, which is a drain on more than just the economy." Later, in their personal conversations, Gorbachev would tell Chernyaev more than once, "I feel that it is our fault that this arms race is still going on."

When Soviet arms negotiators returned to Moscow for their Christmas vacations, Gorbachev summoned them one by one to his Kremlin office for private talks. Ambassador Oleg Grinevsky, who headed the Soviet delegation to the Stockholm-based Conference on Security and Cooperation in Europe (CSCE), remembers Gorbachev encouraging him, " 'It's just the two of us, there's no one listening, don't be afraid to tell me the truth, I want to know only the truth. What's happening at your talks? Is there a possibility of progress and what needs to be done for that?' " He asked everyone the same questions, Grinevsky recalls, and then "literally the next day, he assembled all of us . . . and said, 'Now say what you told me—[but] openly, at the Politburo.' For everyone this was a shock. . . ." The new proposals Gorbachev would shortly offer the United States originated in these reluctant testimonies, but with a twist, Grinevsky reports:

> As a result of this Politburo discussion, which I think was on the 30th of December, the decision was taken to come out with a specific realistic program of disarmament and of policies to decrease tension in the international arena. . . . It included three components: 1) fifty percent reductions in strategic offensive armaments; 2) zero on intermediate- and medium-range missiles [i.e., the United States's zero option for SS-20s and Pershing 2s in Europe]; and 3) solving the issues of the Stockholm conference, in other words, European security. . . . Right from the beginning we ran into enormous resistance from the military. They were supported by the KGB. Basically, they were saying that "we cannot do this, neither fifty percent reduction, nor zero level. It would undermine the basis for the security of the Soviet Union."

The twist came during a meeting of a group of Politburo armsnegotiation experts, the so-called small group of five, that reported to the Big Five commission that supervised such negotiations (representatives of the foreign ministry, the defense ministry, the KGB, the VPK, and the Academy of Sciences). The three-part proposal Grinevsky describes was on the table and up for discussion, and they had begun a long argument about it:

> Suddenly, at the height of this argument, the door opened and Marshal [Sergei] Akhromeyev entered—I wouldn't say he entered, he flew in. He was a very thin, very agile man, he literally flew into the room. I remember General [Valentin] Varennikov said, "Comrade officers, stand up." We started to look at each other, wondering whether to stand or not to stand up, we were confused, not all of us were in the military. Marshall Akhromeyev said, "Forget your program, forget it. General [Nikolai] Chervov just came back from Crimea where Mikhail Sergeyevich Gorbachev was vacationing. I have to tell you an enormous secret. *The general staff, in great secrecy, has been developing a program of liquidating all nuclear arms.* Even members of the delegation, even the military general staff and general cabinet people did not know about it. They are not aware of this secret program, and now finally the program is ready. General Chervov went south to present it to Mikhail Sergeyevich Gorbachev. Gorbachev approved it, so therefore forget your fifty percent reduction of strategic armaments, forget the zero level on medium range missiles. Here is the new agenda and it covers everything."

"We immediately thought that this was all phony," Grinevsky remembers; the small group knew every program developer in the military and knew that none of them had been working on anything so grand. Caucusing in the hallway, Grinevsky and his foreign ministry colleagues agreed that the West would consider such a program propaganda, smacking as it did of the cynical proposals for general and complete disarmament that Khrushchev used to proclaim to stall arms negotiations to lesser ends. To salvage something they decided to recommend including their agenda—50 percent reductions, the zero option, negotiations on conventional forces—in the military's new proposal as stage one. "We pushed it with great difficulties," he recalls, "but we managed to have them accept this as the first stage of their program."

By endorsing a phony but seemingly responsive program, the Soviet military leadership thought it was putting one over on the general secretary. They should have known better. Gorbachev and Shevardnadze had "agreed on the necessity for such a step," Gorbachev wrote, "during a conversation we had soon after his appointment as Foreign Minister"—that is, more than six months earlier. "By the autumn we had made a start—a scientific analysis of the international situation, contacts and meetings we had had in the past months. It was then that we decided to formulate our ideas and intentions in a long-term agenda which would serve as a basis for our 'peace offensive.' "

In the meantime, independently, the military had seized upon a cynical public-relations gambit cobbled together by two specialists on the United States within the foreign ministry and decided to explore its possibilities as a diversion. Sergei Tarasenko and one of his deputies had devised the nuclear-disarmament proposal on their own initiative in April 1985, shortly after Gorbachev took office, expecting that he, like his predecessors, would want something harmless but appropriately spectacular to announce to the world on 9 May 1985, the fortieth anniversary of the Soviet victory over Germany and the end of the Second World War in Europe. "It took us about half a day," Tarasenko concedes. ". . . It was put together based on fairly cynical ideas." He passed it to his boss, who liked it. Then, he says, "the paper vanished." In midsummer, the anniversary having passed, he asked about the proposal. His boss told him, " 'Forget that paper, it does not exist. It's been given away, you've never heard about it.' " Then suddenly, at the end of December, rumors of talk about "a world without nuclear arms" began to circulate through the ministry corridors. "We knew that according to the political order we were small fish—God forbid we should find ourselves under the wheel of history. We kept very quiet about what we had done." What happened, Tarasenko surmises, was that First Deputy Foreign Minister

Georgy Kornienko "talked Akhromeyev into believing that this was not a threatening thing . . . that there would be no immediate disarmament consequences, but as propaganda it sounded good, a nice honorable initiative, and one could get some points for it. I don't know if it went exactly that way, but evidently the proposal did go through Akhromeyev to the military, and the military presented it as their own proposal."

"This was not an 'improvisation,' " on the military's behalf, William Odom confirms, quoting Detinov, "but rather a well-considered tactic, one that made the military look 'eager' to eliminate nuclear weapons while assuring that it 'could hardly lead to any practical results in the foreseeable future.' " The reason the military felt it needed to introduce a diversionary dead end, Odom adds, was that "Gorbachev was building negotiating momentum that would derail some major weapons programs."

Phony or not, the proposal had to look authoritative if it was to be presented to the general secretary as a serious military initiative. Major General Vladimir Slipchenko of the Soviet general staff was one of those who participated in the evaluation process in spring 1985:

> It was very interesting work. Marshall Akhromeyev demanded right away, very urgently, to take the best scientists from the Ministry of Defense. He took twelve people, three people from the strategic missile forces, three people from the navy, three people from the nuclear forces and three people from the general staff. I was in the group from the general staff. . . . We had to solve this task in one month. . . . We were taken to one of the houses of the Ministry of Defense . . . but there was a lot of pressure on us and we were actually asked to present our product in two weeks. . . .
>
> What were we doing? . . . In front of us we had the basic starting point that the Soviet Union would completely abolish its nuclear weapons and we needed to evaluate what would happen in this situation. What other countries would still keep nuclear arms? Who is not going to agree to a one-sided or even multi-sided agreement of liquidation of nuclear arms? . . . The period we were looking at was up to the year 2000. . . .
>
> We produced the information. . . . I think that we might not have completed everything that we had to, but the conclusions that we did make were very shocking for us at that time.
>
> We concluded that there was not one nuclear state which could adequately protect itself through the use of its nuclear arsenal. . . .
>
> The second conclusion was that it is necessary to think about the security of all states, including that of our enemy, in order to ensure our security. So you cannot really use nuclear arms just to protect yourself, you have to consider the safety and security of your potential enemies. . . . We came to the conclusion that we had to start thinking about the inevitability of peaceful coexistence.

Another conclusion was that we had to try to manage all of the existing conflicts on the globe and do everything necessary such that conflicts would never
arise again.

Ordered to evaluate seriously a proposal for nuclear abolition, Akhromeyev's tough military experts discovered themselves to be naked to their
enemies and independently rediscovered the idea of common security. No
wonder they were shocked.

FOR GORBACHEV, the military's cynical proposal for nuclear disarmament
was a godsend: protective cover for his plans. "He promptly put it to the Big
Five," Odom wrote, "who found problems with this 'Gorbachev initiative,' as
it was known thereafter. At Gorbachev's request, [Lev] Zaikov [a Gorbachev
appointee to the Big Five] refereed the dispute in the Big Five between the
[Ministry of Defense] and [Ministry of Foreign Affairs], then submitted the
initiative to the Politburo, where it was quickly endorsed." Asked in retirement if he had encountered much resistance to it, Gorbachev answered,
"Not to the idea, not to the statement. But I must admit that most of the military men thought this was just another propaganda bluff, another deception." In Gorbachev's hands it would be much more. Detinov cites two
important uses to which Gorbachev would put the proposal:

> In and of itself, [it] played a great role in developing the Soviet position at the
> [arms-control] talks. First of all, it demonstrated to the whole world what path
> needs to be taken in order to achieve peace on earth—you need general nuclear
> disarmament. It was a great propaganda slogan. It was an idea to play against
> Reagan's statement that safety can be found in new kinds of armaments, in
> deploying weapons in outer space and creating an anti-missile system. No, we
> said, this was an incorrect path, the better solution lies in the total liquidation
> of nuclear armaments.
>
> Secondly, this document gave Gorbachev an opportunity to feel more sure
> of himself in the future. Once you have a document in your pocket approved
> by the Politburo about the total destruction, down to zero, of all nuclear arma-
> ments, then you are justified in continuing in this policy direction. It is easier to
> speak to the military on those issues once you have such a document.

Thus armed, Gorbachev moved quickly. He wanted to maintain the
momentum of the Geneva summit, such as it was, but he was even more
concerned to broadcast his proposals to the world—and receive its
responses—before the 27th Congress of the Communist Party of the Soviet

Union, forthcoming in February, a meeting that would determine the next Soviet Five-Year Plan; missing that deadline could delay his reforms until 1991. Boris Yeltsin, whom Gorbachev had appointed to the Politburo two days before Christmas, admired the general secretary's maneuvering. "The chief problem of Gorbachev's launching of perestroika," Yeltsin would tell Gorbachev's biographer Archie Brown, "was that he was practically alone, surrounded by the authors and impresarios of Brezhnev's 'era of stagnation,' who were determined to ensure the indestructibility of the old order of things. . . . At that all-important initial moment of his reforming initiative, he operated with amazing finesse. In no way did he frighten the old mafia of the Party apparat, which retained its power for a long time and which, if necessary, might have eaten any general secretary alive without so much as a hiccup."

On 15 January 1986, Gorbachev sent a letter to Reagan outlining his new initiative. Simultaneously he released the text in Moscow, where it was carried in *Pravda* and *Izvestia* and read by announcers on Tass's English-language news and in a Moscow Television Service newscast. It began with a challenge:

[The Soviet Union proposes] a concrete program, calculated for a precisely determined period of time, for the complete liquidation of nuclear weapons throughout the world . . . within the next fifteen years, before the end of the present century. . . .

FIRST STAGE. Over a period of 5–8 years the Soviet Union and the United States will halve the nuclear arms which can reach each other's territory. No more than 6,000 charges [i.e., bombs or warheads] will be retained on the [remaining] delivery vehicles. . . .

It goes without saying that such a reduction is possible only given the mutual renunciation . . . of the development, testing and deployment of space-strike arms. As the Soviet Union has warned repeatedly, the development of space-strike weapons will cancel hopes for the reduction of nuclear arms on earth.

That much had already been debated inconclusively at Geneva. Gorbachev went further, picking up Richard Perle's supposedly unnegotiable zero option without demanding that the regional nuclear powers do more than freeze their arsenals, but also requiring the two superpowers to stop testing:

The first stage will see the reaching and implementation of a decision on the complete liquidation of Soviet and U.S. medium-range missiles in the European zone—both ballistic and cruise missiles—as a first stage on the path to freeing the European Continent of nuclear weapons.

Here the United States must adopt a pledge not to supply its strategic missiles and medium-range missiles to other countries; Britain and France must adopt a pledge not to build up their own corresponding nuclear arms.

Right from the start it is necessary for the Soviet Union and the United States to agree to ending any nuclear [weapons tests] and to call on other states to join in this moratorium as swiftly as possible.

The second stage, Gorbachev continued, would begin no later than 1990 and would last five to seven years. The Soviet Union and the United States would freeze their tactical nuclear weapons and eliminate medium-range nuclear arms while continuing to reduce their strategic weapons. The other nuclear powers would begin nuclear disarmament during this stage, first pledging to freeze numbers and bring the weapons home, then, after the superpowers reached 50 percent reductions, joining them in eliminating tactical nuclear weapons and in banning "space strike arms." All nuclear powers would end nuclear weapons tests.

Finally, during the third stage, beginning no later than 1995, all remaining nuclear arms would be eliminated. "By the end of 1999 no nuclear weapons will be left on earth. A universal accord on ensuring that these weapons are never revived will be elaborated." Another breakthrough that Gorbachev offered at this stage was on-site inspection and verification as well as inspection by "national technical means," meaning satellite intelligence. As a closed society, the U.S.S.R. had long resisted admitting foreign inspectors onto its territory, rejecting them as spies. Offering to abandon that resistance was one more illumination that followed from Gorbachev's policy of glasnost.

Gorbachev knew that the Soviet Union's large stocks of chemical weapons and its purportedly massive advantage in conventional forces in Europe were standard justifications U.S. conservatives used to reject Soviet nuclear-arms-control proposals. In fact, of course, the United States had large stocks of chemical weapons as well, which could quickly be deployed to Europe, and the discrepancy in numbers between Warsaw Pact and NATO forces was illusory. "Actual troop levels on the two sides were not so radically different," writes the IISS research fellow Dana Allin. "In 1985 on the central front (Denmark, the Benelux countries, Germany, Poland and Czechoslovakia), the Warsaw Pact fielded roughly 975,000 troops against NATO's 814,300—a 1.2 to 1 ratio. Overall in Europe, the ratio was about the same, while globally the two alliances had roughly an equal number under arms as well. The Soviets *did* have a large advantage in main battle tanks (16,620 to NATO's 8,050).

NATO had a qualitative superiority in airpower, while the numbers were roughly balanced." The Soviets fielded so many tanks in Europe, according to V. V. Shlykov, a Soviet military intelligence (GRU) department chief, because they expected the majority of them to be destroyed by NATO antitank forces in the early days of a war, and knew that their industry was not capable of replacing them as rapidly as they believed the U.S. industry to be. "It wasn't because we wanted to lunge at Europe," Shlykov told two Western econo-mists studying the collapse of the Soviet economic system in the mid-1990s. He added: "For the very same reason, we accumulated 45,000 nuclear war-heads, which is a lot more than all the Western countries combined. This crazy story is still waiting to be told."

None of these numbers mattered if neither side was planning to start a war, but rather than continue to give U.S. conservatives reasons to reject his initiatives, Gorbachev added proposals to eliminate chemical weapons entirely before the end of the century and to negotiate reductions in conven-tional arms and armed forces. He argued once more, fervently, the folly of SDI:

> Thus, we propose entering the third millennium without nuclear weapons on the basis of mutually acceptable and strictly verified accords. If the U.S. Admin-istration—as it has repeatedly stated—is committed to the goal of completely eliminating nuclear weapons everywhere, it is being given a practical opportu-nity to actually do just that. Instead of spending the next 10–15 years creating new weapons in space, which are extremely dangerous for mankind and are allegedly intended to make nuclear arms unnecessary, is it not more sensible to tackle the destruction of these arms themselves—and ultimately reduce them to zero? The Soviet Union, I repeat, proposes precisely this course.

Gorbachev once more invoked the Palme Commission's idea of common security, emphasizing that the problem of nuclear weapons "is a problem of importance to all mankind; it can and must be resolved jointly. And the faster the program is translated into the language of practical action, the more secure life on our planet will be." In conclusion, he connected the nuclear-arms race to other large challenges the world faced:

> Our new proposals are addressed to the entire world. The switch to active steps to stop the arms race and reduce arms is also a necessary prerequisite for resolving overwhelming global problems: the destruction of man's environ-ment, the need to find new sources of energy and the struggle against eco-nomic backwardness, hunger and disaster.
>
> The principle of armament instead of development imposed by militarism

must be replaced by the reverse order of things—disarmament for development. The noose of the trillion-dollar debt which is now strangling dozens of
countries and entire continents is a direct consequence of the arms race. . . .

We want . . . to complete the 20th century under the sign of peace and
nuclear disarmament. The package of new foreign policy initiatives proposed
by us is designed to ensure that mankind greets the year 2000 beneath peaceful
skies and space, that it does not fear a nuclear, chemical or any other threat of
destruction and is firmly confident of its own survival and the continuation of
the human race.

Many of the proposals that Gorbachev presented to the Reagan administration and the world on 15 January 1986 matched and sometimes even
advanced beyond those developed in the Palme Commission report, which
prefaced its parallel "program of action . . . based on the principle of common security" with a caution Gorbachev clearly heeded: "In the nuclear age,
states cannot achieve security through competition in arms. They must
cooperate to attain the limitation, reduction and eventual abolition of arms."

Chernyaev judges "the very beginning of 1986" to be the exact time "when
Gorbachev placed his stake on a direct dialogue with the American leadership." That is, Gorbachev intended his offer to end the nuclear arms race to
win him the international support and prestige he needed to discredit what
Yeltsin called "the old mafia of the Party apparat" and turn his country away
from militarism. "Disarmament for development," he hoped, would begin at
home.

RONALD REAGAN, AT LEAST, received Gorbachev's letter with enthusiasm. "Gorbachev surprisingly is calling for an arms reduction plan which
will rid the world of nuclear weapons by the year 2000," the president wrote
in his diary that day. "Of course, he has a couple of zingers in there which
we'll have to work around. But at the very least it is a h—l of a propaganda
move. We'd be hard put to explain how we could turn it down." When
George Shultz learned that Gorbachev would publicly announce his initiative that day, he called in Paul Nitze to draft a statement that Reagan could
release to the press. Richard Perle, hearing from Nitze that the statement
would welcome Gorbachev's initiative, worked on Caspar Weinberger to call
Reagan to complain, hoping to beat the State Department to the draw: "Secretary Weinberger had called [the president] with his usual angst," Nitze
confirmed dryly, "after Richard Perle had reported to him what we were
proposing."

In the Oval Office that afternoon, Shultz succeeded in convincing the president to ignore Weinberger's reservations, which may not have been difficult to do; Reagan's first enthusiastic response to Gorbachev's initiative, Nitze reports, was, "Why wait until the year 2000 to eliminate all nuclear weapons?" The White House had already released a statement noting the opening in Geneva the next day of the fourth round of the nuclear and space arms talks. The statement released that afternoon cited Reagan's many previous calls for nuclear abolition, welcomed "the Soviets' latest response," and promised to "give careful study to General Secretary Gorbachev's suggestions." A further statement released the next morning, 16 January 1986, made a point of agreeing with Gorbachev about the malevolence of "space-strike arms" while exempting Reagan's benevolent "strategic defenses."

No one within the Reagan administration whose opinion counted shared the president's enthusiasm for nuclear abolition. The dismissive judgment that day in January and for long after was that Gorbachev's proposal was nothing more than crude Soviet propaganda. Reagan found it interesting that for the first time a Soviet leader had actually set a target date for nuclear disarmament. Unlike his advisers, the president was prepared to put Gorbachev's intentions to the test, as he wrote in his diary in early February after a meeting of the national security planning group, the NSPG, which included, among others, Shultz, Weinberger, William Casey, and Reagan's latest national security adviser, John Poindexter:

> NSPG time in the situation room re Gorbachev's proposal to eliminate nuclear arms. Some wanted to tag it a publicity stunt. I said no. Let's say we share their overall goals and now want to work out the details. If it is a publicity stunt this will be revealed by them. I also propose that we announce we are going forward with SDI but if research reveals a defense against missiles is possible, we'll work out how it can be used to protect the whole world not just us.

Shultz encountered even more naked resistance, which he gleefully exposes in his memoirs. "The naysayers were hard at work," he writes:

> No one could accept the thought of a world moving toward the elimination of nuclear weapons. Richard Perle declared . . . in mid-January that the president's dream of a world without nuclear weapons—which Gorbachev had picked up—was a disaster, a total delusion. Perle said the [National Security Council] should not meet on the idea, because then the president would direct his arms controllers to come up with a program to achieve that result. The Joint Chiefs' representatives agreed with Perle. They feared the institutionalization and acceptance of the idea as our policy.

Shultz disagreed, and more to the point, so did the president. "He thinks it's a hell of a good idea," Shultz told the State Department arms-control group. "And it's a political hot button. We need to work out what a world without nuclear weapons would mean to us and what additional steps would have to accompany such a dramatic change. The president has wanted all along to get rid of nuclear weapons. The British, French, Dutch, Belgians and all of you in the Washington arms control community are trying to talk him out of it. The idea can potentially be a plus for us: the Soviet Union is a superpower only because it is a nuclear and ballistic missile superpower." In another meeting, Shultz writes, "Perle insisted that Gorbachev's letter was not serious, just propaganda. 'We must not discuss it as though it was serious,' he said. The worst thing in the world would be to eliminate nuclear weapons."

Probably because Perle or his lawyers objected, Shultz demoted the last sentence ("The worst thing in the world . . .") to indirect address, but Shultz clearly intends us to construe it to be something he heard Perle say. Why would eliminating weapons of terrible mass destruction be "the worst thing in the world"? Perle himself has never explained in detail why he prefers threats to diplomacy, other than to assert that the Soviets couldn't be trusted, despite the long record across the Cold War of tacit U.S.-Soviet cooperation to keep the peace. One of his reasons may be the reason Shultz's adviser, the ambassador Rozanne Ridgway, offered during another January discussion that Shultz recounts:

> Roz Ridgway broke in. "At dinner last night, Dianne Feinstein [at that time mayor of San Francisco] said, 'Of course people can imagine a nonnuclear world—everybody does.' She was astonished that we had questions about its desirability." But Roz was troubled too. "The loss of nuclear weapons would mean the loss of a special American preeminence; it would change the way we walk down the street. And it can't be done without a gigantic conventional military buildup."
>
> Art Hartman bolstered her point. "In Europe, our allies are up against huge Soviet conventional power. The threatened use of nuclear weapons in order to deter the Soviets is essential to them."

But the conventional advantage in Europe was less than met the Washington eye, as Dana Allin's 1.2-to-1 ratio of Warsaw Pact to NATO forces reveals, and as for a loss of "special preeminence," wasn't that what Shultz had identified as a loss the Soviet Union would sustain from arms reductions, one that could "potentially be a plus for us"? What sort of people build and sustain their "special preeminence," the cocky way they walk down the street, by amassing weapons capable of destroying the human world? If both superpowers shed their vast arsenals, reduced their conventional forces, and settled back into merely major-power status, would the world be better off or worse?

Shultz judged that reducing and eliminating intermediate nuclear forces (INF)—the Pershing 2s, ground-launched cruise missiles (GLCMs), and SS-20s in Europe and Soviet IRBMs in Asia—was the best place to start to test Gorbachev's sincerity. Reagan copied out a seven-page, handwritten letter to that effect in late February. "Our proposal also called for broad cutbacks in conventional forces in Europe," the president later recalled. In response to Gorbachev's more sweeping proposal to begin eliminating nuclear arsenals, Reagan put in another plug for SDI. He did not offer to discontinue nuclear testing.

Gorbachev got the message. "The moratorium helps clarify the real motives of our Western partners," he told the Politburo on 24 March 1986, "precisely that they're not inclined to disarm. When will the new thinking reach them? It's hard to say. But it will come, and maybe even faster than we expect. . . . Maybe we should just stop being afraid of SDI! Of course we can't simply disregard this dangerous program. But we should overcome our obsession with it. They're banking on the USSR's fear of SDI—in moral, economic, political, and military terms. They're pursuing this program to wear us out. So we've decided to say: Yes, we're against SDI, because it destabilizes the peace. But for us it's not a question of fear but responsibility, because the consequences might be unpredictable. SDI doesn't reinforce security, it destroys the remaining security guarantees." At the next Politburo meeting, on 3 April, Gorbachev reminded his colleagues of the new policy of common security that he had announced at the 27th Party Congress in February: "Despite all the contradictions in our relations, the reality is such that we can't do anything without them, and they can't do anything without us. We live on the same planet. We won't be able to preserve peace without America. This is a strong move in our game: [that] we acknowledge their role."

To Reagan, Gorbachev wrote in early April that "more than four months have passed since the Geneva meeting. We ask ourselves: What is the reason for things not going the way they, it would seem, should have gone? Where is the real turn for the better?" He said people were attempting "to portray our initiatives as propaganda." He heard "increasingly vehement philippics addressed to the USSR" and witnessed "quite a few actions directly aimed against our interest. . . . All this builds suspicion as regards to the U.S. policy." Nevertheless, Anatoly Dobrynin, preparing to move back to Moscow as a Gorbachev adviser after twenty-four years as Soviet ambassador to the United States, stopped by Shultz's office a few days later to report, "Gorbachev thinks INF is possible." INF was important—the SS-20s and Pershing 2s with their ten-minute flight times were dangerous—but Gorbachev was playing for the highest stakes. At that point he needed arms reductions to reform his country, not to stay in power. "There have been some questions in the press about whether Gorbachev is in control," Dobrynin volunteered to Shultz. "Let me tell you, *he is in control!*" Arms reductions could only diminish the Soviet threat; why would Reagan's advisers resist them? "The Western governments resorted to their usual strategy of simply ignoring our initiative," Gorbachev writes bitterly.

Among the "actions directly aimed against our interests" Gorbachev would have counted two U.S. Navy intelligence-gathering ships that deliberately approached within six miles of the Soviet Black Sea coastline on 13 March 1986, "part of the worldwide navy program to assert our rights of 'innocent passage,' " Shultz explains, and "not the first time in the Reagan administration when we had made such an assertion close to Soviet shores" but "the first time since the Geneva summit." In March the United States demanded that the Soviet mission to the U.N. be cut back by 170 personnel. On 14 April, responding to a terrorist explosion in a Berlin discotheque frequented by U.S. servicemen, a limited U.S. air strike against Libya killed sixty people, including—when Muammar Gadhafi's personal compound was bombed—Gadhafi's adopted infant daughter; Libya was a Soviet client.

Gorbachev "was disappointed with the way the Americans behaved after Geneva," Chernyaev said later. "He thought that they were just giving the appearance of conducting serious negotiations, but really they were just wasting time. . . . He saw these things as an attempt to irritate him, to test him to see what his reactions would be. He thought it was indicative of a desire to put him in some kind of an awkward situation in front of his own society, in front of his own colleagues. He [had] opened his soul and sincerely offered [Reagan] his suggestions involving these big ideas, and this was the response he received—small and somewhat strange steps."

Matlock, on the other side, remembered a different mood. Gorbachev and his advisers "couldn't yet grasp how important certain issues were to us such as human rights, the breaking down of the Iron Curtain, communications and engaging in reducing the violence in [Third-World conflicts]. . . . The Soviets weren't moving on those things. . . . There were still political prisoners in insane asylums and nothing was being done about it. You still had large numbers of refuseniks. . . . These things weren't moving in 1986. Although we kept saying they are connected for us and that we couldn't go very far in one of these areas without some progress in others, it seemed like we were talking to a wall. It seemed that to the Soviet side, either we simply accept their arms control proposal or nothing's going to happen. . . . This really made everything a little difficult."

Finally, in 1987, Shevardnadze would tell Shultz they were going to deal with human rights in the Soviet Union to improve his country's image in the world, and they made a beginning. At first, said Chernyaev, "we looked at all that as a step back, as a gift—*Okay, we'll do it for the benefit of our dialogue* [with the United States]. . . . Eventually we didn't look at this as a gift or a step back. We started thinking about it as something else. We started thinking about all of these things as momentum, as an issue that is very important for ourselves." For now, his negotiations stalled, Gorbachev pushed on at home.

TWO TECHNOLOGICAL DISASTERS marked the winter and spring of 1986. The U.S. space shuttle *Challenger,* seventy-two seconds into its mission, broke up at an altitude of forty-eight thousand feet over Florida on 28 January 1986 when a seal failed on one of the two solid rocket boosters attached by struts to its external main fuel tank. The failure allowed a blowtorch-like flame of hot gas to jet from the booster casing. The intense flame affected the fuel tank, which was mounted below the winged orbiter that housed the shuttle crew—seven persons including the veteran mission specialist Judith A. Resnik and a Concord, Massachusetts, high school teacher named Christa McAuliffe. Hydrogen gas began discharging from the external fuel tank, which then ruptured, releasing the large volume of liquid hydrogen in the tank just as the rocket booster broke loose and smashed against the orbiter wing. The blowing hydrogen acted as a rocket to drive the hydrogen tank into the oxygen tank directly above it. The oxygen tank ruptured as well, oxygen mixed with hydrogen, and the flame from the booster ignited the hydrogen-oxygen mixture to produce a huge white fireball. Inside the fireball cloud the orbiter swerved sideways into the Mach 2 airstream and broke up. The crew cabin, torn intact from its orbiter housing and with its crew still alive inside, continued ascending up to sixty-five thousand feet before it began to fall back toward the ocean. It fell for almost three minutes, crashing into the ocean at 207 miles per hour—a force on impact of about two hundred times gravity—completely demolishing the crew cabin and crushing to death all seven crew members. The cabin debris was subsequently recovered, but whether or not the crew was conscious at impact was impossible to determine.

The president, personally grieved, said the right things afterward. He said the members of the *Challenger* crew were pioneers. He told the schoolchildren of America, who had been watching the launch in their classrooms because a schoolteacher was aboard, that although painful things sometimes happen, "the future doesn't belong to the fainthearted; it belongs to the brave." He said Sir Francis Drake had died on that date "390 years ago." He quoted a favorite verse of pilots, "High Flight," written in 1941 by an eighteen-year-old American pilot officer, John Gillespie McGee, Jr., during the Battle of Britain, saying that the crew had "slipped the surly bonds of earth" to "touch the face of God." What he did not say, and appears never to have remarked, was the evidence the *Challenger* disaster offered of the great risk of relying on complicated technological systems—such as SDI would have to be—to protect the nation from nuclear attack.

The other disaster, of course, was Chernobyl. When the big RBMK reactor exploded in the northern Ukraine on 26 April 1986, Gorbachev was still thinking through the problem of moving the Reagan administration toward the radical arms-reduction measures he had proposed in mid-January. Andranik Petrosyants, the director of the Soviet atomic energy program, wrote later that "Chernobyl was only a minor event compared with what a nuclear war could be. . . . A one-megaton nuclear bomb explosion would release into the atmosphere one thousand times more radioactivity than a nuclear reactor accident. It would take only one day for seventy percent of the radioactive substances to come back to earth and, at sufficiently high wind velocities, to pollute a vast area. In that case, 1,000 sq. km. [368 square miles] would be covered by lethal fallout."

Petrosyants's comparison of bomb and burning reactor fallout, published in 1988, minimizes Chernobyl's output; a comprehensive scientific review published in 2003 found it to be the equivalent of a twelve-megaton explosion. There is no reason to doubt his bomb fallout estimates, however. By that measure, then, ten thousand megatons might contaminate with lethal fallout an area at least two thousand miles on a side—an area larger than the continental United States. Gorbachev, as he labored in the aftermath of the accident to cope with its enormous demands for relocation and decontamination, saw at first hand what nuclear war would be like and took the lesson to heart. As Shevardnadze would write, the disaster "tore the blindfold from our eyes." Gorbachev made the connection clear to the Warsaw Pact Party secretaries, his counterparts, at a meeting in Budapest on 11 June 1986. In the meeting minutes' paraphrase:

> Comrade Gorbachev stressed that the Soviet Union is currently witnessing serious problems. . . .
> Comrade Gorbachev informed extensively about the accident at the power plant in Chernobyl. . . .
> One should not pretend that nothing happened [Gorbachev said], that everything would be under control. Very serious problems are still to be faced, the majority of which are new to the Soviet Union. . . .
> It was like war. People were evacuated, families were separated and only slowly found their way back to each other. All this was extraordinarily serious. The situation and its impact must not be played down in any way.
> The tragedy of Chernobyl is closely related to the issue of disarmament. Medical experts all over the world clearly state that there would be no medical help in case of a nuclear war. Soviet and American physicians agree on this.

George Shultz was struck by the parallel as well, which may partly explain his somewhat greater enthusiasm for Reagan's commitment to disarmament—greater at least than that of his scornful colleagues. Alexander Bessmertnykh remembered returning from a visit to the United States just weeks after the accident and reporting to Gorbachev "one personal remark that George Schultz had made. He said, 'After Chernobyl, we all now realize the real danger of everything nuclear,' because Chernobyl according to U.S. calculations was something like one-third of the smallest nuclear explosive. And if it caused such great damage to almost half of Europe, what will happen if we shall use all those arsenals we now have in our hands?" Chernyaev concurred: "That phrase, 'Don't put on my desk any war-fighting program,' was uttered [by Gorbachev] before Chernobyl, but I would like very much to endorse what Alexander Bessmertnykh said. Chernobyl had a very significant effect, and it even strengthened Gorbachev's conviction."

In May 1986, Gorbachev took the unprecedented step of calling together in Moscow the entire Soviet foreign-policy establishment—"all the ambassadors and Moscow's 'diplomatic elite,' " he said—to explain and justify to them the "new thinking" in foreign policy and to demand their loyalty to his foreign minister. With all six hundred seats filled in the second-floor auditorium of the foreign ministry where he spoke, he told them "that in today's world of mutual interdependence, progress is unthinkable for any society which is fenced off from the world by impenetrable state frontiers and ideological barriers. A country can develop its full potential only by interacting with other societies, yet without giving up its own identity. We [cannot] ensure our country's security without reckoning with the interests of other countries, and . . . in our nuclear age, you [cannot] build a safe security system based solely on military means. This [prompted] us to propose an entirely new concept of global security, which included all aspects of international relations, including the human dimension." These were not easy ideas to accept, he writes, neither in the Soviet Union nor abroad, and he would continue to shake up and try to reeducate a recalcitrant foreign-policy establishment as well as a recalcitrant military, military-industrial complex, and KGB.

A sour example of his problem with the West occurred shortly after his foreign-policy meeting: Richard Perle, using the hedging of the Soviet leadership about the Chernobyl accident as fresh evidence that the Soviet government was untrustworthy, persuaded Reagan to announce on 27 May that the United States would no longer observe the SALT II agreement, erasing the only restraints on building up strategic weapons then in place between the United States and the U.S.S.R. "From 1986 [onward]," Thomas Graham, Jr., notes, "there were no limitations on strategic offensive arms until the START I Treaty entered into force in December of 1994." The president justified his action with an exaggerated claim Perle had developed to undercut arms agreements: that the Soviets regularly cheated on their commitments to arms control. Ironically, one of Reagan's complaints was that "since the November summit, we have yet to see the Soviets following up constructively on the commitment made by General Secretary Gorbachev and myself to achieve early progress in the Geneva negotiations, in particular in areas where there is common ground." Gorbachev, Chernyaev writes, "was surprised and annoyed by the cautious, unenthusiastic response of the West to his bold and sincere initiatives."

Perle's response was far more than simply cautious and unenthusiastic. He was categorically opposed to arms control, believing dogmatically that it always worked out to the Soviet Union's advantage, and immensely clever at finding ways to convince a secretary of defense inexperienced in the subject of nuclear policy and an equally inexperienced president why they should resist new agreements and repudiate old ones.

Caspar Weinberger "virtually turned over the Pentagon's arms-control portfolio to Perle," Strobe Talbott writes. "In that sense, Weinberger, too, became a member of the Perle mafia [along with Perle's nominal Pentagon superior Fred Iklé, Secretary of the Navy John Lehman, the ACDA's Kenneth Adelman, and others]. And since Weinberger . . . was also a member of President Reagan's inner circle, that gave Perle special advantages." The zero option was Perle's; the so-called broad interpretation of the ABM Treaty that essentially nullified its basic purpose by asserting that it imposed no restrictions on exotic antimissile technologies such as lasers or particle beams was his; a Weinberger letter warning against agreements that was leaked to the press just prior to Reagan's departure for Geneva was his; and the president's decision to cease compliance with SALT II originated with him as well.

Reagan's passion for nuclear abolition greatly worried Perle. When Perle first heard of the president's dream of strategic defense, he dismissed it contemptuously as "the product of millions of American teenagers putting quarters into video machines." After further consideration he realized it might be useful. As Rozanne Ridgway would say later, "There were people who really did want to use SDI, and its implications for the ABM Treaty, to stop the arms control process." Perle was one of those people, and first in line. But since their dispute over SDI alone might not be enough to prevent two such passionate abolitionists as Gorbachev and Reagan from agreeing to eliminate their nations' nuclear arsenals, Perle championed a new poison pill in that spring of 1986. It had originated with Iklé, who had sold it to Perle after talking it over with Max Kampelman. It fit Perle's modus operandi of promoting offers that looked good on paper, that he could sell to Weinberger and Reagan with a straight face, but that he judged the Soviet Union must inevitably refuse. The zero option had been such an offer, and so far, so good. Now, Bach at his harpsichord again, he set about promoting another phony proposal, his ally Edward Rowny recalled:

> Richard Perle called me over . . . and he said, "You know, Reagan is not going to give up this idea of getting rid of all nuclear weapons." I agreed. He said, "I've got an idea. We'll just go ahead and say we'll reduce all ballistic missiles, which are the really dangerous part, but we'll keep sea-launched and ground-launched cruise missiles, and we'll keep bombers." He added, "We'll always have our reserve, and I don't think the French or British will give up their ballistic missiles." So we went in to see Weinberger, and Perle convinced Weinberger and Weinberger himself said, "Yes, I also feel that the President wants to get rid of all nuclear weapons and I can't convince him otherwise. But let's try this ballistic missile proposal out." So we did and it caught on, particularly with Secretary of State Shultz. He had been quite hostile, I think, to Perle up to then. He now thought that Perle was being creative, which he was. Their rapport improved after that.

(In fact, according to Shultz, the secretary of state had been hostile to Perle because he believed Perle had been the high-level Pentagon official who had committed an act of gross disloyalty by secretly encouraging the Japanese and the French to agitate against the president's INF proposals that spring. "On February 21," Shultz writes, "the president handed [his national security adviser John] Poindexter a note on which he had written that the secret approach to the French and Japanese (and probably to other allies) was 'a despicable act.' The president left it up to Cap Weinberger to deal with this breach of discipline and of loyalty to the president. 'These people,' I said, 'are out of control.' To my knowledge, Weinberger did nothing." Shultz says he eventually confronted Perle, "who assured me that he had not been responsible. I accepted his word. By this time, I knew from my own sources that he was not the culprit. The air was cleared, and our relations proceeded amicably." But if not Perle, then who? Who else in the Pentagon had both motive and authority? Despite Shultz's previous indignation, however, he dropped the matter forthwith, except to say that he increasingly found Perle to be "one of the most creative and reliable thinkers on arms control matters.")

Michael Guhin, a counselor to the Arms Control and Disarmament Agency at the time and a senior staff member on the National Security Council, characterizes Perle's proposals more critically. "About this business of doing away with ballistic missiles," he told the Brown conference on the Cold War in 1998—"I think we have to step back from that and say . . . that this was a propaganda ploy. I think zero-zero was [also] a propaganda ploy." Asking the Soviets to give up their ballistic missiles when those missiles constituted the vast majority of their nuclear arsenal, while the United States would retain its more numerous arsenal of bombs, bombers, and air-, sub-marine-, and ground-launched cruise missiles, was not likely to win their agreement, any more than it would have won U.S. agreement were the tables turned. Weinberger and the president thought otherwise, however, when they met to discuss the subject on 12 June 1986. "It made little sense," Weinberger told Reagan, "to commit to share the benefits of advanced defenses with the Soviet Union if the Soviet Union insisted on continuing to retain large numbers of offensive ballistic missiles which would, in turn, attempt to defeat our defenses." Such an argument was doubly cynical—SDI would never be more than a bloated research program, and even if it had been viable, the United States would never have shared it with the Soviet Union—but Weinberger may not have known that. Certainly Perle did. Nitze saw through the Perle initiative immediately. He had one word for it when he heard about it: "ridiculous." By the time the NSC had worked it over and diluted it, it came to very little, although Perle would bring it up again at the next summit meeting to contribute to poisoning the air.

Two important meetings that summer changed Gorbachev's mind about

whether "hopes for major changes in world politics . . . kindled by our summit meeting with President Reagan in Geneva . . . were waning." The French
president, François Mitterrand, visited Moscow in early July. "I do not judge
the American administration as harshly as you do," Mitterrand told Gorbachev after listening to the general secretary's long, angry analysis of Soviet-
U.S. relations. "I admit that the U.S. military-industrial complex puts a lot of
pressure on the U.S. administration. At the same time, we have to bear in
mind that Reagan is the product of his milieu, and he is not without common sense and intuition. . . . In order to break away from the contradictions
in the judgments of his own government, Reagan is moving above them—
into the sphere of prophecies." Here Chernyaev takes up the story:

> "It seems to me," Mitterrand remarked, "that notwithstanding his political
> past, Reagan is one of those statesmen who is intuitively striving to find a way
> out of this dilemma. You may find this judgment contradictory, but it is really
> true. Unlike many other American politicians, Reagan is not an automaton. He
> is a human being."
> "This is extremely important," Gorbachev replied, "and I'm taking special
> note of it." In this way the French president played a major role in eroding the
> remaining stereotypes in Gorbachev's "new thinking."

What Gorbachev himself remembered most vividly of his discussion with
Mitterrand was the French president's report of his meeting a few days previously with Reagan. "He told me that he considered the arguments the
American President had advanced as unconvincing, commenting ironically
that Reagan's belief in the effectiveness of the Strategic Defense Initiative as a
panacea for all ills was, in his view, more mystic than rational."

A week later, in mid-July, Richard Nixon also visited Moscow and talked
with Gorbachev at length. The former president, working on resuscitating
his reputation after the debacle of Watergate, encouraged the general secretary to have patience with Reagan:

> I have known President Reagan for a long time, more than thirty years. I have a
> firm conviction that he considers the matter of American-Soviet relations his
> personal concern. You are right that there are people in the administration who
> do not want agreements with the Soviet Union. They believe that if they can
> isolate the Soviet Union diplomatically, apply economic pressure on it, achieve
> military superiority, then the Soviet order would collapse.* Of course, this is

* A formula for international relations with sovereign states that would find its proponents once again,
after 2000, in the context of U.S. relations with North Korea and Iran.

not going to happen. For years Reagan, as you know, was thought to have been a supporter of the group holding such views [i.e., the Committee on the Present Danger]. But not now. I know from conversations with him that the meeting with you did influence a gradual change in his attitudes. He was very impressed not only by the contents of your exchanges, but also by your personal commitment to peaceful relations between our countries. This he clearly recognized. He also thinks that a certain personal relationship has been formed between the two of you, and consequently believes that you will be able to reach an agreement on the issues of mutual interest.

Despite these encouragements, Gorbachev assessed the letter he received from Reagan on 25 July 1986 as "an attempt to uphold the pretense of a continuing dialogue, another tactical move in the 'double game' played by the Americans." In the letter Reagan offered to continue in compliance with the ABM Treaty for at least the next five years (the Soviets had proposed fifteen or twenty years), after which either country could deploy strategic defenses if it first offered a plan for sharing them and—a vestige of Perle's most recent program of presidential misdirection—a plan for eliminating all ballistic missiles.

Gorbachev was vacationing in the Crimea when the letter came. "Eduard Shevardnadze telephoned me to say that he had already sent a draft reply for approval," he recalls, "adding that we did not need to give a detailed reply since there were no significant proposals in Reagan's message. Still, we could not leave it unanswered." Anatoly Chernyaev had accompanied the Gorbachevs on vacation. The draft reply arrived from Moscow where Shevardnadze's first deputy, Anatoly Kovalev, had supervised its preparation. "I took it to Mikhail Sergeyevich," Chernyaev writes. "He took it and read attentively. Then he tossed it on the table, looked at me, and asked: 'What do you say?' I replied: 'It's no good, Mikhail Sergeyevich!' He said: 'Simply crap!' "

Gorbachev continues:

It was a short, routine statement, and as I was reading it, I suddenly realized that I was gradually being forced into accepting a logic that was alien to me—a logic that was in open contradiction to our new attitude, to the process we had started in Geneva, and—most important—to the hopes of ordinary people. I said that I could not sign such a letter, and told Anatoly about the thoughts that had been haunting me for days. In the end, I decided to take a strong stand, suggesting an immediate summit meeting with President Reagan to unblock the strategic talks in Geneva, which were in danger of becoming an empty rite. A meeting was needed to discuss the situation and to give new impetus to the peace process.

"He started thinking aloud," Chernyaev concludes the story, "and then he said: 'Write this down. Urgently prepare a draft of my letter to the president of the United States of America with a suggestion to meet in late September or early October either in London or,' he paused for a moment, 'in Reykjavik.' I stared at him in surprise. 'Why Reykjavik?' He said, 'It's a good idea. Halfway between us and them, and none of the big powers will be offended!' "

Chernyaev wrote Kovalev on Gorbachev's behalf, directing Shevardnadze's deputy to rethink his department's pedestrian first approach. The memorandum demonstrates that Gorbachev's Reykjavik proposals followed from a serious and continuing effort to rethink Soviet foreign policy from the ground up:

In his [recent Czech newspaper interview] Mikhail Sergeyevich posed the question: "What can we conclude from the Americans' behavior? That they are preparing for war?" It seems that the same question can be asked of the authors of this project. Are we going to fight a war?

Of course the military has its own logic, its interests mean that it's always trying to restrain the politicians. But this doesn't mean that the military should define our general policies. The conclusion of the [27th Party] Congress was that given the right policies—foreign, domestic, economic, in short, policies following the new guidelines—*there will be no war*. This is what our military expectations should be based upon, as well as our military expenditures (although this is a different question). . . .

By keeping our SS-20s in Europe, we'll certainly never get the West Europeans on our side. Besides, do you seriously believe that Thatcher, Mitterrand, or whoever follows them into office, could, in any imaginable situation, press the button to launch their missiles against us? Can this really be what underlies our European strategy?

. . . Going to Reykjavik with little progress beyond that reached over the past year's negotiations in Geneva would condemn this summit to failure and provoke universal disappointment. The summit in Reykjavik is not aimed at experts who know all the fine points of modern weapons, but at nations and states, the world community. Therefore, big politics should be in its forefront, not negotiating minutiae. The world must hear major, sweeping proposals from Reykjavik, in the spirit of the January 15 program.

Shevardnadze personally carried the resulting letter to an angry Reagan in September 1986—the KGB's high-handed arrest of Nicholas Daniloff, an American journalist, had temporarily frozen relations between the two countries—but with the release of Daniloff on 29 September the atmosphere cleared. Reagan announced on 30 September that he would meet with Gorbachev in Reykjavik, Iceland, on 10 through 12 October 1986.

At the Politburo on 4 October, Gorbachev told the group preparing for Reykjavik, "We should not create big hopes for Reykjavik in the press. But for ourselves we should keep in mind that first of all we need to get the Pershing 2s out of Europe. They are a pistol against our head. . . . Our [larger] goal is to prevent the next round of the arms race. If we do not accomplish it, the threat to us will only grow. We will be pulled into an arms race that is beyond our capabilities, and we will lose it, because we are at the limit of our capabilities." To Reagan he had written: "In almost a year since Geneva, there has been no movement on these issues. . . . I have come to the conclusion that the negotiations need a major impulse. . . . They will lead nowhere unless you and I intervene personally."

THIRTEEN LOOKING OVER THE HORIZON

ICELAND, AN ISLAND THE SIZE OF KENTUCKY that rises in the North Atlantic between Norway and Greenland, marks the place where the spreading center of the Atlantic crustal plate—the Mid-Atlantic Ridge—passes over a perpetual upwelling in the earth's mantle called a hot spot. The small island nation is raw and spectacular, still forming from periodic eruptions of basaltic black lava, treeless outside its few cities and towns, with lichen-greened cliffs and glacier-fed waterfalls, mud geysers and steaming blue pools, abrupt canyons, rocky coves, and sandy shores on the cold northern ocean alive with seabirds and migratory ducks and geese. The population of Iceland in 1986 was only 243,000 people, more than half of whom lived in and around Reykjavik, an enlarged fishing village on a peninsula on the southwest coast that juts like a jaw from the west face of the island. The proud nation with the world's oldest parliament was excited to host a Soviet-U.S. summit meeting. It offered a historic white art-nouveau house built for the French consul in 1909, the Hofdi House, as a secure location isolated outside the Reykjavik center. With only ten days' notice, Iceland managed to prepare itself to welcome a crowd of Soviet and U.S. officials and world press. Every inn and hotel room would be filled. Ronald Reagan stayed in the American ambassador's residence. Having been told that Raisa Gorbachev would not attend, Nancy Reagan remained behind in Washington; she was miffed to learn that Raisa showed up after all and upstaged her. The Soviet contingent provided its own housing in the form of an ocean liner, the *George Otts*, chartered over from Tallinn, Estonia and docked in the Reykjavik harbor.

As Reagan explained as he boarded Air Force One for Iceland on 9 October 1986, his administration understood the event to be "essentially a private meeting between [General Secretary Gorbachev and me]. We will not have large staffs with us nor is it planned that we sign substantive agreements. We will, rather, review the subjects that we intend to pursue . . . afterward, looking toward a possible full-scale summit." The summit they were looking toward was to be held in Washington, the date as yet undetermined, but Gorbachev was planning much more for Reykjavik, and he intended to disclose his concessions and proposals as a series of surprises in the hope of a breakthrough. The United States had last-minute intelligence on his plans, however, Paul Nitze told an interviewer. Nitze believed they exposed Gorbachev's intentions for the mini-summit to be basically propagandistic, and his chill recommendation, which he said Shultz and "the others" agreed to, was that they should "await Mr. Gorbachev's marvelous concessions, we should then say we take all those concessions, but we shouldn't give anything more. Therefore we could come out of these negotiations winning without cost." In his memoirs he added, succinctly: "We could pocket what we wished to pocket."

As he had at Geneva, Gorbachev bulked up his Reykjavik delegation with Soviet journalists, scientists, and Central Committee apparatchiks; their purpose, Chernyaev explains, was "to interact around the clock with the Americans and other foreigners who had flocked there in great numbers from all over the world, to explain the policies of new thinking, and to help create a new image of the Soviet Union." What Nitze did not know, or couldn't countenance, was that Gorbachev's strategy for Reykjavik had substance and paralleled his strategy for reforming the Soviet Union itself; he evidently considered wresting changes from a hostile U.S. foreign-policy establishment to be a challenge comparable to his ongoing challenge of wresting changes from a hostile Soviet Communist Party, about which he wrote in his memoirs:

> By the mid-1980s our society resembled a steam boiler. There was only one alternative—either the Party itself would lead a process of change that would gradually embrace other strata of society, or it would preserve and protect the former system. In that case an explosion of colossal force would be inevitable. We also had to consider that only a force that held the reins of power could reform the system, that is, gradually reshape it. Moreover, the very idea of reform could not, at least at first, be a subject for public discussion. This would have immediately provoked rejection and irreparably damaged our work before we even began. It was important to get the "engine of change" started and drive up to a point from which there was no turning back.

In internal discussions earlier in October, Gorbachev had explained why Reykjavik would require concessions and compromise. "We are by no means talking about weakening our security," he told the Politburo. "But at the same time we have to realize that if our proposals imply weakening U.S. security, then there won't be any agreement. Our main goal now is to prevent the arms race from entering a new stage [i.e., into space and into advanced, third-generation nuclear weapons]. If we don't do that, the danger to us will increase. If we don't back down on some specific, maybe even important issues, if we won't budge from the positions we've held for a long time, we will lose in the end. We will be drawn into an arms race that we cannot manage. We will lose, because right now we are already at the end of our tether."

The difference between Gorbachev's approach and that of Reagan's advisers was the difference between common security and the adversarial, zero-sum "realism" that both sides had stubbornly maintained throughout the Cold War and that had stalled meaningful arms negotiations for decades. Gorbachev wanted change. Most of Reagan's advisers did not. Gorbachev's goal then must be to push past the president's advisers and somehow engage the president directly. Knowing that Reagan was totally committed to SDI, his deus ex machina for ending the nuclear-arms race, Chernyaev had advised the general secretary not to link arms reductions to limitations on strategic defense—"otherwise," Chernyaev had written, "it will be another dead end." But Gorbachev had little choice: The Soviet military had been willing to agree to his package of Reykjavik concessions only if he held the line on SDI. "Nobody except the Foreign Ministry was in favor of disarmament," Sergei Tarasenko, a specialist on American affairs, recalled. "The military played hard on Star Wars." Alexander Yakovlev confirmed that "Star Wars was exploited by [Soviet] hardliners to complicate Gorbachev's attempt to end the Cold War." That is, far from forcing Gorbachev to make concessions, as the Reagan conservatives believed, SDI was a key issue Soviet hardliners used to resist the greater concessions Gorbachev wanted to make in the hope of slowing or ending the nuclear-arms race.

When he flew to Iceland on 10 October, Gorbachev left behind grim reminders of the stakes in the debate. That was the time when workers in Kiev were raking up the city's chestnut leaves as the trees shed them into the streets and parks and burying them outside the city to sequester their burden of Chernobyl fallout. At Chernobyl itself, engineers were finishing construction of a makeshift sarcophagus braced around Reactor Number Four, entombing the burned-out reactor within 400,000 cubic meters of reinforced concrete. Only when that work was finished would Number Four cease to dust its surroundings with radiation.

The Hofdi House stood in open grassland next to a breakwater beside a stretch of beach road that U.S. and Soviet security had cordoned off from the unbadged. The 2,600-square-foot house counted two floors and a basement under a mansard roof with gables framing the main entrance. Its builder had ordered it precut from a Norwegian sawmill. By the 1950s it had fallen nearly to ruin when a Reykjavik city engineer had lobbied to have it restored. The two delegations had divided it roughly in half, each group taking two of the five modest rooms on the second floor and sharing the common meeting room between. Security details occupied the basement, leaving the dining room, salon, and sitting room on the main floor for the leaders and their advisers. The foyer was paneled with rustic planking, and an angular spiral staircase in Norwegian dragon style connected the lower and upper floors.

As at Geneva, the president and the general secretary began their discussions—on Saturday morning, 11 October—by meeting privately with only their translators and note-takers at hand. They sat across a table from each other in low-backed tan leather armchairs beside a bay of windows that looked out through the cold morning rain onto the gray sea; the floor was warmed with a large rust-red rug in a Caucasian pattern that must have made Gorbachev feel at home. Gorbachev commented that both of them had a lot of paper with them. Reagan joked that his was to help him recall their Geneva discussions. He was glad Gorbachev had proposed this meeting, he added; it would help make their next one productive.

Their subsequent dialogue was greatly aided by simultaneous translation, which Shultz's people had negotiated and which the Soviet side had previously refused. It allowed each man to respond directly to the other's expressions and body language as well as his words. Much that was said was still redundant or extraneous; I give the gist.

Reagan, note cards in hand: "Which problems should we talk about first? We have a whole set that we didn't finish at Geneva—INF, outer space, the ABM Treaty. . . . I'm proceeding from the assumption that both sides want to rid the world of ballistic missiles and of nuclear weapons in general. The world wants to know if we can make that happen."

Gorbachev: "Mr. President, it would make sense first to talk about why we proposed an urgent meeting with you. Afterward I will explain the concrete ideas I brought to this meeting. For that part it would be helpful to invite Shevardnadze and Shultz to join us. Of course, we're prepared to discuss any issues you wish to raise."

Reagan: "We truly ought to talk about human rights. They have a major influence on how far we can go in cooperating with the Soviet Union given American public opinion."

Gorbachev: "About human rights we have yet to speak. Right now I'd like to give you a general impression of what has happened since Geneva. Then we can move on to the concrete problems of arms control and disarmament."

Reagan: "I agree. I mention human rights only to remind you of what I said about them in Geneva." What Reagan said about human rights in

Geneva he then repeated. Gorbachev listened. (In a transcript of Gorbachev's presentation to the Politburo on 8 October, identified and translated by a young Yale scholar, Michael Mazo, he had already made a beginning. He discussed, Mazo wrote, "the need for a 'serious analysis of the whole situation, of the whole human rights concept, both ours and in the world,' and again at the very end: 'Once more about human rights in our land. Here is also required a "speeding up." No routine any more. We must shake up our agencies—the Interior Ministry [KGB] and so on. See what can be done. It is necessary to open the way back to the Soviet Union for thousands of emigrants, to reverse that flood. And, in general, one should work on these things with greater joy.' ") "But I agree," Reagan concluded, "that these problems can take second place in importance to the problems of nuclear weapons."

Gorbachev began his presentation: "This meeting is being talked about across the world. People have wide-ranging and even contradictory opinions about it. Sitting here now, I'm even firmer in my conviction that the very decision to have this meeting was a crucial step on both sides. It means the Soviet-American dialogue is continuing. If it progresses only with difficulty, still it progresses. This alone justifies our coming to Reykjavik. This meeting is a witness of our joint responsibility before the peoples of our countries and of the whole world."

Reagan: "As I said in Geneva, I consider our situation to be unique. Here we are sitting together in a room, and between us we can resolve the question of whether there is to be war or peace in the world. Both of us want peace, but how do we attain it—how do we strengthen the trust and decrease the mutual suspicions between our two peoples?"

Gorbachev: "That was my second thought. I'd like to develop it, in principle supporting what you just said. After Geneva we set in motion a complex and extensive mechanism for Soviet-American dialogue. It has fallen out of step more than once, we've felt more than a few bumps and bruises, but on the whole, it's moving and gaining momentum. That's the positive side. But on the main question that concerns both governments—how to remove the nuclear threat, how to make use of the helpful impulse of Geneva, how to arrive at concrete agreements—there's no movement, and that troubles us greatly. We're very close to a dead end in our negotiations. That's why we wanted an urgent meeting with you, so that you and I can push the process to arrive at agreements that we can conclude when we meet again in Washington."

Reagan: "I feel the same way." He reverted to the Geneva negotiations, discussed the difficulties there with setting a ceiling on nuclear missile warheads, and proposed a compromise.

Gorbachev: "Let me be as clear as possible: We want such solutions to the arms limitation problem. We approached the proposals I'm making today with the understanding that the interests of both the U.S.A. and the Soviet Union have to be considered in equal measure. If we only consider our own interests—and especially if we give you cause to believe we're trying to attain military superiority—then you aren't going to be interested in seeking agreement. So let me precisely, firmly, and clearly declare: We are in favor of finding a solution that would lead eventually to a complete liquidation of nuclear arms. Along the way to that goal, at every stage, there should be equality and equal security for the U.S.A. and the Soviet Union. Anything less would be incomprehensible, unrealistic, and unacceptable. We expect that the U.S.A. will act in the same way."

Reagan: "We feel exactly the same way. The hard question here is verification. There's a Russian saying about this: *Doveryai no proveryai:* Trust, but verify." (Proud of his three words of Russian, Reagan would repeat this saying so often in his meetings with Gorbachev that the general secretary would eventually cover his ears when he saw it coming.) "You and I were optimistic at Geneva about reducing intermediate-range nuclear missiles in Europe. I can see us completely eliminating this class of weapons. We should be able to make progress on strategic weapons as well. But verification is a necessity. If we can make these things happen, the whole world will welcome it."

Gorbachev: "I agree. We're in favor of effective control over fulfillment of any agreements. We'll go as far as we need to go to give and get an assurance that both sides are doing what they agreed to do. But let me say something about the next meeting, in the U.S.A. We consider Reykjavik a step on the path toward that meeting."

Reagan: "People have been calling it a 'base camp' on the path to Washington."

Gorbachev: "Yes, and they said it was the halfway point—and Reykjavik is almost exactly halfway between Moscow and Washington."

Reagan: "Can we talk about the date of your visit? Will you suggest some possibilities, or should I?" ("Whoops," Matlock, the president's note-taker, says he thought. "He's making the same mistake Gorbachev did in Geneva when he talked about the importance of trade. . . . We had briefed Reagan repeatedly on this point, advising him to play it cool and not appear to want a meeting without results. He would always agree, but at that moment in Reykjavik his eagerness to show Gorbachev the United States got the better of his judgment.")

Gorbachev: "Let me finish my thought. You know I've spoken publicly about the importance of the next meeting leading to palpable accomplishments on the problem that worries the world most—limiting the arms race. You and I can't let the next meeting fail in that sense. People have begun asking what sort of politicians we are that we meet together, make speeches, talk for hours, organize one, then another, and then a third meeting but aren't able to agree on anything. Instead, this meeting in Reykjavik should set the requirements for working out agreements on arms reduction that you and I can sign during my visit to America. For that to happen, we'll have to work hard today and tomorrow to lay everything out for our foreign ministers—and only then can we decide when it would be best to organize my visit."

Reagan reverted to his earlier discussion of strategic missile numbers, raising the question of "maximum throw weight"—throw weight being the weight of the warhead package and guidance system a missile could lift. Gorbachev said impatiently that he would respond to that question as well. An hour had passed, he said. He proposed that they invite in their foreign ministers.

The memoirs of the two leaders give sharply contrasting versions of this first Reykjavik discussion. "Gorbachev and I first met alone briefly with our interpreters," Reagan wrote dismissively, "then he said he wanted to bring in George Shultz and Shevardnadze and that's the way it went for the rest of the two days." Gorbachev to the contrary misremembered that he "outlined the proposals we had prepared in Moscow"—the proposals he would shortly read out to the president and the two advisers—and that Reagan was disconcerted by them:

> Reagan reacted by consulting or reading his notes written on cards. I tried to discuss with him the points I had just outlined, but all my attempts failed. I decided to try specific questions, but still did not get any response. President Reagan was looking through his notes. The cards got mixed up and some of them fell to the floor. He started shuffling them, looking for the right answer to my arguments, but he could not find it. There could be no right answer available—the American President and his aides had been preparing for a completely different conversation.

Factual memory is more fallible than emotional memory; it was so important to Gorbachev to surprise the Americans with his plan for nuclear disarmament, enriched with major concessions, that he recalled doing so once more than he actually did. He expected it to make Reagan fumble—Gorbachev, quick on his feet and vain about it, was always impatient with Reagan's cards—and remembered that it did (it may have done so in the upcoming two-on-two session). Certainly he was accurate in recalling that the Americans had been prepared for a different conversation; the last-minute intelligence about Gorbachev's surprises had not come in time to change the general U.S. mind-set that Reykjavik would be only a warm-up for Washington and needed only limited preparation. By Sunday afternoon, Kenneth Adelman recalled, Reagan would say resentfully, "Hell, this isn't a meeting to prepare for a summit. It's a summit." Gorbachev was "eager to wheel and deal," Adelman continues with unintentional irony, "his briefcase bulging with new ideas, quite in contrast with the old days when only we would propose new ideas and they would mostly say *nyet*." Now it was the United States that would mostly be saying *nyet*.

WITH SHULTZ AND SHEVARDNADZE seated at the table, Gorbachev began reading out his proposals. Both sides agreed, he read, that the principal matter of international politics between their countries was an acknowledgment of the complete liquidation of nuclear arms as a bilateral goal. That goal followed logically from their agreement in Geneva that a nuclear war could not be won and must never be fought.

"How do we imagine moving toward this goal?" he went on. "Our approach is stated in my declarations of 15 January 1986. Corresponding official declarations have also been made on your side. I would like to confirm that our point of view with regard to moving toward this goal is that we should do so in stages, while providing at each stage for an equal degree of security for both sides. We expect that the U.S.A. will feel the same way. Again, such an approach is related to our agreement in Geneva that neither side should acquire military superiority over the other."

He was ready then to state his proposals for strategic nuclear weapons.

Both sides, he read, had proposed a 50 percent reduction in such weapons. They had discussed the reduction at Geneva. But since that time, as many as one hundred variants of that proposal had found their way to the negotiating table and negotiations had stalled. To clarify, he would now confirm that the Soviet leadership was interested precisely in deep, 50 percent reductions in strategic offensive weapons and nothing less. Previously the Soviet position had been for 50 percent reductions in weapons with ranges that could reach each other's territories. Now they were proposing reductions of all strategic weapons and of strategic weapons only. "We are taking into consideration the United States's point of view here," Gorbachev said, "and are making a major concession to them." (Reducing only long-range weapons would have left the Soviets with the capability of attacking U.S. allies in

Europe and Asia with intermediate-range ballistic missiles, a capability the United States would not have had—thus Gorbachev's concession.)

That was concession one.

With the 50 percent reduction, Gorbachev continued, they were prepared to take into consideration the U.S.A.'s concerns with heavy missiles—the throw-weight issue that Reagan had raised—and to significantly reduce that category of weapons as part of the larger reduction—"significantly," Gorbachev underlines, "not cosmetically." In exchange, the Soviet Union expected the United States to address Soviet concerns as well. "The U.S.A. has six thousand five hundred nuclear warheads on submarines scattered all across the world, which constitutes an enormous problem of verification and control. Of these, more than eight hundred warheads are MIRVed. We hope the U.S.A. will meet the Soviet Union halfway here."

Reducing the Soviet Union's heavy missiles instead of holding them back in the 50 percent that would remain active was Gorbachev's second concession.

Next Gorbachev turned to intermediate-range nuclear forces, INF: the SS-20s in Europe and Asia, the Pershing 2s and GLCMs in Europe. The Soviet Union had been leery of Perle's zero option in Europe and unwilling as well to give up maintaining a fleet of SS-20s facing China from the far-eastern U.S.S.R. It had also insisted that French and British missiles be counted on the NATO side. Now Gorbachev proposed "a total liquidation of both the USSR's and the U.S.A.'s missiles of this class in Europe. We are making a major concession—we are removing the question of [counting] the nuclear powers England and France." In return, he asked the United States to "make a concession and remove the question of Soviet INF in Asia, or at the very least, agree to begin negotiations about nuclear weapons—Soviet and American—in Asia."

That was concession number three.

This third concession was less than it appeared, George Shultz would write: "He proposed a freeze on deployment of short-range INF systems, knowing that we had none deployed. The freeze would be followed by negotiations to reach some permanent understanding about these weapons. I thought to myself, if we have none and they have 120 and the deployments are frozen, we would be frozen into a permanent disadvantage."

These, Gorbachev summarized, were his proposals on nuclear weapons. He hoped the American leadership appreciated the broad scope of his compromises.

Next Gorbachev turned to the question of the ABM Treaty and of a ban on nuclear testing. The treaty needed to be strengthened, he said, to serve as a foundation for nuclear disarmament. He proposed a compromise that would "accept the American approach" of a fundamental time period during which neither side would withdraw from the treaty followed by a time period when they would negotiate over the treaty's future. "Under these terms," he emphasized, "development and testing of strategic defense systems would be allowed in a laboratory setting, but tests outside the laboratory would be prohibited." For time periods, he proposed not less than ten years of nonwithdrawal, followed by three to five years of negotiation on the treaty's future. Antisatellite technologies would be prohibited as well, since creating such technologies might allow the development of antimissile systems.

As for nuclear tests, Gorbachev said, they had studied the problem comprehensively and at length. "It might be understandable, as long as both sides were not moving toward major reductions, to question the advisability of ceasing nuclear testing. Now, however, in the context of the proposals I have made, any such doubts should fall by the wayside. We should come to agreement on the complete and final prohibition of nuclear tests.

"That, Mr. President," Gorbachev concluded his long reading, "is our package of proposals on all the fundamental aspects of nuclear-weapons reductions. I propose that you and I, here in Reykjavik, give directions to our aides to jointly work out draft agreements that you and I can then approach and sign during my visit to Washington." Having perhaps overlooked it earlier, Gorbachev mentioned that the Soviet Union was prepared to use all means necessary to make these proposals work, including on-site inspections. Whereupon he handed Reagan an English translation of his proposal text.

Shultz characterized the general secretary's presentation wryly: "Gorbachev was brisk, impatient and confident, with the air of a man who is setting the agenda and taking charge of the meeting. Ronald Reagan was relaxed, disarming in a pensive way and with an easy manner. He could well afford to be, since Gorbachev's proposals all moved toward U.S. positions in significant ways."

Shultz's assessment ignored Gorbachev's proposals of a comprehensive nuclear test ban and an ABM Treaty agreement that would strangle SDI in its crib. Reagan, however, instantly spotted the threat to his cherished program and reacted. "What you have just said gives us cause for hope," he told Gorbachev. "But I did notice several differences in our positions." He mentioned reductions in SS-20s in Asia to go with the zero option in Europe. He said the

United States would like to reduce strategic nuclear weapons not merely by 50 percent but to zero. "As I already said in Geneva," he explained, "SDI would make sense only if strategic weapons are eliminated. Therefore, along with reducing strategic weapons, we propose that you sign a treaty that would replace the ABM Treaty." (I find no previous reference to this idea in the record, but Thomas Graham, Jr., recalls that there was discussion in conservative circles at this time of an "SDI cooperation treaty" to replace the ABM Treaty. Gorbachev ignored the proposal, and nothing seems to have come of it.)

"In this [new] treaty," Reagan told Gorbachev, "both sides would carry out research on strategic defense as allowed in the ABM Treaty. If either side approached the limit of what is allowed under the ABM Treaty, then experiments could continue with the other side present—so if we were the first to approach the boundary, then we would invite you to observe our experiments. And if the experiments were successful, then this treaty would require us to share such a system. In the course of two or three years of negotiations, both sides would agree on the mutual use of such a system. In exchange, both sides would be bound to completely eliminate strategic weapons. The reason for this approach is that both sides will continue to be able to produce offensive weapons—after all, we certainly know how—and we need a guarantee that if anyone does, either one of us or a maniac like Hitler, that we have a defense against it. So we propose defending ourselves once and for all time against the recurrence of strategic weapons in the world, and on this basis to build our future for many years to come."

Matlock says Gorbachev was "obviously disappointed that Reagan did not show greater enthusiasm for his proposals." To Shultz, Gorbachev seemed "somewhat taken aback at President Reagan's pleasant but argumentative reaction." Considering how hard Gorbachev had fought at home to wrest his proposals from the reluctant conservatives in his military and his government, he was probably furious. He sounds furious even through the muffling screen of note-taking and translation, scolding Reagan as if the president were a student who had failed to pay attention and spoke without thinking:

Let me react to your remarks. First, we will consider your statements to be preliminary. I have only just now made some completely new proposals; they have not yet been discussed in any negotiations. Therefore I would ask you to pay them their due attention, and to state your reaction later. Second, what you said just now is on the very same level, on the same plane, as what the American negotiators in Geneva are saying. We value the efforts of experts in the detailed working out of questions, but they do not move the matter forward; we need a new contribution, a new impulse. We want to create this with our proposals. But how is the American side proceeding? We propose accepting the American "zero" in Europe and sitting down at the negotiating table about Asia within the framework of the IRBM problem—but you are now departing from your former position. We do not understand this. Now, regarding ABM. We propose preserving and strengthening this fundamentally important agreement, but you propose rejecting it and destroying a mechanism that has created the foundation of strategic stability. We do not understand this. Now, about the SDI. You need not worry. We have studied this problem, and if the USA creates a three-layered system of ABMs, then we will find a response. It is not this that concerns us, but rather the fact that the SDI would signify a shift of the arms race into a new environment, the raising of it to a new stage, the creation of new types of weapons, destabilizing the strategic situation in the world. If this is the goal of the U.S.A. that is one thing. But if they want greater security for the American people, for the whole world, then their position contradicts this goal and is downright dangerous. I hope, Mr. President, that you will study our proposals and respond to them point by point as to what you agree with, what you disagree with and what you're bothered by.

Reagan acknowledged that they would continue to discuss Gorbachev's proposals that afternoon. He couldn't let Gorbachev's attack on SDI go unanswered, however. "For now," he said, "let me just make one remark. The Soviet side refuses to see the point of SDI. If we were proposing to do research on strategic defensive systems under conditions where we had refused to reduce our offensive weapons, then we could be accused of creating a cover for first-strike capabilities. But that's not our position. We propose giving up offensive strategic systems. The treaty that I proposed would prohibit us from developing a strategic defense system until such time as we reduce our offensive weapons. This system would be our defense, together with you, from unforeseen situations—a sort of gas mask." Not for the first time, nor the last, the president explained to the impatient general secretary the similarity between strategic defenses and gas masks, concluding, "We need a gas mask here. But we can discuss this in more detail at our next meeting."

"Fine," Gorbachev said abruptly, and the principals left the table.

GEORGE SHULTZ RECALLED THAT HE "was relieved. Gorbachev had introduced new and highly significant material. Our response, I knew, must be prepared with care. . . . I was glad we had on hand a knowledgeable team with all the expertise we needed. They could rework the president's talking points during the break. Excitement was in the air. I felt it, too. Perhaps we were at a moment of breakthrough after a period, following the Geneva summit, of stalemate in our negotiations." Back at the American Embassy, Shultz assembled Donald Regan, John Poindexter, Paul Nitze, Richard Perle, Max Kampelman, Kenneth Adelman, and Poindexter's military assistant, Robert Linhard, inside what Adelman calls "the smallest bubble ever built"— the Plexiglas security chamber, specially coated to repel electromagnetic radiation and mounted on blocks to limit acoustic transmissions, that is a feature of every U.S. Embassy in the world. Since the State Department had seen no need for extensive security arrangements for negotiating U.S. relations with little Iceland, the Reykjavik Embassy bubble was designed to hold only eight people. When Reagan arrived, the air-lock-like door swooshed and everyone stood up, bumping into each other and knocking over chairs in the confusion. Reagan put people at ease with a joke. "We could fill this thing with water," he said, gesturing, "and use it as a fish tank." Adelman gave up his chair to the president and sat on the floor leaning against the tailored presidential legs, a compass rose of shoes touching his at the center of the circle.

"Why did Gorbachev have more papers than I did?" Reagan kidded his secretary of state. Nitze volunteered that the Soviet proposal was "the best we have received in twenty-five years." Perle complained that the zero option wouldn't work if the Soviets kept missiles in Asia, since they could always shift them back to Europe. When Reagan mentioned Gorbachev's proposed ban on antisatellite testing, Adelman blurted, "Tell him it's a done deal. The Congress gave that away yesterday." Shoulder to shoulder, the president and his advisers talked for most of an hour about strategy. Then some of them went to a baked chicken lunch in the embassy dining room while others prepared a new set of talking points, six pages of single-spaced text. Reagan rehearsed reading the talking points. Gorbachev and his advisers, lunching on the main deck of the *George Otts,* discussed their afternoon's strategy.

THE TWO LEADERS CONVENED AGAIN with their two foreign policy advisers at Hofdi House at 3:30 p.m. Reagan began reading. In the first paragraph his document resurrected Perle's ballistic-missiles dodge, and even had the chutzpah to attribute "the focus . . . placed on ballistic missiles" to Gorbachev. "We are prepared for appropriate corresponding reductions in all ballistic missile systems," Reagan read, "including in our sea-launched ballistic missile force . . . as suggested. Additionally, we need throw-weight reductions, additional sub-limits and effective verification."

Reagan's advisers wanted to limit air-launched cruise missiles as well, but to exclude "other bomber weapons, gravity bombs and short-range attack missiles [for bomber defense]." Why exclude bombers? "Bombers fly slow and face unconstrained Soviet air defenses." "Unconstrained" was a Perle term of art, implying that Soviet air defenses were so good, or could be made so good, that they could effectively shield the Soviet Union from U.S. bombers—which would certainly have come as a surprise to the Strategic Air Command and Prime Minister Stanley Baldwin. "You cannot equate bomber weapons with missile warheads," Reagan read on, "and this was not done in past arms control agreements. But we can consider a sublimit of 350 bombers, thus bounding bomber weapons." The United States was prepared to accept an "aggregate ceiling on bombers and ballistic missiles" of 1,600. Bombers, of course, could carry multiple bombs, and the Soviet Union had only a limited bomber fleet.

Reagan said that he was disappointed with Gorbachev's position on INF. Intermediate-range missiles had to be controlled globally, he asserted, not simply in Europe. He would accept a global limit of one hundred each, with verification.

Turning now to SDI, Reagan told Gorbachev, confusingly, that his SDI cooperation treaty would not eliminate the ABM Treaty but simply take precedence over certain of its provisions. It would, he said, "establish a mechanism for the two sides to move together toward increasing reliance on defense." One by one Reagan repeated his old arguments. SDI would not be used to attack the Soviet Union. It would not be used to attack from space to earth—ballistic missiles were much better at long-distance attack. It would not be used to cover a first strike—to assure Gorbachev of that was the reason he was proposing to eliminate all ballistic missiles. Defenses would reinforce stability. They would protect against cheating. The United States would share them. If the two sides eliminated all ballistic missiles, their remaining forces would be far more stable. "Neither bombers nor cruise missiles are suitable for surprise attack. They are slow and vulnerable to unconstrained Soviet air defenses."

Rather than agree to a comprehensive test ban, Reagan said that the United States needed "verification improvements" in the Threshold Test Ban Treaty and the Peaceful Nuclear Explosions Treaty, negotiated in 1974 and 1976 but not yet ratified by the U.S. Senate. "Let's agree to fix those treaties," Reagan said, but he also said that "neither a test moratorium nor a comprehensive test ban is in the cards for the foreseeable future."

There was more, but the president finally concluded by proposing that they direct their experts that night to work through all the issues the leaders had identified: strategic offensive weapons, intermediate-range nuclear forces, defense and space, nuclear testing. He said Nitze, Kampelman, Perle, Edward Rowny, and Adelman would be prepared to work with Gorbachev's team there in Hofdi House beginning at eight o'clock that night. And believe it or not, he told Gorbachev, he had come to the end of his reading.

To clarify, Gorbachev asked if Reagan had agreed to his proposal for 50 percent reductions in strategic offensive missiles.

"Yes," Reagan said.

Gorbachev said sublimits for different systems had been the bane of the Nuclear and Space Talks going on in Geneva. His proposal had been to reduce all the strategic systems on both sides by 50 percent, he said, calling Perle's bluff. He meant land-based, sea-launched, and those carried by strategic bombers. "The force structures have evolved historically," he explained, "and if we proceed to reduce them by fifty percent across the board, we will reduce the level of strategic confrontation. The structure will remain the same, but the level will be lower, and this will be clear to everyone. Then the disputes which have been going on for years about limits and sublimits will be superseded by fifty-percent reductions. The level of confrontation will be cut in half." He included the SS-18 heavy missiles that the United States worried so much about, he added. Shultz, he said, was hearing that concession for the first time. We should act to untie the knot, he urged. Otherwise Kampelman and Karpov (Viktor Karpov, Kampelman's Soviet negotiating counterpart in Geneva) would continue beating around the bush.

It was an interesting idea, Reagan countered, but since the Soviet forces outnumbered the U.S. forces "by a lot," cutting by 50 percent wouldn't redress the imbalance. Gorbachev had a data sheet showing both U.S. and Soviet nuclear forces; he passed it to Reagan. Here is the data, he said. Let us cut this in half. Reagan said the experts should take it up. Gorbachev said it wasn't a matter for the experts; it needed a political decision. I *said* it was an interesting idea, Reagan bristled; Gorbachev should give the U.S. side a chance. Shultz spoke up to calm the waters: It's a bold idea, he interjected, and they needed bold ideas. Gorbachev agreed. Otherwise, he joked, it went back to Karpov and Kampelman, and that meant *kasha* forever (i.e., the same old porridge).

Reagan asked if he could keep the data sheet. Gorbachev said he could. Now the president had all their secrets, he added. He shrugged: There was no other way out of the forest. But if the United States tried to outsmart him, that would be the end of their negotiations. Reagan reassured him that such was not his intention.

They debated the zero option once more. Reagan claimed the United States had no missiles in Asia. But you have nuclear weapons in South Korea, Gorbachev insisted, on bases in Asia, and forward-based naval vessels as well; it doesn't matter to us if the bomb dropped on us came from an aircraft carrier or a base on land. Back and forth they argued, and finally the general secretary asked: "If we find a solution on Asian missiles, do you accept zero in Europe?" "Yes," Reagan said—a major breakthrough and a defeat for Perle, but one he later claimed to be a victory.

They came then again to SDI. If they were really beginning to reduce strategic missiles, Gorbachev argued, and eliminate medium-range missiles, which would itself be a tense business, how could they destroy the ABM Treaty, the only brake they had on dangerous developments? How could they abandon it when they should be strengthening it? Both sides had proposed not to withdraw from the treaty for a number of years; numbers were the only difference between the two positions. The Soviet side had proposed ten years, during which large-scale reductions would be taking place. That much time would certainly be needed. So it was logical to commit to ten years and limit strategic defense work to laboratory research only. They weren't far apart on testing, either, Gorbachev added, since negotiating a total ban would take time, and in the meantime they could begin reducing test yields and numbers and discuss the future of the test-ban treaties.

Gorbachev's points were interesting, Reagan responded, and their people should take them up. We believe you've already violated the ABM Treaty, he said, with the defenses you've built. He himself thought that SDI was the greatest opportunity of the twentieth century for peace. He wasn't proposing that they annul the treaty, but rather that they add something to it.

Dryly Gorbachev agreed that their experts should meet at eight that evening to consider all the ideas they had discussed. He would be instructing his people to look for genuine solutions in all areas of nuclear arms, he said, including verification. Now that they were getting down to specifics, his people would be fighting for verification. They would want it three times as much as the U.S. side.

We're both civilized countries, Reagan countered passionately, civilized people. "I'm older than you are," he told Gorbachev. "When I was a boy, women and children could not be killed indiscriminately from the air. Wouldn't it be great if we could make the world as safe today as it was then?"

He was proposing something to change this barbarism, he said. It was something to be shared. It was not for one country only. It would protect people if a madman wanted to use such weapons. Take Gadhafi—if he had them he would certainly have used them. Defense couldn't happen in their time; it would be in someone else's time. But he asked Gorbachev to think about the two of them standing there and telling the world that they had this protection, and asking others to join them in getting rid of these terrible systems.

By now, Rozanne Ridgway remembered, "It was a shouting match. Not angry, but two people passionate in their views, with diametrically opposed positions."

Gorbachev went through his arguments yet again, concluding that his concerns about SDI were not military. They had to do with convincing his people, and the Soviet Union's allies, that they should be prepared to begin reductions while the ABM Treaty was being destroyed. That wasn't logical, and his people and allies wouldn't understand it.

All the United States was saying, Reagan shot back, was that in addition to the missiles covered by the ABM Treaty, SDI was something bigger that he wanted the world to have. The United States was not building it for superiority—it wanted every country to have it. With the progress he and Gorbachev were making, he claimed, they didn't need ten years. He couldn't have said that a few years ago, but he didn't think it would take that long. He felt they were making progress. (In the end, SDI was a $44 billion failure; it was abandoned in 1993 for a program of research into ground-based ballistic-missile defense.)

After more discussion of meeting schedules, Reagan said he had one closing remark. Gorbachev had said the Soviet Union didn't need SDI and had a better solution. (Gorbachev had said his country had a cheaper solution, referring among other things to the Topol ballistic missile that Soviet designers were developing.) Perhaps both sides should go ahead, Reagan said, and if Gorbachev's people did better, the Soviet Union could give the United States theirs.

"Gorbachev finally exploded," Matlock recalls. " 'Excuse me, Mr. President,' he said, voice rising, 'but I cannot take your idea of sharing SDI seriously. You are not willing to share with us oil well equipment, digitally guided machine tools, or even milking machines. Sharing SDI would provoke a second American revolution! Let's be realistic and pragmatic.' "

Reagan responded with evident sincerity that if he thought the benefits wouldn't be shared, he would give up the project himself. Gorbachev scoffed that he doubted if the president even knew what the project contained.

MARSHAL SERGEI AKHROMEYEV, small and wiry, with pale blue eyes, at sixty-three the chief of the Soviet general staff, told George Shultz he was the last of the Mohicans—the last Soviet commander still active who had fought against the German Army in the Second World War. The Americans had wondered what his role would be at Reykjavik. He appeared that evening as the leader of the Soviet arms-negotiation expert group. (Gorbachev thus exquisitely co-opted the Soviet military after its attempt to manipulate him with its vacuous plan for complete disarmament.) A story Akhromeyev told over dinner that evening revealed both his stoicism and his survival instincts: Early in the war, he said, he had been assigned the task of blocking the advance of the German Army on a particular stretch of road leading into Leningrad. With his tank battalion he guarded that road for eighteen months, through the terrible Soviet winter, and never once in all those months went indoors. Shultz praised his patriotism. "Mr. Secretary," the marshal responded, "there was that, but I knew that if I had left that road, Stalin would have had me shot."

Akhromeyev's counterpart on the U.S. side was Paul Nitze, then seventy-nine. The Soviet team also included Viktor Karpov, Yevgeni Velikhov, and Georgi Arbatov; the U.S. team was Kampelman, Perle, Adelman, Rowny, and Linhard. A second pair of negotiating teams under Rozanne Ridgway and Alexandr Bessmertnykh met in another room to deal with human rights and regional issues. Ridgway and Bessmertnykh finished a little after midnight. The Nitze-Akhromeyev teams ran a marathon across more than ten hours of negotiation.

Akhromeyev made it clear at the beginning that he was there to push for change. "I'm no diplomat, like you," he told the Americans—reminding his own team as well. "I'm not a negotiator, like you. I'm a military man. Let's not repeat all the familiar arguments. Let's see how much progress we can make tonight. That's what I want and that's what Gorbachev wants."

They focused on three issues. Akhromeyev reverted to Gorbachev's original formula of an across-the-board 50 percent cut in strategic weapons. Since, theoretically, that formula would have left the United States at a disadvantage, with fewer ICBMs than the Soviets, Nitze argued for an agreement that equalized the numbers. An equal outcome, of course, meant that the Soviets would have to eliminate more ICBMs than the United States. They debated the question for six hours, along with a subsidiary question: How many warheads should a bomber count for? The U.S. side was adamant that bombs in no way equaled ballistic-missile warheads. (Certainly there were differences in time to target and perhaps in vulnerability to Soviet defenses, but the largest weapons in the U.S. arsenal were bombs, for the obvious reason that a bomber could carry more weight than a missile.)

Sometime after midnight, Rowny, who was greatly worried that the

United States might give something away, disagreed with Nitze on rules for counting missile warheads. Nitze called a caucus to hash out the difference, but the other members of the team backed Rowny. Akhromeyev had a similar argument with Karpov about the equal-outcomes problem in his caucus. Both sides returned to the table and debated some more. "At two o'clock in the morning," Nitze recalled in an interview, "Marshal Akhromeyev suddenly rose from his chair. He said that he was leaving, and I thought that that was the end of the negotiations, at least for that night. But then he turned at the door as he was leaving the room, and he said, 'I will be back at three o'clock.' So Bob Linhard . . . and I talked about it and we decided to go to the hotel at which Secretary George Shultz was staying and wake him up, and tell him exactly where we were in the negotiations, and get guidance from him as to what we should do next." Nitze and Linhard "hopped into a car and drove through the frigid Icelandic night to our hotel and woke up Secretary Shultz. He received us in his suite in robe and pajamas, surprisingly alert for that hour." Shultz listened, advised, and made it clear that Nitze was the boss of his team and didn't have to count heads. Nitze apologized for waking Shultz in the middle of the night. Shultz laughed: "Who do you think Akhromeyev woke up?"

Back at Hofdi House, Nitze continues, "Marshal Akhromeyev walked in and he sat down and he said, 'I'm authorized to change the position which I have been insisting upon up to now.' We on our side agreed to look for an equal end point through unequal reductions. So that on the main thing that had been blocking us, apparently Mr. Gorbachev had authorized him to move to our position, and it was at that point that I thought that with that basic change in the Soviet position, we probably could move on from there to really, finally working out an agreement that we could live with, and which they would accept."

For negotiating the START treaty the numbers they agreed on were six thousand weapons and sixteen hundred delivery vehicles. But how should they count bombers? Without long-range stand-off air-launched nuclear cruise missiles, Nitze argued, "it was unlikely our bombers could get to their targets against heavy Soviet air defenses, which were not to be limited." Whatever the authority of that argument Akhromeyev agreed to count bombers with bombs and defensive short-range attack missiles (SRAMs) as one each in the weapons category and the delivery vehicle category—a significant concession.

They were unable to agree on Asian INF limits. "It became clear," Nitze explains, "that Akhromeyev was not authorized to negotiate on the Asian level." They would have to leave that problem for the principals. So also the last frustrating hour-and-a-half debate over how to count such difficult-to-verify weapons as sea-launched cruise missiles carried out of sight on ships and submarines.

All in all, the night had been a success. "We made an immense amount of progress during those few hours, from three o'clock a.m. to 6:30 a.m.," Nitze said. "Defining strategic systems," Adelman concurs, "excluding bomber weapons, and closing on limits is one amazing night's work, indisputably more progress than we achieved in thousands of hours in hundreds of meetings over the previous five years." Then they had to work together to prepare a memorandum to be included in the final Reykjavik joint communiqué. Hofdi House was devoid of copiers; to make copies as they drafted the memorandum they had to borrow some old-fashioned Soviet carbon paper, which Akhromeyev provided—with a joke about superior Soviet technology. It was still dark when they finished; the sun would not rise for another hour. Nitze went off to brief Shultz, Akhromeyev to brief Gorbachev. "Damn good!" Shultz told Nitze. "It's what we came for!" Nitze, for whom negotiation was a professional sport, finally relaxed. "I haven't had so much fun in years," he confided.

The Reykjavik base camp was scheduled to fold its tents that Sunday morning after one more meeting between the principals. Schedule or no, Gorbachev and Reagan still had a range of mountains left to climb.

"FOR THE SUNDAY MORNING SESSION," George Shultz remembered, "we took our whole delegation to Hofdi House. People wandered about the upstairs sitting rooms, where huge oil paintings of subjects such as American astronauts in surreal landscapes hung on the wall." (U.S. astronauts had trained for their moon walks on the Iceland barrens.) "The president, in our pre-meeting discussion, agreed that our working group had made great progress in fleshing out and strengthening material developed during the first day. But the president also saw, as we all did, that much work remained."

In fact, both Reagan and Gorbachev were sharply disappointed. When they sat down together they proceeded to debate SS-20s in Asia, then nuclear testing. Reagan proposed turning the SDI issue over to their negotiators to explore areas of possible agreement. Gorbachev said the proposals he had brought to Reykjavik had been highly constructive, they had made real concessions, but the United States hadn't budged an inch. If anything, it was trying to drag things backward. They sparred a little more on INF.

Reagan said that the Soviet Union and the United States were the only two real nuclear powers; other countries had nuclear weapons basically for defense. (So the two superpower arsenals were weapons of war in Reagan's mind; so much for deterrence theory.) If the United States and the Soviet Union, Reagan said eagerly, were to start reducing their nuclear forces to zero, and stood shoulder to shoulder telling other nations that they must eliminate their nuclear weapons as well, it would be hard to imagine a country that wouldn't do so.

Gorbachev agreed. He felt, in fact, that the present opportunity might not come again. He had not been in a position a year ago, to say nothing of two or three years ago, to make the proposals he had made at Reykjavik. Ominously, he said he might not be able to make the same proposals in another year. Time passed, things changed; Reykjavik would be only a memory.

Reagan said they were both in the same boat, but that meant it was all the more important to use the time they had to free the world from the nuclear threat. Gorbachev said that given the proposals he had brought to Reykjavik, his conscience was clear. Abruptly he offered a major concession, another formula for agreeing on INF: zero U.S. and Soviet intermediate-range weapons in Europe, French and British forces excluded, one hundred warheads on Soviet systems in Asia, and one hundred U.S. warheads based on its own territory. (As they had discussed earlier, that meant the United States would be free to locate Pershings or similar weapons in Alaska, within range of the Soviet East.) The Soviets would accept this formula, Gorbachev said, even though it would require them to reduce their forces in Asia by an order of magnitude he could not even compute. Since the United States insisted on posing ultimata, Gorbachev added bitterly, and since the president was unwilling to make proposals of his own, the Soviet Union would accept these terms—which should show how serious his country was about reaching agreements.

Reagan said he agreed to the INF proposal Gorbachev had described, putting it in his pocket. That was good, Gorbachev said sarcastically, and when would the United States start making concessions of its own? He listed where they had found agreement: to reduce strategic forces by 50 percent; to eliminate intermediate nuclear forces from Europe; to freeze and begin to negotiate shorter-range INF; to reduce Soviet Asian warheads to one hundred, with the United States to have the right to the same number on its own territory. These were unprecedented steps, Gorbachev said, and they would require responsible implementation, including stringent verification—and the United States would find the Soviet Union even more vigorous than the United States in insisting on verification.

But the ABM Treaty was the crux of the matter, Gorbachev told Reagan. We understood before we came here that you were attached to the SDI program. We took that into account when we proposed that SDI-related research could continue in the laboratory for ten years. Ten years would allow the two sides to solve the problems of reducing nuclear weapons. This arrangement wouldn't impede SDI politically, practically, or technically.

What the hell was it that they were defending? Reagan erupted, revealing his real feelings about the ABM Treaty. The treaty restricted defenses to one hundred ground-based antiballistic missiles on each side, he said—which the United States had never deployed. That meant our only defense was retaliation if someone wanted to blow us up. That didn't give protection—it limited protection. Why the hell, the president went on, should the world have to live for another ten years under the threat of nuclear weapons when we'd decided to eliminate them? He failed to see the magic of the ABM regime. Far better to eliminate the missiles, so that our populations could sleep in peace. With strategic defense they could give the world a means of putting the nuclear genie back in the bottle. The next generation would reap the benefits when he and the general secretary were no longer around.

So it went through the morning and an hour past the time scheduled for lunch. Gorbachev reminded Reagan that "it takes two to tango" and asked if the president was ready to dance. Reagan reminded Gorbachev "once burned, twice shy," and recalled Soviet perfidies. Reagan quoted Marx and Lenin; Gorbachev said history was full of examples of those who had sought to overcome Marxism and Leninism by force and all had failed.

Shultz intervened and listed the points he felt they'd agreed upon. Both leaders took a deep breath. Reagan said he hoped he had made it clear that he would not give up SDI. Gorbachev said with a laugh that some had accused him of trying to encourage the development of SDI to increase the United States's defense burden—backhanding the notion popular among Reagan's national security advisers that SDI would weigh down the Soviets with the burden of trying to keep up.

Finally Gorbachev called time. On the first two questions, he said—strategic weapons reductions and INF—they could say there were common points. On the second two—the ABM Treaty and banning nuclear testing—there had been a meaningful exchange of views, but no common points. With that, Gorbachev said somberly, the meeting could end. It had not been in vain. But it had not produced the results that he had expected. Probably the same could be said for the United States. One had to be realistic. In political life one had to follow reality. "No, let's go home," he concluded. "We've accomplished nothing."

Were they truly to depart with nothing? Reagan asked plaintively. Gorbachev said they should talk about the humanitarian and regional issues, and they did. After a while Shultz asked to read some language he had formulated on nuclear security. Gorbachev rejected one paragraph and accepted a second. Then, relenting from his determination to break off negotiations, he proposed that the two foreign ministers meet over lunch to see what they could come up with. He didn't mind waiting an hour or two, he added. If the president agreed, he proposed they meet again at three p.m.

"The president agreed," the Sunday morning memorandum of conversation concludes, "and escorted Gorbachev from the room, ending the session." The two very frustrated men who led the two most powerful nations in the world would give ending the nuclear arms race another chance.

SHULTZ PULLED HIS TEAM TOGETHER. "It's been a slugging match all the way," he told them. "We're going to have one more round." They talked for a few minutes. The Soviet team joined them. Shultz began summarizing what the leaders had agreed on. Shevardnadze stopped him. "He was cold," Shultz recalls, "almost taunting. The Soviets had made all the concessions, he said. Now it was our turn: there was no point in trying to perfect language on other issues. Everything depended on agreement on how to handle SDI: a ten-year period of nonwithdrawal and strict adherence to the terms of the ABM Treaty during that period. That was their bottom line."

At the other end of the table, Linhard and Perle scribbled away on a yellow pad. When they were finished, the pad passed to Poindexter, Linhard's boss, and from Poindexter to Shultz. Shultz read it, explained to Shevardnadze that it was "an effort by some of us here to break the impasse" and read it aloud. It proposed limiting work on strategic defense to the research, development, and testing allowed by the ABM Treaty for five years, during which time the sides would achieve a 50 percent reduction in "strategic nuclear arsenals." After five years, the sides would continue reducing "the remaining ballistic missiles" with the goal of eliminating all "offensive ballistic missiles" at the end of a second five-year period. After ten years, "with all offensive ballistic missiles eliminated," either side could deploy defenses if it chose.

Gorbachev and Reagan returned. The leaders retreated upstairs with their teams. Reagan's advisers briefed him in the only place where they could meet in private, Rowny recalled, "a little ten by twelve bathroom where about ten of us crowded in. Several stood in the bathtub, Reagan was on the throne. I was agitated, I was worried about the idea of giving up all nuclear weapons."

Reagan reviewed the Linhard-Perle formulation. He liked it. "He gets his precious ABM Treaty," the president said, "and we get all his ballistic missiles. And after that we can deploy SDI in space. Then it's a whole new ball game." Reagan had the formulation typed up and took it with him when he descended the Norwegian dragon stairway to meet Gorbachev, with Shultz, Shevardnadze, two interpreters, and two note-takers to assist.

Shevardnadze had briefed Gorbachev on the Linhard-Perle formulation, and he and Gorbachev had formulated a paragraph. Back at the table with Reagan, the general secretary led off by reading his formulation aloud: no right of withdrawal from the ABM Treaty for ten years, all its provisions strictly observed during that period, testing of any components of an ABM system prohibited "except research and testing conducted in laboratories." Fifty percent reductions in strategic offensive weapons within five years, the remaining strategic offensive weapons eliminated during the second five years. "Thus by the end of 1996, the strategic offensive weapons of the USSR and the United States will have been totally eliminated."

Gorbachev made no immediate comment about the distinction in the Linhard-Perle formulation between "strategic nuclear arsenals" and "offensive ballistic missiles," the latter being the idea Perle had flogged around the White House earlier that year. The general secretary may not have noticed the distinction yet, or he may simply have decided to deal with his more fundamental objections first. In any case, the most obvious differences between the two formulations concerned how SDI research would be limited and whether or not strategic defenses after a ten-year limitation would be explicitly endorsed.

Reagan and Gorbachev hacked away at those differences for an hour. Gorbachev, evidently still believing he could swing the president over to his side, held himself calm while Reagan battered him: Why would Gorbachev object to SDI deployment after ten years, the president asked sarcastically—if, that is, he wasn't planning to develop a nuclear weapon or to pull one out of hiding somewhere? And if Gorbachev was so decidedly set on strengthening the ABM Treaty, how was Reagan to understand the Krasnoyarsk radar (a large radar station the Soviets were building in a location the treaty prohibited and that Gorbachev eventually would order to be torn down)?

When battering didn't work, Reagan unveiled a curious scenario complete with the happy ending he always sought as an outcome for the conflicts in his life: If the two countries completely eliminated their nuclear arsenals, why would Gorbachev be troubled if the United States or the Soviet Union put up a defense system against nonexistent weapons, just in case? Other people could build missiles. But if both countries completely eliminated their weapons, he could imagine, ten years from now, the two of them returning to Iceland with the last two missiles in the world. Reagan would be so old that Gorbachev wouldn't recognize him. He'd say, "Hello, Mikhail," and Gorbachev would say, "Ron, is that you?" The two of them would destroy the last missiles, and then the whole world would have a tremendous party.

The origin of Reagan's fantasy is revealing. It first appeared in notes he wrote for a speech he delivered to a governors' conference in 1963, "Are Liberals Really Liberal?" Criticizing the current U.S. "policy of accommodation with the Soviet Union," he mocked what he called the "liberal . . . answer to the bomb threat":

> The theory goes something like this: As time goes on the men in the Kremlin will come to realize that dogmatic communism is wrong. The Russian people will want a chicken in every pot, and decide some features of decadent capitalism may make for more plentiful poultry, while their system hasn't even provided a pot. By a strange paradox us decadent capitalists will have discovered in the meantime that we can do without a few freedoms in order to enjoy government by an intellectual elite which obviously knows what is best for us. *Then on some future happy day Ivan looks at Joe Yank, Joe looks at Ivan, we make bridge lamps out of all those old rockets, and discover the cold war just up and went away.* To bring all this about it is of course necessary that we whittle the back edge of our heels round so we can lean over backwards in an all out effort to prove to Ivan that we aren't mad at anybody.

At the end of his speech, Reagan offered an alternative to round-heeled accommodation: "We can make those rockets into bridge lamps," he concluded, "by being so strong the enemy has no choice, or we can bet our lives and freedom on the cockeyed theory that if we make him strong enough he'll learn to love us." His editors describe this 1963 speech as "an unvarnished statement of the strategy for dealing with the Soviet Union that he would follow, some twenty years later, as president." Unfortunately for Reagan's strategy, he had not, by his own estimate, come to Reykjavik stronger than the enemy, the men in the Kremlin had indeed begun to realize that dogmatic Communism was wrong, and they were still proving vigorously resistant to his plans.

Charmed despite himself by Reagan's Mikhail-and-Ron last rocket routine, Gorbachev said he wasn't sure he would survive until then.

Reagan: Well, I'm sure that I will.

Gorbachev: Oh, you'll survive. You've already passed the dangerous age for a man. You'll have smooth sailing until you're one hundred. I still have all the dangers ahead that catch up with a man at around sixty. And furthermore, I'll still have to meet with President Reagan, who, as I have learned, hates to concede a point. President Reagan wants to emerge the victor. But here, in these questions, there can't be one victor: Either we both win, or we both lose. We're both in the same boat.

Reagan: I know I won't live to see a hundred if I have to live in fear of these damned missiles.

Gorbachev: Then let's reduce them and liquidate them.

Reagan: This is a very strange situation. You want a ten-year period. I won't give up SDI. But both of us insist that the most important issue is eliminating our nuclear arsenals.

Gorbachev: You wouldn't even have to give up SDI, you know, since you could continue with research and testing at the laboratory scale. But I'm categorically opposed to a result where one of us wins and the other loses. Equality is essential at every stage. Only if the document takes into consideration the interests of both the U.S.A. and the U.S.S.R. will it be worthy of ratification and support. If one of us won and the other lost, that would come out at the next stage and the loser would leave everything in a ruin.

They went back to haggling.

Shultz interrupted to point out the "offensive ballistic missile" variation in the second five years of the Linhard-Perle formulation. He may have done so to remind Reagan of the terms he was offering—the president had never been entirely clear about the different kinds of nuclear delivery systems. Gorbachev found the variation bewildering. He thought they'd already agreed yesterday, he said, to reduce the entire triad of strategic weapons (i.e., missiles, submarines, bombers). Let's agree, he proposed, that we're speaking not only of missiles but of all strategic offensive weapons in this case as well.

At that point Reagan suggested they recess to meet with their advisers to see what was keeping them apart.

HIS TEAM AT HAND, INTENSELY EXCITED, Gorbachev paced an upstairs room. "Everything could be decided right now," he said.

In the room where Reagan met, it was. Richard Perle's biographer Jay Winik describes the crucial exchange as Perle described it to him:

The president first looked at Perle. "Can we carry out research under the restraints the Soviets are proposing?"

Perle's mouth was dry; he felt short of breath. Reagan was asking him for a reason. If he said yes, it gave Reagan cover with the conservatives to confine SDI to the laboratory ("Richard Perle assured me . . ."); if he said no, he would be arguing against Shultz.

But his view was an unequivocal no. "Mr. President, we cannot conduct the research under the terms he's proposing. It will effectively kill SDI."

The president paused and weighed this, and then turned to Nitze and Shultz. They both counseled him to accept the language proposed by Gorbachev, and suggested that they would worry about whether research could be conducted in the laboratory later.

Perle stared hard at Reagan. What was he going to do?

What indeed. In Winik's telling, which came from Perle, Perle was left in doubt until the principals met again. But in fact Reagan accepted Perle's argument immediately, over the arguments of his most experienced counselors, Nitze and Shultz, as Perle revealed in a later interview:

> Some of the people present urged [the president] to go forward and thought that there were ways we could work around these limitations. . . . I expressed the categorical view that there was no way you could see the program through to a successful conclusion if we accepted the constraints that Gorbachev had in mind. . . . And upon hearing that, [Reagan] turned to Don Regan, his Chief of Staff, and said, "If we agree to the Gorbachev limitations, won't we be doing that simply so we can leave here with an agreement?" And it was a rhetorical question, of course, and you knew the moment he put it that he'd made his decision.

Just as Reagan's Joe Yank and Ivan story anticipated his Mikhail-and-Ron routine, so also did Reagan's 1963 condemnation of round-heeled liberals anticipate his rhetorical question. Was he trying to explain to his advisers, and justify to himself, why he should pass up the historic breakthrough, then so near at hand, that he so eagerly wanted? "Round-heeled" in the president's generation was a pejorative for women who were easily seduced; Reagan, and perhaps Gorbachev too, were both struggling not to be easily seduced. They were both men who prided themselves on their persuasive powers. Reykjavik was solving the old riddle of what happens when the Irresistible Force meets the Immovable Object; the answer was impasse.

I asked Perle why he felt limiting SDI to the laboratory would kill it. "The president went round the room," he told me, "to see if the others agreed. Ken Adelman did, but Don Regan wanted an agreement badly and so did the representative of the Joint Chiefs. The president saw the danger." I asked if Perle was concerned primarily with congressional support under such limiting conditions. "Yes," he said emphatically. "But I also didn't see how you could keep scientists interested in SDI for so many years with those limitations." I didn't ask Perle to address the question of the substance of the SDI program. He spoke of it in 2006, long after its demise, as he had spoken of it in Reykjavik, as a real phenomenon, not as the politically useful chimera that it was.

Reagan, having made his decision, sent Linhard and Perle off to revise their formulation, instructing them to reframe it in Gorbachev's format—but also, crucially, to remove the word "laboratory" from the result. With no other private space available where they could work, the two conspirators once more commandeered the upstairs bathroom, laying a board across the bathtub for a desk.

AT FIVE THIRTY P.M. on that cold, blustery October day, long after their discussions were supposed to have concluded, Reagan, Gorbachev, Shultz, and Shevardnadze met one last time. The several thousand journalists, photographers, and radio and television correspondents clamoring beyond the Hofdi House barriers understood the message of the afternoon's delay: The leaders were working on a major breakthrough. A Soviet press secretary had violated the press blackout early that afternoon to announce as much—another way Gorbachev put pressure on Reagan to come to agreement.

Reagan apologized for keeping Gorbachev waiting. You know how much trouble Americans have getting along with each other, he joked. He held up what he called "the final version we can offer you" and proceeded to read it:

> The USSR and the United States undertake for ten years not to exercise their existing right of withdrawal from the ABM Treaty, which is of unlimited duration, and during that period strictly to observe all its provisions while continuing research, development and testing, which are permitted by the ABM Treaty. Within the first five years of the ten-year period (and thus through 1991), the strategic offensive weapons of the two sides shall be reduced by 50 percent. During the following five years of that period, all remaining offensive ballistic missiles of the two sides shall be reduced. Thus by the end of 1996, all offensive ballistic missiles of the USSR and the United States will have been totally eliminated. At the end of the ten-year period, either side could deploy defenses if it so chose unless the parties agreed otherwise.

How do you feel about this formula? Reagan asked.

Gorbachev: I have two questions for you by way of clarification. You speak of "research, development and testing" as allowed by the ABM Treaty. Any mention of laboratory testing has disappeared from your formula. Was this done on purpose?

Reagan: The two sides have different views on what the treaty permits. This is something that ought to be decided in Geneva.

Gorbachev: I'm asking you, did you drop the mention of laboratories consciously or not?

Reagan: Yes, consciously—what's the problem?

Gorbachev: I'm simply clarifying your position; so far, I'm not commenting on it. One more question: In the first part of this formula you speak of reducing the strategic offensive weapons of the parties by 50 percent in the first five years. But in the second part, where you speak of the second five years, you mention offensive ballistic missiles. What's that about? Why such a difference in approach?

Reagan responded with a remarkable answer. During the recess, he said, while he was upstairs, he had received the message that the Soviets were mainly interested in ballistic missiles. He had thought earlier that they were thinking of everything nuclear, and then he had heard it was ballistic missiles. That's why we included that formula, he said. It's true that in the first part they had spoken of all types of strategic nuclear weapons including bombs on bombers and [cruise] missiles. But in the second part the United States spoke of ballistic missiles because he understood that's what Gorbachev wanted.

Gorbachev had been clear throughout the negotiations that he meant for all strategic nuclear weapons to be included in the agreement; he had reiterated the point just prior to the last break for consultations at four thirty that afternoon. Could Reagan have become confused? Evidently he could; for the next ten minutes the two leaders sparred over the question, and Reagan, increasingly testy, blamed the confusion on Gorbachev:

Gorbachev: We both agreed a long time ago that the terms include all components of the triad.

Reagan: So am I to understand that by the end of 1996 all strategic offensive ballistic missiles will be eliminated?

Gorbachev: What about planes?

Reagan: But what I want to know is, will all offensive ballistic missiles be eliminated?

Gorbachev: In the first part of your formulation . . .

Reagan: Is that the only thing you're opposed to?

Gorbachev: I'm simply trying to clarify this question.

Reagan: We'll have to figure it out.

Gorbachev: We really need both formulations to be identical.

Reagan: Apparently we simply misunderstood you. But if that's what you want—okay.

Was Reagan being disingenuous? Did someone deliberately mislead him? He said specifically that they had received a message. It would not have come from the Soviet side, since limiting disarmament to ballistic missiles was against Soviet interests, given the U.S. preponderance in bombers and cruise missiles. Who on the American side had lied to the president and misled him? Whoever it was, no one is telling; none of the post-Reykjavik accounts of the meeting even mentions the exchange.

Shultz jumped in to save the ballistic missile bait-and-switch by raising questions about other categories of ballistic missiles, evidently trying to confuse Gorbachev. He didn't succeed.

The president listened as the general secretary traded details with the secretary of state. The details—ballistic missiles versus ballistic missiles, cruise missiles, and bombers, Shultz's interjection of short-range and intermediate-range missiles—seem to have clarified for Reagan the scale of what Gorbachev was proposing, and he rejoined the conversation with an eager question.

Reagan: Let me ask, do we mean that by the end of the two five-year periods all nuclear explosive devices will be eliminated, including bombs, battlefield weapons, cruise missiles, sub-launched, everything? *It would be fine with me if we got rid of them all.*

Gorbachev: *We can do that. We can eliminate them all.*

Shultz: *Let's do it!*

Reagan: If we agree that by the end of the ten-year period all nuclear weapons will be eliminated, we can send that agreement to Geneva. Our teams can put together a treaty and you can sign it when you come to Washington.

Gorbachev, seemingly startled, agreed. Then he raised the red flag of confining SDI to the laboratory.

Reagan reacted angrily. We've come a long way, he said. The ABM Treaty sets the limits, and what the hell difference does it make anyway? He was just trying to protect the United States, to make a sort of gas mask against the danger of nuclear maniacs.

Yes, Gorbachev said with contempt, he'd already heard about the gas mask and the maniacs, about ten times. But Reagan still hadn't convinced him, he said.

Upstairs, where the two teams of advisers had gathered, the mood was increasingly grim. "I remember tension growing," Chernyaev writes, "as both we and our American colleagues awaited the end of the meeting. We didn't want to talk about anything anymore. We stood by the windows, looking out on the dark ocean. Waiting, waiting, hoping."

More debate: "A matter of principle." "But you're burning all my bridges."

Gorbachev: Is that your final position? If so, then I think we can end our meeting on that.

Reagan: Yes. It's final. You must understand that experiments and research cannot always remain within laboratory walls—sometimes it's necessary to go outside.

Gorbachev: And you understand me too. The question of the laboratory for us isn't a matter of being stubborn or hardheaded. It's not casuistry. We're agreeing to deep reductions and in the final analysis to the destruction of nuclear arms. But at the very same time, the American side is pushing us to agree to allow them the right to create space weapons. That's unacceptable to us. If you agree to restrict your research to the laboratory, without going into space, then in two minutes I'll be ready to sign the treaty.

But Reagan couldn't agree; as Perle had assured him, restricting SDI to laboratory research must kill it.

Gorbachev gave it one more try: Mr. President, allow me to speak in confidence and with frankness. If we sign a package containing huge concessions on the part of the Soviet Union on the cardinal problems, then you will become, without exaggeration, a great president. You're literally two steps away from there. If not, then we may as well go home and forget about Reykjavik. But there won't be another chance. I know I won't have another chance. I believed strongly in the possibility of coming to agreement. Otherwise I wouldn't have proposed holding an urgent meeting with you and I wouldn't have come here in the name of the Soviet leadership with a solid supply of serious compromises. I counted on their being met with understanding and support and on our being able to come to agreement. If that did happen, even now, if we were able to attain the destruction of nuclear arms, then none of your critics will be able to say a word, because the vast majority of people in the world would welcome our success. If we're unable to agree, however, then obviously this will become a matter for another generation of leaders: You and I no longer have any time left. The American side has not made any substantive concessions at all, not a single large step to meet us even partway. It's hard to conduct business on this basis.

Shevardnadze jumped in. He said he would speak very emotionally, because he felt they had come very close to accomplishing a historic task, to decisions of historic significance. If future generations read the minutes of these meetings, the foreign minister said, and saw how close the two countries had come before they let these opportunities pass—those generations would never forgive them.

Reagan: It's a question of one word. If I give you what you're asking, it will cause me great damage at home.

Gorbachev: Let's end it there, then. We can't agree to what you're asking—that's all I have to say.

Reagan: Are you really, for the sake of one word, going to reject the historic possibility of an accord?

Gorbachev: It's not just a question of a word, but a question of principle. If I return to Moscow and say that I agreed to allow you to test in the atmosphere and in space, they would call me a fool and not a leader.

Reagan: I ask you for a personal favor, one that would have enormous impact on our future relations, and you refuse me.

Gorbachev: There are different kinds of favors. What you're asking of the U.S.S.R. would never be acceptable to the United States.

Reagan: One word. I ask you again to change your mind as a favor to me, so that we can go to the people as peacemakers.

Gorbachev: It's unacceptable. Agree to a ban on tests in space and in two minutes we'll sign the document. We can't agree on anything else. What we could agree to, we already have. We can't be reproached for anything. I have a clear conscience before my people and before you. I did all that I could.

Reagan: It's a pity. We were so close to agreement. I think, after all, that you didn't want to reach an agreement. I'm sorry.

Gorbachev: I'm also sorry this happened. I did want an agreement, and I did everything I could for it, if not more.

Reagan: I don't know when we'll have another chance like this, or if we'll be able to meet soon.

Gorbachev: I don't know either.

REAGAN STOOD UP FIRST. "LET'S GO, GEORGE," he said to Shultz. He wrote later that he was getting "angrier and angrier," and his face was knotted with anger when he and Gorbachev emerged together into the television lights. "More than body language conveyed a message," Shultz said. "Our faces looked stricken and drained."

"It was a dark day," Chernyaev recalled, "with huge waves coming off the beach. We all crowded outside.... The time was late.... The stress was incredible. The tension was so high that we couldn't talk. We were just making strange, low sounds. Then the door opened . . . and we saw there the grave faces of the leaders. The Americans looked graver and more disappointed than the others. Gorbachev also looked very unhappy."

Gorbachev wrote that he and the president "left the house as it was getting dark. We stood by the car." Everyone was in a bad mood.

"Reagan reproached me. 'You planned from the start to come here and put me in this situation!'

" 'No, Mr. President,' I replied. 'I'm ready to go right back into the house and sign a comprehensive document on all the issues agreed if you drop your plans to militarize space.'

" 'I'm really sorry,' was Reagan's reply. We made our farewells and he left in his car."

Dobrynin, who was standing with the men when they reached Reagan's car and served as an impromptu interpreter, adds two more lines to their dialogue. "Gorbachev," he wrote, "his voice ringing with bitterness he could hardly hide, said: 'Mr. President, you have missed the unique chance of going down in history as a great president who paved the way for nuclear disarmament.' Reagan replied gloomily, 'That applies to both of us.' "

Reagan remembered a different exchange:

I realized [Gorbachev] had brought me to Iceland with one purpose: to kill the Strategic Defense Initiative. . . .

When we reached our cars before leaving Reykjavik, Gorbachev said, "I don't know what else I could have done." I said, "I do. You could have said yes." In my diary that night, I wrote:

He wanted language that would have killed SDI. The price was high but I wouldn't sell and that's how the day ended. All our people thought I'd done exactly right. I'd pledged I wouldn't give away SDI and I didn't, but that meant no deal on any of the arms reductions. He tried to act jovial but I was mad and showed it. Well, the ball is now in his court and I'm convinced he'll come around when he sees how the world is reacting.

I was very disappointed—and *very* angry.

Whose victory, whose defeat? I asked Thomas Graham, Jr., who was the general counsel to the Arms Control and Disarmament Agency at the time of the Reykjavik summit, about Perle's part in encouraging the president to hang a potentially world-transforming breakthrough on a specious concern for testing outside the "laboratory" systems that had hardly yet even entered the laboratory in 1986. "Perle regarded his successful frustration of agreement at Reykjavik as one of his most important achievements," Graham responded.

Reykjavik was not quite over. Reagan, still furious, returned to the American Embassy to reframe the standoff as a victory. Shultz told the waiting press that all was not in vain, but his quivering lip said otherwise.

Gorbachev, prepared in his anger to condemn the American side and call the meeting a failure, turned himself around in the space of the few minutes it took him to reach the press center:

> I walked from the building where the talks had been held. It was a distance of some 400 meters and I was feverishly collecting my thoughts. One thing preyed on my mind—had we not reached an agreement both on strategic and intermediate-range missiles, was it not an entirely new situation, and should it be sacrificed for the sake of a momentary propaganda advantage? My intuition was telling me that I should cool off and think it all over thoroughly. I had not yet made up my mind when I suddenly found myself in the enormous press conference room. About a thousand journalists were waiting for us. When I came into the room, the merciless, often cynical and cheeky journalists stood up in silence. I sensed the anxiety in the air. I suddenly felt emotional, even shaken. These people standing in front of me seemed to represent mankind waiting for its fate to be decided.
>
> At this moment I realized the true meaning of Reykjavik and knew what further course we had to follow.
>
> My speech has been published in newspapers and commented on by scores of journalists, political scientists and politicians. I therefore do not quote it *in extenso*. The key phrase of the speech was: *"In spite of all its drama, Reykjavik is not a failure—it is a breakthrough, which allowed us for the first time to look over the horizon."* The audience came out of its state of shock, greeting the sentence with thunderous applause. One journalist wrote later in an article characterizing the mood of the press conference: "When the General Secretary presented the failure of the Reykjavik meeting as a victory, Raisa Gorbachev was sitting in the conference hall, looking with awe at her husband, with tears rolling down her face."

In that extraordinary press conference, in private remarks to Chernyaev during their flight home to Moscow, and in talks to the Soviet people afterward, Gorbachev evaluated Reykjavik for the complicated but ultimately productive confrontation it was:

> The position of the American side in Reykjavik on the ABM issue has clearly shown that they have not abandoned the quest for superiority. That is why they

did not have enough character, responsibility or political decisiveness to step over that threshold.

It seems to me that America has yet to make up its mind.

We felt that there was a definite lack of a new way of thinking at this meeting. And the ghost of pursuit of military superiority re-emerged. This summer I met with Mr. Nixon, and he said to me then: I have grounds to say, on the basis of my vast political and life experience, that the search for the ghost of superiority has taken us too far. Now we do not know how to break away from the mounded stockpiles of nuclear weapons. All this is complicating and poisoning the situation in the world.

I think nevertheless that the entire meeting here was of major significance. We did, after all, come close to reaching agreements; only they have yet to be endorsed.

Reykjavik generated more than just hopes. Reykjavik also highlighted the difficulties encountered on the way to a nuclear-free world.

After all, a start has to be made somehow. . . . If we always turn to the past for advice and make use of what belongs to very different times, without considering where we are today and where we will be tomorrow, and that there may be no tomorrow at all if we act in this way, there will be no dialogue whatsoever. There must be some way of making a start.

FOURTEEN

THE SOVEREIGN RIGHT TO CHOOSE

IN THE SPRING OF 1992, MIKHAIL GORBACHEV visited Stanford University as a guest of George Shultz. Before dinner at Shultz's house, the former secretary of state recalled, "We sat in the back yard, and I said to him, 'When you entered office, and when I entered, the Cold War was about as cold as it got, and when we left office it was over. So what do you think was the turning point?' And he didn't hesitate one second. He said, 'Reykjavik.' I said, 'Why do you say that?' He said, 'For the first time, the real leaders got together and really talked about the important subjects.' "

Gorbachev's answer was perhaps tinged with nostalgia; compared to the domestic political struggles that challenged him after Reykjavik, the debate with Ronald Reagan must have come to seem benign. At the time it left him with mixed feelings of anger, frustration, and hope; he said later that its effect on him was "comparable to Chernobyl." In his 1987 book *Perestroika,* he wrote that "the meeting in Iceland was a landmark [that] signified completion of one stage in the disarmament effort and the beginning of another." After Reykjavik, however, he added, "the objective is nearer and more palpable, while the situation has grown more complex and contradictory." Shortly after returning from Iceland he also told the Politburo that it had botched the job of modernizing Soviet industry fifteen years ago and that the country couldn't afford such "irresponsibility" again. "The fate of the country is on the line," Gorbachev reproached his colleagues, "and we are really at a historical turning point. *They look at us in the West and wait for us to drown.*" He said reducing the defense burden was crucial to the success of perestroika.

Gorbachev was ready to negotiate seriously the reduction and even abolition of nuclear weapons, replacing nuclear deterrence with common security. He had learned at Reykjavik that Reagan was also ready, but believed fervently that nuclear abolition required the protection of strategic defense. The U.S. rejection of the grand bargain Gorbachev had offered at Reykjavik—strategic nuclear disarmament, zero INF in Europe, a comprehensive test ban, intrusive on-site inspection in exchange for restricting SDI to the laboratory—supplied confirming evidence, as he told Chernyaev on the way home, that "SDI is the main obstacle to nuclear disarmament." But shockingly, neither he nor Eduard Shevardnadze had been clear at Reykjavik on what restricting SDI to laboratory research actually meant when they insisted on it so vehemently.

"A few days after Gorbachev came back," Roald Sagdeev told me, "Shevardnadze called me. 'Could you come talk to me?' he asked. So I came. He said, 'You know what happened. Gorbachev insisted on a laboratory level of activity and it stalemated the negotiations.' Shevardnadze asked me, 'Can you explain to me what is a laboratory in this context? Is it a small room down in the basement tinkering with something, or what is it?' I told him, 'Eduard Ambrosievich, it's too late to interpret "laboratory" as a room in a building, because if you open *Pravda* in the last couple of years, you'll find a story almost every day reporting about the success of our orbital laboratory—the *Salud* orbital station.'

"This interested Shevardnadze very much," Sagdeev continued. "He said, 'This is important.' And then he did something very interesting. He said, 'Can you fly to New York and give a talk about what you understand a laboratory to be in the context of strategic defense research?' So in two or three days I was given a diplomatic passport and a ticket. I flew to New York, where a press conference had been arranged at the United Nations [on 29 October 1986]. I said some tests could be carried on in space, because we scientists consider manned space stations to be orbital laboratories. It's the amplitude of activity that's important—the power of a laser and so on. Tests with modest instruments—devices, not actual components—would be admissible under the ABM Treaty. So next day the *Washington Post* reported, 'Soviet scientist says "modest" SDI testing is compatible with ABM pact.' It was Shevardnadze who promoted this understanding. He was far ahead of anyone in trying to reach practical agreement. I personally think Shevardnadze played a tremendous role at that time."

Realizing that the West would never acknowledge progress in glasnost while the Soviet physicist and Nobel Peace Prize laureate Andrei Sakharov and his physician wife, Elena Bonner, continued to live in forced exile in the city of Gorky, which was off-limits to the Western press, Gorbachev moved in early December to arrange their return to Moscow.* Fortuitously, Sakharov began criticizing the Reykjavik all-or-nothing negotiation almost as

---

* In Moscow in 1992, Bonner told me bitterly of reviewing her husband's KGB file and discovering that at a Politburo meeting Gorbachev had attributed Sakharov's stubborn dissent to the influence on him of

soon as he and Bonner stepped off the overnight train at Yaroslavl Station in Moscow on 23 December 1986. He spoke to an international audience on the subject at a forum called *For a Nuclear-Free World and the Survival of Humanity* in Moscow in mid-February 1987. The forum included a delegation from the Federation of American Scientists, the successor organization to the original associations organized by the scientists of the Manhattan Project in 1945. The two leaders of the FAS delegation, the Princeton physicist Frank von Hippel and the CEO of the Federation, Jeremy Stone, shared Gorbachev's table at the forum's final banquet and supported Sakharov's arguments. Sakharov dismissed SDI as a "Maginot line in space—expensive and ineffective." He favored abandoning the all-or-nothing "package principle," he said, because doing so "would create a new political and strategic climate in which the U.S. would not deploy antimissile defenses in space" or, alternatively, if they did so, "we would simply revert to the current situation [of mutual deterrence], with appreciable political gains for the USSR."

Gorbachev untied SDI from at least the INF negotiations in a television address on 1 March 1987. Three days later the United States offered a draft treaty with comprehensive provisions for verification. Shultz traveled to Moscow in April, and he and Gorbachev discussed the idea of reducing or eliminating not only intermediate nuclear forces but also short-range nuclear forces. A Soviet treaty draft followed.

Soviet military leaders strongly resisted an INF treaty; some even dared to warn Gorbachev to slow down, the journalist Don Oberdorfer reports. Again fortuitously, a nineteen-year-old German student named Mathias Rust, who had earned his private pilot's license around the time of the Reykjavik summit, decided to take East-West relations into his own hands. He said later that he was "very political," followed Reykjavik closely, and out of that experience formed a belief that "the aircraft was the key to peace. I could use it to build an imaginary bridge between East and West." On 13 May 1987, Rust rented a Cessna 172B, a four-seat light aircraft with a range of about 625 miles (1,005 kilometers), and began a fifteen-day odyssey that culminated in a shocking penetration of Soviet airspace that decisively refuted Richard Perle's contention of unconstrained and supposedly impenetrable Soviet air defenses.

"that Jewish bitch," meaning Bonner. The file has since been published and I do not find the phrase there, but it may have been purged. Gorbachev in the course of manipulating his colleagues often pretended to share their values. Certainly he felt ambivalence about Sakharov, and may well have been prepared to blame Bonner.

Rust flew first from Hamburg to Iceland, presumably to visit the scene of the Reykjavik summit. From Iceland he flew to Norway, then on to Helsinki. When he left Helsinki on the morning of 28 May, he filed a flight plan for Stockholm. Once over the Baltic, however, he turned east and followed the coastline toward Leningrad, about 180 miles, then turned southeast, dove beneath Soviet radar, and beelined across 400 miles of Soviet territory into Moscow, the combined distance nearly emptying the Cessna's fuel tanks. (When a Soviet Air Defense pilot spotted and reported the border violation, his ground commander refused to believe him. The Finns thought Rust had crashed into the Baltic and mounted a major search-and-rescue effort.) "My plan was to land in Red Square," the German student said, "but there were too many people and I thought I'd cause casualties. I had thought about landing in the Kremlin, but there wasn't enough space. I wanted to choose somewhere public, because I was scared of the KGB." He buzzed Red Square three times before he noticed a wide highway bridge paralleling the large parking area behind St. Basil's Cathedral. "I landed there and taxied into Red Square. As it turned out, the day I chose [for the flight] was the [national] holiday of the border patrol. I suspect that's how I got away with it." Alien in a red flight suit and wearing a motorcycle helmet, Rust climbed down from his plane and informed the citizens crowding around him that he carried a twenty-page plan for nuclear disarmament to deliver to Gorbachev. The KGB eventually hauled him away. He served 432 days in Lubyanka prison— KGB headquarters—before returning home.

The results of Rust's peaceful mission, which drew Gorbachev and the senior leadership of the Politburo back early from a Warsaw Pact meeting in Berlin, came to be called the Rust Massacre. Gorbachev used the embarrassing event to sack the resistant defense minister, Sergei Sokolov, and replace him with a younger and more pliant general, Dmitri Yazov, who was a perestroika enthusiast within the military. "Gorbachev also ordered far-reaching military reform," the historian Robert English summarizes, "including a purge of the officer corps, that shattered the morale and unity of the brass. With his opponents temporarily reeling, and with public opinion increasingly assertive and increasingly hostile to them, Gorbachev now prevailed in pushing through the concessions necessary for the INF treaty, for an Afghan settlement and for progress on issues from human rights to third world conflicts." The joke around Moscow was that Rust should get the Order of Lenin.

In the United States, the Iran-Contra affair became public in November 1986. The revelation that the Reagan administration had been defying Congress and the Constitution to sell arms to Iran to raise money to support the right-wing militia fighting to overthrow the revolutionary government of Nicaragua preoccupied and politically wounded Reagan that winter. The scandal allowed Shultz to gain leverage against the neoconservatives who were resisting post-Reykjavik arms reductions. Frank Carlucci replaced John Poindexter as national security adviser. Perle, who had complained for years that government service was impoverishing, resigned in the spring as deputy secretary of defense to write his novel and make some money. When Caspar Weinberger stepped down in November 1987, Carlucci replaced him as secretary of defense and Colin Powell moved up to national security adviser. Despite the neoconservatives, Shultz pursued arms negotiations vigorously with Shevardnadze and Gorbachev because he believed that one of the most popular presidents in American history had the right and the mandate to end the nuclear arms race and the Cold War.

For Thomas Graham, Jr., who participated in the INF treaty negotiations, Reykjavik was "the true watershed of modern arms control." Everything changed when Gorbachev agreed to the principle of intrusive on-site inspection, Graham writes:

> In 1987 the Soviets at INF were prepared to exchange more data on their systems than the [U.S. Joint Chiefs of Staff] wanted, as there was a limit to what the JCS was prepared to turn over. In the last week of the INF negotiations the Soviet officer making the presentation said, "A week ago I would have been shot for what I am doing today" (he really meant a year ago). Gorbachev agreed to the U.S. proposal, pressed during 1986 in Geneva, of double zero. There were, first, a ban on all intermediate-range, ground-launched nuclear missiles (both ballistic and cruise) of ranges from 1,000 to 5,500 kilometers and a ban on all short-range, ground-launched nuclear missiles of ranges 500 to 1,000 kilometers. The higher range ban captured the U.S. Pershing II and GLCM as well as the Soviet SS-20. There were no systems between the range of Pershing II (1,800 km) and Pershing I (950 km). The Soviet SS-23 had a 500-km range and was caught by the lower range ban. In 1981 Richard Perle had urged Ronald Reagan to propose a zero solution for INF. It looked good. Dutch peace groups had proposed it, but it was virtually out of the question that the Soviet Union would accept it given their advantage of about 1,200 to zero in INF systems. But lo and behold, five years later Gorbachev was accepting not one, but two zeros, the famous INF double-zero solution.

Negotiations and preparations were barely completed in time for the treaty to be signed at the Washington summit on 8 December 1987 at 1:45 p.m., an hour Nancy Reagan's astrologer had declared to be propitious. In his memoirs, Gorbachev would call the Soviet deployment of SS-20s, which had started the whole complicated problem, "an unforgivable adventure embarked on by the previous Soviet leadership under pressure from the military-industrial complex"; the INF Treaty, he wrote with relief, "removed a pistol held to our head." This "first nuclear arms reduction treaty," he added, ". . . set the whole process in motion. It is doubtful whether we would ever have been able to sign the subsequent agreements without it—the INF treaty represented the first well-prepared step on our way out of the Cold War, the first harbinger of the new times." There had not been time to devise a verification regime; the United States's Sandia National Laboratories learned in December that it had six weeks to develop a prototype and two months to deliver—which it did. During negotiations, the United States had insisted on the right to station inspectors at the plant that had built the SS-20s and would continue producing the SS-25 Topol, the Votkinsk Machine-Building Plant in the town of Votkinsk, in the Ural Mountains. "A reciprocal right was granted the Soviet Union," Graham notes with amusement, "at a former U.S. Pershing II production facility at Magna, Utah . . . much to the surprise of the Hercules Corporation, whose site it was."

"A great number of missiles were [eventually] destroyed," the Soviet arms control expert Nikolai Detinov recalls. "I can tell you how many. On May 31, 1991, we [finished liquidating] 889 intermediate-range missiles, including 654 SS-20 missiles, as well as 957 shorter-range missiles, including 239 SS-23 missiles. The United States during that time liquidated 234 Pershing II missiles and 443 cruise missiles and 169 Pershing I missiles. That was the end, I hope, of intermediate-range missiles in Europe." The INF Treaty eliminated a whole class of nuclear-weapons systems, the first treaty ever to do so.

EARLY IN THE COLD WAR, when someone insisted that the Soviet Union and the United States would come to blows one day, Enrico Fermi, the Italian-born Nobel-laureate physicist who coinvented the nuclear reactor, had asked dryly, "Where will they fight?" Fermi meant that the two nations lacked a traditional cause for armed belligerence—they contested no territory—and technically that was true, but the answer to his question through the years of U.S.-Soviet conflict was always Europe. Since the Russian Revolution, the wealthy elite of the United States had feared that the red tide of Communism would flood across the world if it was not resolutely stanched. The Soviet victory over Nazi Germany, Stalin's evident determination to dominate Eastern Europe, his reluctance to quit northern Iran after the end of the Second World War, all reinforced Western fears. Two world wars had begun in Europe, and it seemed to the architects of containment—Dean Acheson and George Kennan first of all but Paul Nitze enduringly—that the United States had suffered for not engaging with and guarding Europe to prevent those earlier conflicts. They also intended to prevent German rearmament.

NATO originated in those concerns. So did arming NATO with nuclear weapons and threatening their first use when Soviet conventional forces fell into formation along the NATO nations' eastern borders. At the height of the confrontation, no continent on earth was more heavily armed than Europe. The Cold War was not, first of all or fundamentally, the clash between radically different and incompatible ideologies that American policymakers claimed for it in order to encourage and sustain popular American support; it was first of all and fundamentally an effort to prevent a third conflagration (and this one potentially nuclear) from catching fire in the unstable space where two previous world wars had burned. George H. W. Bush confirmed this analysis, mutatis mutandis, in a memoir he wrote in retirement with Brent Scowcroft:

> I always have believed that the United States bears a disproportionate responsibility for peace in Europe and an obligation to lead NATO. In the 1930s, we learned the hard way that it was a mistake to withdraw into isolation after World War I. We watched as Europe struggled with fascism, but were drawn inevitably into battle to restore its freedom. When the Cold War began, Western Europe became the front line against a Soviet threat, and our allies depended on the United States to point the direction for NATO; the American president was to lead the way.

It followed that if Europe could be stabilized—if the confrontation between the two alliances could be neutralized there—then the Cold War would lose its real purpose and would very likely melt away.

The question of reducing Soviet *conventional* forces in Europe had already come up briefly at the Geneva and Reykjavik summits, but Gorbachev had focused first of all on unloading the nuclear pistol pointed at his head. With the changes of military leadership that followed the Mathias Rust invasion and the conclusion of the INF Treaty, he was ready to begin negotiating conventional-force reductions. One reason certainly was to save the expense, but such economy would not have won Politburo backing until the logic of common security and Gorbachev's conviction that the West had no intention of starting a war made such massive deployment both superfluous and unnecessarily provocative.

At a meeting in Moscow between Gorbachev and Shultz on 28 February 1988, the two "briefly touched on the question of conventional forces, agreeing that we 'should push on.' " Push on they did. At the Moscow summit at the end of May 1988 where Reagan and Gorbachev signed the instruments of ratification of the INF Treaty, the two leaders discussed conventional forces; the discussion, Gorbachev writes, "was facilitated by the fact that only two weeks before, George Shultz and Eduard Shevardnadze had finally agreed on the agenda for negotiations: armed forces, conventional weapons and equipment—all types would be included in the negotiations"—an important preliminary agreement.

Gorbachev's continuing concern for nuclear as well as conventional forces emerged at a private dinner the Gorbachevs and the Shevardnadzes gave during the Moscow summit for the Reagans and the Shultzes. Shultz, in a memo to Reagan written shortly afterward, documented for the president "the remarkable evening . . . at the Tsarist palace . . . the liveliness of the conversation and the easy conviviality." He was struck, Shultz wrote, "by how deeply affected Gorbachev appeared to be by the Chernobyl accident. He commented that it was a great tragedy which cost the Soviet Union billions of rubles and had only been barely overcome through the tireless efforts of an enormous number of people. Gorbachev noted with seemingly genuine horror the devastation that would occur if nuclear power plants became targets in a conventional war, much less a full nuclear exchange. . . . It was obvious from that evening that Chernobyl has left a strong anti-nuclear streak in Gorbachev's thinking."

Alexander Yakovlev, Gorbachev's primary idea man, was writing a book that year, a furious book about what he called "the fate of Marxism." Gorbachev could not have missed hearing its arguments. They reflected the increasing sense of urgency that the Soviet leader and his reformers felt as Party, military, and bureaucratic resistance to perestroika increased. The time was "merciless," Yakovlev wrote, but it was "also a tragic and cleansing time," a "great time of a Great Sobering. It has been a tortuous and contradictory path from the hopes and illusions of the Social Experiment of the Twentieth Century to *an understanding* of the depths of the abyss of our national fate, most of all for those who sincerely believed, sincerely hoped, sincerely blundered." As for the present day, 1988:

> Our country is now morally and physically exhausted. Naturally, various people assess the reasons for this exhaustion in various ways and see different paths out of the situation. Right-wingers of all stripes have constantly reiterated that

perestroika has brought the country to a state of collapse. If we get rid of perestroika, they say, we will live like human beings again, as we lived in "the good
old times of stagnation."

But how did we live?

Irresponsibility, lack of discipline and elementary order, and unrestrained
drunkenness litter the landscape of both our private and our public existence.
There are millions of micro- and macro-Chernobyls, from the actual tragedy
of the nuclear power station, to pollution of the sea, air and land, to the lack of
nitroglycerine [tablets for angina] in our drugstores. Time bombs are constantly going off and will continue to explode until normal economic relations
prevail.

For decades, cast iron, coal, steel and petroleum had priority over food,
housing, hospitals, schools and services. The claim that "it had to be that way"
is fallacious. Because of the economic re-feudalism of management, the price
of industrialization has been disastrously high in both human and material
terms. Disregard for the individual has known no bounds.

We will not brag about the absence of unemployment under the old system.
There was no unemployment under serfdom, either. . . .

The country, the people, and the young generations are having to pay for the
past. That is why no turning back, no restoration of the past in new forms is
possible—with or without perestroika, with the reforms or in spite of them,
with democracy or dictatorship. Those who maintain otherwise either do not
understand what is at stake or understand and are deliberately deceiving the
people. . . . History may be maimed, mutilated, falsified, concealed, rewritten,
or treated in any fashion whatsoever, but it cannot be deceived.

By the end of October 1988, increasingly frustrated with the Reagan
administration's inertia, Gorbachev was planning a spectacular speech at the
United Nations. It was to be, he wrote, "the exact opposite of Winston
Churchill's famous [Iron Curtain] speech." By then Gorbachev felt that he
and his reformers had "fully developed both the conceptual basis and the
policies of our new political thinking." Among other policies, "everyone
agreed that the time had come to make significant cuts in our armed forces
and that the next five-year period should be dedicated to disarmament."
Through the Soviet Defense Council, now run by one of his appointees, Gorbachev ordered the Defense Ministry to begin planning the withdrawal of
Soviet forces from Eastern Europe, a fact attested to in Soviet documents
since made public that confirm Gorbachev's determination to allow the
European satellite nations to choose their own way. For now, at the U.N., he
intended to announce major unilateral force reductions, which Akhromeyev
worked with him to plan.

Before announcing his new policies to the world, Gorbachev had to bully them through the Politburo. He had already told the 29th Party Congress in June 1988 that his predecessors should be faulted for their reliance on military muscle rather than politics and negotiation to protect the country. "As a result," he said, "we let ourselves be drawn into the arms race, which was bound to affect the socio-economic development of the country and its international position." Now he challenged the Politburo members directly and personally. He began casually, saying that he'd talked with Nikolai Ryzhkov, the chairman of the council of ministers, and Yuri Maslyukov, the deputy chairman in charge of the military-industrial complex, had read letters from the people and met with young Komsomol members at the Palace of Youth, and these encounters had forced him "finally to give some serious thought to the question Komsomol members have asked: 'Why do we need such a big army?' " The truth is, he said, "we need quality, not quantity. Now the time has come to make major decisions. Yes, we're taking 'little steps' on medium- and short-range missiles and some other things. But they don't change the situation principally." By now "agitated and tough," Chernyaev records, Gorbachev barreled on:

> Our announced military doctrine contradicts our actual military programs. . . . Our military expenses are 2.5 times larger than those of the United States. No country in the world—except the "underdeveloped" ones, whom we flood with arms without ever being paid back—spends more per capita on the military sector. . . .
>
> We won't solve the problems of *perestroika* if we leave the army as it is. As before, it still gets the best scientific and technical talent, the best financial support, always provided for without question. . . . The Komsomol kids are right—what do we need such an army for? Six million people!
>
> . . . What are we doing? Knocking our best young talent out of the intellectual pool! Who are we going to implement reforms with? We have a strong tank attack force in the GDR [i.e., the German Democratic Republic, East Germany] plus pontoon equipment. With all this "hanging over them" how can the Americans and the others believe in our defense doctrine?

At which point Ryzhkov jumped in to be the first to agree with him: "If we don't do it, we can forget about any increase in the standard of living." Gorbachev immediately turned Ryzhkov's intervention into a call for endorsement:

> *Gorbachev:* If we all agree and if we come to make major decisions, including unilateral reductions and not just what's required by the agreement on

medium- and short-range missiles and the Vienna mandate, I think I'll announce it in my U.N. speech.

Everyone: Yes, yes!

Gorbachev: After the medium- and short-range missile agreement and the decision to pull out of Afghanistan, this will make a huge impression. They'll see that we aren't just blowing smoke, but making real politics for the whole world. The main reason why we're doing this is *perestroika.* Nikolai Ivanovich is right, without reductions in the army and the military-industrial complex we won't be able to deal with *perestroika*'s tasks. . . . There's no question about it, we can't afford not to be militarily strong. But for the purposes of security, not intimidation.

Chernyaev wrote these notes; his acute sense of irony colors that obsequious "Yes, yes!" from the Politburo collectivity. Gorbachev had already decided to announce reductions in conventional forces in his U.N. speech. He wanted the Politburo members on the record so they would have to share responsibility afterward for the decision.

George H. W. Bush, Reagan's vice president, had been president-elect for one month when Gorbachev flew to New York to speak at the United Nations on 7 December 1988, a brisk, windy New York winter day. They would meet after the speech along with Reagan on Governors Island in the East River. Gorbachev wanted to assess Bush's enthusiasm for continued cooperation. He also, he writes candidly, "hoped that a positive international response to my [speech] would strengthen my position [at home] and help overcome the growing resistance to change in the Soviet Union." By then he was a world celebrity; the U.N. speech was his first to that institution, and expectations were high. He did not disappoint them.

"I started speaking somewhat hesitantly," Gorbachev remembers, "with occasional pauses. But gradually I felt the growing interest of the audience, sensing that my words and ideas were coming across and gaining self-confidence and perhaps eloquence." He spoke for an hour, in general terms first, then about world problems and possible solutions. Near the end he turned to the subject of disarmament. The following day would be the first anniversary of the signing of the INF Treaty, he said. The world was "witnessing the emergence of a new historic reality—a turning away from the principle of superarmament to the principle of reasonable defense sufficiency." And then he offered his "deeds":

Today, I can report to you that the Soviet Union has made a decision to reduce its armed forces.

Within the next two years their numerical strength will be reduced by

500,000 men. The numbers of conventional armaments will also be substantially reduced. This will be done *unilaterally,* without relation to the [negotiations ongoing in Vienna].

By agreement with our Warsaw Treaty allies, we have decided to withdraw by 1991 six tank divisions from the German Democratic Republic, Czechoslovakia and Hungary, and to disband them.

Assault landing troops and several other formations and units, including assault-crossing support units [i.e., that "pontoon equipment"] with their weapons and combat equipment, will also be withdrawn from the groups of Soviet forces stationed in those countries.

Soviet forces stationed in those countries will be reduced by 50,000 men and 5,000 tanks.

All Soviet divisions remaining, for the time being, in the territory of our allies are being reorganized. Their structure will be different from what it is now: a large number of tanks will be withdrawn, and they will become clearly defensive.

At the same time, we shall reduce the numerical strength of the armed forces and the numbers of armaments stationed in the European part of the USSR.

In total, Soviet armed forces in this part of our country and on the territory of our European allies will be reduced by 10,000 tanks, 8,500 artillery systems and 800 combat aircraft.

He also said his country would work toward a treaty on a 50 percent reduction in strategic offensive arms, a convention on the elimination of chemical weapons ("we believe that 1989 may be a decisive year in this regard") and negotiations on the reduction of conventional arms and armed forces in Europe.

"After an hour of holding its breath," Chernyaev reports, "the audience erupted in an endless ovation." Robert Kaiser of the *Washington Post* called it "a speech as remarkable as any ever delivered at the United Nations."

Gorbachev was elated, but news that had first come to him the previous evening by telegram from his good friend Margaret Thatcher preoccupied him: A magnitude 6.9 earthquake had shaken northwestern Armenia, followed four minutes later by a magnitude 5.8 aftershock. Though it was far less powerful than the magnitude 7.8 earthquake in China in 1976 that killed more than 240,000 people, it caused great damage and many deaths, the U.S. National Oceanic and Atmospheric Administration reports: "Swarms of aftershocks, some as large as magnitude 5.0, continued for months in the area. Direct economic losses were put at $14.2 billion (U.S.) at the United Nations official exchange rate. Twenty-five thousand were killed and 15,000 were injured by the earthquake. In addition 517,000 people were made homeless."

On Governors Island, Gorbachev met with Reagan and Bush, the general secretary advising the president-elect over lunch, "I know what people are telling you now that you've won the election: you've got to go slow, you've got to be careful, you've got to review. That you can't trust us, that we're doing all this for show. You'll see soon enough that I'm not doing this for show and I'm not doing this to undermine you or to surprise you or to take advantage of you. I'm playing real politics. I'm doing this because I need to. I'm doing this because there's a revolution taking place in my country. I started it. And they all applauded me when I started it in 1986 and now they don't like it so much, but it's going to be a revolution nonetheless." Bush was noncommittal, and although he phoned Gorbachev within days of his 20 January 1989 inauguration to promise "no foot-dragging" on arms control, "weeks and months passed," Gorbachev writes, with little initiative from the American side. He and his advisers took to calling the period "the pause." The Bush administration was in no hurry to develop Soviet-American relations. Scowcroft; the CIA director, Robert Gates; the NSC's Condoleezza Rice; and others agreed that Moscow should be left to struggle for a while, to soften it up for future concessions.

Bush appointed Richard Cheney as secretary of defense in March 1989 when his first choice, John Tower, failed to win Senate approval. Since serving as Gerald Ford's chief of staff, Cheney had been elected a Republican member of the House of Representatives from Wyoming; he left the job of House minority whip, with a 100 percent conservative voting record, to join Bush's Cabinet. Cheney was convinced that Gorbachev was a fraud and a failure. He told CNN in April, journalists Franklin Foer and Spencer Ackerman write, "that Gorbachev would 'ultimately fail' and a leader 'far more hostile to the West' would follow." The policy within the administration— discussed among Bush; his new secretary of state, James Baker III; Scowcroft; and Rice—was to support Gorbachev and perestroika, however cautiously. Cheney disagreed, Foer and Ackerman report:

> Cheney believed that, with a gust of aggressive support for alternatives to Gorbachev, the United States could dismember its principal adversary once and for all.
>
> To craft an alternative strategy, Cheney turned to alternative experts. On Saturday mornings, [undersecretary of defense for policy Paul] Wolfowitz's deputies convened seminars in a small conference room in the Pentagon's E Ring, where they sat Cheney in front of a parade of Sovietologists. . . . Out of

these Saturday seminars, Cheney's Soviet position emerged—with concepts and rhetoric that perfectly echo the current [2004 George W.] Bush administration's Iraq policy. *They would push regime change in the Soviet Union, transforming it into a democracy.* . . . Cheney was unsuccessful in pushing the White House away from Gorbachev. After he mused aloud about Gorbachev's shortcomings in a 1989 TV interview, Baker called Scowcroft and told him, "Dump on Dick with all possible alacrity."

Gorbachev's answer to the collective skepticism of the Bush administration was to continue to follow through on his program of "new thinking" while agitating for further change. In 1988 he discontinued production of highly enriched uranium (HEU) for weapons, although the Soviet military-industrial complex continued to process HEU for other purposes until 1990. According to two U.S. military historians, Joseph Harahan and John C. Kuhn III, Gorbachev volunteered a breakthrough during this period that "changed the course of all previous negotiations [on conventional forces] by conceding that since the Soviet Union had numerically superior conventional forces in Europe, the NATO nations might reasonably conclude that these forces were a threat. He further stated that under any negotiated all-European arms-control treaty, the side with the greater number of forces ought to take a larger share of the reductions, provided there was adequate verification through on-site inspections." The Warsaw Pact endorsed Gorbachev's initiative. On 15 February 1989, Lieutenant General Boris Gromov, who commanded Soviet forces in Afghanistan, crossed the Termez bridge from Afghanistan into the Soviet Union, closing out the war. Thirty-six thousand young Soviet men and women had died in the ten-year course of the bloody project and about one million Afghanis, most of them civilians.

If preventing another world war from starting in Europe had been the fundamental object of the Cold War, it followed that ending the Cold War would require both sides to stand down not only their nuclear but also their conventional forces in Europe, with "Europe" defined, as the French defined it, as extending from the Atlantic coast to the Ural Mountains (ATTU, the negotiators called it—Atlantic to the Urals), and thus including a large swath of Soviet territory as well as the NATO and Warsaw Pact alliances. The negotiating entity that had been pursuing such improvements in security was called the Conference on Security and Cooperation in Europe (CSCE), an ongoing consultation among thirty-five nations that had begun meeting in 1973. The Helsinki Final Act of 1975 had been the CSCE's first important agreement. Confidence-building measures followed, including a requirement that every CSCE nation notify all its counterparts three weeks in advance of any large (more than twenty-one thousand in personnel) military exercise it intended to undertake. In 1983, the CSCE nations agreed to begin negotiating not only new confidence-building measures but also gradual European disarmament. In 1986, with Gorbachev now in power in the Soviet Union, the CSCE nations agreed to require notification of military exercises involving as few as thirteen thousand personnel with provision for on-site inspection of larger-scale (more than seventeen thousand in personnel) exercises. "Known as the Stockholm Document of 1986," Harahan and Kuhn write, "this was the first multinational agreement that the Soviet Union signed permitting on-site inspection of its own territory to verify an arms control accord."

It was in the context of these CSCE negotiations—the "Vienna talks" Gorbachev sometimes referred to—that the Soviet leader proposed that the Warsaw Pact should bear the burden of larger cutbacks in troops and equipment in the interest of achieving balanced force reductions. Why such a seemingly overgenerous concession? Gorbachev explains:

> For us, it was essential to break the stalemate in the talks on armed forces reduction in Europe, which had been dragging on since the early 1970s. The time had come for us to acknowledge that, even by Cold War logic, Soviet superiority in conventional weaponry in Europe stopped making political sense the moment we had reached nuclear parity with the United States. On the contrary, this situation helped to maintain the image of the Soviet Union as the enemy, thus creating ever new threats to our own security. Soviet conventional superiority served as a pretext for the United States and NATO to push through all sorts of military programs, including the upgrading of nuclear weapons—in a sense, we were even giving them a hand with it!

Other negotiations followed, culminating in January 1989 in a Mandate for Negotiation on Conventional Armed Forces in Europe, agreed upon among sixteen NATO states and seven Warsaw Treaty Organization (WTO) states. The mandate laid down the ground rules for negotiating a Conventional Armed Forces in Europe (CFE) Treaty, which would be designed to prevent surprise attacks across national borders by asymmetrically reducing offensive military equipment—tanks, artillery, and armored combat vehicles—with extensive on-site inspections to police the agreement. According to Thomas Graham, Jr., who participated in the CFE negotiations, the Soviet Union "wanted to include combat aircraft and attack helicopters" as well, but the NATO side disagreed. "But in March of 1989,

President Bush decided to concede on this point and the CFE negotiations finally began."

Bush and Gorbachev were both committed to the negotiations, which made for rapid progress. Gorbachev had already promulgated what he called "the principle of reasonable sufficiency in defense," which was an extension to conventional forces of the idea of minimal deterrence: enough to defend but not enough to threaten offensively. "Developing this new doctrine had been far from easy," he writes. ". . . Indeed, two factors formed one psychological knot: on the one hand, the constant worry about a secure peace (the Soviet people remembered Hitler's attack in 1941) and, on the other, the need drastically to reduce our defense budget—an indispensable condition for improving our economy." He adds of the CFE negotiations, "For us, it was essential to prevent upgrading of any types of weapons; this would have dealt a fatal blow to everything we had achieved by then and to the trust we had taken such pains to establish."

In April, Graham took it upon himself to prepare, with a colleague, a "bare-bones draft CFE Treaty" based on the January mandate:

> I called [the U.S. negotiator, Ambassador Stephen] Ledogar and told him that he needed a lawyer and a treaty, that I was a lawyer, that I had a draft treaty, and that I was coming over to see him. He did not say no, so I was off to Vienna in June to persuade the U.S. CFE delegation that they in fact did need a lawyer and a treaty. . . .
>
> When I returned to Washington [a week later] I could say that I had a draft treaty text which had been approved by the delegation. All of this was made up from whole cloth. Of course, no one had asked for a draft treaty text; I was just saying we needed one and here it is. CFE was blessedly different from the SALT/START process, however. It was a negotiation everyone wanted and one that had been authorized and advocated by the president. Thus, there was not a high degree of bureaucratic infighting of the type that characterized those processes. I remember remarking what a pleasure it was working on a negotiation that everyone, in the U.S. government at least, wanted.

Nineteen eighty-nine was the year Eastern Europe pulled free of Soviet domination. In a May entry, Chernyaev sketched the turmoil in his journal:

> All around, Gorbachev has unleashed irreversible processes of "disintegration" which had earlier been restrained or covered up by the arms race, the fear of war, myths about the international communist movement, the socialist community, the worldwide revolutionary process, and proletarian internationalism. . . .

Socialism in Eastern Europe is disappearing. Communist parties are col-
lapsing in Western Europe and everywhere else where they couldn't "latch
onto" the national idea. In other words, what has long been brewing has now
boiled over and is following its natural course. Everywhere things are turning
out different from what had been imagined and proposed.

The Baltic states—Latvia, Estonia, and Lithuania—went first, not without
resistance, harassment, and violence on the part of the Soviet Union despite
Gorbachev's promises. With a tin ear for ethnic nationalism, his tragic flaw,
he distinguished sharply between nations like the Baltic states that the
U.S.S.R. had absorbed and those like Poland and Hungary that it had only
dominated; he feared that if he allowed the Baltic states to withdraw from
the U.S.S.R., other ethnic nationalities would want to secede as well—as
indeed they would and did. Estonia and Lithuania nevertheless bravely
declared their sovereignty on 18 May 1989; Latvia followed on 29 July. In elections in Poland in June, candidates affiliated with Solidarity, the labor union
led by Lech Walesa, overwhelmingly defeated Communist Party candidates.
Shortly afterward, in a speech to the European parliament, Gorbachev
encouraged Eastern European reformers by insisting that "respect for the
sovereign right of every people to choose its own social system" was an
"important precondition . . . for a normal European process." Change in the
social and political order of a country, he added, "is exclusively a matter for
the people themselves to decide. It is their choice." Shevardnadze reemphasized the point over dinner with James Baker, the secretary of state, at the
Soviet Embassy in Paris on 29 July 1989. "If we were to use force," the Soviet
foreign minister told Baker, "then it would be the end of *perestroika*. We
would have failed. It would be the end of any hope for the future, the end of
everything we're trying to do, which is to create a new system based on
humane values. If force is used, it will mean that the enemies of *perestroika*
have triumphed. We would be no better than the people who came before us.
We cannot go back."

In August, after interagency vetting, Graham's CFE treaty draft became
the official NATO treaty text. Graham himself followed his draft to Vienna at
the beginning of September as the U.S. delegation's legal adviser and ACDA
representative. Ten days later, Hungary opened its border with Austria and
thousands of East Germans who had traveled to Hungary to wait crossed
into the West, to be followed in the weeks ahead by thousands more.

On 9 November 1989, East Germany capitulated and allowed its citizens
to travel freely. Crossing points along the Berlin Wall opened and East Germans streamed into glittering West Berlin. I visited Berlin two weeks later

and watched a flow of people on foot, on bicycles, or driving shabby Trabants passing through a crossing point and flooding out into the city. Not much of the Wall had yet been torn down—the concrete of its composition had been mixed with asbestos to make it tough and it was difficult to break. The cold Berlin winter air, air that a writer in an earlier era had described as "always bright, as if it were peppered," was criss-crossed with sulfury scent trails of cream of broccoli soup from soup kitchens the Red Cross had set up to feed lunch to the visitors, who seldom possessed even a Deutschmark of West German coin. Returning to the East at dusk, many of them carried brightly printed plastic bags, usually empty, as souvenirs of their first free encounter with Western capitalism; the books I bought the next day at a government bookstore in dark, sooty East Berlin were wrapped begrudgingly in brown paper tied up with twine.

Watching the same scenes "on a television set in his small study adjoining the Oval Office," Michael Beschloss and Strobe Talbott write, "Bush knew what this meant. He told his aides, 'If the Soviets are going to let the Communists fall in East Germany, they've got to be really serious—more serious than I realized.' " The two historians add: "Before the fall of that year, Bush had been able to argue, as Kissinger had done before the inauguration, that the changes wrought by Gorbachev were 'cosmetic' and easily reversible. But with the Berlin Wall down and Eastern Europe as a whole leaving the Soviet sphere, it was almost impossible to maintain that the world was in imminent danger of returning to the Cold War as everyone had known it." Some years later I had occasion to ask the former congressman Lee Hamilton of Indiana, a leader astute in foreign affairs, why the United States had been so slow to recognize the validity of the revolution Gorbachev was piloting. Hamilton thought a moment and answered, "You know, we were so used to thinking of the Soviets as the enemy that when they changed, we just couldn't turn ourselves around that fast." Certainly not George H. W. Bush, a dogged champion of the status quo guided by a national security adviser, Brent Scowcroft, who cautioned Condoleezza Rice in 1989 to avoid saying publicly that the Cold War was over because once it was said, it couldn't be rescinded, and Congress would use it as an excuse to cut the defense budget.

The CFE negotiations, Graham writes, "lasted about twenty months"— record time for so complicated an agreement. During that time, "five negotiating parties changed their names and one disappeared (the German Democratic Republic . . . merged into the Federal Republic of Germany on October 3, 1990)." When the treaty was signed, in Paris on 19 November 1990, there were twenty-two signatories. Two days earlier, the delegations had gathered in a room at the Hofburg Palace in Vienna, where the negotiations had been held, for the initial exchange of information about their "treaty-limited equipment" (TLE)—the tanks, armored combat vehicles, artillery, and aircraft they had agreed to reduce. "It was like a bazaar," Graham recalls. "Tables were set up around the room with each delegation handing out books containing the initial date exchange—the one to take place at the time of signature—with appropriate pictures of weapons systems, tanks and the like. There were the Soviets, the French, the Germans and all the rest, hawking their data presentations. Some of the delegations had slicker presentations than others but all were comprehensive. It was quite a scene."

The CFE Treaty, limiting NATO and Warsaw Pact hardware to equivalent levels, resulted in major reductions for the Warsaw Pact. A "sufficiency rule" restricted the numbers of treaty-limited equipment belonging to any one country within the Eastern or Western bloc to one-third of the bloc total, which meant proportionally even larger cuts for the Soviet Union. "In 1988," Graham writes, "the Soviets alone had 41,000 battle tanks, 57,000 ACVs and 42,000 pieces of artillery in the area of application [i.e., the ATTU]. Under the sufficiency rule, the Soviets were permitted only 13,000 battle tanks, 20,000 armored combat vehicles, 13,700 artillery pieces, 5,150 combat aircraft and 1,500 attack helicopters. Thus, the sufficiency rule itself imposed a very significant reduction in Soviet military power."

The numbers of machines actually withdrawn and destroyed—chopped up or smashed according to an agreed protocol—were staggering: 40 percent of Warsaw Pact tanks, 26 percent of Pact artillery, 30 percent of armored combat vehicles, 19 percent of aircraft. When the dust cleared, conventional Western and Eastern bloc forces were equal and balanced from the Atlantic to the Urals. "The CFE Treaty," Graham writes with justifiable pride, "ended the Cold War and is one of the central pillars of European security." The leaders who signed the treaty in Paris concurred, the political scientist Matthew Evangelista found. "They declared a formal end to the Cold War, stated they were 'no longer adversaries,' and pledged to 'build new partnerships and extend to each other the hand of friendship.' "

BEFORE THE CONVENTIONAL ARMED FORCES in Europe Treaty was signed, Mikhail Gorbachev had finally agreed with his scientists and other advisers to unlink the Strategic Arms Reduction Treaty (START) negotiations in Geneva from limitations on SDI. With the George H. W. Bush administration's renewed commitment as well, START negotiators were able to resolve many issues in 1989 and 1990 while the CFE negotiations were ongoing. In October 1990, Gorbachev was awarded the Nobel Peace Prize—considered a scandal by those who despised his politics and human rights record, a well-deserved honor by those who admired his work for common security and disarmament. He called again for a moratorium on nuclear testing on 24 October, when the Soviet Union conducted its last nuclear weapons test.

At a summit in Washington at the beginning of June 1990, Gorbachev writes, "we finally managed to settle the basic provisions for the strategic arms reduction treaty, which was designed to cut our strategic arsenals by fifty percent—an idea launched four years ago in Reykjavik. The remaining disagreements were finally resolved." The summit, he added, "significantly increased the pace of the clean-up of the gigantic powder magazine left over from the Cold War." The two presidents—Gorbachev became the first and last Soviet president—in 1990—agreed to sign START I in Moscow on 31 July 1991. That agreement "put the negotiations in overdrive," Graham notes, "and somehow the delegations were able to complete the treaty with its many associated documents and side agreements and deliver it to Moscow in time to be signed." As the U.S. ambassador and arms negotiator James Goodby summarized the agreement: "START I . . . limited the United States and the Soviet Union to 6,000 accountable strategic nuclear warheads and 1,600 nuclear delivery vehicles on each side." It was not nuclear abolition, but it was a measurable stride down that road.

The last trip wires in the nuclear forest were so-called tactical nuclear weapons: bombs, artillery shells, rocket and missile warheads, land mines, demolition munitions, and depth charges intended for use in land and sea battles, primarily in and around Europe, that ranged in yield from a fraction of a kiloton up to as much as one megaton (i.e., one thousand kilotons; by comparison, the Nagasaki bomb yielded twenty-two kilotons). At his first summit meeting with Bush, at Malta in December 1989, Gorbachev had told the U.S. president, "the strategic component is part of the Geneva talks; the tactical nuclear weapons remain. We propose that they be eliminated completely. Such a radical solution would also simplify verification procedures." The previous April, the Soviet Union had formally proposed negotiations on tactical nuclear weapons reductions, and Gorbachev had also announced the unilateral withdrawal of tactical nuclear weapons from Eastern Europe. The United States had not responded, however, even though the Soviet Union stocked some twenty-two thousand tactical nuclear weapons at that time. (The United States stocked twenty-three thousand.) Attention was still focused on strategic and conventional weapons and forces, but already in 1989, an interagency group led by Condoleezza Rice, under a directive from Scowcroft to "put on your Kremlin-watcher's hat . . . and start asking questions about what we do if various nightmare scenarios come true," had concluded that keeping Soviet nuclear weapons, particularly tactical weapons, under secure control was essential. The fact is, the United States had (and has) very little intelligence about either numbers or disposition of Soviet (or Russian) tactical nuclear weapons.

The abortive Soviet coup of August 1991, only days after Bush and Gorbachev had signed START, reminded the Bush administration that tactical nuclear weapons could easily fall into the wrong hands. When eight nervous plotters with hesitant support from the Soviet military isolated Gorbachev at his vacation compound at Foros, in the Crimea, and tried to turn the clock back to 1984, Boris Yeltsin, now the president of the Russian Republic, denounced them as no more than "a right-wing junta" and called out the Moscow citizenry to surround and protect the Russian Republic building— the "White House"—where he and his advisers had barricaded themselves. Under Yeltsin's bare-knuckle tank-turret leadership, the coup quickly failed. One of its casualties was Marshal Sergei Akhromeyev, who had been involved only peripherally but who shot himself the day after the collapse, convinced that Gorbachev's reforms had destroyed what he had spent his life building and protecting. "During the coup," wrote James Baker, "U.S. intelligence had picked up several anomalous indicators involving the Strategic Rocket Forces (SRF), the nuclear arm of the Soviet military. While there had been no indications that the threat of a nuclear accident had increased, these anomalies quite naturally concerned [the president]."

Gorbachev returned to find his power base gone. While Gorbachev was still assessing the damage, Senator Sam Nunn, Democrat of Georgia, who at the time was the chairman of the Senate Armed Services Committee, saw the handwriting on the wall. "I was in Budapest at a meeting when the coup began," Nunn told me. "A Russian friend of mine had to leave the meeting to rush back to Moscow. When Gorbachev was released, my friend invited me to come to Moscow, and I went. I listened to the debate in the Duma about forming a commonwealth of states. I could see all sorts of troubles coming, and after I got back to Washington I introduced the Nunn-Lugar program legislation." The Nunn-Lugar program, cosponsored by Senator Richard Lugar, Republican of Indiana, passed both houses of Congress in November 1991. Initially it provided funds from the U.S. Defense Department budget to secure Soviet nuclear weapons and material—the best investment in defense the DoD ever made.

Eliminating tactical nukes had long been one of Colin Powell's "hobby-horses," he writes in a memoir. As the chairman of the Joint Chiefs of Staff under Defense Secretary Richard Cheney, Powell had ordered a study of their usefulness. "The staff's recommendation," he recalls, "was to get rid of the small, artillery-fired nukes because they were trouble-prone, expensive to modernize and irrelevant in the present world of highly accurate conventional weapons." The four service chiefs, lobbied by the Army artilleryman among them—"the nukes were a matter of prestige to the artillery," Powell explains without apparent irony—rejected the recommendation. "The report went up to the Pentagon policy staff, a refuge of Reagan-era hardliners, who stomped all over it, from Paul Wolfowitz on down." Cheney rejected it as well.

At a meeting of the National Security Council on 5 September 1991, which Bush called, according to Scowcroft, to review possible arms-control initiatives "while there were [Soviet and Russian] leaders in power . . . who would work with us," Cheney strongly resisted pursuing further cuts; he distrusted arms negotiations and feared they would encourage reductions in the defense budget. He had already decided that there would be no peace dividend from the demise of the Soviet Union, declaring in a speech the previous summer, "I don't think the notion of a military threat to the interests of the United States was invented by the Communist Party of the Soviet Union, and I think it will be there long after the Communist Party of the Soviet Union no longer wields the interest [sic] that it has in the past." (Powell thought otherwise. "I'm running out of demons," he told the *Army Times* that year. "I'm running out of villains. I'm down to Castro and Kim Il Sung.") Bush was determined, however, and at the end of the meeting he charged Cheney, Powell, Scowcroft, and the rest of the NSC, "I want to see some new ideas on nuclear disarmament. I don't want talk. I want solid proposals."

Given "Cheney's distaste for negotiated arms control," Scowcroft writes, it occurred to Bush's national security adviser after the NSC meeting that unilateral cuts in the U.S. nuclear arsenal might be a more effective approach, one that could "take advantage of the situation to solve a number of tactical nuclear weapons questions at the same time." Cheney himself had proposed reviewing the basing of tactical nukes in Germany, an embarrassment now that its two states were reunited. South Korea wanted U.S. nuclear weapons removed from its territory as part of its new initiative toward the North, but effecting such a removal in isolation might look like a U.S. withdrawal, which was not a signal the United States wanted to send to Kim Il Sung, the North Korean dictator. Navy ships carrying tactical nuclear weapons caused problems in countries such as Japan and New Zealand, which refused to allow nuclear weapons on their territory. "The sum of all these issues," Scowcroft concludes, "led me to suggest that we unilaterally declare we were getting rid of all tactical nuclear weapons (except air-delivered ones)." Cheney, skeptical at first, signed on when Scowcroft agreed that the weapons would be withdrawn but not destroyed. You can't be too careful: Like the troll under the bridge, watching out for billy goats, Cheney was determined to husband the republic's resources.

In his memoir, Powell sorts out the pile of proposals, which "far exceeded the elimination I had urged of artillery-launched nukes":

> Get rid of short-range nuclear weapons, like the Army's Lance missiles. Ground the Strategic Air Command bombers that had been on alert for the previous thirty-two years, and offload their nukes. Remove nuclear weapons from all ships, except for strategic missiles on Trident submarines. Get rid of multiple-warhead intercontinental ballistic missiles [i.e., MIRVs] and stick to single-warhead ICBMs. Shut down as many Minuteman missile silos as we dared.

"The chiefs," Powell concludes, "now responding to a radically changing world, signed on, as did Paul Wolfowitz and his hardliners. Cheney was ready to move with the winds of change. Within three weeks, on September 27, President Bush announced these unilateral nuclear reductions to the world."

Gorbachev, in what would turn out to be his last arms-control venture, welcomed Bush's initiative and responded a week later with initiatives of his own. Bush summarizes most of them in his memoir:

He wanted to destroy tactical nuclear weapons on sea forces and was prepared to make further cuts in strategic weapons. The Soviets would also take their heavy bombers off alert and stockpile their weapons. He proposed a one-year moratorium on testing, and was ready to discuss a plan to reduce fissionable materials. In addition, the Soviets would reduce their army by 700,000. [Bush had announced a 500,000-man U.S. reduction.] There were some differences in our positions, but on balance it was very positive and forthcoming. Mikhail told me he had spoken with Yeltsin, and indicated that Yeltsin was in agreement.

One offer Bush chose not to mention was Gorbachev's possibly tongue-in-cheek adoption of Ronald Reagan's pledge to share research on SDI: "We propose to study the possibility of creating joint systems to avert nuclear missile attacks with ground- and space-based elements."

In the wake of the dissolution of the Soviet Union, the United States would have to negotiate with a crowd of nuclear-armed successor states to win their commitment to these initiatives—another story for another book. Nevertheless, the unilateral initiatives of autumn 1991 may fairly be counted as the final, historic acts of demolition in the termination of the superpower nuclear-arms race that had burdened and threatened the world since 1949. After 1991 there would be a diminished second-tier arms race between India and Pakistan and efforts toward nuclear proliferation in North Korea, Libya, and Iran, aided by a private black-market operation out of Pakistan led by a Pakistani metallurgist named A. Q. Khan. The terrorist attacks on New York and Washington of 11 September 2001 would raise fears of an undeterrable terrorist nuclear strike with a stolen or homemade arsenal—the ultimate argument for complete, worldwide control of fissile materials and nuclear abolition. But such mutually arrogant, economically disastrous, self-defeating, and mortally dangerous nuclear militarism as that of the Soviet Union and the United States in the years of the Cold War will almost certainly never repeat itself on so large a scale, if only because no other nation, seeing the crushing folly of the first round, would choose to waste the resources.

MIKHAIL GORBACHEV WAS NO SAINT. He came to office fully committed to Soviet Communism, believing that its troubles and failures were the result of the corruption and incompetence of its leaders, not inherent in the system itself. Whether or not he ever completely gave up that belief continues to be a contentious question. His biographer Archie Brown offers one answer, based on the testimony of Gorbachev adviser Georgi Shakhnazarov:

Gorbachev and Reagan met for the first time at the Geneva summit in November 1985. The Soviet premier broached the idea of "common security" rather than unending competition and attacked Reagan's Strategic Defense Initiative. The president defended his dream of a shield against nuclear weapons and surprised his advisers by offering to share the system. *Below:* Two months later the space shuttle *Challenger* exploded on ascent when hot gas leaked from a failed seal—a lesson, ignored by Reagan, in the unpredictability of complex technological systems.

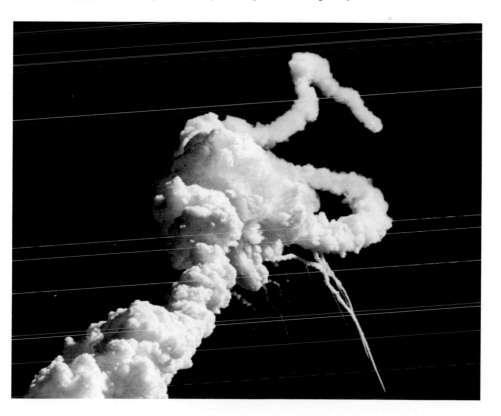

Gorbachev borrowed the idea of common security from a U.N. commission led by Sweden's Olof Palme *(left);* Gorbachev adviser Georgi Arbatov *(left in group photo at bottom),* a member of the commission, carried the message home. The new approach originated in the *Ostpolitik* of German chancellor Willy Brandt and his adviser Egon Bahr *(above).* "No longer against each other," Bahr wrote, "but only with each other shall we be secure." A back channel of Soviet and American scientists also encouraged arms reduction: Gorbachev advisers Yevgeny Velikov *(left),* Roald Sagdeev and Nikolai Shishlin *(bottom, with Susan Eisenhower).* Eisenhower, the president's granddaughter, and Sagdeev would marry, another opening between the two nations.

The scientists' back channel: Richard Garwin, Ann Druyan, Evgeny Chasov, Bernard Lown, Carl Sagan. *Center left:* Stanford physicist Sidney Drell. *Center right:* Gorbachev released Andrei Sakharov from exile to demonstrate his commitment to glasnost.

Gorbachev maneuvered the Soviet military to support nuclear abolition. *Below right:* Marshall Sergei Akhromeyev. Paul Nitze *(below)* advised pocketing Gorbachev's offers at the October 1986 Reykjavik summit without offering concessions.

Gorbachev arrived at Reykjavik with major arms concessions, including eliminating medium-range missiles in Europe and all strategic nuclear weapons. At one point he and Reagan nearly agreed to abolish all nuclear weapons if Reagan would limit SDI to laboratory research for ten years. On Richard Perle's advice, Reagan refused. An angry Reagan left the meeting feeling cheated, but Gorbachev saw that they had broken through.

German student pilot Matthias Rust's penetration of Soviet air defenses allowed Gorbachev to purge his military of resistance to perestroika.

Below: Lithuania led the way in breaking free of Soviet rule. KGB violence there tarnished Gorbachev's record.

At the UN on 7 December 1988 Gorbachev proposed reducing strategic arms and withdrew half a million troops from Europe.

Below: A year later, in November 1989, the Berlin Wall fell.

Right: A new administration doubted Gorbachev's sincerity and sat on its hands. Cheney thought that encouraging regime change could make the U.S.S.R. a democracy. *Left to right:* Wolfowitz, Cheney, George H. W. Bush, vice president Dan Quayle, chief of staff John Sununu.

Left: Cooperation between the U.S.S.R. and the U.S. during the first Gulf War improved relations; Secretary of State James A. Baker III and Foreign Minister Eduard Shevardnadze (seen here fishing at Baker's ranch in Jackson Hole) became good friends.

The signing of the Conventional Forces in Europe Treaty in November 1990 marked the real end of the Cold War. Under its terms, Warsaw Pact and NATO forces had to be equal and balanced, making aggressive war impossible. The Soviets destroyed 28,000 battle tanks.

Above: In August 1991, when a right-wing junta arrested Gorbachev and tried to stage a coup, Boris Yeltsin rallied Muscovites to resist. Gorbachev returned to find his presidency obsolete.

Below: Nationalism and ethnic identity proved to be the centrifugal forces that pulled the U.S.S.R. apart. Ukraine's Leonid Kravchuk, Shushkevich of Belarus, and Yeltsin met in December to draft the document that dissolved the Soviet Union. Gorbachev resigned on Christmas Day, 1991.

Dismissing the myth—increasingly disseminated both in Russia and abroad in 1991—that Gorbachev wished merely "to perfect the system" while "not touching its essence," Shakhnazarov quoted verbatim from his December 1989 conversation with Gorbachev in which Gorbachev said:

"Don't think that something will stop me, that there is a threshold through which I shall not be able to pass. Everything that is needed for the very deepest transformation of the system I accept without embarrassment. I will go as far as it is necessary to go for that. And if we speak about the final goal, insofar as it is possible today to be definite, that is integration into the world community by peaceful means. By conviction I am close to social democracy."

Anatoly Chernyaev, frustrated in the summer of 1990 with Gorbachev's seeming equivocation with Communist Party resistance to reform, has described this exchange with the Soviet president:

Gorbachev, while seeing and understanding everything, once again failed to draw the necessary conclusions. After meeting with secretaries of city, regional, and district Party committees during the Congress he told me: "Self-interested scum, they don't want anything except a feeding trough and power. . . ." He swore at them in the foulest language. I replied: "To hell with them, Mikhail Sergeyevich. You're the president. You see what kind of Party this is. And [so long as you remain at its head] you'll be its hostage, its permanent whipping boy." He replied:

"You know, Tolya, you think I don't see. But I do, and I've read your notes. And those of Arbatov and Shmelev too. All arguing the same thing, as if by design. That I should give up the general secretary's post [i.e., now that he was president]. But you must understand me, I can't let this lousy, rabid dog off the leash. If I do that, all this huge structure will be turned against me."

In an article defending perestroika written at Foros only days before the August 1991 coup, Gorbachev himself had this to say:

In the most general terms, the aims of *perestroika* are: economic freedom, political freedom, escape from isolation and the inclusion of the country in the mainstream of civilization. And the fundamental principle, if you look at it on a philosophical level, is the unacceptability of any ready-made models which might once again, however good the intentions, be imposed on society, to bring people happiness "from above."

. . . We did not realize immediately, of course, how far we had to go and what profound changes were needed. This gave rise to mistakes. . . .

All that is true. But we had to get involved practically in the new work, to acquire experience, look deep into the public mind as it was found to be after seventy years of an extraordinary regime and isolation from the rest of the world, and to learn to take account of all its specific qualities. It was only then that we came to the final conclusion that *perestroika* was not to be measured by the usual criteria or directed according to the principles of a previously dominant ideology. In the end we saw also that *perestroika* would not succeed within the framework of the old system, however much we tried to renew it and improve it. What was needed was a change of the whole economic and political system, the reform of the whole multinational state; that is, in all aspects a real revolution which had been prepared by all our own past and by worldwide progress.

At least two of those who participated directly at the highest level in bringing an end to the superpower nuclear-arms race gave Gorbachev the credit that the evidence demonstrates he properly deserved. François Mitterrand had this to say to Gorbachev at the G7 meeting in London in the summer of 1991:

> In the final analysis, you could have behaved like your predecessors, and the result would be catastrophic. History will record this. It will note not only the fact that you are transforming a country that does not have democratic traditions, but also how its relations with other countries have changed. Nations have been freed from the presence of foreign troops. Germany has been unified. All this is a result of your policy.

And James Baker, a tough, experienced politician, told Gorbachev in Moscow in September 1990, when Gorbachev and Bush were working together to confront Saddam Hussein's invasion of Kuwait:

> Mr. President . . . nobody in the world has ever tried what you and your supporters are trying today. We're talking about breaking a pattern of thinking that had been formed over seven decades. Naturally, it has to be done gradually, step by step, in order to be successful. . . . I'm not a rookie in politics, I've seen a lot, but I've never met a politician with as much bravery and courage as you have. I know that you have to deal with various limitations, to work within a certain political framework. I know how tough the steps you're so bravely taking are. And I'd like to tell you that President Bush shares this opinion.

Gorbachev himself, as it happens, unlike many Reagan and George H. W. Bush administration alumni, has been more than happy to share the credit for ending the Cold War—provided that the United States is willing to share the blame as well:

Both the Soviet Union and the United States bear their share of the responsibility for the fact that the post-war period was marked by a wasteful and dangerous confrontation, which exhausted resources and distorted not only the economy but society as a whole. In an unprecedented, far-reaching move, these same two countries took upon themselves the responsibility for dismantling, as soon as possible, the existing mechanisms of military confrontation between East and West, in order to employ the resources freed by disarmament to improve the well-being of the people. If it is true that the world has changed in the past few years, moving towards a period of genuine peace, the decisive contribution was made by the Soviet Union and the United States of America.

SPEAKING IN MUNICH IN LATE JANUARY 1987, not long before he resigned as assistant secretary of defense, Richard Perle ridiculed the idea of a nuclear-free world as "foolishness" that was "in no way mitigated by the conditions that Western statesmen routinely attach to its achievement in order to avoid dismissing the idea as the empty propaganda that it is." Perle disguised his ex cathedra censure of nuclear abolition as a deconstruction of Gorbachev's surprising proposals at Reykjavik, but his reference to "Western statesmen" makes it clear that he also meant to condemn Ronald Reagan's dream. "To argue that eliminating all nuclear weapons is a good idea," Perle went on, "but the year 2000 is too soon, or to suggest that it must proceed by steps or stages, or that it must await a more favorable conventional balance or the settlement of regional disputes, is a self-defeating obfuscation. These arguments—rationalizations, really—are deployed by officials and politicians who fear that the public would not support them if they simply rejected outright Mr. Gorbachev's beguiling maneuver."

Perle's conviction that fielding a nuclear arsenal is self-evidently necessary and useful raises the interesting question of whether nuclear weapons served the purposes that national leaders and deterrence theorists attributed to them during the years of the Cold War. The evidence indicates they did not.

Anatoly Dobrynin, for example, points out that both the United States and the Soviet Union based their military planning on the assumption that the other side would initiate a war with "a nuclear first strike with maximum devastation." At a conference in 1994 attended by Carter administration principals Cyrus Vance, Zbigniew Brzezinski, and Harold Brown, however, Dobrynin learned that "the Carter administration did not work under a first-strike doctrine against the Soviet Union (though Carter—like his predecessors—considered the possibility of using nuclear weapons first in case of a mass Soviet attack by conventional forces in Europe)." At the same conference, two high-ranking Russian generals, "both of them participants in nuclear war planning during the cold war, also confirmed that the Soviet government and general staff never followed a first-strike doctrine because, contrary to its public statements in the 1960s, they were convinced that nuclear war would cause unacceptable damage to both countries." Dobrynin concludes: "Nevertheless, hundreds of billions were spent to counterbalance the mutual fear of a sudden nuclear attack when—as we now know—neither side ever conceived of such a strategy because it knew what horrors it would visit on both."

The activist-scholar Richard J. Barnet, approaching the question from another angle, notes that although the United States "came out of World War II the most powerful nation on earth—perhaps, briefly, the paramount nation of all time—it has not won a decisive military victory since 1945 despite the trillions spent on the military and the frequent engagement of its military forces." What the United States got instead of victory, Barnet writes, was a national security state with a permanent war economy maintained by a military-industrial complex—much like the Soviet Union in those departments, but with a far greater reserve of resources to squander. "The national security state structures could not accomplish their task unless the American people were socialized to accept the idea that the only peace possible is a form of permanent war. . . . A threat of one sort or another to justify the continuous flow of resources to the military was now a fixture of American life."

Threat inflation, as I hope I have shown, was crucial to maintaining the defense budgets of the Cold War. The practice was carried to its extreme by Ronald Reagan, who with neoconservative coaching actually claimed that the U.S. nuclear arsenal was dangerously inferior to the Soviet arsenal, vulnerable to the first strike that Dobrynin reports was never a part of Soviet planning—and inflated his defense budgets accordingly. In words published in 1985 that describe the post-2000 George W. Bush years as well as the years of the Cold War, Barnet adds, "It is one of history's great ironies that at the very moment when the United States had a monopoly of nuclear weapons, possessed most of the world's gold, produced half the world's goods on its own territory, and laid down the rules for allies and adversaries alike, it was afraid." Fear was part of the program, the psychological response to threat inflation that delivered reliable votes. How did we come to such a pass? I was raised to believe that Americans were a courageous people. Weren't you?

All of these indignities to the person of the American electorate might have been justified if nuclear deterrence in its vast, glittering malevolence had actually deterred. The political scientist Jacek Kugler has his doubts, although he acknowledges the difficulty of proving the case. A good case can still be made, however.

"Deterrence," Kugler writes, "is more than simply avoiding massive war." Deterrence—limited conflict or nuclear threat—can only be called success-ful when nations can use it to achieve policy goals. "Nuclear nations . . . should consistently [be able to] impose their own policy preferences in dis-putes with nonnuclear nations, and should achieve draws with equivalent nuclear powers." If they don't—if a weaker nation achieves its goals in con-flict with a nuclear nation—then the technical term for the policy of the nuclear nation is not deterrence but appeasement. Yet "of the forty-odd crises since 1945 that involved nuclear powers directly," Kugler finds, refer-ring to the Berlin airlift, the Korean War, the Soviet invasion of Hungary, the building of the Berlin Wall, the Vietnam War, the Soviet war with Afghanistan, and a number of other such events, "over one-fourth escalated to the point that nuclear weapons were an important factor in the eventual settlement. Hence, the risk of nuclear war did not inhibit the escalation of crisis. In the remaining thirty crises that were not serious enough to warrant any nuclear threats, the nonnuclear nations attained desired policy objec-tives as many times as they failed." Thus, "nuclear nations have not *consis-tently* prevented opponents from attaining contested policy objectives. Of . . . fourteen extreme cases considered, five are resolved in favor of the nuclear contenders and nine produced outcomes that favor nonnuclear challengers." That is, in a large majority of cases, nuclear weapons failed to deter. Conventional forces, Kugler discovered, accounted far more precisely for the outcome of extreme conflicts in the nuclear era than did nuclear capabilities. "Paradoxically, the addition of nuclear considerations *detracts* from the effective accounting of crisis outcomes." Kugler draws surprising and promising conclusions from his analysis:

> The main and disturbing result of this investigation is that nuclear weapons, despite their massive destructive potential, may not be the unique element that accounts for the absence of massive war in the international system in the last 35 years [Kugler published his study in 1984]. Several indirect evaluations lead to this conclusion. First, nuclear nations do not have an obvious and direct advantage over other nuclear or nonnuclear nations in extreme crises. Rather, conventional capabilities are the best predictor of outcome of extreme crises regardless of their severity. Second, nuclear preponderance, which, logically, should enhance the likelihood of war, does not lead to demonstrably different

or less stable behavior than nuclear parity. . . . Finally, the most consistent reason for the absence of major war in the nuclear era seems to be the relative congruence of policy objectives among the nuclear powers, and this congruence cannot be directly traced to the buildup of nuclear arsenals.

If the failure of nuclear arsenals to reliably deter undercuts the arguments of those who believe in maintaining the national security state despite its parasitism, it also, Kugler pointed out, undercuts the arguments of those who believe the answer lies in arms control:

> Challenging the persuasive and ingrained notion that war can be prevented by the deployment of nuclear arsenals deprives decision makers of the one manipulatable tool in their possession to control conflict of great magnitude. Also, by questioning, even indirectly, the implication that nuclear arsenals can prevent massive conflict, one challenges other long-held deductions. One can no longer argue with impeccable logical conviction that effective arms limitations increase the likelihood of peace, or that, in the absence of arms limitation agreements, one can find reassurance in the buildup of nuclear arsenals capable of destroying the opponent. . . . The need to open fresh arenas in the search for peace is indeed urgent. To do otherwise is to believe in magic.

(One fresh arena that needs to be opened, it seems to me, is nuclear abolition, but that too must be the subject of another book.)

How much we have believed in magic in space, on earth, and under the sea is measured by a little-known story told in hearings before the Senate Armed Services Committee in late April 1986. Looking for arguments to defeat congressional endorsement of the Nuclear Freeze movement then rallying millions of citizens in the United States and Europe, the Department of Energy produced a report of past problems with U.S. nuclear warheads. The point of the report was to justify nuclear testing. In pursuit of that point, it revealed that "at times in the past, the warheads for a large part of the U.S. Fleet Ballistic Missile force [i.e., ballistic missile submarines] have been found to be badly deteriorated. At different times, a large fraction of the warheads either obviously or potentially would not work; they were obvious or potential duds." And not only were U.S. nuclear submarines patrolling the seas across the years of the Cold War with dud warheads on their missiles. At various times, there were duds among Minuteman ICBM warheads ("In late 1963 the AEC had to rebuild all the W56 warheads of the Minuteman ICBM force") and W45 warheads used in the Army's Little John tactical missile, the Navy's Terrier surface-to-air missile and the Marines' atomic demolition munition. In other words, at various times throughout the Cold War we were naked to our enemies. No doubt the Soviets had such troubles as well. Yet both sides plowed on, following the blind, plodding oxen of mutual belligerence, believing ourselves to be protected. Magic indeed: a house of cards, with all our lives at risk.

AFTER A SHAKEN MIKHAIL GORBACHEV RETURNED from Foros in late August 1991, Boris Yeltsin's Russia rapidly divested him of his powers. Gorbachev resigned as general secretary of the Communist Party of the Soviet Union on 24 August 1991, the same day Ukraine declared its independence. Belarus, Moldova, Azerbaijan, Uzbekistan, Kyrgyzstan, and Tajikistan followed. Kazakhstan's president, Nursultan Nazarbayev, closed the nuclear-weapons test site at Semipalatinsk. Yeltsin in turn closed Novaya Zemlya, the other Soviet test site, in October. "The coup had given a strong impulse to disintegration," Gorbachev writes. "All the republics declared their independence in September and October 1991. The separatists felt that their day had come." The Congress of People's Deputies had functioned as an interim parliament, but with republics spinning off right and left it no longer had a constituency. Under Gorbachev's guidance it issued a resolution supporting central control over Soviet nuclear weapons and NPT membership as a requirement for independence and then dissolved itself.

Stanislav Shushkevich, the nuclear physicist who had cursed Gorbachev after Chernobyl for Moscow's refusal to authorize potassium iodide tablets for Byelorussian children, had gone into politics when glasnost had opened up the opportunity. By the time Byelorussia declared its independence and renamed itself Belarus, Shushkevich was head of the Belarusian Supreme Soviet, and thus became the first Belarusian head of state. He, Yeltsin, Nazarbayev, and other heads of state tried to work with Gorbachev in October 1991 to negotiate an all-union treaty that would hold the former Soviet Union together in a confederative state. "In Gorbachev's conception of the union," Yeltsin writes, "a strong center would be preserved that would determine matters of defense and some fiscal issues. A single president would remain . . . [to] represent the Union of Sovereign States . . . in dealings with foreign countries." But "to Gorbachev's immense consternation, one after another of the former Union republics began to drop out. . . . They all dreamed of elevating their own status; all of them wanted to become full-fledged members of the UN." It was obvious, Yeltsin concludes, "that Gorbachev, not because of anyone's ill will, was, historically speaking, painting himself into a corner."

The people of Ukraine endorsed independence with an overwhelming majority vote on 1 December 1991 and elected Leonid Kravchuk as their first president. At that point Yeltsin, Shushkevich, and Kravchuk realized, Yeltsin writes, that they "had to find another way" than Gorbachev's desperate union, which Kravchuk, on behalf of his new nation, refused to join. When the union treaty had fallen apart in October, Gorbachev had stalked off in fury to his office. Shushkevich and Yeltsin had been delegated to go to him and coax him back. "Yeltsin and I went off to make peace," Shushkevich told me in one of our conversations, "walking down the hall in the Kremlin. I said to Yeltsin, 'You have a beautiful place, but we have a beautiful place in Belarus. Come and visit.' Yeltsin said, 'Sure.' " The beautiful place Shushkevich had in mind was the Bison Lodge in the Belovezhskaya Pushcha nature reserve in western Belarus, a semi-wilderness where the last of Europe's ancient forest bison, relatives of the bison that once populated the American West, had been restored across the decades by German and Soviet wildlife experts to cater to the hunting tastes of German generals and Soviet premiers. It had been a Brezhnev favorite.

A week after the vote in Ukraine at the beginning of December, Yeltsin, Kravchuk, and Shushkevich met at the Bison Lodge in the Belovezh forest. "We were meeting," Yeltsin writes, "to decide the fate of the Soviet Union." Shushkevich told me less dramatically that he met "not to consider dissolution but problems in Belarus. We had to do something, because an economic crisis was looming. Gas and oil were impossible. Belarus and Ukraine would have frozen and starved." But when they got together and talked it over, Shushkevich added, "we realized the whole system didn't work."

Yeltsin recalled "a wonderful winter evening with a soft snowfall." He felt a certain imperial discomfort when he thought about letting go of Ukraine and Belarus "perhaps forever, offering them in a new agreement a guaranteed status on a par with Russia." Shushkevich suggested they go hunting or walk in the woods, Yeltsin says, "but no one felt like strolling. We were all too overwrought." Yeltsin's aides had prepared documents—"an enormous amount of work"—which suggests that the meeting in the Bison Lodge was less indefinite than the participants present it to be. So does the fact that it was kept a close secret, "even guarded," Yeltsin writes, "by a special security division." Shushkevich told me at another time of the purpose of the meeting. "Something had to be done. Everyone had his own agenda. Yeltsin wanted to get rid of Gorbachev. I wanted independence for Belarus. And Krauchuk wanted independence for Ukraine." The documents Yeltsin offered, and over which the three heads of state then labored in turn, resulted in an agreement dissolving the old Soviet Union and replacing it with a

Commonwealth of Independent States, with Minsk as its capital. Other republics could join if they chose, or go their own ways.

Separating from the Soviet Union compromised Belarus's economy, Shushkevich told me. Under the old system, essentially colonial, the region had been designated an industrial center, sending finished machinery and goods to Moscow in exchange for food and energy supplies produced elsewhere in the U.S.S.R. Separating would compromise that arrangement. Then why break away? I asked him, expecting, from someone trained in science and skillful at statecraft, a pragmatic answer. His explanation, which parallels Yeltsin's explanation of Russia's separation, surprised me with its vehement nationalism:

> First a little history. In 1918, Byelorussian patriots resolved that Byelorussia should be an independent state. At about the same time, Ukraine, Lithuania, Latvia, Estonia, and Finland also announced the formation of independent states. This actually worked for some of them (Finland, for example), but not for others. Later on, people who had such intentions were relentlessly destroyed by the Bolsheviks. We came back to the idea only in 1990. On 27 July 1990, the [Byelorussian] Supreme Soviet that had been elected to office in 1990 passed the Declaration of State Independence. This had only symbolic meaning, since Russia—which had also announced its own sovereignty earlier—had intended Ukraine and the other republics to be its constituent parts.
>
> By 1991, an advantageous situation had developed: Boris Yeltsin wanted to become the sovereign ruler of Russia, and had the right to do so, since he had been elected president by the people of Russia. But Gorbachev believed that he outranked Yeltsin, since he had been elected president by the Congress of People's Deputies of the U.S.S.R. Given this situation, Yeltsin decided that the easiest solution would be to strip Gorbachev of his authority by officially declaring the cessation of the U.S.S.R.'s functions as a subject of international law. This was fairly logical, since it wasn't a union of states anymore (Moscow no longer controlled this large conglomerate); but the U.S.S.R. officially continued to exist. Moreover, fearing that a breach of the Yalta Agreements might lead to chaos or even to nuclear war, President Bush (Senior) announced in an October 1991 speech in Kiev that the West would recognize the U.S.S.R. only as a complete whole and warned about the danger of its disintegration, supposing that this would give rise to several new countries with nuclear weapons. For these reasons, Kravchuk and I took advantage of Yeltsin's desire to become the sole master of Russia and helped him to make Gorbachev the de jure president of a nonexistent state. We believed our primary achievement to be Russia's recognition of the independence of Belarus and Ukraine (as well as that of the other republics of the former Soviet Union).

Yeltsin's explanation:

The idea of a new kind of state system had not been born yesterday, and not just in my head or that of Shushkevich or Kravchuk. If we recall the years 1917–1918, immediately after the democratic February revolution [i.e., the liberal socialist democratic Russian Provisional Government under Alexander Kerensky], the republics immediately began the process of succession, eventually moving toward independence. Several new national governments were declared in the territory of the Russian empire, including in the Caucasus and Central Asia. Ukraine led the process. The Bolsheviks managed to suppress all the nationalist uprisings, forcing peasants and soldiers into a civil war, although the revolution was supposedly spontaneously proletarian. With an iron fist, the Soviets strangled the liberation struggles, executed the national intelligentsia and dispersed national parties.

Seventy-three years later, the wheel had come full circle. As Yeltsin, Kravchuk, and Shushkevich signed the historic documents, they discovered that no one had thought to provide a copying machine, just as there had not been one at Reykjavik, and because of the extreme security they couldn't call for one. Rather than use carbon paper they set two fax machines side by side and faxed the documents from one to the other to make copies. Yeltsin made a point of calling Bush first (after which he asked Shushkevich to call Gorbachev, who was predictably furious). "On December 8, 1991," Bush writes, ". . . Boris Yeltsin called me from a hunting lodge near Brest, in Belarus. Only recently elected President of the Russian Republic, Yeltsin had been meeting with Leonid Kravchuk, President of Ukraine, and Stanislav Shushkevich, President of Belarus. 'Today a very important event took place in our country,' Yeltsin said. 'I wanted to inform you myself, before you learned about it from the press.' Then he told me the news: the Presidents of Russia, Belarus, and Ukraine had decided to dissolve the Soviet Union."

SOVEREIGNTY, ONCE ATTRIBUTED TO DIVINE RIGHT, later to the people, today has an additional locus of authority: control of a nation's nuclear weapons. When George H. W. Bush delivered his notorious "Chicken Kiev" speech in Kiev on 1 August 1991, for example, cautioning the Ukrainians against separating from the Soviet Union, he was motivated in part by his fear of what Shushkevich described to me as "Bush realizing that the nuclear monster could split up into many little monsters." The ambassador and arms negotiator James Goodby remembers Baker using the phrase "Yugoslavia with nukes" to characterize what Goodby calls "the nightmare that could result from a loss of central authority and control over [Soviet] nuclear weapons." After the meeting at the Bison Lodge, Shushkevich told me, "there was a second meeting in Alma-Ata [the capital of Kazakhstan, now Almaty] to discuss the transfer of nuclear weapons to the CIS." That meeting, held on 21 December, after Gorbachev had announced his forthcoming resignation, gave the other new republics an opportunity to join the CIS, which most of them did.* Four leaders, Shushkevich said, would officially take control of the former Soviet nuclear arsenal: "Yeltsin, Nazarbayev, Kravchuk and Shushkevich. The day after that meeting we received the communications equipment that would connect these four people—it was called 'Metal'—and there was always a man around us carrying it. We only tried it once, and it worked. But it was all a farce. All those weapons of course were controlled by Yeltsin, which we understood. And you Americans also understood that it was a pretense." Pretense or not, Belarus alone had eighty-one MIRVed mobile missiles on its territory, "sufficient to eradicate Europe and the United States." There were hundreds more ICBMs on the territories of Ukraine and Kazakhstan, a problem that Baker would undertake to solve in the immediate months ahead. In the end it would take five years.

It remained then for Gorbachev to transfer the *chemodanchik,* the "little suitcase" that contained the missile launch codes, to Yeltsin. The two bitter rivals met for the last time in Gorbachev's Kremlin office on 24 December, had what Yeltsin calls a "protracted and difficult" conversation, and formally accomplished the transfer. After the meeting, the two officers assigned to protect the *chemodanchik* left with Yeltsin. "It was like being in the front line of a war," Gorbachev said of his years as general secretary and then president. "I lived through several lives, and I don't know how I survived."

Gorbachev called Bush at Camp David on Christmas morning 1991. "My dear George," he said, "greetings! Let me begin with something pleasant. Merry Christmas to you and Barbara and your family!" He went on, Bush writes, "to sum up what had happened in his country: the Soviet Union had ceased to exist. He had just been on national TV to confirm the fact, and he had transferred control of Soviet nuclear weapons to the President of Russia."

"I attach great importance to the fact that this aspect is under effective control," Gorbachev concluded. "I've signed a decree on this issue that will come into effect immediately after my final statement. You may therefore feel at ease as you celebrate Christmas, and sleep quietly tonight."

---

* The exceptions were the three Baltic states and Georgia.

THE SUPERPOWER NUCLEAR-ARMS RACE had ended after forty-two dangerous years. Afterward, some of those in America who had promoted that confrontation with inflated threats, fearmongering, and misleading or fraudulent intelligence claimed shamelessly that the United States had won the Cold War. The world had won with the two superpowers at least partly disarmed. The Soviet Union had dissolved into its original components, a socioeconomic disaster for most of the new nations and especially for Russia, where life expectancy continued to decline, descending to a truncated 59.0 years for Russian males in 2000, and the population to plummet from a wide excess of deaths over births. The United States was left still standing, seemingly triumphant, but across the Cold War, nuclear weapons and weapons-related programs alone had cost the nation at least $5.5 trillion. Carl Sagan estimated in 1992 that other Cold War costs took the total even higher, to about $10 trillion. That, Sagan wrote in indignant benediction, was "enough to buy everything in the United States except for the land." What we bought for a waste of treasure unprecedented in human history was not peace nor even safety but a pervasive decline in the capacity and clemency of American life. As in the countries of the former Soviet Union, but not so severely, even American male life expectancy stalled compared to the European democracies and Japan.

The investment banker and Federal Reserve Board Chairman Marriner Eccles argued as long ago as the 1960s that "over-kill spending of the military" was "responsible for our financial inability to adequately meet the problems of our cities (poverty, crime, riots, pollution) and our rapidly expanding educational requirements." The Columbia University economist Seymour Melman noted in 1974 that "the extent of economic deterioration in the cities of the U.S. would be a mystery forever if we had no way of explaining the unique consequences of nonproductive [military] economic activity. After all, the decay of America's cities occurred during a period of economic growth in the United States. . . . [But] the additional taxes generated by the new income were being preempted for the military." Melman dismisses the triumphalist right-wing claim that the United States with its superior economy could afford to spend the Soviet Union into bankruptcy—one argument offered for the huge defense budgets of the Reagan years. "The purveyors of this shrewd idea," he writes, "never allowed themselves to admit the possibility that the American war economy could also devour the civilian economy of the United States." Further, "the assumption that sustained war economy brings economic and allied well-being encounters a cruel contrast in the shape of what is forgone in the United States in health care, housing, education and minimum nutrition. These are all recognized areas of public responsibility partly because the consequences of deficiencies in these realms have blighting effects on the entire society." Melman quotes the Yale scholar Bruce Russett on the long-term effects of investing in military power rather than civilian needs:

> Since future production is dependent upon current investment, the economy's *future* resources and power base are thus much more severely damaged by the decision to build or employ current military power than is current indulgence. According to some rough estimates . . . an additional dollar of investment in any single year will produce 20–25¢ of annual additional production in perpetuity. Hence, if an extra billion dollars of defense in one year reduced investment by $292 million, thenceforth the level of output in the economy would be *permanently* diminished by a figure on the order of $65 million per year.

"The dollars that pay for the operation of the military system," Melman concludes, "finally represent something forgone from other aspects of life, especially those parts that are also dependent on financing from the community's public budgets." Which should be indisputable, since civil destitution is exactly what happened to the Soviet Union.

Some argue that the buoyant American economy of the 1990s disproved these economic predictions. The defense budget began declining in the late 1980s and was cut by about $10 billion per year during the Bill Clinton presidency, but such deep budget deficits had accumulated during the Reagan era that the savings went largely to deficit reduction. A "Report Card for America's Infrastructure" issued for the year 2001 by the American Society of Civil Engineers (ASCE) confirms the continuing and even worsening decrepitude of the United States's physical plants in the years after the Cold War. For 2001, the nation's civil engineers gave American infrastructure the following grades:

Aviation: D
Bridges: C
Dams: D
Drinking Water: D
National power grid: D+
Hazardous waste: D+
Navigable waterways: D+
Roads: D+
Schools: D–

Solid waste: C+
Transit: C–
Wastewater: D

Nor had these grades increased by more than a plus sign by 2005; in the
majority of categories they had further declined. The ASCE estimated at that
time that "all levels of government and the private sector" would need to
invest $1.6 trillion over a five-year period to correct the pervasive deficiencies
it found.

Far from victory in the Cold War, the superpower nuclear-arms race and
the corresponding militarization of the American economy gave us ram-
shackle cities, broken bridges, failing schools, entrenched poverty, impeded
life expectancy, and a menacing and secretive national-security state that
held the entire human world hostage. "If you try to look at [the Cold War]
from today's point of view," Gorbachev's adviser Georgi Shakhnazarov concluded at the 1998 Brown conference, "from the height of a bird's flight, so to
speak, the politics of both sides were not moral. Each side, of course, thought
they were doing the right thing."

The politics of both sides were not moral because they put the human
world at mortal risk, with no reasonable gain in security, for domestic
advantage and the international play of power. Robert Oppenheimer saw the
dishonesty as early as 1953, when he wrote sardonically in *Foreign Affairs*:

> The very least that we can say is that, looking ten years ahead, it is likely to be
> small comfort that the Soviet Union is four years behind us, and small comfort
> that they are only about half as big as we are. The very least we can conclude is
> that our twenty-thousandth bomb, useful as it may be in filling the vast muni-
> tions pipelines of a great war, will not in any deep strategic sense offset their
> two-thousandth. . . . We may anticipate a state of affairs in which two Great
> Powers will each be in a position to put an end to the civilization and life of the
> other, though not without risking its own. We may be likened to two scorpions
> in a bottle, each capable of killing the other, but only at the risk of his own life.

The discovery of how to release nuclear energy was a fact, not a choice, a
new understanding of the natural world. It revealed that there was no limit
to the amount of energy that might be packaged into small, portable, and
relatively inexpensive weapons; that there could be no defense against such
weapons, each of which could destroy a city; that therefore a policy of common security in the short run and a program of abolition in the long run
would be necessary to accommodate the new reality and avoid disaster.

Recoiling from such urgencies, which would require negotiation, compromise, and a measure of humility, we chose instead to distend ourselves into the largest scorpion in the bottle. Obstinately misreading the failure of our authoritarian counterpart on the other side of the world, to our shame and misfortune, we continue to claim an old and derelict sovereignty that the weapons themselves deny.

NOTES

ONE TO THE CHERNOBYL SARCOPHAGUS

3 BYELORUSSIAN INSTITUTE RADIATION EVENTS: Irina and S. Shushkevich interviews, April 2003; Alexievich (1997), pp. 180–81; Yaroshinskaya (1995), p. 16; Scherbak (1989), p. 26.

4 A LARGE CACHE OF MONEY: Volkogonov (1998), p. 430.

4 "I WAS THE FIRST . . . WALL": S. Shushkevich interview, Apr. 2003.

4 "WE JUST . . . THIS": Gorbacheva (1991), p. 5.

4 "I EMPHASIZED . . . ORGANIZATIONS": Gorbachev (1995), p. 167.

4 "THE ELIMINATION . . . DEVELOPMENT": ibid., p. 173.

4 SOVIET MILITARY-INDUSTRIAL COMPLEX . . . STATE BUDGET: Gorbachev, in his *Memoirs*, gives this number as a percent of "the state budget": Gorbachev (1995), p. 215. For a different view see Vitaliy V. Shlykov, The structural militarization of the Soviet economy: the unknown phenomenon, in Genin (2001), p. 101: "Research conducted at the end of the 1980s by the Institute for Economic Forecasting of the Soviet Academy of Sciences, showed that if the output of the USSR machine-building industry were to be rated at world market prices, the share of military equipment would account for more than 60 percent of the output, and consumer goods not more than 5 percent." See also Reed (2004), p. 219; Clem (1986), p. 3.

4 "A CONCRETE . . . CENTURY": quoted from *Izvestia* in Mazo (2004), p. 16.

5 AT 2:30: Alexievich (1997), p. 181.

5 DETAILS OF PROMPT CRITICAL EXCURSION: John Dunster, *Nature* 333, 811 (30 June 88); Wilson (1987), p. 1636.

5 THE *PYATACHOK* "BEGAN TO . . . DANCE": Josephson (2000), p. 256.

6 ABOUT HALF THE TOTAL RADIATION: Z. Medvedev (1990), p. 45.

6 EXPLOSION DETAILS: see in particular ibid., p. 28ff.

6 A CONTAINMENT DOME WOULD HAVE CONFINED THE REACTION: "Had the Soviet Union built its RBMKs with a containment shield, the world community would have been spared the events at Chernobyl and their aftermath." Ebel (1994), p. x.

6 CONTAINMENT DOME BEYOND SOVIET CAPACITY: Z. Medvedev (1990), p. 232.

6 INFORMATION ABOUT ACCIDENTS DENIED: Potter emphasizes this point: Potter (1989), p. 12.

6 THIRTEEN ACCIDENTS: see list at Potter (1989), pp. 9–12. Also see Z. Medvedev (1990), pp. 17–19.

7 "SOMETHING AWFUL . . . EXPLOSION": this and the following quotation cited in *Nature* 342 (10) (2 Nov. 1989).

7   BRYUKHANOV DELAY ALERTING KIEV: Mould (2000), p. 300, n. 13.

7   FIREFIGHTERS: Ebel (1994), pp. 6–7.

7   SEVEN A.M.: Z. Medvedev (1990), p. 44.

7   "1-2-3-4": Legasov (2000), p. 289.

7   CIVIL DEFENSE ALERTED TWO HOURS AFTER EXPLOSIONS: Potter (1989), p. 58.

8   GORBACHEV ALERTED, POLITBURO MEETING: Gorbachev (1995), p. 189.

8   EIGHT P.M. GOVERNMENT COMMISSION ARRIVAL: Legasov (2000), p. 291.

8   "THE REACTOR . . . HOSPITALIZED": ibid., p. 290.

8   "THEY HAD . . . SPOT": ibid., p. 293.

8   "A *WHITE* . . . LUMINESCENCE": ibid., p. 291. Original italics.

8   GRAPHITE BURNING RATE: ibid., p. 292.

9   PRIPYAT TOWN COMMITTEE . . . SANDBAGS: Shcherbak (1989), pp. 57–58.

9   ANTOSHKIN ARRIVAL: Potter (1989), pp. 50–51.

9   "THE FIRST . . . RUNS": *Current Digest of the Soviet Press* 38 (19), p. 10.

9   "[AT 110 . . . SACKS": quoted in Z. Medvedev (1990), pp. 168–69. Ellipses in original text.

9   "IF YOU . . . LEAD": quoted in Schmid (2005), p. 285, n. 53. I altered Schmid's translation slightly to save the rhyme.

9   20 TO 80 RADS PER FLIGHT: Z. Medvedev (1990), p. 168.

10   DEATHS AMONG LIQUIDATORS: "The Ukrainian government has estimated the number of deaths among cleanup workers alone as 7,000–8,000. Total civilian casualties are not known and may never be known." Marples (1996a), p. 1. Marples's total is disputed by knowledgeable Russian authorities (Sig Hecker, personal communication, Oct. 2006).

10   "THEY FLUNG . . . REACTOR": Alexievich (1997), p. 76.

10   QUENCHING MATERIALS: Z. Medvedev (1990), p. 56.

10   MORE THAN ELEVEN MILLION POUNDS: 5,000 tonnes. Mould (2000), p. 45.

10   REM LEVELS: Wilson (1987), p. 1637.

10   KIEV BUSES AND TRUCKS: Mould (1988), p. xiii.

10   THE DRIVERS . . . SECRECY: Hopkins (1993), p. 41.

10   "HAVE YOUR . . . YOU": Shcherbak (1989), p. 64.

11   10 REM PER HOUR: Wilson (1987), p. 1637.

11   DECONTAMINATION CENTER: *Current Digest of the Soviet Press* 36 (23), p. 14.

11   POTASSIUM IODIDE DISPENSED: G. Medvedev (1991), p. 186.

11   POTASSIUM IODIDE EFFECTIVENESS: Zanzonico and Becker (2000).

11   "IN EVERY . . . TABLETS": S. Shushkevich interview, Apr. 2003.

12   NESTERENKO NARRATIVE: Alexievich (1997), p. 210ff.

12   "EVERY POLITICAL . . . ACCIDENT' ": S. Shushkevich interview, Apr. 2003.

13   "THE WORST . . . AVERTED": Gorbachev (1987c), p. 522.

13   "THAT WAS . . . HATED HIM": S. Shushkevich interview, Apr. 2003.

13   "IN THOSE FIRST . . . MILLIONS": Alexievich (1997), p. 185.

13   "OPINION CHANGED . . . SILO": Mould (2000), pp. 48–49.

14   BRITISH GOVERNMENT INFORMED: ibid., p. 49.

14   HELSINKI RADIATION LEVELS: Rippon (1986).

14   CROSSED INTO SWEDEN, STUDSVIK, FORSMARK: Hopkins (1993), pp. 37–38; Z. Medvedev (1990), pp. 195–96; L. Devell et al. (1986). "Initial Observations of Fallout from the Reactor Accident at Chernobyl." *Nature* 321 (192) (15 May 1986).

14   "COMBINED WITH . . . WEAPONS": L. Devell et al., "Initial Observations."

14   RUTHENIUM . . . VAPORIZED: ibid.; Z. Medvedev (1990), p. 2.

15 THE GOVERNMENT COMMISSION . . . MEETING: Z. Medvedev (1990), p. 53; Gorbachev (1995), p. 189.

15 "WE CATEGORICALLY . . . TRUTH": quoted in Shevardnadze (1991), p. 173.

15 "HOW CAN . . . THINKING": Shevardnadze (1991), pp. 173–74.

15 "POSSESSED BY . . . CAMP": Vitaliy V. Shlykov, The Soviet system of mobilization preparedness, in Genin (2001), p. 66.

15 "IT WAS . . . EASY": Shlykov in Genin (2001), p. 68.

15 RBMK ADAPTED IN THE 1970S: Marples (1996a), p. 3.

16 GORBACHEV TRUSTING THE EXPERTS: Chernyaev (2000), p. 65.

16 "UNSHEATHED . . . CLAWS": Shevardnadze (1991), p. 174.

16 "NOTHING TERRIBLE . . . IT": Gorbachev (1995), p. 191.

17 "FROM THE . . . CREATED": quoted in Marples (1986), p. 1.

17 "I WAS PHONED . . . IT": Hans Blix interview, Las Vegas, Sept. 2005.

17 POLITBURO OPERATIONAL GROUP: Yaroshinskaya (1995), p. 123.

17 "THE EMISSION . . . NORMALLY": Current Digest of the Soviet Press 38 (16), 21 May 1986, p. 1.

18 TEN-KILOMETER . . . ZONE: Mould (1988), p. xiii.

18 A NEW . . . THREAT: see Z. Medvedev (1990), p. 57ff.

18 MONDAY LEVEL: ibid., p. 61.

18 "AT FIRST . . . HEROES": Alexievich (1997), pp. 76–77.

19 116,000 PEOPLE, 86,000 CATTLE: Mould (1988), p. xiii.

19 "WE DIDN'T . . . LIVES": Alexievich (1997), p. 34.

19 "IT COULD . . . SOLID": Z. Medvedev (1990), pp. 57–58.

19 LIQUID NITROGEN PROJECT: ibid., p. 60.

19 PUMPING OUT BUBBLER POOL: Shcherbak (1989), p. 98.

19 FILLING POOL: Z. Medvedev (1990), p. 58; Potter (1989), p. 56.

20 "WE SAT . . . ANYTHING": Alexievich (1997), p. 146.

20 "IN SERIOUS . . . VICTIMS": Current Digest of the Soviet Press 38 (16), 21 May 1986, p. 3.

20 SECRET PROTOCOLS: These documents were subpoenaed by a Russian parliamentary commission investigating the Chernobyl accident late in 1991. See Yaroshinskaya (1995), p. 123ff.

20 "1,882 PEOPLE . . . CONDITION": Yaroshinskaya (1995), p. 124.

20 BLIX MOSCOW BRIEFING: Petrosyants (1988), pp. 43–44.

20 "I KNOW . . . CONTINUED": Hans Blix interview, Sept. 2005.

20 "SO THAT . . . MUCH": Shevardnadze (1991), p. 174.

20 "THE NUMBER . . . CHILDREN": quoted in Yaroshinskaya (1995), p. 124.

21 "IN ONE . . . 34": quoted in ibid., p. 125.

21 "WE CIRCLED . . . HAPPENED": Hans Blix interview, Sept. 2005.

21 "THE HELICOPTER . . . OVER": Petrosyants (1988), pp. 44–45.

21 3.5 REM PER HOUR: Z. Medvedev (1990), p. 68.

21 "AND THEN . . . ENOUGH": Hans Blix interview, Sept. 2005.

21 CHERNOBYL FALLOUT . . . TNT: Paton et al. (2003), p. 5.

21 "THE SOVIET . . . ACT": Director-General's statement for Roundtable 7, "The Future of Nuclear Power," World Energy Conference, 13th Congress, Cannes, Oct. 1986.

22 "IT WAS . . . JUDGMENT": Z. Medvedev (1990), p. 70.

22 "SHED LIGHT . . . REFORMS": Gorbachev (1995), p. 193.

22 "SEVERELY AFFECTED . . . TRACKS": ibid., p. 189.

22 GORBACHEV SPEECH, 14 MAY 1986: Gorbachev (1987c), p. 519ff.

22 POLITBURO PROTOCOL FOR 12 MAY: Yaroshinskaya (1995), p. 125.

23 THIRTEEN KILOTONS: the current (c. 2006) official yield of the Hiroshima bomb.

24 THREE HUNDRED THOUSAND TONS OF LEAVES: Mould (1988), p. xiv.

24 "WE BURIED . . . LIVE": Alexievich (1997), pp. 93–94.

24 "MORE THAN . . . ANALYSIS": quoted in Mould (2000), pp. 198–99.

24 " 'CHERNOBYL DAY' . . . EYES": Shevardnadze (1991), p. 175.

24 "CHERNOBYL HAPPENED . . . CHANGED": Alexievich (1997), p. 170.

24 7 MAY 1986 AGRICULTURAL PRODUCTS BAN: "The Soviets End Their Silence—But the Damage Keeps Mounting," *Business Week*, 19 May 1986, p. 44.

25 "THE DECISION . . . PRIORITY": Z. Medvedev (1990), pp. 241–42.

25 27TH PARTY CONGRESS GOALS: ibid., p. 69.

25 "CHERNOBYL WAS . . . FAILED": Shevardnadze (1991), p. 176.

25 " 'PROFOUNDLY REALISTIC' . . . WEAPONS": Volkogonov (1998), p. 482.

25 "SENIOR POLISH . . . WAR": Potter (1989), p. 83.

25 "I WAS . . . EXCHANGE": George Shultz to Ronald Reagan, reproduced in Reagan (1990), p. 710.

26 "HIS MIND . . . 'DE-IDEOLOGIZATION' ": Chernyaev (2000), p. 67.

26 "CHERNOBYL . . . HANDS?": Wohlforth (1996), p. 33. (Translation slightly corrected.)

26 "GLOBAL NUCLEAR . . . POLITICS": quoted in Volkogonov (1998), p. 483.

26 "WHAT HAPPENED . . . IT": quoted in Chernyaev (2000), p. 67.

TWO **MOSCOW DOES NOT BELIEVE IN TEARS**

27 "FREE AND EASY": Remnick (1994), p. 152.

27 "MY [MATERNAL] GRANDFATHER . . . LAND": Gorbachev and Mlynar (2002), p. 14. Emphasis added.

27 "LENIN GAVE . . . SAYS": Gorbacheva (1991), p. 16. Emphasis added.

28 "NOT REALLY . . . PROCEEDS": Conquest (1986), p. 108.

28 "HE PARTICIPATED . . . CHAIRMAN": Gorbachev (1995), p. 23.

28 "LOYALTY TO . . . OFFICE": Dolot (1985), p. 93.

28 "THE LIQUIDATION . . . CLASS": quoted in Conquest (1986), p. 117.

28 "THE CAPITALISTS . . . VILLAGE": quoted in Gareth Jones, "Seizure of Land and Slaughter of Stock," *The Western Mail*, 8 Apr. 1933.

28 CONQUEST ESTIMATES . . . PEOPLE": Robert Conquest, hearing testimony, U.S. Commission on the Ukraine Famine, 8 Oct. 1986.

28 TEN MILLION SMALL FARMS: Conquest (1990), p. 18.

28 KULAK TRANSPORT AND TEMPORARY HOUSING: Viola (2001), pp. 735–41.

28 8.5 TO 9 . . . VORTEX": Volkogonov (1988), p. 166.

29 "EVEN BY . . . RUINS": Conquest hearing testimony, 8 Oct. 1986; ibid.

29 "THE STAVROPOL . . . DISTRICT": Conquest (1986), p. 123.

29 "IT IS . . . TEARS": ibid., p. 130.

29 "HOW INSIGNIFICANT . . . FARMS": Doder and Branson (1990), p. 11.

29 "UP TO . . . CAMPAIGN": Dolot (1985), p. 137.

29 "WITH COLLECTIVIZATION . . . INDUSTRY": Malia (1990), p. 311.

30 INDUSTRIALIZATION . . . 12.5 MILLION: Conquest (1986), p. 168.

30 "THIS INCREASE . . . 26 PERCENT": ibid., pp. 168–69.

30 GRAIN REQUISITIONS: ibid., p. 174.

30   "ALL TOO . . . FAMILIES": Khrushchev (1974), p. 108, quoted in Conquest (1986), p. 176.

30   "I REMEMBER . . . ORDEAL": Dolot (1985), pp. 137–38.

30   "ONE OF . . . LAW": ibid., pp. 156–57.

31   PASSPORTS DENIED TO RURAL POPULATION: Gorbachev (1995), p. 36.

31   "THE FAMINE . . . ESCAPE": Carynnyk et al. (1988), p. 259.

32   "PEOPLE HAVE . . . SEVERELY": ibid., p. 264.

32   "FOR NOT . . . YEAR": quoted in Remnick (1994), p. 149.

32   "THE FAMINE . . . YEARS": Gorbachev (1995), p. 27.

32   "BEARING TWO . . . IMMEDIATELY": ibid.

32   A MILLION, FIVE MILLION: Volkogonov (1988), p. 307.

33   "FIRST REAL TRAUMA": Gorbachev (1995), p. 24.

33   "AFTER GRANDFATHER'S . . . SINCE": ibid.

33   "THE HEAD . . . PRISON": ibid., p. 26.

33   "I REMEMBER . . . ELSE": ibid.

33   "HE WAS . . . MISFORTUNES": ibid.

34   "THE TRAGEDY . . . PERVERSION": Remnick (1994), p. 149.

34   "IN THE . . . LIVES": Dolot (1985), p. 92.

34   "NOT ONLY . . . POSSIBLE": Gorbachev and Mlynar (2002), p. 17.

34   "THE SHOPS . . . THEN": Gorbachev (1995), pp. 27–28.

35   "THE THIRD . . . COUNTRYSIDE": Conquest (1986), p. 181.

35   2,500 MTS, PARTY OFFICIALS, AND SECRET POLICE: ibid., pp. 181–2.

35   "THE VILLAGE . . . GONE": Gorbachev (1995), p. 28.

35   "GORBACHEV PASSED . . . GOLD": Sheehy (1990), p. 47.

35   ON THE RARE . . . PROBLEMS: ibid.

35   "UNBEARABLE TERROR": Gorbachev (1995), p. 29.

35   "FIERY ARROWS . . . SOUND": ibid.

35   "RUMORS OF . . . GAS": ibid., p. 30.

36   GORLOV TOLD SHEEHY: Sheehy (1990), p. 46.

36   GORBACHEV HIDDEN; MONTHS OF OCCUPATION: Gorbachev (1995), p. 30.

36   "FELT AS . . . WOOD": ibid., p. 31.

36   "THE FAMILY . . . WELL": ibid., p. 33.

36   "I WROTE . . . US": ibid.

36   "UNSPEAKABLE HORROR . . . WORLD": ibid., p. 34.

37   "SPREADING THE . . . RUSSIA": first Komsomol program, quoted at http://www.iremember.ru/nagrady/Komsomol.htm (accessed 5 Oct. 2005).

37   "A GREAT . . . FRIENDS": Gorbachev (1995), p. 36.

37   "CORRECTING TEACHERS . . . MEETING": quoted (apparently from a *Washington Post* story by David Remnick) in Doder and Branson (1990), p. 7.

38   "DISLIKE OF . . . GENERICALLY": Doder and Branson (1990), p. 31.

38   THIRTY-SEVEN MILLION TONNES, SEVENTEEN MILLION TONNES: Gorbachev (1995), p. 38.

38   "VERY, VERY . . . YEARS": Sheehy (1990), p. 49.

38   120 MILLION TONNES: compiled from USDA National Agricultural Statistics Service Track Records, U.S. Crop Production (April 2003), online.

38   "WE SOMEHOW . . . WINTER": Gorbachev (1995), p. 38.

38   "THE TERRIBLE . . . DROUGHT": ibid.

39   "I WAS . . . AWARDS": ibid.

39   "THE PROBLEM . . . RUSSIA": Mlynar (1980), pp. 10–11.

39　"ABSENCE OF . . . COMMUNISM": ibid., p. 11.

39　GORBACHEV HAD HOPED TO STUDY PHYSICS: See his statement to that effect quoted in Doder and Branson (1990), p. 8.

39　SAGDEEV ON GORBACHEV DENIED ACCESS TO PHYSICS COURSE: See Sagdeev (1994), pp. 25–26.

40　SAKHAROV RECRUITED WHILE A POSTDOC: See Sakharov (1990), p. 94ff.

40　LENIN: a connection made by Doder and Branson (1990), p. 8.

40　"I HAD . . . ME": Gorbachev (1995), p. 41.

40　ROMANTIC AND INNOCENT: See Doder and Branson (1990), p. 14.

40　"THE SOVIET . . . COURTYARD": Mlynar (1980), p. 20.

40　"EVERYTHING WAS . . . PASSIONATELY": Gorbachev (1995), p. 42.

40　ALUMNI REMEMBER: see, e.g., Remnick (1994), p. 160.

41　PARTY MONITOR AND ORGANIZER: Doder and Branson (1990), p. 10.

41　"MASSIVE IDEOLOGICAL . . . CONCLUSIONS": Gorbachev (1995), p. 45.

41　"BEFORE THE . . . PROCESS": Gorbachev and Mlynar (2002), p. 23.

41　STALIN DEATH SCENE: Volkogonov (1988), p. 574.

41　"THE INSTRUCTOR . . . LIFE": Gorbachev (1995), p. 47.

41　" 'MISHA, WHAT'S . . . KNOW' ": Gorbachev and Mlynar (2002), p. 21.

41　"WE ADVANCED . . . PLACE": Gorbachev (1995), p. 47.

41　"THE DENSITY . . . AWAY": Mlynar (1980), p. 25.

42　"A STONY . . . FEELINGS": Gorbachev (1995), p. 47.

42　"THE GENERATION . . . -OLDS": Gorbacheva (1991), p. 47.

42　"THE NEVER-ENDING . . . LIKE?": ibid., p. 17.

42　"AT THE . . . PEOPLE' ": ibid., pp. 16–17.

42　"I DO . . . PEOPLE' ": ibid., pp. 186–87.

43　MAXIM TITORENKO'S TRANSFER TO CHERNIGOV: Jürgens (1990), p. 18.

43　TITORENKO PURGED: The German biographer who offers this information says it came from "Lydia Budyka, a pediatrician [who] is one of Raisa's closest friends" and who was willing to talk "only under certain conditions: following each interview, she had to refer back to Raisa"—who then allowed or disallowed the information to be used. I find no evidence that Raisa Gorbachev ever publicly disputed or repudiated the biographer's information. Nor, of course, did she endorse it, and the conditions under which Budyka spoke with the biographer allowed Raisa Maximovna deniability. See Jürgens (1990), p. 12.

43　"I REMEMBER . . . OUT": Gorbacheva (1991), p. 18.

44　"A DAILY . . . SOCIAL": ibid., p. 20.

44　"I RECEIVED . . . HISTORY": ibid.

44　"IN OUR . . . SYSTEM": ibid., p. 93.

44　"OUR RELATIONSHIP . . . MARRIED": ibid., pp. 61–62.

45　"A BEAUTIFUL . . . IT": Gorbachev (1995), p. 51.

45　"YOU'VE GOT . . . INCENTIVE": ibid., p. 50.

45　"I KNOW . . . INTELLECT": quoted in Gorbacheva (1991), p. 69.

45　"I HAD . . . BEFORE": Gorbachev (1995), p. 50.

THREE　**A HIERARCHY OF VASSALS AND CHIEFS**

46　"STAVROPOL STRUCK . . . EVERYWHERE": Gorbacheva (1991), p. 76.

46　AGRICULTURAL REFORMS: See Fainsod (1956), p. 32.

46　"SHEER MISERY . . . MIND": Gorbachev (1995), p. 59.

47 "I DON'T . . . LIFE": Gorbacheva (1991), p. 83.

47 "THE CHIEF . . . TERROR": Berman (1963), p. 933. Berman discusses the Special Board's abolition.

47 "HUNDREDS . . . REFORMS": Berman (1963), p. 936.

48 "A SUBSTANTIAL . . . CITIZENS": ibid., p. 944.

48 "THE MAIN . . . DEVELOPMENT": Gorbachev and Mlynar (2002), p. 27.

48 "PRACTICED BRUTAL . . . [HIM]": Paul Halsall, *Modern History Sourcebook: Nikita Khrushchev, Secret Speech, 1956*, excerpts, www.fordham.edu/halsall/mod/khrushchev-secret.html (accessed 1 Aug. 2005).

48 "LENIN HAD . . . REVOLUTION": Volkogonov (1998), p. 203.

48 "HOW WERE . . . INTIMIDATION": ibid., p. 205.

48 "MORALLY DISCREDITED . . . SYSTEM": Gorbachev (1995), p. 70.

48 "I WAS . . . 1930S": quoted in Archie Brown (1996), p. 39.

48 "I HAD . . . REVELATIONS": Gorbachev and Mlynar (2002), p. 20.

48 "THE CONCRETE . . . MIND": Mlynar (1980), p. 27.

49 "TO UNDERSTAND . . . WAS": Gorbachev and Mlynar (2002), p. 21.

49 "AM I . . . DID?": quoted in Remnick (1994), p. 150.

49 "I DID . . . FUTURE": Gorbachev and Mlynar (2002), p. 25.

49 "WE HAD . . . LIFE": Shevardnadze (1991), p. 23.

49 "SHAKEN . . . FAITH": ibid., p. 20.

49 "THE EAST . . . 1960S": ibid., p. 21.

50 "IT IS . . . POLITICS": ibid., pp. 20–21.

50 "IF WE . . . ADD HUNGARY": János M. Rainer, "Decision in the Kremlin, 1956—the Malin notes," posted at The Institute for the History of the 1956 Hungarian Revolution, http://www.rev.hu/intezet/index.html (accessed 25 Jan. 2006).

51 "I WAS . . . KRAI": Gorbachev (1995), pp. 73–74.

51 "BOTH THE . . . SYSTEM": Gorbachev and Mlynar (2002), p. 48.

51 "THE PEASANT . . . BOOTS": Gorbacheva (1991), pp. 94–96.

52 "AND NOT . . . CONCEPTS": ibid., p. 96.

52 "THE TRADITIONAL . . . CITIZEN": Gorbachev (1995), p. 118.

52 FOOD RATIONING, VIOLENT DEMONSTRATION: Malish (1984), p. 301.

52 "THE LEADERSHIP . . . BREAD' ": ibid.

52 "FROM 13.1 . . . 1963": Volkogonov (1998), p. 211.

52 "A REFINED . . . ME": Gorbachev (1995), p. 74.

53 "A MILD . . . MAN": Volkogonov (1998), p. 262.

53 "WE . . . STALINISM": Gorbachev and Mlynar (2002), pp. 31–32.

53 THE GORBACHEVS' TRAVELS ABROAD: Doder and Branson (1990), p. 20; Archie Brown (1996), p. 328, n. 14.

53 "MY PREVIOUS . . . COUNTRIES?": Gorbachev (1995), pp. 102–3.

53 YEFREMOV WAS FURTHER FRUSTRATED AND ANGERED: According to ibid., pp. 79–80. Volkogonov (1998), p. 440, claims that Yefremov supported Gorbachev's appointment for second secretary as well as, later, first secretary.

54 "I SUDDENLY . . . US": Gorbachev and Mlynar (2002), p. 43.

54 "THE KGB . . . COUP": quoted in Kramer (1992), p. 21.

54 SOVIET NUCLEAR ALERT: This discussion follows Kramer (1992), pp. 42–43.

54 "ENGENDERED A . . . STAGNATION": Gorbachev and Mlynar (2002), p. 65.

54 "PRACTICALLY PUT . . . MANAGEMENT": Gorbachev (1995), p. 83.

54 "GRADUALLY, AND . . . CENTER": Gorbachev and Mlynar (2002), p. 47.

55 "MANIPULATORS . . . PUNISHABLE' ": Gorbachev (1995), p. 94.

55   GORBACHEV "WAS . . . CREATURE": Doder and Branson (1990), pp. 30–31.

55   "WE MADE . . . RIGHT": Gorbachev (1995), pp. 95–96.

55   "THE ENTIRELY . . . FUTURE": quoted in Arbatov (1992), p. 259.

55   "A BRILLIANT . . . STAVROPOL": quoted in Archie Brown (1996), p. 50.

56   "GORBACHEV COULD . . . LANGUAGE": Remnick (1991), n.p.

56   "DOES NOT . . . BELIEVE": quoted in Scheer (1988), p. 147.

56   "MY TRIPS . . . THEMES": Gorbachev and Mlynar (2002), p. 50.

56   "I AM . . . COMPLICITY": quoted in Doder and Branson (1990), p. 21.

56   "I HEARD . . . WHOLE": Gorbacheva (1991), p. 119.

57   KULAKOV'S MANNER OF DEATH: Kotkin (2001), p. 39. Gorbachev (1995), p. 97, has
     Kulakov dying of "heart failure."

57   "THOSE BASTARDS . . . MOSCOW": Arbatov (1992), p. 259.

57   "THE TRAIN'S . . . WELL": Doder and Branson (1990), p. 39.

57   "MY CHARACTER . . . AUTUMN": Gorbachev (1995), p. 105.

57   FOOD IMPORT COSTS: Doder and Branson (1990), p. 40.

58   GROSS OUTPUT: Malish (1984), p. 308, Table 3. Rubles converted at the rate of five
     rubles to the dollar.

58   1972 WHEAT DEAL DESTABILIZING: See Luttrell (1973).

58   LIBYA, $20 BILLION: Gates (1996), p. 77.

58   OIL AND GAS PRODUCTION AND PRICES: Reed (2004), p. 215.

58   "THE CARELESS . . . PEOPLE": Gorbachev (1995), p. 118.

58   ELECTRICAL SUPPLY: ibid.

58   "DESPITE THE . . . ENTERTAINMENT": ibid.

58   "ONE-FIFTH . . . THEM": Doder and Branson (1990), pp. 40–41.

58   "MUCH MORE . . . COUNTRYSIDE": Gorbachev (1995), p. 120.

59   SEVENTEEN MILLION TONNES: ibid., p. 116.

59   "THE GROWING . . . RESOURCES": Arbatov (1992), p. 215.

59   "GROMYKO AND . . . GRAIN": Gorbachev (1995), pp. 116–17.

59   FOOD PROGRAM: See Malish (1984), p. 302ff.

59   40 BILLION RUBLES: Gorbachev (1995), p. 121.

59   "THIS PROBLEM . . . SAVINGS": ibid.

60   "N. K. BAIBAKOV . . . RESOURCES": ibid.

60   "WE BOTH . . . TURF": ibid.

60   "WITH TECHNOLOGICAL . . . PREGNANT": Gorbachev et al. (1996).

60   "THE MILITARY-INDUSTRIAL . . . MILITARY": Arbatov (1992), p. 201.

61   "I LEARNED . . . IN": Chernyaev (2000), p. 26.

61   "ARGUING . . . SENSELESS": Chernyaev (2000), p. 26.

61   "A PRETTY . . . AID": Arbatov (1992), p. 198.

61   MINISTRY OF DEFENSE INSISTED: ibid., citing Oleg Kalugin and "quite a few other
     pieces of information."

61   "AS A . . . WEAPONS": Arbatov (1992), p. 203.

61   "SOMETHING LIKE . . . SATURATED WITH THEM": Vitaliy L. Katayev, MIC: the
     view from inside, in Genin (2001), pp. 54–56.

62   "TO KEEP . . . 'WARM' ": Shlykov in Genin (2001), p. 85.

62   1930S POLICY: ibid., p. 82.

62   "UNDERMINED WESTERN . . . RACE": Arbatov (1992), p. 203.

62   "THE REGIME . . . TROUBLE": Pryce-Jones (1995), p. 39.

62   $1 BILLION ANNUALLY PER $1 PRICE DECLINE, "THE CREAKY . . . HOUSE": Reed
     (2004), p. 215.

62   "STRAIGHT FROM . . . APPARAT": Arbatov (1992), p. 191n.

62 "ANDROPOV AND . . . IT": Gorbachev (1995), p. 146.

63 "LEADING . . . THINKERS": Chernyaev (2000), p. xxi.

63 "THE RELATIONS . . . COUNTRY": quoted in Ellman and Kontorovich (1997), p. 263.

63 110 STUDIES: according to Nikolai Ryzhov, quoted in Archie Brown (1996), p. 64.

63 "THEIR ANALYSIS . . . PERESTROIKA": Gorbachev (1987a), p. 27.

63 YAKOVLEV CRITICISM OF BREZHNEV CULT: Yakovlev's exile is usually attributed to his 1972 article on Soviet nationalism, but see Kaiser (1991), p. 110, for this explanation, Yakovlev's own.

63 "TERRIBLY ASHAMED": quoted in Kaiser (1991), p. 108.

63 "WE SPOKE . . . PRINCIPLES": quoted in Archie Brown (1996), p. 81.

63 "MY CANADIAN . . . THOUGHT": Gorbachev (1995), p. 149.

64 "HE REALIZED . . . SYSTEM": ibid., p. 153.

64 "INDECISIVENESS . . . GENERATION": Arbatov (1992), p. 258.

64 "KOSTYA [CHERNENKO] . . . CHOSEN": quoted in Roxburgh (1991), p. 18.

64 "LOOKED AT . . . ELSE": Chernyaev (2000), p. 7.

64 "NOT PSYCHOLOGICALLY . . . PERSON": Archie Brown (1996), p. 69.

64 "BRILLIANTLY": quoted in Archie Brown (1996), p. 73.

64 "I LIKE . . . TOGETHER": Margaret Thatcher Foundation Archive.

65 " 'EVERYTHING'S ROTTEN . . . PITSUNDA": Shevardnadze (1991), p. 37.

65 GORBACHEV SPEECH OF 10 DECEMBER 1984: Unless otherwise cited, all extracts are taken from "Gorbachev Keynotes Ideological Meeting," *Current Digest of the Soviet Press* 36 (5), 9 Jan. 1985, pp. 1–5, 26–27.

65 GORBACHEV INTRODUCED . . . WORLD: He had used "perestroika" before, but not in the same context; see Archie Brown (1996), pp. 122–23.

65 "PRICES . . . CREDIT": omitted from *Pravda* transcript but quoted in Kaiser (1991), p. 77.

65 " 'WAS UNAMBIGUOUSLY . . . FAR": Archie Brown (1996), p. 80.

66 GORBACHEV MEETING WITH GROMYKO: Gorbachev (1995), p. 164.

66 "MIKHAIL . . . THIS": Gorbacheva (1991), pp. 4–5.

66 "THE HALL . . . APPLAUSE": Chernyaev (2000), pp. 19–20.

FOUR **"THE BOMBER WILL ALWAYS GET THROUGH" (I)**

69 WEAPONS NUMBERS AND YIELD; "A FEW . . . WELL": McNamara (1986), p. 5.

69 "IT MUST . . . WEAPON": Otto Robert Frisch and Rudolf Peierls, quoted in Rhodes (1986), p. 325. The complete Frisch-Peierls memorandum is reprinted in Ronald W. Clark, *Tizard*, MIT Press, 1965, p. 214ff.

70 NATIONS THAT WORKED ON NUCLEAR-WEAPONS DEVELOPMENT: James Walsh, panel discussion, "Why Do States Abandon Nuclear Ambitions," United Nations, NPT RevCon, 10 May 2005.

71 "A SCIENTIFIC . . . PROGRAMS": Memorandum for the President from Secretary of Defense Robert McNamara, "The Diffusion of Nuclear Weapons With or Without a Test Ban Agreement," 16 Feb. 1963, National Security Archive Electronic Briefing Book *The Making of the Limited Test Ban Treaty, 1958–1963*, Document 47, at http://www.qwu.edu/~nsarchiv/index.html (accessed 6 Mar. 2006).

71 "PERSONALLY, I . . . HAZARD": John F. Kennedy, News Conference Number 52 (21 Mar. 1963), transcription at http://www.jfklibrary.org/jfkpressconference_630321 .html (accessed 9 Mar. 2006).

71 SOVIET UNION'S FIRST PROPOSAL: Graham and LaVera (2003), p. 29.

71 "ALL NUCLEAR . . . MONITORED": Eisenhower News Conference, 11 Feb. 1960, partial text at http://www.clw.org/archive/coalition/eis0260.htm (accessed 9 Mar. 2006).

72 IRELAND'S PROPOSAL TO U.N. GENERAL ASSEMBLY: Graham and LaVera (2003), p. 100.

72 CONCERNS OF NONNUCLEAR STATES: See full discussion at Graham and LaVera (2003), pp. 102–5.

72 "TO NEGOTIATE . . . ARSENALS": Graham and LaVera (2003), p. 102.

73 TEXT OF NPT: See ibid., pp. 108–12.

73 TREATIES: for texts and commentary See Graham and LaVera (2003).

74 "THE CENTRAL . . . CIVILIZATION": Schneider and Dowdy (1998), p. 189.

74 BERIA ORDERED COPY: Yuli Khariton, personal communication, 1992.

74 RDS-1 PILOT SERIES: Podvig (2001), p. 2. For the full story of the early years of the Soviet nuclear-weapons program see this reference, Holloway (1994), and Rhodes (1995).

74 RDS-1 SERIAL PRODUCTION: Podvig (2001), p. 2.

75 STOCKPILE NUMBERS: Norris and Arkin (1994).

76 "SUCH A . . . LIGHT": quoted in Rhodes (1995), pp. 401–2.

76 "THE NOTION . . . WEAPONS": ibid., p. 403.

76 THE JOINT . . . 1950: ibid., pp. 406–7.

77 JOINT CHIEFS HAD ENDORSED SURPRISE ATTACK: See Rhodes (1995), p. 225.

77 "OFFENSE . . . DEFENSE": JCS 169 1/7 (30 June 1947), quoted in Rhodes (1995), p. 225.

77 "WHAT THE . . . IT": quoted in Rhodes (1995), p. 407.

77 "TO CONTINUE . . . SUPER-BOMB": ibid.

77 "WE HAD . . . RUSSIANS": ibid.

78 SOVIET FULL-SCALE THERMONUCLEAR WEAPONS PROGRAM APPROVED: Podvig (2001), p. 74.

78 "HE SAID . . . KIDS' ": quoted in Herken (1980), p. 11.

78 "TO HAVE . . . ONE": Millis (1951), p. 458.

78 "A SYSTEM . . . 1948": Rosenberg (1983), pp. 11–12.

78 "SINCE WE . . . WEAPONS": quoted in Rosenberg (1983), p. 22.

79 "LED PRESIDENT . . . OFF": Robert Bowie in Hunter and Robinson (2005), Chapter 7.

79 1950, 1953 SITES AND EMPLOYEES: Douglas Lawson, in Hunter and Robinson (2005), Chapter 8.

79 6.7 PERCENT; CAPITALIZATION: Anders (1987), p. 4.

79 1953–1955 STOCKPILE NUMBERS AND YIELDS: Norris and Arkin (1994), p. 4.

79 "IS FAR . . . WHOLESALE": quoted in Rosenberg (1983), pp. 26–27.

79 "THE WAR . . . MEN": quoted in Rhodes (1995), p. 583.

79 "WERE ALL . . . JAPAN": Rosenberg (1983), p. 20.

79 "THAT JUST . . . GOVERNMENT": ibid., p. 31.

79 "FIRMLY CONVINCED . . . III": William B. Moore memorandum, appended to Rosenberg and Moore (1981–1982), p. 27.

80 "WITH THE . . . INCIDENTAL": Rosenberg (1983), p. 15.

80 "WHAT WAS . . . INDUSTRY?": quoted in Rosenberg (1983), p. 15.

80 "THE GENERAL . . . DIRT' ": Gates (1996), p. 21.

80 "THE BOMBER . . . THEM": MacArthur (1999), pp. 125–26.

80 "NO AIR . . . PREPARED": quoted in Rhodes (1995), pp. 227–28.

81 "IN GENERAL . . . U.S.": Samuel E. Anderson briefing, appended to Rosenberg and Moore (1981–1982), p. 32.

81   "IN LIGHT . . . UNTHINKABLE": Bundy (1969), pp. 9–10.

81   "I COULDN'T . . . AGAIN": quoted in Holloway (1994), p. 339.

81   "THE RETALIATORY . . . COUNTRY": Tannenwald (1999), p. 51.

82   "HE SAID . . . SECURITY": ibid., p. 23.

82   "THESE WEAPONS . . . WEAPONS": Todd White in Hunter and Robinson (2005), Chapter 2.

83   "THE LARGE . . . REQUIREMENTS": Douglas Lawson in Hunter and Robinson (2005), Chapter 8.

83   "IT WAS . . . BE": Leon Smith in Hunter and Robinson (2005), Chapter 8.

83   "WE WERE . . . ALONG": John Foster in Hunter and Robinson (2005), Chapter 5.

FIVE   **"THE BOMBER WILL ALWAYS GET THROUGH" (II)**

84   THREE CATEGORIES OF TARGETING: see Rosenberg (1983), pp. 16–17.

84   "ALL BUT . . . LEVEL": Rosenberg and Moore (1981–1982), p. 11.

84   1,700 DGZS: Moore memorandum, appended to Rosenberg and Moore (1981–1982), p. 18.

84   "LAY DOWN . . . HOURS": Moore memorandum, appended to Rosenberg and Moore (1981–1982), p. 25.

84   AS FAR . . . THE BETTER: See Rosenberg's description of the Navy's "devastating critique" of Air Force targeting plans, and USAF chief of staff Thomas White's rebuttal, at Rosenberg (1983), p. 51.

85   SHARES OF DEFENSE APPROPRIATIONS: Rosenberg (1983), p. 29.

85   BISON A, BISON B: Podvig (2001), p. 341; p. 376, Table 6A.3.

85   "DEPLOYED ON . . . ALERT": Podvig (2001), p. 342.

85   REFUELING ON ICE AIRSTRIPS: ibid.

85   "SUCH ACTION . . . US": quoted in Sagan (1987), p. 31, n. 28.

85   1960 WEAPONS NUMBERS AND YIELDS: Norris and Arkin (1994), p. 4.

86   "THE RULE . . . DESTRUCTION": ibid., p. 2.

86   FOUR ICBMS: Kaplan (1983), p. 286.

86   SOVIET VULNERABILITIES: Sagan (1987), pp. 27–29.

86   "THE SOVIETS . . . STATES": James Schlesinger in Hunter and Robinson (2005), Chapter 16.

86   "IT BECAME . . . WEAPONS": General Lyman L. Lemnitzer in Sagan (1987), p. 41.

86   WEAPON SHARES TO SAC AND THEATER COMMANDERS: ibid.

86   "THE COMPLEX . . . PLAN": Burr (2004), Document 28, p. 3.

86   "TIME OVER TARGET" CONFLICTS: Burr (2004), Document 28, p. 4; Sagan (1987), p. 42, n. 1.

87   "ATOMIC OPERATIONS . . . POSSIBLE": quoted in Burr (2004), Document 28, p. 4.

87   KENNEDY'S SIOP-62 BRIEFING: Sagan (1987), pp. 41–51.

87   "WE ESSENTIALLY . . . POLAND?' ": Robert McNamara in Hunter and Robinson (2005), Chapter 16.

87   3,153 WEAPONS, MEGATONNAGE: Norris and Arkin (1994), p. 4.

87   "BECAUSE OF . . . MEASURE": Sagan (1987), p. 51.

87   285 MILLION DEAD: Kaplan (1983), p. 269.

87   GENERAL DAVID SHOUP STORY: ibid., p. 270.

88   ONE HUNDRED KILOTONS: Eden (2004), p. 27.

88   "ONLY BLAST . . . SIOP": Burr (2004), Document 20, p. 3.

88   KISTIAKOWSKY TO OMAHA: Kistiakowsky (1976), p. 403.

88   "THE JSTPS . . . REQUIREMENTS' ": Burr (2004), Document 23, p. 1914.

88 "MIGHT ACTUALLY . . . ATTACK": Solomon and Marston (1986), p. 17.

88 "THE EXTRAORDINARILY . . . SPEEDS": Eden (2004), p. 27.

89 "GROUND WINDS . . . ELSE": ibid., pp. 25–26. For Eden's Washington scenario see p. 15ff.

89 "A NUCLEAR . . . WEAPON": Solomon and Marston (1986), p. 52.

89 "ABOUT 300 . . . SECOND": Eden (2004), p. 16.

89 "WE MUST . . . D.C.": quoted in Eden (2004), p. 16.

89 "TOSSING IT . . . BARREL": Hap Arnold, quoted in Eden (2004), p. 72.

90 "THE WORLD . . . EQUIPMENT": Eden (2004), p. 290.

90 "WE DON'T . . . IMPORTANT": quoted in Eden (2004), p. 276.

90 "ADMIRAL COLLEY . . . SENSE": Eden (2004), p. 276.

90 EDEN LISTS: ibid., p. 228.

91 "ULTIMATE . . . DETERRENT": quoted in Rosenberg (1983), p. 52.

91 BURKE TOLD THE JOINT CHIEFS: as described in Rosenberg (1983), p. 57.

91 "THE NAVY . . . PROBLEM": Rosenberg (1983), p. 57.

92 "THAT MILITARY . . . RESERVE' ": ibid., p. 55.

92 "THAT IN . . . SUFFICIENT": Burr (2004), Document 1, p. 4.

92 SOVIETS LIMITED BOMBERS: Podvig (2001), p. 4.

93 "THEATER" NUCLEAR MISSILES, SUBMARINES: ibid., p. 3.

93 PODVIG WRITES: ibid., p. 5.

93 "THE LEVEL . . . DEPLOYMENT": ibid.

93 TWENTY-FOUR HOURS TO LAUNCH: ibid., p. 181, Table 4A.2.

93 "COULD DELIVER . . . TERRITORY": ibid., p. 4.

93 1,576 SAC BOMBERS: Cowley (2005), p. 223.

94 "THE U.S. . . . CRISIS": Podvig (2001), p. 6.

94 "THE RESULTS . . . PROBLEM": Tannenwald (1999), p. 24.

94 "WELL, MR. . . . AGAIN": quoted in Powers (1996), n.p.

94 "HUMILIATION IN . . . STATE": Gates (1996), p. 29.

94 "DURING THE . . . HARD": Tannenwald (1999), pp. 24–25.

94 "A SIMPLE . . . STATES": Podvig (2001), p. 201.

95 SS-9: ibid., p. 127.

95 SOVIET SUBMARINES PATROLLING COASTS: ibid., p. 7.

95 "WERE QUIETLY . . . BUILDUP": Reed (2004), p. 96.

95 FRACTIONAL-ORBITAL SS-9: Podvig (2001), p. 196.

95 "THE SOVIETS . . . WELL": Gates (1996), p. 29.

95 U.S. STOCKPILE AT 32,200: Schwartz (1998), p. 45.

96 "ONE OF . . . OURS": Sheldon (2004), p. 68.

96 "OTHER CONSIDERATIONS . . . CHOICE": Bundy (1988), p. 551.

96 "WOULD BE . . . SYSTEM": ibid.

96 "THE INADEQUACY . . . ANYWAY": Alexei Arbatov, Verification: servant or master of disarmament? Carnegie International Nonproliferation Conference "Sixty Years Later," Washington, D.C., 7–8 Nov. 2005.

97 U.S. REMAINED AHEAD: See Norris and Arkin (1994), Estimated U.S. and Soviet/Russian nuclear stockpiles, 1945–94.

97 "MASSIVE AND . . . EFFORT": Nitze (1976), p. 3.

97 "A NUCLEAR- . . . SIDE": ibid., p. 5.

97 "UNLESS ACCURACIES . . . THEM": Lodal (1976), p. 3.

97 "THAT IMPLEMENTATION . . . SURVIVE": Nitze (1976), p. 3.

98 "WE DID . . . PROGRAM": Sheldon (2004), p. 68.

98 "Q.—MCNAMARA . . . EACH": Burr (2004), Document 24B, p. 4.

99 "EACH INDIVIDUAL . . . INSANE": Robert McNamara, personal communication, Washington, D.C., Nov. 2005.

99 "EACH OF . . . SUPPORT": McNamara (1986), pp. 5–6.

99 "DESPITE AN . . . CATASTROPHE": ibid., p. 44.

100 "MOVED FROM . . . CERTAINTY": McNamara (1995), p. 341. The number 162 is McNamara's.

100 "WE ARE . . . SECURITY": quoted in Gaddis (1997), p. 221.

100 "GREATER THAN . . . STAFF": quoted in Rodberg and Shearer (1970), p. 300.

100 MCNAMARA TOLD JOHNSON: Kaplan (1983), p. 317; Kunsman and Lawson (2001), p. 49.

101 "WE HAD . . . UNION": Sheldon (2004), p. 69.

101 "YOU CAN'T . . . STREETS": quoted in Kunsman and Lawson (2001), p. 121.

101 "WE ARE . . . WAR": Nielsen (1963).

101 THIRTY-ONE OTHER MEMBERS: Cahn (1998), p. 30.

SIX **THE SORCERER'S APPRENTICES (I)**

102 "WERE NOT . . . ONE": Nitze (1989), p. 43.

103 "THIS EXPERIENCE . . . CONCEPT": "Interview with Secretary of the Navy Nitze," by Alfred Goldberg, 15 June 1966, Burr and Wampler (2004), Document 6, p. 1.

103 "TO UNDERTAKE . . . UNION": quoted in NSC-68 (1950), p. 2.

104 "THE PURPOSE . . . OUT": quoted in Sanders (1983), p. 31.

104 "WANTED TO . . . THREAT": Paul Y. Hammond, quoted in Sanders (1983), p. 30.

104 "ANIMATED BY . . . ANNIHILATION": NSC-68 (1950), I, p. 3.

104 "THE DESIGN . . . DESIGN": ibid., I, p. 4.

104 "THUS UNWILLINGLY . . . POWER": ibid., I, p. 5.

104 SOVIET WAR LOSSES: cited from several contemporary sources in Rhodes (1995), p. 179.

105 "DRIV[ING] TOWARD . . . DAMAGE THIS COUNTRY": NSC-68 (1950), I, pp. 12–13.

105 "TO CHECK . . . DOMINATION": ibid., III, p. 13.

105 "A RAPID . . . WORLD": ibid., III, p. 12.

106 "ONCE THE . . . PACTS": Karl R. Bendetsen Oral History Interview, 21 Nov. 1972, Harry S. Truman Presidential Library.

106 "NOT ONLY . . . NOT": Hobbes (1651), Chapter VI, cited in Robin, 2004, p. 43.

106 "DIMENSION OF . . . INFERENCE": Robin (2004), p. 43.

106 "ADDRESSED WHAT . . . WAY?": Nitze (1989), p. 95.

107 "AT THE . . . THROUGH": Academy of Achievement (1990), p. 8.

107 "WE LIVED . . . JUNGLE": Nitze (1989), p. xi.

108 "ONE TIME . . . GANG": Academy of Achievement (1990), p. 9.

108 "TO HAVE . . . STRATEGY": quoted in Sanders (1983), p. 256.

108 "IN THAT . . . CONSPIRACY": NSC-68 (1950), II, p. 3.

108 "A PRINCIPAL DRAFTSMAN": Bundy (1988), p. 337.

108 "YOU HAVE . . . TIME": Herbert York interview, National Security Archive.

109 "THE USSR . . . PROGRAMS": Burr and Wampler (2004), Document 2, p. 14.

109 "PREDICTED A . . . U.S.": Kistiakowsky (1979), p. 6.

109 "NO MORE . . . 1961": Wohlstetter, Nitze, et al. (1974), p. 85.

109 "MANNED BOMBERS . . . U.S.": Burr and Wampler (2004), Document 2, p. 16.

109 1959 SOVIET BOMBER FORCE: Podvig (2001), p. 350, Table 6.1.

109 "A SPECTRUM . . . NUCLEAR WEAPONS": Burr and Wampler (2004), Document 2, p. 4.

109 1959 SOVIET NUCLEAR ARSENAL: Norris and Arkin (1994), p. 4.

110 "FROM 80 . . . 600": Burr and Wampler (2004), Document 2, p. 6.

110 "A NATIONWIDE . . . POPULATION": Burr and Wampler (2004), Document 2, p. 8.

110 "HE KNEW . . . SIGNIFICANT": Bundy (1988), p. 338.

110 "MORAL FIBER": quoted in Callahan (1990), p. 106.

110 "HE WAS . . . SURRENDER": Nitze (1989), pp. 168–69.

110 "PROMINENT MEMBERS . . . PARTICULAR": ibid., p. 294.

111 "LACKING FUNDS . . . PERLE": ibid., p. 295.

111 "WOHLSTETTER . . . MISSILES": Winik (1996), p. 50.

112 "THE NUMBER . . . ENEMY": Gates (1996), p. 82.

112 450 TO 150: Graham and LaVera (2003), p. 337.

112 50 PERCENT, 30 PERCENT: Fosdick (1990), p. 136.

112 "A LONGTIME . . . COALITION": Cahn (1998), p. 39.

112 "TO SEEK . . . UNION": Fosdick (1990), p. 153.

112 "KEY NUCLEAR . . . 1960S": Kull (1988), p. 34, Table 2.1.

113 "THE GAME . . . PEOPLE": ibid., p. 127.

113 "IF YOU . . . DUBIOUS": ibid., p. 139.

113 "STRATEGIC WEAPONS . . . CATEGORY": ibid., p. 116.

113 "LET'S PUT . . . IT": ibid., p. 299.

114 "HE PUSHES . . . MASTERED": Scheer (1988), p. 189.

114 "PARTICIPATION IN . . . CONTROL": Gates (1996), p. 46.

114 "BECAUSE FEAR . . . FEAR": Robin (2004), p. 43.

115 "MOST THREATENING . . . REPERCUSSIONS": Graham (2002), p. 54.

115 " 'ONE OF . . . IT?' ": quoted in Nacht (1975), p. 163.

115 "THOSE WERE . . . REGRET": William Hyland, quoted in Cahn (1998), p. 66.

115 "THE CRITICS . . . DISAPPEAR": Cahn (1998), p. 15.

115 SANTA MONICA DINNER, RAND CONFERENCE: ibid., pp. 9, 11.

115 WOHLSTETTER PAPER: Wohlstetter (1974); Wohlstetter, Nitze, et al. (1974).

115 "THE UNITED . . . RACE": Wohlstetter (1974), p. 71.

116 WOHLSTETTER'S "CONCLUSIONS . . . COMPARISONS": Cahn (1998), p. 13.

116 "STOPPED WITH . . . SUBS": ibid.

116 WARHEAD TOTALS; "FOR THE . . . WARHEADS": Nacht (1975), p. 170.

116 "NOT LIVED . . . SERVED": ibid., p. 177.

116 "HIS PROBLEM . . . ELSE": Sidney Drell, personal communication, Stanford University, Sept. 2005.

116 "WOHLSTETTER'S CHARGES . . . UNION": Cahn (1998), p. 15.

116 "TO DEFEND . . . WERE": Gates (1996), pp. 47–48.

117 "DECLINED SHARPLY . . . FLAT": Cahn (1998), p. 196.

117 "SOVIET . . . CHANGES,"; "A BALANCE . . . DOGMA": quoted in Sanders (1983), p. 150.

117 "THE DEMOCRATIC . . . PUBLICITY": quoted in Callahan (1990), p. 174.

SEVEN **THE SORCERER'S APPRENTICES (II)**

118 "CHENEY WAS . . . RULES": Hartmann (1980), p. 283.

119 "RUMSFELD AND . . . IDEAS": Blumenthal (2005).

119 "IF THE . . . SYSTEM": Cahn (1998), p. 95.

119   SS-9 FIVE-KILOMETER MAXIMUM ERROR: Podvig (2001), p. 198, Table 4A.7.

120   CIA DISAGREEMENT: Cahn (1998), p. 97.

120   "THAT WHAT . . . PLAN": ibid., p. 112.

120   TELLER DRAFT DOCUMENT: "An Alternative NIE," 18 June 1975, cited in Cahn
       (1998), p. 113, n. 55.

120   "TELLER QUICKLY . . . NIE": Cahn (1998), p. 113.

121   TELLER AND FOSTER TO THE CIA: ibid., pp. 114–15.

121   "IT IS . . . PREPARE": quoted in Cahn (1998), p. 119.

121   "FOSTER AND . . . PREDECESSORS": ibid., p. 130.

121   "BUSH WAS . . . PREDECESSOR": Blumenthal (2005).

121   TEAM B EXPERIMENT: described at Cahn (1998), p. 139.

121   B TEAMS: Cahn (1998), pp. 141–47.

121   CHENEY CONNECTION: Blumenthal (2005).

121   RUMSFELD AND PAUL WOLFOWITZ: ibid.

122   "IMPORTED TO . . . JACKSON": Blumenthal (1987b), p. 6.

122   TELLER, FOSTER, WOHLSTETTER'S ESSAYS CONSULTED: Cahn (1998), p. 151.

122   "MEMBERS OF . . . CONSENSUS": Burr and Wampler (2004), Document 10: Report
       of Team "B," p. iii.

122   "ACQUIRED A . . . NEGOTIATIONS": Pipes (1986), pp. 25–26.

122   "SO PERSUADED . . . FLAT": ibid., p. 26.

122   "THE ONLY . . . LOW LEVEL": ibid., pp. 26–27.

123   "I WILL . . . FACT": Wiesner (1984), p. 736.

123   "SIMPLY IGNORED . . . STANFORD": Pipes (1986), p. 28.

124   "HIS DEEP . . . SOUL": quoted in Herken (1985), p. 276.

124   "WE HAVE . . . WARS": quoted in Kull (1988), p. 23.

124   "IGNORE THE . . . WAR": Burr and Wampler (2004), Document 10: Report of Team
       "B," p. 2.

125   "A REALISTIC . . . EFFORT": ibid., p. 16. Original italics.

125   "THE IMPLICATION . . . YEARS": ibid., p. 32.

125   "YES, THAT'S . . . THAT": Curtis (2005), Part I.

125   "THE POSSIBILITY . . . THREAT": Burr and Wampler (2004), Document 10: Report
       of Team "B," p. 4.

125   "AN INTENSIFIED . . . LEVEL": ibid., pp. 45–47.

125   "ALL OF . . . THEM": Curtis (2005), Part I. N.B.: Cahn misstates the location of the
       imaginary laser-beam weapon-test facility as Krasnoyarsk in her interview with Cur-
       tis; I have corrected her misstatement by inserting text from Cahn (1998), p. 167.

126   "SEVERAL [SOVIET] . . . 'COMPENSATE' ": Kull (1988), p. 287.

126   "WHAT WAS . . . INSTALLATION": Sakharov (1990), p. 97.

127   VIKTOR GIRSHFELD: identified after the dissolution of the Soviet Union.

127   "COL. X . . . WRONG": quoted in Kull (1988), p. 290; original source: "Colonel X's
       Warning: Our Mistakes Plus Your Hysteria," Detente, No. 1, Oct. 1984, pp. 2–3.

127   "THERE WAS . . . SECURE' ": Kull (1988), p. 291.

127   "THERE WAS . . . PROGRAMS": Tannenwald (1999), p. 34.

128   "WE DID NOT . . . GENUINE": ibid., pp. 56–57.

128   "THERE IS . . . WORLD!' ": Ellman and Kontorovich (1998), pp. 41–42.

129   "THERE WERE . . . [PEOPLE]": Tannenwald (1999), pp. 32–33.

130   "APES ON A TREADMILL": Warnke (1975).

130   "WE COULDN'T . . . CURRENCY": ibid., p. 24.

130   "NOT A . . . UNION": ibid., p. 28.

130   "ONE SOURCE . . . POINTS' ' ": Murrey Marder, "Carter to Inherit Intense Dispute on Soviet Intentions," *Washington Post,* 2 Jan. 1977, p. A1.

130   "IT MEANS . . . VIEW' ": ibid.

131   "SABOTAGE SALT II . . . STATES": quoted in Pipes (1986), p. 35.

131   "TO CRITICS . . . THREAT' ": Callahan (1990), p. 380.

131   "THAT SOVIET . . . OURS": Cox (1980), pp. 4–5.

131   "IF THE . . . ALONE": quoted in Cahn (1998), p. 137.

132   "A COUPLE . . . IT?": quoted in Sanders (1983), p. 152.

132   "A CLEAR . . . PREVENT": SCHENCK *v.* UNITED STATES, SUPREME COURT OF THE UNITED STATES 249 U.S. 47 (3 Mar. 1919).

132   CPD ROSTER: Sanders (1983), p. 154ff.

133   "HE NEEDED CREDENTIALS": Winik (1996), p. 110.

133   "THE PRINCIPAL . . . POWER": quoted in Winik (1996), pp. 110–11.

133   "NITZE WAS . . . APPROACH": quoted in Talbott (1988), p. 149.

133   "WE WERE . . . FRIGHTENING": quoted in Winik (1996), p. 111.

133   "TO TRY . . . ARSENALS]": Interview with President Jimmy Carter, Cold War Interviews, Episode 18, National Security Archive.

134   BRZEZINSKI AND PERLE DRAFTED CARTER PROPOSAL: Thomas Graham, Jr., personal communication, Sept. 2006.

134   WOHLSTETTER AND THE EUROPEAN-AMERICAN WORKSHOP: For details see Kaplan (1979).

134   "OWING TO . . . EUROPE": Schmidt (1981), p. 3.

134   "ARMS CONTROL . . . DEPLOYMENTS": Graham (2002), p. 107.

135   "IN THE RANGE . . . WELL": Garthoff (1983), pp. 205–6.

135   "WAS A . . . FAVOR": ibid., pp. 876–78.

136   "POLICY OF . . . RUINS": Fosdick (1990), p. 167.

136   "THE CONGRESS . . . UNION": Interview with President Jimmy Carter, Cold War Interviews, Episode 18, National Security Archive.

136   CARTER PULLED THE TREATY: Thomas Graham, Jr., personal communication, Sept. 2006.

136   "I COULD . . . NATION": Interview with President Jimmy Carter, Cold War Interviews, Episode 18, National Security Archive.

136   REASON FOR SOVIET INVASION: Garthoff (1985), p. 920; Westad (2001), p. 130.

136   "THE USA . . . ALARMING": Gorbachev (1995), p. 116.

136   LIST OF SANCTIONS: Garthoff (1985), p. 951.

136   "BY THE 1980 . . . SPENDING": Cahn (1998), p. 49.

137   OFFICIAL SOVIET RESPONSE: Garthoff (1985), p. 998ff.

EIGHT   **DECAPITATION**

138   JACKSON ACCUSING CARTER OF APPEASEMENT: quoted in Whelan (1988), p. 82.

138   CARTER COMPARED TO CHAMBERLAIN; "REAGAN OPENLY . . . COLLAPSE": Blumenthal (1986), p. xiii.

138   "SOME BIZARRE . . . WRITTEN": quoted in Beth A. Fischer (1997), p. 19.

138   "BY VIRTUE . . . TEAM B": Cahn (1998), p. 191.

138   "A STUDY . . . U.S.S.R.' ": ibid.

139   INFORMATION WENT TO PFIAB: ibid., p. 192.

139   "BY ANY . . . NATIONS": ibid., p. 193.

139   "THE MORE . . . ERA": quoted in Stone (1973), p. 2.

139 "CANNOT BE . . . POWER": ibid.

140 "IN SOCIALIST . . . PERCENT)": ibid., pp. 3–4.

140 "PENCHANT FOR . . . PROPHESYING": Janos Radvanyi, review of *The Final Fall* in *Russian Review* 39 (1) (Jan. 1980), p. 97.

140 "INTERNAL PRESSURES . . . SYSTEMS": Todd (1979), p. 3.

141 "SHABBY AND . . . DATA": ibid., p. 10.

141 "HAVE FIXED . . . SAME": ibid., pp. 10–11.

141 "THERE WILL . . . WAGES?": ibid., pp. 58–62.

141 "THE DEGREE . . . ALIENATION": ibid., pp. 40–43.

141 CHINA: TWENTY ICBMS: CRS (2006), p. 11.

141 "BY THE . . . EXPLOITED": Todd (1979), p. 72. Original italics.

142 "CONSIDER THAT . . . LIFE-STYLES?": ibid., pp. 68–69. Original italics.

142 "IN 1976 . . . ECONOMY": ibid., p. 71. Original italics.

143 "TO TRANSFORM . . . SURVIVE": ibid., p. 40.

143 "IS THE . . . PRODUCTIVITY": ibid., pp. 78, 81.

143 "THE BEGINNING . . . CYCLE": ibid., p. 222.

143 "NO ONE . . . WEALTH": ibid., (emphasis in original).

143 "SUFFER . . . UPHEAVAL": ibid., p. 202.

143 "THE SUCCESSIVE . . . FUSS": ibid., p. 204.

143 "COULD NOT . . . COME": ibid., p. 202.

144 THE NATO DECISION: discussed at Guadeloupe in Jan. 1979, issued in final form in Dec. Gates (1996), p. 112.

144 "EVEN THE . . . STATES": Mastny and Byrne (2005), Document No. 84, pp. 418–19.

144 "THE THREAT . . . PERCEPTIONS": Nuenlist (2001), pp. 22–23.

145 "[THE KGB CHIEF . . . JUSTIFIED": Quoted in Benjamin B. Fischer, Intelligence and disaster avoidance: the Soviet war scare and US-Soviet relations, in Cimbala (1999), p. 90. Fischer cites (and translates from) the German edition of Wolf's memoir; a less detailed version of the encounter appears in Wolf (1997), p. 221.

145 "WHEN CARTER . . . THINGS' ": Wolf (1997), p. 223.

145 "ON AT . . . SURPRISE ATTACK": Gates (1996), p. 114.

145 "AS HE . . . THOUGH": ibid., pp. 114–15.

146 "AND BY JUNE . . . WAR' ": Fischer, in Cimbala (1999), p. 91.

146 "IF DETERRENCE . . . ATTACK": quoted in Fischer, in Cimbala (1999), p. 92.

146 "THE MOST . . . ANARCHY": Gray and Payne (1980), p. 21.

147 SEVEN HUNDRED BUNKERS, FOURTEEN HUNDRED SILOS: Fischer in Cimbala (1999), p. 92.

147 MINUTEMAN II, TRIDENT C4 CHANGES: John Prados, personal communication, May 2006.

147 W86, W85 PERSHING 2 CHANGES: Robert S. Norris, personal communication, June 2006.

147 THIRTY-ONE APPOINTEES: Cahn (1998), p. 30.

148 " 'IT WAS . . . HOME' ": Schweizer (1994), pp. 8–9.

148 PROBES BEGAN MID-FEBRUARY: ibid., p. 9.

148 CARTER INCREASE: Stockman (1986), p. 107.

148 "A PARTING . . . ADMINISTRATION": ibid.

149 "WE HAD . . . 1986": ibid., pp. 108–9.

149 "WE'D LAID . . . DOLLARS!": ibid., p. 108.

149 "THE FEBRUARY . . . COMPLEX": ibid., p. 109.

149 REAGAN'S DEFENSE SPENDING COMPARISONS: Wirls (1992), pp. 35–36.

149 "FOR FISCAL . . . *PERCENT*": ibid., p. 54.

149 "EXTRAORDINARY SURGE . . . PROGRAM": ibid., p. 37.

149 "IN ALL . . . STATES": Fitzgerald (1976), p. 58.

150 "FEWER THAN . . . PURPOSES": Steinbruner (1981), p. 18.

150 "COMMAND VULNERABILITY . . . SIZE": ibid., p. 22.

150 "AS SEEN . . . WAR": ibid., p. 27.

151 PROJECT RYAN, ANDROPOV SPEECH: Andrew and Gordievsky (1991), p. 67.

151 "THOSE IN . . . USTINOV": Gates (1996), p. 270.

151 "WHAT APPEARS . . . REVERSE": quoted in Blake (1990), pp. 267–68.

151 "PARTICIPATION IN . . . READY": Mastny and Byrne (2005), Document No. 92, p. 449.

151 "RYAN . . . MORE": Andrew and Mitrokhin (1999), p. 214.

152 "ONLY ADDED . . . RYAN": Gates (1996), p. 271.

152 REAGAN'S SPEECH BASED ON NSDD-32; "THE DISSOLUTION . . . EMPIRE": Reed (2004), p. 237.

152 "WAS NO . . . LOSE": ibid., p. 236.

152 "INCLUDE . . . ACTION": ibid., p. 237.

152 "THE PRESIDENT . . . INEVITABLE": Maynes (1982), p. 86.

152 "SOME SOVIET . . . LATE": ibid., pp. 100–101.

152 "A SPECTACULAR . . . ENEMY' ": Benjamin Fischer, in Cimbala (1999), pp. 95–96.

153 "THE REAGAN . . . BEFORE": Mastny and Byrne (2005), Document No. 96, pp. 466–68.

NINE **REHEARSING ARMAGEDDON**

154 "ZERO SOLUTION"; "ILLUSORY": Talbott (1985), pp. 56–57.

154 "INTENDED . . . UNACCEPTABLE": Graham (2002), p. 107.

154 "I DO . . . AGGRESSIVE": Tannenwald (1999), p. 136.

154 "AT LEAST . . . TOMAHAWKS: Talbott (1985), p. 57.

155 "COMPACT . . . RESERVED": Perle (1992), p. 5.

155 "CONVINCED THAT . . . WAR": ibid., p. 36.

155 "UNLIKELY THE . . . AGREE": ibid., p. 95.

155 "ZERO . . . EARS": ibid., p. 91.

155 "URBANE GUERRILLAS . . . LEAKS": ibid., p. 5.

155 "WHAT IS . . . ACTIVITY": Robin W. Winks, review of *Hard Line* by Richard Perle, *Washington Post Book World*, 9 June 1992.

155 CUBAN MISSILE CRISIS: as Andropov told Oleg Grinevsky from his deathbed in December 1983: see Tannenwald (1999), p. 15. Grinevsky's information disqualifies any claim that Andropov was simply cranking up the Cold War to encourage his people to work harder, although that was certainly one of the uses to which he put the U.S. arms buildup and the Reagan administration's belligerence, as he does in this speech.

156 EXCERPTS FROM ANDROPOV 1983 SPEECH: Mastny and Byrne (2005), Document No. 98, pp. 472–79.

156 KGB DOCUMENTS: Andrew and Gordievsky (1991), pp. 69–81.

157 EVIL EMPIRE SPEECH MEANT TO WIN FUNDAMENTALIST SUPPORT: Oberdorfer (1992), p. 24.

157 "THE MILITARY . . . WAR": quoted in Wittner (2004), p. 1.

157 "FORWARD STRATEGY," "HIGH-THREAT": quoted in Hersh (1986), p. 17.

157 "was one . . . boss": Hersh (1986), p. 17.

157 "three aircraft . . . there' ": ibid.

157 "impotent and . . . themselves": Ronald Reagan, "Address to the Nation on Defense and National Security," 23 Mar. 1983.

158 "that was . . . president": quoted in Lettow (2005), p. 114.

158 "took prodigious . . . cloth": Shvets (1994), p. 75.

159 "the rhetoric . . . war": Andrew and Gordievsky (1991), p. 81.

159 "paid a . . . war": James Buchan in Morton (2005).

159 "civilians debated . . . nuances": Powers (1996), p. 10.

159 "unable to . . . strike": quoted in Lettow (2005), p. 114.

159 "a bid . . . threat": quoted in Oberdorfer (1992), p. 29.

159 "one night . . . higher": Hersh (1986), pp. 17–19.

160 "read together . . . down": Sayle (1993), p. 95.

160 "unprecedented sharpening . . . mankind": Andrew and Gordievsky (1991), p. 81.

160 "if we . . . ~~weap~~[ons]": quoted in Oberdorfer (1992), p. 38.

160 advice of william clark: Shultz (1993), p. 360. Clark replaced Richard Allen on 4 Jan. 1982.

161 kamchatka fighter tanks light: Sayle (1993), p. 98.

161 "provisionally . . . rc-135": ibid.

161 "the air . . . flashing": quoted in Dallin (1985), p. 24.

161 andropov reviewed files: Sayle (1993), p. 97.

162 "the soviet . . . missiles' ": ibid., p. 99.

162 "i have . . . attack": quoted in Dallin (1985), p. 25.

162 "were mandated . . . intrusion": Sayle (1993), p. 100.

162 "the murder . . . airliner": quoted in Cannon (1991), p. 476.

162 "was astonishingly brutal": Shultz (1993), p. 369.

162 "the meeting . . . it": ibid., p. 370.

162 "the 747 . . . plane": Beth Fischer (1997), p. 126.

163 kennan described: according to Talbott (1984), p. 23.

163 "a militarist . . . implanted": Talbott (1984), "Yuri Andropov Statement," pp. 119–27.

163 able archer, autumn forge: Maloney (2004), pp. 607–8.

164 "to ascertain . . . nato": Andrew and Gordievsky (1991), p. 76.

164 leaders' approval: Benjamin Fischer (1997), p. 16.

164 "i had . . . planned": quoted in Beth Fischer (1997), p. 123.

164 mcfarlane scrubbed: Oberdorfer (1992), p. 65.

164 thatcher, kohl: Beth Fischer (1997), p. 123.

164 "the sudden . . . ryan": quoted in *CNN Cold War, Episode 22: Star Wars* at http://www.cnn.com/SPECIALS/cold.war/episodes/22/spotlight.

164 "they were . . . deployments": Morton (2005).

164 "the entire . . . 'pre-war' ": Benjamin Fischer, in Cimbala (1999), p. 93.

164 "some clandestine . . . analysts: *CNN Cold War, Episode 22: Star Wars.*

165 "when the . . . america?": Beth Fischer (1997), p. 132.

165 soviets and nato starting war from within exercise: Gen. Eugene Habiger, personal communication, Nov. 2005.

165 "the exercise . . . war' ": Gates (1996), p. 271.

165 "between november . . . 10": ibid., p. 272.

165 "the group . . . germany": Paul Dibb, in Morton (2005).

166   "INFORMATION ABOUT . . . MISPLACED": Gates (1996), p. 273.
166   "LIFTING ITS . . . COUNTRIES": Mastny and Byrne (2005), Document No. 102, p. 490.
167   "NEVER, PERHAPS . . . EIGHTIES": Gorbachev, speech to the 27th Communist Party Congress, quoted in Newhouse (1989), I: 39.
167   "I FEEL . . . WANT?": Reagan (1990), p. 589.
167   "DO YOU . . . ABOUT": quoted in Oberdorfer (1992), p. 67.

TEN THE WARHEADS WILL ALWAYS GET THROUGH

168   "COLUMBUS DAY . . . WAR": quoted in Reagan (1990), p. 585.
169   NUCLEAR WINTER *SCIENCE* PAPER: R. P. Turco, O. B. Toon, T. P. Ackerman, J. B. Pollack, and C. Sagan (1983). Nuclear winter: global consequences of multiple nuclear explosions. *Science* 222, 1283–92.
169   "I KNEW . . . CELLULOID": quoted in Cannon (1991), p. 157.
169   "WHEN BILL . . . PRODUCE' ": Cannon (1991), pp. 156–57.
169   "THE FIRST . . . DEPRESSED' ": Morris (1999), p. 498.
170   SIOP TARGETS: Oberdorfer (1992), p. 65.
170   "WAS 'CHASTENED' . . . SCENARIO' ": Beth Fischer (1997), p. 121. Fischer believes that this late-October briefing was Reagan's first, but Thomas Reed reports attending a SIOP briefing with the president during the IVORY LEAF exercise of 1–4 March 1982. See Reed (2004), p. 243.
170   "A MOST . . . CRAZY": Reagan (1990), pp. 585–86.
170   "ANECDOTALLY, NOT ANALYTICALLY": Gelb (1985), p. 2.
170   "FIRSTHAND DISCOVERIES . . . EXPERIENCE": Cannon (1991), p. 287.
170   "MOST OF . . . LAZY": ibid., p. 55.
171   "THE SAD . . . RESPECT": ibid., p. 427.
171   "NOT ONE . . . BOOKS": Gelb (1985), pp. 1–2.
171   "REAGAN'S SEEMINGLY . . . IT' ": Cannon (1991), p. 308.
171   "HIS BIGGEST . . . COLLEGE": ibid., p. 130.
171   ("PLAYING IT . . . CAMPUS"): Wills (1987), p. 67.
172   "REAGAN COULD . . . ANALOGY": Pious (1991), p. 500.
172   "WITH HIM . . . FORCE": Blumenthal (1986), pp. 241–42.
172   "EVERYTHING IS . . . CHRIST": Cannon (1991), pp. 288–89.
172   "TWICE TEN . . . WORMWOOD": Revelation 9:18; Revelation 8:10–11 (RSV).
173   "WAS SIEZED . . . TRIUMPH": Cannon (1991), p. 288.
173   "FROM THE . . . EARTH": quoted in Cannon (1991), p. 290.
173   "HE WOULD . . . ARMAGEDDON": Cannon (1991), p. 291.
173   "HAIL AND . . . GRASS": Revelation 8:7 (RSV).
174   "GOD HAS . . . EVERYONE": quoted in Lettow (2005), p. 8.
174   "SEVEN SUMMERS . . . YOURSELF' ": Reagan (1965), pp. 19, 22.
174   "WE CAN . . . CREDIT": quoted in Clark's foreword to Reagan (2000), p. 9.
174   "THE SDI . . . PERSONAL": Wohlforth (1996), p. 35.
174   "I'VE BEEN . . . MORE": quoted in Lettow (2005), p. 117.
174   "IT KIND . . . DID": quoted in Lakoff and York (1989), pp. 6–7.
175   "ULTIMATE GOAL . . . OBSOLETE": Ronald Reagan, "Address to the Nation on Defense and National Security," 23 Mar. 1983.
175   "THAT MIGHT . . . RAIN": Ronald Reagan, "Remarks at the High School Commencement Exercises in Glassboro, New Jersey," 19 June 1986.

175   "LIFEGUARDS ARE . . . RESCUE": quoted in Lettow (2005), pp. 8–9.

175   "THE SUM . . . CAN DO IT": Freedman et al. (2005), p. 66.

175   "IN THE . . . TIME' ": Reed (2004), pp. 234–35.

176   "REAGAN THOUGHT . . . WEAPONS": Lettow (2005), pp. 30–31.

176   "ONE OF . . . WAR": Reagan (1990), p. 550, cited in Beth Fischer (1997), p. 104.

176   "HE WAS . . . WARFARE": Freedman et al. (2005), p. 67.

176   "REAGAN . . . WAR": Lettow (2005), p. 51.

176   "WHATEVER HAPPENS . . . CAN": quoted in Lettow (2005), p. 50.

177   "MADE ME . . . WAR": ibid.

177   "MATLOCK . . . UNACCEPTABLE' ": Lettow (2005), p. 133.

177   "I LISTENED . . . ANIMALS": Shultz (1993), p. 513.

177   "REAGAN ASKED . . . RESPOND": Newhouse (1989), I, p. 39.

178   REAGAN LAMENTED FAILURE OF BARUCH PLAN: See Lettow (2005), p. 75: "On several occasions, Reagan publicly expressed regret that the Soviets had not accepted the Baruch Plan of 1946, which would have abolished nuclear weapons and internationalized nuclear energy."

178   WEST POINT ADDRESS: Ronald Reagan, "Address at Commencement Exercises at the United States Military Academy," 27 May 1981.

178   "THE BEST . . . DEFENSE": quoted in Beth Fischer (1997), p. 106.

179   "THIRD GENERATION . . . WEAPONS": Teller, House Armed Services Committee testimony, Apr. 1983, quoted in Broad (1992), p. 143.

179   "NO DOCUMENTARY . . . 1967": Lettow (2005), p. 254, n. 92.

179   "HE TOOK . . . MIND": Strober and Strober (1998), p. 232.

180   "I WOULD . . . ENTIRELY": quoted in Oberdorfer (1992), p. 129.

180   "THE TRUTH . . . OF": Hunter (1992), p. 94.

180   "PRESIDENT REAGAN . . . CRISIS' ": Beth Fischer (1997), p. 134.

181   JAPANESE DIET SPEECH: Ronald Reagan, "Address Before the Japanese Diet in Tokyo," 11 Nov. 1983.

181   A CONVICTION EXPRESSED BEFORE: Ronald Reagan, "Radio Address to the Nation on Nuclear Weapons," 17 Apr. 1982; "Address Before the 38th Session of the United Nations General Assembly in New York, New York," 26 Sept. 1983.

181   "WHEN I . . . HANDS": Shultz (1993), p. 376.

181   16 JANUARY 1984 SPEECH: Ronald Reagan, "Address to the Nation and Other Countries on United States–Soviet Relations," 16 Jan. 1984.

181   FIFTY-FIVE HUNDRED NEW WARHEADS: Newhouse (1989), I, p. 42.

182   REAGAN ALLUDING TO WAR SCARE: "McFarlane, who helped draft the speech, notes that the president's references to 'dangerous misunderstandings and miscalculations' referred to the Soviet response to the war game. In a thinly veiled statement, Reagan declared that he sought to find 'meaningful ways to reduce the uncertainty and potential for misinterpretation surrounding military activities and to diminish the risk of surprise attack.' Likewise, the president's assurances that the United States 'poses no threat to the security of the Soviet Union' were meant to clarify U.S. intentions for the Kremlin." Beth Fischer (1997), p. 135–36.

182   "HACKNEYED PLOY": quoted in Newhouse (1989) I, p. 50.

182   FIVE LETTERS; TASS COMPARISON; "A SHAMELESS . . . END": Shultz (1993), p. 476.

182   "WHAT IS . . . SYSTEMS": quoted in Shultz (1993), p. 474.

182   NANCY REAGAN WORRIED: Newhouse (1989), I, p. 51. See also Prados in Cowley (2005), p. 451.

182   "HINTS CAME . . . PRESIDENT": Shultz (1993), p. 480.

183   "THE PRESIDENT . . . WEAPONS' ": ibid., p. 484.

183   "WHATEVER IS . . . OPERATIONS": Gorbachev (1995), p. 161.

183   "THE SOVIET . . . WEAPONS": quoted in Shultz (1993), p. 507.

183   "GORBACHEV HAD . . . SDI": Memorandum of Conversation, Meeting with British Prime Minister Margaret Thatcher, 22 Dec. 1984, p. 6 (online version), Margaret Thatcher Foundation Archive.

183   "THE TOUGHEST . . . TABLE": Shultz (1993), p. 504.

183   "RONALD REAGAN'S . . . GROUND": ibid., p. 505.

184   "TO SEE . . . GROMYKO": ibid., p. 515.

184   "THE SIDES . . . EVERYWHERE": quoted in Shultz (1993), p. 519.

184   "THE USSR . . . NOW": ibid., p. 530.

184   "THE RESULT . . . AIR": Shultz (1993), p. 532.

184   "A PERSONAL . . . UNDERSTANDING": quoted in Shultz (1993), p. 534.

184   "WE WERE . . . WAR": Shultz (1993), p. 501.

ELEVEN   GOING AROUND IN CIRCLES

187   "THE NEXT . . . OFF?": quoted in Kuhn (2004), p. 168.

187   GENEVA SUMMIT SESSIONS: this and all further session discussions paraphrased from the corresponding U.S. Memoranda of Discussions, available online in the Margaret Thatcher Foundation Archives.

189   "SECURITY CAN . . . SECURE": quoted in Sigal (2000), p. 317, n. 4.

189   ("WE MET . . . MEMOS"): quoted in English (2000), p. 324, n. 44.

189   GORBACHEV MEETING PALME: "Throughout that period, Arbatov was working with Gorbachev, and when the Commission met in Moscow in June 1981, Palme and a few members went to see Gorbachev and spoke with him and talked about their ideas and the Commission." Barry Blechman interview, Washington, D.C., Nov. 2005.

189   SOVIET MILITARY STRATEGY: see Odom (1998), passim.

189   "SHARED THE . . . CREDIBILITY": Brandt (1989), p. 396.

190   "I NEVER . . . DEFENSES": Knott Selverstone et al. (2002), p. 13.

190   "THERE WERE . . . THAT": Knott and Riley (2002), p. 10.

190   "NONE OF . . . END": Tannenwald (1999), p. 88.

190   "REAGAN'S SECOND . . . PEOPLE": Dobrynin (1995), p. 610.

190   "THROUGHOUT THE . . . DEVELOPED?": ibid., p. 611.

191   "ALTHOUGH THE . . . SPENDING": Gorbachev (1995), p. 405.

191   "WHAT ARE . . . NOT": quoted in Chernyaev (2000), p. 83.

191   "SINCE THERE . . . START": Wohlforth (1996), p. 37.

191   "MANY HUNDREDS . . . DISARMAMENT": Assembly of presidents of scientific academies and other scientists convened by the Pontifical Academy of Scientists, "Declaration on Prevention of Nuclear War," 24 Sept. 1982.

192   "MADE A . . . CONCLUSIONS": Cohen and vanden Heuvel (1989), p. 160.

192   "THE TASK . . . MEANS": quoted in Sigal (2000), p. 19.

192   "IN OUR . . . DESTRUCTION": ibid., p. 20.

192   "I CRITICIZED . . . UNION' ": Brandt (1989), pp. 65–66. Emphasis added.

192   "RENUNCIATION OF . . . EUROPE": Bahr (2003), p. 138.

193   "RAISE OUR . . . ACT": ibid., p. 140.

193   "THE PRINCIPLE . . . THEM": Palme (1982), p. 176.

193   "MAKE REFERENCE . . . PROBLEMS": Bahr (2003), p. 141.

194   "THE BLANK . . . PAPER"): Chernyaev diary, 24 Nov. 1985. National Security Archive

Electronic Briefing Book No. 192. (N.B.: Translation used here from an earlier posting, "Excerpt from Anatoly Chernyaev's Diary," same site.)

194 "HE WOULD . . . PRESIDENT' ": Alexander Yakovlev, Memorandum prepared on request from M.S. Gorbachev and handed to him on 12 Mar. 1985, National Security Archive Electronic Briefing Book No. 168.

195 "BUD AND . . . MEETING": Kuhn (2004), p. 169.

195 "ARE YOU . . . IS": Knott, Selverstone, et al. (2002), p. 26.

195 "RIPPED MY . . . SHEVARDNADZE": Kuhn (2004), p. 170.

195 "WREATHED IN SMILES": ibid.

197 "ASTONISHED": Tannenwald (1999), p. 68.

198 "SUCCEEDED IN . . . PROBLEMS"): Krepon (1989), p. 258.

198 "THEY ASKED . . . DINOSAUR!' ": Gorbachev interviewed on CNN *Perspectives*, *Episode 22: Star Wars.*

199 "THE FIRST . . . EASE": Chidester et al. (2003), p. 56; Adelman (1989), pp. 122–23. I have merged these two variant versions of Adelman's story.

200 "BLEEDING WOUND": Gorbachev first used this phrase publicly in his speech to the 27th Party Congress in Feb. 1986. Archie Brown (1996), p. 221.

201 "I CAN'T . . . DID": quoted in Lakoff and York (1989), p. 362, n. 68.

201 SDI AND REDUCTIONS IN OFFENSIVE MISSILES: according to Matlock (2004), p. 158.

201 "WE WILL . . . THUNDERED": quoted in Matlock (2004), p. 157.

202 "I OBSERVED . . . CHIN": Matlock (2004), p. 156.

202 "VELIKHOV AND . . . THING' ": Roald Sagdeev interview, Washington, D.C., Dec. 2003.

202 "GORBACHEV'S GENUINE . . . ECONOMY": Sagdeev (1994), p. 273.

203 "VACCINATIONS . . . 1972": Velikhov (1991), p. 368.

203 "A SPACE-BASED . . . DOWN": ibid., p. 369.

203 "THE 'BALANCE . . . EXPANDED": Velikhov et al. (1986), p. 112.

204 "OUR RESPONSE . . . SDI": Chernyaev (2000), p. 57.

204 TOPOL: Uhler (2003); Podvig (2001), pp. 230–34; www.globalsecurity.org, Weapons of Mass Destruction (WMD): RT-2UTTH - Topol-M (SS-27).

204 312 DEPLOYED BY 2006: See Podvig at http://russianforces.org/missiles/ (accessed 4 Aug. 2006). The Topol entered active service in Dec. 2006.

204 "HOW COULD . . . SILLY?": quoted in Robert Cottrell, "An Icelandic Saga," *NYRB* 51 (17), 4 Nov. 2004, n. 6 (online edition).

204 COMPOSITION OF VPK: Odom (1998), p. 51.

204 "EXPERTS AT . . . STATES' ": Oberdorfer (1992), pp. 29–30.

205 "A SURPRISINGLY . . . POSITIONS": Odom (1998), p. 115.

205 "CUTTING MILITARY . . . LEADERSHIP": ibid., p. 119.

206 "WITH RIGHTEOUS . . . DESTRUCTION": Gorbachev (1995), p. 406.

206 "WE HAD . . . WACKO": Chidester et al. (2003), p. 52.

206 "SHARPLY DISAGREE[D] . . . UNION": Second Reagan-Mondale debate, 21 Oct. 1984, Kansas City, Mo.

207 ("IF THE . . . 1985"): Mastny and Byrne (2005), Document No. 106, p. 509.

207 "RONALD REAGAN'S . . . REPLIED": Gorbachev (1995), p. 407.

208 "AND BESIDES . . . MOVIES": Arbatov (1992), p. 320.

208 "THE WALK . . . ME": Gorbachev (1995), p. 407.

209 "WITH SOME . . . SPHERE?": Memorandum of Conversation, Reagan-Gorbachev Afternoon Tête-à-Tête, 19 Nov. 1985, pp. 3–4. Margaret Thatcher Archives.

210 "WE WERE . . . MOSCOW": Gorbachev (1995), p. 408.

210   "THE DAY . . . POLITICS": Tannenwald (1999), p. 115.

210   "WE HAD . . . IT' ": Knott (2002), p. 21.

210   TWO A.M.: Gorbacheva (1991), p. 169.

211   "TRULY HISTORIC DOCUMENT": Gorbachev (1995), p. 411.

211   "THE SIDES . . . STABILITY": quoted in Oberdorfer (1992), p. 153.

TWELVE **NAYSAYERS HARD AT WORK**

212   "NOT ONCE . . . STATE": Reagan (1990), p. 641.

212   "GORBACHEV . . . WAS . . . IMPRESSION' ": Zubok (2000), p. 5.

212   "NUCLEAR WAR . . . WEAPONS": Gorbachev (1995), p. 411.

212   "DECIDED THAT . . . OFF": quoted in Newhouse (1989), II, p. 58.

212   "OBVIOUSLY THERE . . . ALL": Reagan (1990), p. 643.

213   "GORBACHEV TOLD . . . UNRESOLVED": Tannenwald (1999), pp. 112–13.

213   "IMPRESSION THAT . . . ECONOMY": Chernyaev (2000), pp. 45–46.

213   "I FEEL . . . ON": Tannenwald (1999), p. 79.

213   " 'IT'S JUST . . . SHOCK": ibid., p. 121.

214   "AS A . . . UNION": ibid.

214   "SUDDENLY, AT . . . EVERYTHING' ": Tannenwald (1999), p. 122. Emphasis added.

215   "WE IMMEDIATELY . . . PHONY": ibid., p. 122.

215   "WE PUSHED . . . PROGRAM": ibid., p. 123.

215   "AGREED ON . . . OFFENSIVE' ": Gorbachev (1995), p. 411.

215   TARASENKO PROPOSAL: For details see Tannenwald (1999), p. 124ff.

215   "IT TOOK . . . PROPOSAL": Tannenwald (1999), pp. 124–25.

216   "THIS WAS . . . FUTURE' ": Odom (1998), p. 127.

216   "GORBACHEV WAS . . . PROGRAMS": ibid.

216   "IT WAS . . . AGAIN": Tannenwald (1999), pp. 136–38.

217   "HE PROMPTLY . . . ENDORSED": Odom (1998), p. 127.

217   "NOT TO . . . DECEPTION": quoted in Evangelista (2001), p. 20.

217   "IN AND . . . DOCUMENT": Tannenwald (1999), p. 113.

218   "THE CHIEF . . . HICCUP": Archie Brown (1996), pp. 93–94.

218   GORBACHEV 15 JANUARY 1986 TEXT: *FBIS Daily Report,* 16 Jan. 1986, Vol. 3, No. 11, pp. AA1–AA9 (hereafter "FBIS 16 Jan. 86").

218   "[THE SOVIET . . . EARTH": FBIS 16 Jan. 86, pp. AA1–AA2.

218   "THE FIRST . . . POSSIBLE": ibid., p. AA2.

219   SECOND STAGE OF GORBACHEV'S PLAN: ibid.

219   "BY THE . . . ELABORATED": FBIS 16 Jan. 86, p. AA3.

219   ON-SITE INSPECTION: ibid.

219   "ACTUAL TROOP . . . BALANCED": Allin (1994), p. 82.

220   "IT WASN'T . . . TOLD": Ellman and Kontorovich (1998), p. 43.

220   "THUS, WE . . . COURSE": FBIS 16 Jan. 86, p. AA3.

220   "IS A . . . BE": ibid.

220   "OUR NEW . . . RACE": FBIS 16 Jan. 86, pp. AA7–AA8.

221   "PROGRAM OF . . . ARMS": Palme (1982), p. 177.

221   "THE VERY . . . LEADERSHIP": Chernyaev (2000), p. 59.

221   "GORBACHEV SURPRISINGLY . . . DOWN": Reagan (1990), pp. 650–51.

221   PERLE, HEARING FROM NITZE: Shultz (1993), p. 669.

221   "SECRETARY WEINBERGER . . . PROPOSING": Nitze (1989), p. 422.

222   "WHY WAIT . . . WEAPONS?": ibid.

222   WHITE HOUSE STATEMENTS: Statement on the Soviet–United States Nuclear and Space Arms Negotiations, 15 Jan. 1986; Statement on the Soviet Proposal on Nuclear and Space Arms Reductions, 15 Jan. 1986; Statement by Principal Deputy Press Secretary Speakes on the Soviet Proposal on Nuclear and Space Arms Reductions, 16 Jan. 1986, Public Papers of Ronald Reagan.

222   "NSPG TIME . . . US": Reagan (1990), p. 651.

222   "THE NAYSAYERS . . . POLICY": Shultz (1993), p. 701.

223   "HE THINKS . . . WEAPONS": ibid.

223   COLD WAR TACIT COOPERATION: See, e.g., Kanet and Kolodziej (1991).

223   "ROZ RIDGWAY . . . THEM' ": Shultz (1993), pp. 704–5.

224   "OUR PROPOSAL . . . EUROPE": Reagan (1990), p. 658. For excerpts from Reagan's 22 Feb. 1986 letter see pp. 656–58.

224   "THE MORATORIUM . . . GUARANTEES": Chernyaev (2000), pp. 56–57; Gorbachev Foundation Archive (combining variant translations).

224   "DESPITE ALL . . . ROLE": 3 Apr. 1986 Politburo meeting (Chernyaev's notes), Gorbachev Foundation Archive.

224   "MORE THAN . . . BETTER?": Reagan (1990), p. 662.

224   "TO PORTRAY . . . POLICY": ibid., pp. 662–63.

225   "GORBACHEV . . . CONTROL!": Shultz (1993), p. 709.

225   "THE WESTERN . . . INITIATIVE": Gorbachev (1995), p. 412.

225   "WAS DISAPPOINTED . . . STEPS": Tannenwald (1999), pp. 154–55.

225   GORBACHEV AND . . . DIFFICULT": ibid., pp. 153–54.

226   SHEVARDNADZE ON DEALING WITH HUMAN RIGHTS: according to Jack Matlock in Tannenwald (1999), p. 178.

226   "WE LOOKED . . . OURSELVES": Tannenwald (1999), p. 196.

226   FORTY-EIGHT THOUSAND FEET: Many accounts give forty-six thousand, but cf. Joseph P. Kerwin, M.D., to Rear Admiral Richard H. Truly, 28 July 1986, at http://history.nasa.gov/kerwin.html, an official report on the deaths of the Challenger astronauts, which says forty-eight thousand. Details of the accident from this source and from James Oberg, "7 Myths about the Challenger Shuttle Disaster," Space News, MSNBC.com.

227   "THE FUTURE . . . GOD": Ronald Reagan, "Address to the Nation on the Explosion of the Space Shuttle Challenger," 28 Jan. 1986.

227   "CHERNOBYL WAS . . . FALLOUT": Petrosyants (1988), p. 54.

227   "TORE THE . . . EYES": Shevardnadze (1991), p. 175.

228   "COMRADE GORBACHEV . . . THIS": Mastny and Byrne (2005), Document No. 115, pp. 531–32.

228   "ONE PERSONAL . . . HANDS?": Wohlforth (1996), p. 33.

228   "THAT PHRASE . . . CONVICTION": ibid., p. 37.

228   "ALL THE . . . ELITE' ": Gorbachev (1995), p. 402.

228   LOCATION OF MEETING: Oberdorfer (1992), p. 162.

228   "THAT IN . . . DIMENSION": Gorbachev (1995), pp. 402–3.

229   THESE WERE NOT . . . KGB: e.g., ibid.

229   "FROM 1986 . . . 1994": Graham (2002), p. 51.

229   RICHARD PERLE ARGUMENT: "He persuaded Mr. Reagan to repudiate the SALT II treaty": "The Light and Darkness of Richard Perle," New York Times editorial, 16 Mar. 1987.

229   "SINCE THE . . . GROUND": Ronald Reagan, "Statement on Soviet and United States Compliance with Arms Control Agreements," 27 May 1986.

229 "WAS SURPRISED . . . INITIATIVES": Chernyaev (2000), p. 58.

229 CASPAR WEINBERGER . . . ADVANTAGES": Talbott (1985), p. 17.

230 ABM TREATY'S "BROAD" INTERPRETATION: For a full treatment of this controversy see T. Graham (2002), pp. 143–84.

230 "THE PRODUCT . . . MACHINES": quoted in David (2000), p. 3 (online version).

230 "THERE WERE . . . PROCESS": Wohlforth (1996), p. 41.

230 IKLÉ, KAMPELMAN: Oberdorfer (1992), p. 171.

230 "RICHARD PERLE . . . THAT": Tannenwald (1999), p. 143.

231 "ON FEBRUARY . . . NOTHING": Shultz (1993), p. 708.

231 "WHO ASSURED . . . AMICABLY": ibid., p. 719.

231 "ONE OF . . . MATTERS": ibid.

231 "ABOUT THIS . . . PLOY": Tannenwald (1999), p. 148.

231 "IT MADE . . . DEFENSES": quoted in Lettow (2005), pp. 209–10.

231 "RIDICULOUS": quoted in Oberdorfer (1992), p. 173.

232 "HOPES FOR . . . WANING": Gorbachev (1995), p. 429.

232 "I ADMIT . . . PROPHECIES": Transcript of Conversation Between Mikhail Gorbachev and François Mitterrand, 7 July 1986, Gorbachev Foundation Archives, in document collection for Brown University Conference "Understanding the End of the Cold War," archival document no. 25.

232 " 'IT SEEMS . . . THINKING' ": Chernyaev (2000), p. 76.

232 "HE TOLD . . . RATIONAL": Gorbachev (1995), p. 430.

232 "I HAVE . . . INTEREST": Transcript of Mikhail Gorbachev–Richard Nixon conversation, Gorbachev Foundation Archives, 18 July 1986, p. 14 (translation from the Russian), in Mazo (2004), p. 20, and Zubok (2000), p. 10.

233 "AN ATTEMPT . . . AMERICANS": Gorbachev (1995), p. 414.

233 "I TOOK . . . CRAP!' ": Chernyaev (2000), p. 78.

233 "IT WAS . . . PROCESS": Gorbachev (1995), p. 414.

234 "HE STARTED . . . OFFENDED!' ": Chernyaev (2000), p. 78.

234 "IN HIS . . . PROGRAM": quoted in Chernyaev (2000), p. 79.

234 "WE SHOULD . . . CAPABILITIES": Transcript of Chernyaev notes from Politburo session of 4 Oct. 1986, Gorbachev Foundation Archives, in document collection for Brown University Conference "Understanding the End of the Cold War," archival document no. 32.

235 "IN ALMOST . . . PERSONALLY": Reagan (1990), p. 672.

THIRTEEN **LOOKING OVER THE HORIZON**

236 "ESSENTIALLY A . . . SUMMIT": Ronald Reagan, "Remarks on Departure for Reykjavik, Iceland," 9 Oct. 1986.

237 "THE OTHERS . . . COST": Academy of Achievement (1990), p. 2.

237 "WE COULD . . . POCKET": Nitze (1989), p. 429.

237 "TO INTERACT . . . UNION": Chernyaev (2000), p. 84.

237 "BY THE . . . BACK": Gorbachev (1995), p. 349.

237 "WE ARE . . . TETHER": quoted in Chernyaev (2000), pp. 83–84.

238 "OTHERWISE . . . DEAD END": Chernyaev (2000), p. 82.

238 "NOBODY EXCEPT . . . WARS": quoted in Pryce-Jones (1995), p. 114. See also Don Oberdorfer, quoting Chernyaev, in Wohlforth (1996), p. 5.

238 "STAR WARS . . . WAR": Lebow and Stein (1994), p. 37.

238 KIEV LEAVES: Mould (1988), p. xiv.

238 SARCOPHAGUS FINISHED: Z. Medvedev (1990), p. 80.

238 HOFDI HOUSE DETAILS: "Hofdi: The City of Reykjavik's House for Official Recep-
tions," Reykjavikurborg official pamphlet, 1996, courtesy Terri and Randy Reece.

239 A LOT OF PAPER: All direct and indirect quotations from principals at Reykjavik are
drawn from U.S. or translated Soviet memoranda of conversations unless otherwise
indicated. U.S. memoranda online at Margaret Thatcher Archives. Soviet memoranda from the Gorbachev Foundation Archives. First and final session Soviet memoranda translated by Glen Worthy. I have sometimes compressed "direct" quotations,
which are not verbatim in the original.

240 "THE NEED . . . JOY' ": Mazo (2004), pp. 30–31.

241 "WHOOPS . . . HIS JUDGMENT": Matlock (2004), p. 220.

242 "GORBACHEV AND . . . DAYS": Reagan (1990), p. 675.

242 "OUTLINED THE . . . CONVERSATION": Gorbachev (1995), p. 416.

243 "HELL, THIS . . . NYET": Adelman (1989), p. 44.

244 "HE PROPOSED . . . DISADVANTAGE": Shultz (1993), p. 759.

245 "GORBACHEV WAS . . . WAYS": ibid., p. 758.

246 "SDI COOPERATION TREATY": Thomas Graham, Jr., personal communication,
Sept. 2006.

246 "OBVIOUSLY DISAPPOINTED . . . PROPOSALS": Matlock (2004), p. 221.

246 "SOMEWHAT TAKEN . . . REACTION": Shultz (1993), p. 760.

247 "WAS RELIEVED . . . NEGOTIATIONS": ibid.

248 "THE SMALLEST . . . TANK": Adelman (1989), p. 46.

248 "WHY DID . . . YEARS": Shultz (1993), p. 760.

248 "TELL HIM . . . YESTERDAY": Adelman (1989), p. 47.

248 GORBACHEV AND ADVISERS ON THE MAIN DECK: Chernyaev (2000), p. 84.

250 KASHA FOREVER: quoted in Oberdorfer (1992), p. 196.

251 "I'M OLDER . . . THEN?": quoted in Winik (1996), p. 506.

252 "IT WAS . . . POSITIONS": Rozanne Ridgway interview, CNN Perspectives, Episode
22: Star Wars.

252 "GORBACHEV FINALLY . . . PRAGMATIC' ": Matlock (2004), p. 222.

253 LAST OF THE MOHICANS: Shultz (1993), p. 763.

253 "MR. SECRETARY . . . SHOT": quoted in Chidester et al. (2003), p. 37.

253 "I'M NO . . . WANTS": quoted in Winik (1996), p. 507, and (a variant) Adelman
(1989), p. 49.

254 ROWNY DISAGREEMENT AND CAUCUS: Adelman (1989), p. 50.

254 AKHROMEYEV AND KARPOV: Shultz (1993), p. 763.

254 "AT TWO . . . NEXT": Academy of Achievement (1990), p. 3.

254 "HOPED INTO . . . HOUR": Nitze (1989), p. 430.

254 "WHO DO . . . UP?": Shultz (1993), p. 764. Shultz misremembers Perle and others
accompanying Nitze and Linhard; both Nitze and Rowny recalled otherwise.

254 "MARSHAL AKHROMEYEV . . . ACCEPT": Academy of Achievement (1990), pp. 3–4.

254 "IT WAS . . . LIMITED": Nitze (1989), p. 431.

254 "IT BECAME . . . LEVEL": ibid.

255 "WE MADE . . . A.M.": Academy of Achievement (1990), p. 4.

255 "DEFINING STRATEGIC . . . YEARS": Adelman (1989), p. 53.

255 SOVIET CARBON PAPER: ibid.

255 "DAMN GOOD . . . YEARS": Shultz (1993), pp. 764–65.

255 "FOR THE . . . REMAINED": ibid., p. 765.

257 "NO, LET'S . . . NOTHING": Oberdorfer (1992), p. 196.

258   "IT'S BEEN . . . ROUND": quoted in Winik (1996), p. 512.

258   "ALMOST TAUNTING . . . LINE": Shultz (1993), p. 768.

258   "AN EFFORT . . . IMPASSE": ibid.

258   "A LITTLE . . . WEAPONS": Tannenwald (1999), pp. 188–89.

259   LINHARD-PERLE PROPOSAL: quoted in full in Shultz (1993), p. 769.

259   "HE GETS . . . BALL GAME": quoted in Oberdorfer (1992), p. 199.

259   GORBACHEV PROPOSAL: quoted in full in Shultz (1993), p. 769.

260   "RON, IS THAT YOU?": Besides the official memorandum of conversation, this reconstruction draws on Mazo (2004), p. 52; Schell (2004), p. 7; and Shultz (1993), p. 771.

260   "POLICY OF . . . ANYBODY": Skinner et al. (2001), pp. 439–40. Emphasis added.

260   "WE CAN . . . US": ibid., p. 442.

260   "AN UNVARNISHED . . . PRESIDENT": ibid., p. 438.

262   "SOME OF . . . DECISION": quoted in Bosch (1998), p. 284.

262   "THE PRESIDENT . . . LIMITATIONS": Richard Perle conversation, Hoover Institution, Oct. 2006.

263   "THE USSR . . . OTHERWISE": quoted in Shultz (1993), pp. 770–71.

266   "I REMEMBER . . . HOPING": Chernyaev (2000), p. 86.

267   "ANGRIER AND ANGRIER": Reagan (1990), p. 679.

267   "MORE THAN . . . DRAINED": Shultz (1993), p. 773.

267   "IT WAS . . . UNHAPPY": Tannenwald (1999), p. 199.

268   "LEFT IN HIS CAR": Gorbachev (1995), pp. 418–19.

268   "GORBACHEV . . . US' ": Dobrynin (1995), p. 621.

268   "I REALIZED . . . ANGRY: Reagan (1990), p. 679.

269   "PERLE REGARDED . . . ACHIEVEMENTS": Thomas Graham, Jr., personal communication, Sept. 2006.

269   "I WALKED . . . FACE' ": Gorbachev (1995), p. 419. Emphasis added.

269   "THE POSITION . . . THRESHOLD": Thoughts about Reykjavik, Chernyaev notes, 12 Oct. 1986, Gorbachev Foundation Archives.

270   "IT SEEMS . . . MIND": Gorbachev (1987b), p. 29.

270   "WE FELT . . . ENDORSED": ibid., p. 25.

270   "REYKJAVIK GENERATED . . . WORLD": ibid., p. 66.

270   "AFTER ALL . . . START": ibid., p. 19.

FOURTEEN   **THE SOVEREIGN RIGHT TO CHOOSE**

271   "WE SAT . . . SUBJECTS' ": Knott, Selverstone, et al. (2002), p. 8.

271   "COMPARABLE TO CHERNOBYL": quoted in Zubok (2000), p. 8.

271   "THE MEETING . . . CONTRADICTORY": Gorbachev (1987a), pp. 240–41.

271   "IRRESPONSIBILITY" . . . DROWN": Chernyaev notes, 16 Oct. 1986, Gorbachev Foundation Archives, in document collection for Brown University Conference "Understanding the End of the Cold War," archival document no. 24. Emphasis added.

272   "SDI IS . . . DISARMAMENT": Chernyaev notes, 12 Oct. 1986, Brown University Conference, archival document no. 23.

272   "A FEW . . . TIME": Roald Sagdeev interview, Washington, D.C., Dec. 2003. *Washington Post* story: Walter Pincus, " 'Modest' SDI Testing Called Compatible with BM Pact," 30 Oct. 1986.

273   "MAGINOT LINE . . . USSR": Sakharov (1991), pp. 22–23.

273 WARNED GORBACHEV TO SLOW DOWN: Oberdorfer (1992), p. 230. Oberdorfer gives many of the details of Rust's excursion that follow.

273 "VERY POLITICAL . . . WEST": Carl Wilkinson, "What Happened Next?" *Guardian Observer*, 27 Oct. 2002.

274 "MY PLAN . . . IT": ibid.

274 RUST MASSACRE, ORDER OF LENIN: Oberdorfer (1992), p. 230.

274 "GORBACHEV ALSO . . . CONFLICTS": English (2002), p. 84.

275 "THE TRUE . . . CONTROL": T. Graham (2002), p. 124.

275 "IN 1987 . . . SOLUTION": ibid., p. 125.

275 ASTROLOGER PICKED SIGNING TIME: Oberdorfer (1992), p. 259.

276 "AN UNFORGIVABLE . . . HEAD": Gorbachev (1995), pp. 443–44.

276 "FIRST NUCLEAR . . . TIMES": ibid., pp. 442–43.

276 SANDIA AND VERIFICATION REGIME: Dori Ellis, personal communication, Nov. 2005.

276 "A RECIPROCAL . . . WAS": T. Graham (2002), p. 111.

276 "A GREAT . . . EUROPE": Tannenwald (1999), pp. 206–7.

276 "WHERE WILL THEY FIGHT?": Emilio Segré, personal communication, 1982.

277 "I ALWAYS . . . WAY": Bush and Scowcroft (1998), p. 60.

278 "BRIEFLY TOUCHED . . . ON' ": Gorbachev (1995), p. 451.

278 "WAS FACILITATED . . . NEGOTIATIONS": ibid., p. 455.

278 "THE REMARKABLE . . . THINKING": Reagan (1990), p. 710.

278 "MERCILESS" . . . BLUNDERED": Yakovlev (1993), p. 3.

278 "OUR COUNTRY . . . DECEIVED": ibid., pp. 73–75.

279 "THE EXACT . . . DISARMAMENT": Gorbachev (1995), p. 459.

279 GORBACHEV ORDERING DEFENSE MINISTRY TO PLAN TROOP WITHDRAWALS: Evangelista (2001), p. 27.

279 AKHROMEYEV WORKED WITH HIM: Gorbachev (1995), p. 459.

280 "AS A . . . POSITION": quoted in Ellman and Kontorovich (1997), p. 267.

280 "FINALLY TO . . . INTIMIDATION": Chernyaev (2000), pp. 193–95.

281 "HOPED THAT . . . UNION": Gorbachev (1995), p. 460.

281 "I STARTED . . . ELOQUENCE": ibid., p. 461.

281 "TODAY, I . . . AIRCRAFT": Gorbachev (1990), pp. 36–37.

282 "AFTER AN . . . OVATION": Chernyaev (2000), p. 201.

282 "A SPEECH . . . NATIONS": quoted in Gorbachev (1995), p. 462.

283 "I KNOW . . . NONETHELESS": quoted in Oberdorfer (1992), p. 321.

283 "WEEKS . . . PASSED": Gorbachev (1995), p. 496.

283 MOSCOW SHOULD BE LEFT TO STRUGGLE: See Beschloss and Talbott (1993), p. 106.

283 "CHENEY BELIEVED . . . ALACRITY": Foer and Ackerman (2003), pp. 3–4. Emphasis added.

284 HEU PRODUCTION: ISIS, Military and Excess Stocks of Highly Enriched Uranium (HEU) in the Acknowledged Nuclear Weapon States, 11 June 2004, Revised 25 June 2004, Table 1, n. 1.

284 "CHANGED THE . . . INSPECTIONS": Harahan and Kuhn (1996).

284 GROMOV CROSSING, WAR DEATHS: Oberdorfer (1992), p. 243.

284 CSCE: For a detailed account of this and the following discussion, see Harahan and Kuhn (1996).

285 "KNOWN AS . . . ACCORD": Harahan and Kuhn (1996), Chapter 1a., p. 2.

285 "FOR US . . . IT!": Gorbachev (1995), p. 502.

285 "WANTED TO . . . BEGAN": T. Graham (2002), pp. 190–91.

286 "THE PRINCIPLE ... ESTABLISH": Gorbachev (1995), p. 437.

286 "BARE-BONES ... WANTED": T. Graham (2002), p. 192.

286 "ALL AROUND ... PROPOSED": Chernyaev (2000), p. 226.

287 "RESPECT FOR ... CHOICE": quoted in Kramer (2001), p. 126.

287 "IF WE ... BACK": quoted in Beschloss and Talbott (1993), p. 96.

287 GRAHAM HIMSELF ... REPRESENTATIVE: T. Graham (2002), p. 193.

288 "ALWAYS BRIGHT ... PEPPERED": Alex de Jonge, *The Weimar Chronicle*, London: Paddington Press, 1978, p. 130.

288 "ON A ... REALIZED' ": Beschloss and Talbott (1993), p. 132.

288 "BEFORE THE ... IT": ibid., p. 166.

288 "YOU KNOW ... FAST": Lee Hamilton, conversation, Washington, D.C., 2004.

288 "LASTED ABOUT ... 1990)": T. Graham (2002), p. 185.

289 "IT WAS ... SCENES": ibid., p. 203.

289 "IN 1988 ... POWER": Graham and LaVera (2003), p. 594.

289 "THE CFE ... SECURITY": T. Graham (2002), p. 209.

289 "THEY DECLARED ... FRIENDSHIP' ": Evangelista (2001), p. 23.

FIFTEEN **THE LITTLE SUITCASE**

290 "WE FINALLY ... WAR": Gorbachev (1995), pp. 538–39.

290 "PUT THE ... SIGNED": Graham and LaVera (2003), p. 885.

290 "START I ... SIDE": Jentleson (2000), p. 111.

291 TACTICAL NUKE YIELDS: Millar (2002), p. 1.

291 "THE STRATEGIC ... PROCEDURES": Gorbachev (1995), p. 514.

291 TWENTY-TWO THOUSAND SOVIET TACTICAL NUKES: Millar (2002) p. 4, n. 6.

291 TWENTY-THREE THOUSAND U.S.: Powell (1995), p. 541.

291 "PUT ON ... TRUE": quoted in Beschloss and Talbot (1993), p. 316.

291 RICE INTERAGENCY GROUP: ibid.

291 "A RIGHT-WING JUNTA": quoted in Bush and Scowcroft (1998), p. 527.

291 "DURING THE ... PRESIDENT]": Baker (1995), p. 526.

292 "A RUSSIAN ... LEGISLATION": Sam Nunn, conversation, Washington, D.C., Sept. 2005.

292 "WHILE THERE ... US": Bush and Scowcroft (1998), p. 544.

292 "I DON'T ... SUNG": quoted in Nichols (2004), p. 108.

293 "I WANT ... PROPOSALS": quoted in Powell (1995), p. 541.

293 "CHENEY'S DISTASTE ... TIME": Bush and Scowcroft (1998), pp. 544–45.

293 "THE SUM ... ONES)": ibid., p. 545.

293 CHENEY SIGNED ON: ibid.

293 "FAR EXCEEDED ... WORLD": Powell (1995), p. 541.

294 "HE WANTED ... AGREEMENT": Bush and Scowcroft (1998), p. 547.

294 "WE PROPOSE ... ELEMENTS": "Text of President Gorbachev's Televised Statement on Nuclear Weapons," 5 Oct. 1991, Tass, Moscow.

295 "DISMISSING THE ... DEMOCRACY": Archie Brown (1996), pp. 101–2.

295 "GORBACHEV, WHILE ... ME' ": Chernyaev (2000), p. 280.

295 "IN THE ... PROGRESS": Gorbachev (1991), pp. 104–5.

296 "IN THE ... POLICY": quoted in Gorbachev (1995), p. 614.

296 "MR. PRESIDENT ... OPINION": quoted in Chernyaev (2000), p. 274.

297 "BOTH THE ... AMERICA": Gorbachev (1995), p. 539.

297 "FOOLISHNESS" ... MANEUVER": quoted in John H. Cushman, Jr., "Defense Aide Rejects Concept of a World Free of Atomic Arms," *New York Times*, 1 Feb. 1987.

297 "A NUCLEAR . . . BOTH": Dobrynin (1995), pp. 468–69.

298 "CAME OUT . . . LIFE": Barnet (1985), pp. 484–90.

298 "IT IS . . . AFRAID": ibid., p. 490.

299 "DETERRENCE . . . FAILED": Kugler (1984), pp. 474–76.

299 "NUCLEAR NATIONS . . . OUTCOMES": ibid., pp. 478–79.

299 "THE MAIN . . . ARSENALS": ibid., p. 501.

300 "CHALLENGING THE . . . MAGIC": ibid.

300 SENATE HEARINGS: *Nuclear Testing Issues:* Hearing before the Committee on Armed Services, United States Senate, 99th Congress, 2nd Session, 29–30 April 1986.

300 "AT TIMES . . . DUDS": Rosengren (1983), p. 13.

300 "IN LATE . . . FORCE": ibid., p. 21.

300 MINUTEMAN AND W45S: ibid., pp. 21–22.

301 "THE COUP . . . COME": Gorbachev (1995), p. 646.

301 "IN GORBACHEV'S . . . CORNER": Yeltsin (1994), pp. 109–10.

302 "HAD TO . . . WAY": ibid., p. 111.

302 "WE WERE . . . UNION": ibid.

302 "A WONDERFUL . . . DIVISION": Yeltsin (1994), pp. 111–12.

303 "FIRST A . . . UNION)": Stanislav Shushkevich, personal communication, Aug. 2005.

304 "THE IDEA . . . PARTIES": Yeltsin (1994), p. 112.

304 FAX MACHINES: ibid.

304 "ON DECEMBER . . . UNION": Reed (2004), pp. 1–2.

304 "YUGOSLAVIA WITH . . . WEAPONS": Jentleson (2000), p. 111.

305 "THERE WAS . . . PRETENSE": Shushkevich interview, April 2003.

305 "PROTRACTED AND DIFFICULT": Yeltsin (1994), p. 121.

305 "IT WAS . . . SURVIVED": quoted in Archie Brown (1996), p. 342, n. 104, quoting Gorbachev interview with Jonathan Steele, *Guardian,* 24 Dec. 1992.

305 "MY DEAR . . . FAMILY!": quoted in Beschloss and Talbot (1993), p. 461.

305 "TO SUM . . . RUSSIA": Reed (2004), p. 2.

305 "I ATTACH . . . TONIGHT": quoted in Beschloss and Talbot (1993), p. 461.

306 $5.5 TRILLION: Schwartz (1998), p. 3.

306 "ENOUGH TO . . . LAND": C. Sagan (1992), p. 24.

306 "RESPONSIBLE FOR . . . REQUIREMENTS": quoted in Barnet (1971), pp. 171–72.

306 "THE EXTENT . . . MILITARY": Melman (1974), p. 122.

306 "THE PURVEYORS . . . SOCIETY": ibid., p. 123.

307 "SINCE FUTURE . . . YEAR": quoted in Melman (1974), pp. 122–23.

307 "THE DOLLARS . . . BUDGETS": Melman (1974), p. 117.

307 ASCE REPORT CARD: "2005 Report Card for America's Infrastructure," www.asce.org (accessed 6 Dec. 2006).

308 "ALL LEVELS . . . SECTOR": ASCE press release, 9 Mar. 2005, available at http://www.asce.org/reportcard/2005/page.cfm?id=108 (accessed 6 Dec. 2006).

308 "IF YOU . . . THING": Tannenwald (1999), pp. 52–53.

308 "THE VERY . . . LIFE": Oppenheimer (1953), pp. 527–29.

BIBLIOGRAPHY

Academy of Achievement (1990). Paul H. Nitze Interview, 20 October 1990. Academy of Achievement, Washington, D.C.

Adelman, Kenneth L. (1989). *The Great Universal Embrace: Arms Summitry, A Skeptic's Account.* New York: Simon & Schuster.

Alexievich, Svetlana (2005). *Voices from Chernobyl.* K. Gessen, Trans. Normal, IL: Dalkey Archive Press.

Allin, Dana H. (1998). *Cold War Illusions: America, Europe and Soviet Power, 1969–1989.* New York: St. Martin's Press.

Anders, Roger M. (1987). *Forging the Atomic Shield.* Chapel Hill: University of North Carolina Press.

Anderson, Martin (1990). *Revolution: The Reagan Legacy.* Stanford, CA: Hoover Institution Press.

Andrew, Christopher, and Oleg Gordievsky (1990). *KGB: The Inside Story of Its Foreign Operations from Lenin to Gorbachev.* New York: HarperCollins.

Andrew, Christopher, and Oleg Gordievsky, Eds. (1991). *Instructions from the Centre: Top Secret Files on KGB Foreign Operations 1975–1985.* London: Hodder & Stoughton.

Andrew, Christopher, and Vasili Mitrokhin (1999). *The Sword and the Shield: The Mitrokhin Archive and the Secret History of the KGB.* New York: Basic Books.

Anspaugh, Lynn R., Robert J. Catlin, and Marvin Goldman (1988). The global impact of the Chernobyl reactor accident. *Science* 242 (4885), 16 Dec., 1513–19.

Arbatov, Georgi (1992). *The System: An Insider's Life in Soviet Politics.* New York: Times Books.

Armstrong, David (2002). Dick Cheney's song of America. *Harper's* 305 (1829).

Arnold, Lorna (2001). *Britain and the H-Bomb.* Basingstoke, Hampshire: Palgrave.

Bahr, Egon (2003). Statements and discussion: Egon Bahr. *German Historical Institute Bulletin, Supplement 1: American Detente and German Ostpolitik, 1969–1972,* 2003, 137–43.

Baker, James A., III (1995). *The Politics of Diplomacy: Revolution, War and Peace, 1989–1992.* New York: G. P. Putnam's Sons.

Ball, Desmond, and Jeffrey Richelson, Eds. (1986). *Strategic Nuclear Targeting.* Ithaca, NY: Cornell University Press.

Barnet, Richard J. (1971). *The Economy of Death.* New York: Atheneum.

———(1985). The ideology of the national security state. *Massachusetts Review* 26 (Winter), 483–500.

Baucom, Donald R. (1990). Hail to the chiefs: The untold history of Reagan's SDI decision. *Policy Review* 53 (Summer), 66.

Bearden, Milt, and James Risen (2003). *The Main Enemy: The Inside Story of the CIA's Final Showdown with the KGB.* New York: Random House.

Berman, Harold J. (1963). The dilemma of Soviet law reform. *Harvard Law Review* 76 (5), 929–51.

Beschloss, Michael R., and Strobe Talbott (1993). *At the Highest Levels: The Inside Story of the End of the Cold War*. Boston: Little, Brown.

Betts, Richard K. (2003). Striking first: A history of thankfully lost opportunities. *Ethics and International Affairs* 17 (1) (Spring).

Blacker, Coit D. (1993). *Hostage to Revolution: Gorbachev and Soviet Security Policy, 1985–1991*. New York: Council on Foreign Relations Press.

Blake, George (1990). *No Other Choice: An Autobiography*. New York: Simon & Schuster.

Bleek, Philipp C. (2001). U.S. and Russian/Soviet strategic nuclear forces. *Arms Control Today,* May.

Blinken, Antony J. (2003). From preemption to engagement. *Survival* 45 (4) (Winter), 33–60.

Blumenthal, Sidney (1986). *The Rise of the Counter-Establishment*. New York: Times Books.

———(1987a). Richard Perle, disarmed but undeterred. *Washington Post,* 23 Nov.

———(1987b). Richard Perle's nuclear legacy. *Washington Post,* 24 Nov.

———(1987c). Perle and the diminished dream. *Washington Post,* 25 Nov.

———(2005). The long march of Dick Cheney. *Salon,* http://www.salon.com/opinion/blumenthal/2005/11/24/cheney/ (accessed 24 November 2005).

Bosch, Adriana (2000). *Reagan: An American Story*. New York: TV Books.

Brandt, Willy (1989). *My Life in Politics*. New York: Viking.

Broad, William J. (1992). *Teller's War: The Top-Secret Story Behind the Star Wars Deception*. New York: Simon & Schuster.

Brook-Shepherd, Gordon (1989). *The Storm Birds: Soviet Postwar Defectors*. New York: Weidenfeld & Nicolson.

Brown, Archie (1996). *The Gorbachev Factor*. New York: Oxford University Press.

Brown, Michael (1996). Phased Nuclear Disarmament and US Defense Policy (Occasional Paper No. 30). The Henry L. Stimson Center, Oct.

Bundy, McGeorge (1969). To cap the volcano. *Foreign Affairs* 48 (1) (Oct.).

———(1988). *Danger and Survival: Choices About the Bomb in the First Fifty Years*. New York: Random House.

Bunn, George (2003). The Nuclear Nonproliferation Treaty: History and current problems. *Arms Control Today,* Dec.

Burnham, James (1945). Lenin's heir. *Partisan Review* 12 (Winter), 61–72.

Burr, William, Ed. (2004). *The Creation of SIOP-62: More Evidence on the Origins of Overkill*. Washington, D.C.: National Security Archive Electronic Briefing Book No. 130.

———. (2005). *"To Have the Only Option That of Killing 80 Million People Is the Height of Immorality": The Nixon Administration, the SIOP, and the Search for Limited Nuclear Options, 1969–1974*. Washington, D.C.: National Security Archive Electronic Briefing Book No. 173.

Burr, William, and Robert Wampler, Eds. (2004). *"The Master of the Game": Paul H. Nitze and U.S. Cold War Strategy from Truman to Reagan*. Washington, D.C.: National Security Archive Electronic Briefing Book No. 139.

Bush, George H. W., and Brent Scowcroft (1998). *A World Transformed*. New York: Vintage.

Butler, Richard, Lee Butler, et al. (1996). *Report of the Canberra Commission on the Elimination of Nuclear Weapons*. Department of Foreign Affairs and Trade, Commonwealth of Australia.

Cahn, Anne Hessing (1998). *Killing Detente: The Right Attacks the CIA*. University Park: Pennsylvania State University Press.

Calabrese, Edward J., and Linda A. Baldwin (2003). Toxicology rethinks its central belief. *Nature* 421, 13 Feb., 691.

Callahan, David (1990). *Dangerous Capabilities: Paul Nitze and the Cold War.* New York: HarperCollins.

Cannon, Lou (1991). *President Reagan: The Role of a Lifetime.* New York: Simon & Schuster.

Carynnyk, Marco, Lubomyr Y. Luciuk, and Bohdan S. Kordan, Eds. (1988). *The Foreign Office and the Famine: British Documents on Ukraine and the Great Famine of 1932–1933.* Kingston, ON: Limestone Press.

Chernyaev, Anatoly (2000). *My Six Years with Gorbachev.* University Park: Pennsylvania State University Press.

Chidester, Jeff, Stephen F. Knott, and Robert Strong (2003). Interview with Kenneth Adelman, University of Virginia, 30 Sep. Charlottesville, VA: Ronald Reagan Oral History Project, Presidential Oral History Program, Miller Center of Public Affairs.

Cimbala, Stephen J., Ed. (1999). *Mysteries of the Cold War.* Aldershot, England: Ashgate.

Clem, Ralph S. (1986). The Soviet Union: Crisis, stability or renewal? *Air University Review* (Nov.–Dec.), http://www.airpower.au.af.mil/airchronicles/aureview/1986/nov-dec/clem .html (accessed 24 June 2005).

Cochran, Thomas B., et al. (1991). Report on the Third International Workshop on Verified Storage and Destruction of Nuclear Warheads held in Moscow and Kiev, Natural Resources Defense Council. Dec. 16–20.

Cohen, Avner (1998). *Israel and the Bomb.* New York: Columbia University Press.

Cohen, Avner, and Thomas Graham, Jr. (2004). An NPT for non-members. *Bulletin of the Atomic Scientists* 60 (3) (May/June), 40–44.

Cohen, Avner, and Steven Lee, Eds. (1986). *Nuclear Weapons and the Future of Humanity.* Totowa, NJ: Rowman & Allanheld.

Cohen, Stephen F. (2000). *Failed Crusade: America and the Tragedy of Post-Communist Russia.* New York: W. W. Norton.

Cohen, Stephen F., and Katrina vanden Heuvel (1989). *Voices of Glasnost: Interviews with Gorbachev's Reformers.* New York: W. W. Norton.

Conquest, Robert (1986). *The Harvest of Sorrow: Soviet Collectivization and the Terror-Famine.* New York: Oxford University Press.

———(1990). *The Great Terror: A Reassessment.* New York: Oxford University Press.

Cottrell, Robert (2004). An Icelandic Saga: Review of *Reagan and Gorbachev: How the Cold War Ended,* by Jack F. Matlock, Jr. *New York Review of Books* 51 (17), 4 Nov.

Cowley, Robert, Ed. (2005). *The Cold War: A Military History.* New York: Random House.

Cox, Arthur Macy (1975). *The Myths of National Security: The Peril of Secret Government.* Boston: Beacon Press.

———(1980). The CIA's tragic error. *New York Review of Books* 27 (17), 6 Nov., 1–8 (online version).

CRS (Congressional Research Service) (2006). U.S. Conventional Forces and Nuclear Deterrence: A China Case Study. Bolkom, Christopher, et al. 11 Aug.

Curtis, Adam (2005). *The Power of Nightmare* (BBC three-part series), DVD edition.

Dahl, Robert (1985). *Controlling Nuclear Weapons: Democracy Versus Guardianship.* Syracuse, NY: Syracuse University Press.

Dallin, Alexander (1985). *Black Box: KAL 007 and the Superpowers.* Berkeley: University of California Press.

Dam, Kenneth W. (1983). Challenges of U.S.-Soviet relations at the 50-year mark: Address before the International House, Chicago, 31 Oct. *Department of State Bulletin* (Dec.), 26–30.

David, Mark W. (2000). Reagan's real reason for SDI. *Policy Review* (103) (Oct.–Nov.), online version.

Department of State (1950). *NSC 68: United States Objectives and Programs for National Security.* 7 Apr.

Dobrynin, Anatoly (1995). *In Confidence: Moscow's Ambassador to Six Cold War Presidents.* Seattle: University of Washington Press.

Doder, Dusko (1988). *Shadows and Whispers: Power Politics Inside the Kremlin from Brezhnev to Gorbachev.* New York: Penguin.

Doder, Dusko, and Louise Branson (1990). *Gorbachev: Heretic in the Kremlin.* New York: Viking.

Dolot, Miron (1985). *Execution by Hunger: The Hidden Holocaust.* New York: W. W. Norton.

Ebel, Robert E. (1994). *Chernobyl and Its Aftermath: A Chronology of Events.* Washington: Center for Strategic and International Studies.

Eden, Lynn (2004). *Whole World on Fire: Organizations, Knowledge and Nuclear Weapons Devastation.* Ithaca, NY: Cornell University Press.

Ehrman, John (1995). *The Rise of Neoconservatism: Intellectuals and Foreign Affairs 1945–1994.* New Haven, CT: Yale University Press.

Eisenhower, Susan (1995). *Breaking Free: A Memoir of Love and Revolution.* New York: Farrar, Straus & Giroux.

Ellman, Michael, and Vladimir Kontorovich (1997). The collapse of the Soviet system and the memoir literature. *Europe-Asia Studies,* 49 (2) (March), 259–79.

Ellman, Michael, and Vladimir Kontorovich, Eds. (1998). *The Destruction of the Soviet Economic System: An Insiders' History.* Armonk, NY: M. E. Sharpe.

English, Robert D. (2000). *Russia and the Idea of the West: Gorbachev, Intellectuals and the End of the Cold War.* New York: Columbia University Press.

———(2002). Power, ideas, and new evidence on the Cold War's end: A reply to Brooks and Wohlforth. *International Security* 26 (4) (Spring), 70–92.

Ermarth, Fritz W. (2003). Observations on the "war scare" of 1983 from an intelligence perch. Parallel History Project on Cooperative Security, http://www.php.isn.ethz.ch/collections (accessed 11 Mar. 2007).

Evangelista, Matthew (1999). *Unarmed Forces: The Transnational Movement to End the Cold War.* Ithaca, NY: Cornell University Press.

———(2001). Norms, heresthetics and the end of the Cold War. *Journal of Cold War Studies* 3 (1) (Winter), 5–35.

Fainsod, Merle (1956). The Communist Party since Stalin. *Annals of the American Academy of Political and Social Science* 303 (Jan.), 23–36.

Feiveson, Harold A., Ed. (1999). *The Nuclear Turning Point: A Blueprint for Deep Cuts and De-Alerting of Nuclear Weapons.* Washington, D.C.: Brookings Institution Press.

Fischer, Benjamin B. (1997). A Cold War Conundrum. Center for the Study of Intelligence, Central Intelligence Agency.

———, Ed. (1999). *At Cold War's End: US Intelligence on the Soviet Union and Eastern Europe, 1989–1991.* Washington, D.C.: GPO.

Fischer, Beth A. (1997). *The Reagan Reversal: Foreign Policy and the End of the Cold War.* Columbia: University of Missouri Press.

Fischer, David (1997). *History of the International Atomic Energy Agency: The First Forty Years.* Vienna: IAEA.

FitzGerald, Frances (1976). The warrior intellectuals. *Harper's,* May, 45–64.

———(2000). *Way Out There in the Blue: Reagan, Star Wars and the End of the Cold War.* New York: Simon & Schuster.

Foer, Franklin, and Spencer Ackerman (2003). The radical. *New Republic* (1 Dec.), 3–4.

Fosdick, Dorothy, Ed. (1990). *Henry M. Jackson and World Affairs: Selected Speeches, 1953–1983.* Seattle: University of Washington Press.

Foster, Kenneth R., David E. Bernstein, and Peter W. Huber, Eds. (1993). *Phantom Risk: Scientific Inference and the Law*. Cambridge, MA: MIT Press.

Freedman, Lawrence (2000). Does deterrence have a future? *Arms Control Today*, Oct.

Freedman, Paul B., Stephen F. Knott, et al. (2001). Interview with Stuart Spencer, University of Virginia, 15–16 Nov. Charlottesville, VA: Ronald Reagan Oral History Project, Presidential Oral History Program, Miller Center of Public Affairs.

Gaddis, John Lewis (1997). *We Now Know: Rethinking Cold War History*. Oxford: Clarendon Press.

Garthoff, Raymond L. (1983). The NATO decision on Theater Nuclear Forces. *Political Science Quarterly* 98 (2) (Summer), 197–214.

———(1985). *Detente and Confrontation: American-Soviet Relations from Nixon to Reagan*. Washington, D.C.: The Brookings Institution.

Garton Ash, Timothy (1993). *In Europe's Name: Germany and the Divided Continent*. New York: Vintage.

Gates, Robert M. (1996). *From the Shadows: The Ultimate Insider's Story of Five Presidents and How They Won the Cold War*. New York: Simon & Schuster.

Gelb, Leslie H. (1984). Is the nuclear threat manageable? *New York Times Magazine*, 4 Mar. (online version).

———(1985). The mind of the President. *New York Times Magazine*, 6 Oct. (online version).

Genin, Vlad E., Ed. (2001). *The Anatomy of Russian Defense Conversion*. Walnut Creek, CA: Vega Press.

Gilpatrick, Roswell, et al. (1965). A report to the President by the Committee on Nuclear Proliferation. The White House, 21 Jan. National Security Archives.

Glaser, Charles L. (1990). *Analyzing Strategic Nuclear Policy*. Princeton, NJ: Princeton University Press.

Goldman, Marshall I. (1986). Keeping the Cold War out of Chernobyl: Just as the Soviets must be more open, so we in the West must not gloat. *Technology Review* 89 (2) (July), 18–19.

Gorbachev, Mikhail (1984). The people's vital creativity. *Current Digest of the Soviet Press* 35 (24), 9 Jan. 1985 (*Pravda*, 11 Dec. 1984), 1–10, 24, and No. 25, pp. 1–8.

———(1987a). *Perestroika: New Thinking for Our Country and the World*. New York: Harper & Row.

———(1987b). *Reykjavik: Results and Lessons*. Madison, CT: Sphinx Press.

———(1987c). *Selected Speeches and Articles*. Second Updated Ed. Moscow: Progress Publishers.

———(1990). *A Road to the Future: Complete Text of the December 7, 1988 United Nations Address*. Santa Fe, NM: Ocean Tree Books.

———(1991). *The August Coup: The Truth and the Lessons*. New York: HarperCollins.

———(1995). *Memoirs*. London: Doubleday.

———(2000). *On My Country and the World*. G. Shriver, Trans. New York: Columbia University Press.

Gorbachev, Mikhail, and Zdenek Mlynar (2002). *Conversations with Gorbachev on Perestroika, the Prague Spring, and the Crossroads of Socialism*. New York: Columbia University Press.

Gorbachev, Mikhail, et al. (1996). What did we end the Cold War for? *New Perspectives Quarterly* (Winter).

Gorbacheva, Raisa (1991). *I Hope*. D. Floyd, Trans. New York: HarperCollins.

Graham, Bradley (2001). *Hit to Kill: The New Battle Over Shielding America from Missile Attack*. New York: Public Affairs.

Graham, Thomas, Jr. (2002). *Disarmament Sketches: Three Decades of Arms Control and International Law*. Seattle: University of Washington Press.

Graham, Thomas, Jr., and Damien J. LaVera (2003). *Cornerstones of Security: Arms Control Treaties in the Nuclear Era.* Seattle: University of Washington Press.

Graham, Thomas, Jr., and Douglas B. Shaw (1998). Viewpoint: Nearing a fork in the road; Proliferation or nuclear reversal? *Nonproliferation Review* (Fall), 70–76.

Gray, Colin S., and Keith Payne (1980). Victory is possible. *Foreign Policy* 39 (Summer), 14–27.

Gusterson, Hugh (1996). *Nuclear Rites: A Weapons Laboratory at the End of the Cold War.* Berkeley: University of California Press.

Hadley, Stephen, Robert G. Joseph, et al. (2001). Rationale and Requirements for U.S. Nuclear Forces and Arms Control. National Institute for Public Policy (NIPP). Jan.

Hafemeister, David (1997). Reflections on the GAO Report on the nuclear triad: How much was enough to win the Cold War; was it Freud or Newton? (Occasional Report). *Science & Global Security* 6, 383–93.

———(2005). A secrecy primer. *Bulletin of the Atomic Scientists* (May/June), 23–25.

Harahan, Joseph P., and John C. Kuhn III (1996). *On-Site Inspections Under the CFE Treaty: A History of the On-Site Inspection Agency and CFE Treaty Implementation, 1990–1996.* Washington, D.C.: On-Site Inspection Agency, U.S. Dept. of Defense (online at www .fas.org).

Hartmann, Robert T. (1980). *Palace Politics: An Inside Account of the Ford Years.* New York: McGraw-Hill.

Hayes Holgate, Laura S. (1991). Fallout in the Fifties: The beginnings of environmentalism as arms control. *Breakthroughs* (Spring), 14–19.

Heilbrunn, Jacob (1996). Who won the Cold War? *The American Prospect* 7 (28) (Sept.).

Hendrickson, David C. (2002). Toward universal empire: The dangerous quest for absolute security. *World Policy Journal* (Fall), 1–10.

Herken, Gregg (1980). *The Winning Weapon.* New York: Alfred A. Knopf.

———(1985). *Counsels of War.* New York: Alfred A. Knopf.

Hersh, Seymour M. (1986). *"The Target Is Destroyed": What Really Happened to Flight 007 and What America Knew About It.* New York: Random House.

Hobbes, Thomas (1651). *Leviathan.* Reprinted by Oxford: Clarendon Press, 1909.

Hollander, Paul (1999). *Political Will and Personal Belief.* New Haven, CT: Yale University Press.

Holloway, David A. (1994). *Stalin and the Bomb.* New Haven, CT: Yale University Press.

Hopkins, Arthur T. (1993). *Unchained Reactions: Chernobyl, Glasnost and Nuclear Deterrence.* Washington, D.C.: National Defense University.

Hudson, George E., Ed. (1990). *Soviet National Security Policy Under Perestroika.* Mershon Center Series on International Security and Foreign Policy, Vol. IV, C. F. Hermann, Ed. Boston: Unwin Hyman.

Hunter, Kerry L. (1992). *The Reign of Fantasy: The Political Roots of Reagan's Star Wars Policy.* New York: Peter Lang.

Hunter, Thomas O., and C. Paul Robinson, Eds. (2005). *U.S. Strategic Nuclear Policy: An Oral History, 1942–2004* (4 DVDs). Albuquerque, NM: Sandia National Laboratories.

IAEA, Ed. (1997). *International Atomic Energy Agency: Personal Reflections.* Vienna: IAEA.

Iklé, Fred Charles (1973). Can nuclear deterrence last out the century? *Foreign Affairs* (Jan.), 267–85.

Jaworowski, Zbigniew (1999). Radiation risk and ethics. *Physics Today,* Sept. 1999, 24–29.

Jentleson, Bruce W. (2000). *Opportunities Missed, Opportunities Seized: Preventive Diplomacy in the Post-Cold War World.* Latham, MD: Rowman & Littlefield.

Jervis, Robert (1989). *The Meaning of the Nuclear Revolution: Statecraft and the Prospect of Armageddon.* Ithaca, NY: Cornell University Press.

Johnson, Chalmers (2004). *The Sorrows of Empire*. New York: Henry Holt.

Joseph, Paul (1983). Nuclear strategy and American foreign policy. In *The Socialist Register 1983*, R. Miliband and John Saville, Eds., pp. 202–18. London: Merlin Press.

Josephson, Paul R. (2000). *Red Atom: Russia's Nuclear Power Program from Stalin to Today*. New York: W. H. Freeman.

Jürgens, Urda (1990). *Raisa: The 1st First Lady of the Soviet Union*. S. Clayton, Trans. New York: Summit.

Kaiser, Robert G. (1992). *Why Gorbachev Happened*. New York: Simon & Schuster.

Kanet, Roger E., and Edward A. Kolodziej, Eds. (1991). *The Cold War as Cooperation*. Baltimore, MD: Johns Hopkins University Press.

Kaplan, Fred (1979). Warring over new missiles for NATO. *New York Times Magazine* (9 Dec.).

———(1983). *The Wizards of Armageddon*. New York: Simon & Schuster.

Keeney, L. Douglas (2002). *The Doomsday Scenario*. St. Paul, MN: MBI Publishing.

Kegley, Charles W., Jr. (1994). How did the Cold War die? Principles for an autopsy. *Mershon International Studies Review* 38 (1) (Apr.), 11–41.

Khrushchev, Nikita (1974). *Khrushchev Remembers: The Last Testament*. S. Talbott, Trans. Boston: Little, Brown.

Kistiakowsky, George (1976). *A Scientist at the White House: The Private Diary of President Eisenhower's Special Assistant for Science and Technology*. Cambridge, MA: Harvard University Press.

———(1979). False alarm: The story behind SALT II. *New York Review of Books* 26 (4), 22 Mar. (online version.)

Klotz, Frank Graham (1980). The U.S. President and the Control of Strategic Nuclear Weapons. D. Phil. Oxford University.

Knight, Amy (2003). The KGB, perestroika, and the collapse of the Soviet Union. *Journal of Cold War Studies* 5 (1) (Winter), 67–93.

Knott, Stephen, and Russell L. Riley (2002). Interview with Caspar Weinberger, University of Virginia, 19 Nov. Charlottesville: Ronald Reagan Oral History Project, Presidential Oral History Program, Miller Center of Public Affairs.

Knott, Stephen, Marc Selverstone, and James Sterling Young (2002). Interview with George Shultz, University of Virginia, 18 Dec. Charlottesville: Ronald Reagan Oral History Project, Presidential Oral History Program, Miller Center of Public Affairs.

Knott, Stephen, James Sterling Young, and Allison Asher (2001). Interview with Martin Anderson, University of Virginia, 11–12 Dec. Charlottesville: Ronald Reagan Oral History Project, Presidential Oral History Program, Miller Center of Public Affairs.

Kotkin, Stephen (2001). *Armageddon Averted: The Soviet Collapse, 1970–2000*. New York: Oxford University Press.

Kramer, Mark (1992). New sources on the 1968 Soviet invasion of Czechoslovakia. *Cold War International History Project Bulletin* 2 (1) (Fall), 4–13.

———(2001). Realism, ideology and the end of the Cold War: A reply to William Wohlforth. *Review of International Studies* 27 (1) (January), 119–30.

Kramish, Arnold (1993). Proliferation 101: The Presidential faculty. *Global Affairs*, Spring, 110.

Krepon, Michael (1989). *Arms Control in the Reagan Administration*. Lanham, MD: University Press of America.

Kristensen, Hans M., Matthew G. McKinzie, and Robert S. Norris (2004). The protection paradox. *Bulletin of the Atomic Scientists* 60 (2) (Mar./Apr.), 68–77.

Kugler, Jacek (1984). Terror without deterrence: Reassessing the role of nuclear weapons. *Journal of Conflict Resolution* 28 (3) (Sept.), 470–506.

Kuhn, Jim (2004). *Ronald Reagan in Private*. New York: Sentinel.

Kull, Steven (1988). *Minds at War: Nuclear Reality and the Inner Conflicts of Defense Policy-makers*. New York: Basic Books.

Kunsman, David M., and Douglas B. Lawson (2001). A Primer on U.S. Strategic Nuclear Policy. Sandia National Laboratories. January.

Kurtz, Lester R. (1988). *The Nuclear Cage: A Sociology of the Arms Race*. Englewood Cliffs, NJ: Prentice Hall.

Lakoff, Sanford, and Herbert F. York (1989). *A Shield in Space? Technology, Politics, and the Strategic Defense Initiative*. Berkeley: University of California Press.

Lambright, W. Henry (2002). Changing course: Admiral James Watkins and the DOE nuclear weapons complex. In *Security in a Changing World: Case Studies in U.S. National Security Management*, V. C. Franke, Ed., 55–80. Westport, CT: Praeger.

Lebow, Richard Ned, and Janice Gross Stein (1994). Reagan and the Russians. *Atlantic* 273 (2) (Feb.), 35–37.

Leebaert, Derek (2002). *The Fifty-Year Wound: The True Price of America's Cold War Victory*. Boston: Little, Brown.

Leffler, Melvin P. (1991). Was the Cold War necessary? *Diplomatic History* 15 (2), Spring, 265–75.

Legasov, Valery (2000). Testament. In *Chernobyl Record*, R. F. Mould, Ed., 289–303. Bristol, England: Institute of Physics Publishing.

Lettow, Paul (2005). *Ronald Reagan and His Quest to Abolish Nuclear Weapons*. New York: Random House.

Levoy, Peter R. (2004). Predicting nuclear proliferation: A declassified documentary record. *Strategic Insights* 3 (1) (Jan.) (online).

Lodal, Jan M. (1976). Assuring strategic stability: An alternate view. *Foreign Affairs* 54 (3) (Apr.) (online version).

Luttrell, Clifton B. (1973). The Russian wheat deal: Hindsight vs. foresight. *Federal Reserve Bank of St. Louis Review* (Oct.), 2–9.

MacArthur, Brian, Ed. (1999). *The Penguin Book of Twentieth-Century Speeches*. London: Penguin Books.

MacLean, Douglas, Ed. (1984). *The Security Gamble: Deterrence Dilemmas in the Nuclear Age*. Totowa, NJ: Rowman & Allanheld.

Madariaga, Salvador de (1929). *Disarmament*. New York: Coward-McCann.

Malia, Martin ("Z," pseudonym) (1990). To the Stalin mausoleum. *Daedalus* 119 (1) (Winter), 295–344.

Malish, Anton F. (1984). Soviet agricultural policy in the 1980s. *Policy Studies Review* 4 (2) (Nov.), 301–10.

Maloney, Sean (2004). Fire brigade or tocsin? NATO's ACE mobile force, flexible response and the Cold War. *Journal of Strategic Studies* 27 (4) (Dec.), 585–613.

Mann, James (2004). *Rise of the Vulcans: The History of Bush's War Cabinet*. New York: Viking.

Marples, David R. (1986). *Chernobyl and Nuclear Power in the USSR*. New York: St. Martin's Press.

———(1993). Chernobyl's lengthening shadow. *Bulletin of the Atomic Scientists* 49 (7) (Sept.), 38–43.

———(1996a). *Belarus: From Soviet Rule to Nuclear Catastrophe*. New York: St. Martin's Press.

———(1996b). The Chernobyl disaster: Its effect on Belarus and Ukraine. In *The Long Road to Recovery: Community Responses to Industrial Disaster*, J. K. Mitchell, Ed. New York: United Nations University Press. Full text online (accessed 6 Oct. 2005).

Masters, Roger D. (1964). World politics as a primitive political system. *World Politics* 16 (4) (July), 595–619.

Mastny, Vojtech (2003). Did East German spies prevent a nuclear war? Parallel History Project on Cooperative Security, online at http://www.php.isn.ethz.ch/collections/coll_stasi/mastny.cfm (accessed 12 Mar. 2007.)

Mastny, Vojtech, and Malcolm Byrne, Eds. (2005). *A Cardboard Castle? An Inside History of the Warsaw Pact, 1955–1991.* Budapest: Central European University Press.

Matlock, Jack F., Jr. (1995). *Autopsy on an Empire: The American Ambassador's Account of the Collapse of the Soviet Union.* New York: Random House.

———(2004). *Reagan and Gorbachev: How the Cold War Ended.* New York: Random House.

Maynes, Charles William (1982). Old errors in the new Cold War. *Foreign Policy* 46 (2) (Spring), 86–104.

Mazo, Michael (2004). The Peak: Nuclear Arms Control and the End of the Cold War at the Reykjavik Summit. B.A. thesis, Yale University.

McLean, Scilla, Ed. (1986). *How Nuclear Weapons Decisions Are Made.* Basingstoke, England: Macmillan.

McNamara, Robert S. (1986). *Blundering into Disaster: Surviving the First Century of the Nuclear Age.* New York: Pantheon.

———(1995). *In Retrospect: The Tragedy and Lessons of Vietnam.* New York: Vintage.

Medvedev, Grigori (1991). *The Truth About Chernobyl.* New York: Basic Books.

———(1993). *No Breathing Room: The Aftermath of Chernobyl.* New York: Basic Books.

Medvedev, Zhores (1990). *The Legacy of Chernobyl.* New York: W. W. Norton.

Melman, Seymour (1970). *Pentagon Capitalism: The Political Economy of War.* New York: Basic Books.

———(1974). *The Permanent War Economy: American Capitalism in Decline.* New York: Touchstone.

Millar, Alistair (2002). The pressing need for tactical nuclear weapons control. *Arms Control Today,* May 2002, 1–5, online at http://www.armscontrol.org/act/2002_05/millarmayo2.asp (accessed 12 Mar. 2007).

Millis, Walter, Ed. (1951). *The Forrestal Diaries.* New York: Viking.

Mlynar, Zdenek (1980). *Nightfrost in Prague: The End of Humane Socialism.* P. Wilson, Trans. New York: Karz.

Morris, Edmund (1999). *Dutch: A Memoir of Ronald Reagan.* New York: Random House.

Morton, Tom (2005). Episode 1: The Nuclear War We Nearly Had in 1983. In *Torn Curtain: The Secret History of the Cold War.* ABC Radio National. Australia.

Mould, Richard F. (1988). *Chernobyl: The Real Story.* Oxford: Pergamon Press.

———(2000). *Chernobyl Record: The Definitive History of the Chernobyl Catastrophe.* Bristol, England: Institute of Physics Publishing.

Moynihan, Daniel Patrick (1990). How America blew it. *Newsweek* (10 Dec.), 14.

Mueller, John (1988). The essential irrelevance of nuclear weapons. *International Security* 13 (2) (Fall), 55–79.

Nacht, Michael L. (1975). The delicate balance of error. *Foreign Policy* 19, (Summer), 163–77.

Newhouse, John (1989). Annals of diplomacy: "The Abolitionist" I & II. *New Yorker;* I: 2 Jan., 37–52; II: 9 Jan., 51–72.

Nichols, John (2004). *The Rise and Rise of Richard B. Cheney: Unlocking the Mysteries of the Most Powerful Vice President in American History.* New York: New Press.

Nielsen, J. Rud (1963). Memories of Niels Bohr. *Physics Today,* Oct.

Ninsic, Miroslav (1988). The United States, the Soviet Union and the politics of opposites. *World Politics* 40 (4) (July), 452–75.

Nitze, Paul (1976). Assuring strategic stability in an era of detente. *Foreign Affairs* 54 (2) (Jan.), 1–16 (online version).

———(1989). *From Hiroshima to Glasnost: At the Center of Decision.* New York: Grove Weidenfeld.

Nolan, Janne E. (1989). *Guardians of the Arsenal: The Politics of Nuclear Strategy.* New York: Basic Books.

Norris, Robert S., and William M. Arkin (1994). Estimated U.S. and Soviet/Russian nuclear stockpiles, 1945–1994. *Bulletin of the Atomic Scientists* 50 (6) (Nov.–Dec.), 58–59.

Nuenlist, Christian (2001). Cold War generals: The Warsaw Pact Committee of Defense Ministers, 1969–1990. Parallel History Project on Cooperative Security, online at http://www.php.isn.ethz.ch/ (accessed 12 March 2007).

Nye, Joseph S., Jr. (1987). Nuclear learning and U.S.-Soviet security regimes. *International Organization* 41 (3) (Summer).

Oberdorfer, Don (1992). *The Turn: From the Cold War to a New Era; The United States and the Soviet Union 1983–1990.* New York: Simon & Schuster.

Odom, William E. (1998). *The Collapse of the Soviet Military.* New Haven, CT: Yale University Press.

Oppenheimer, Robert (1953). Atomic weapons and American policy. *Foreign Affairs* 31 (4) (July), 525–35.

Palme, Olof (Independent Commission on Disarmament and Security Issues) (1982). *Common Security: A Blueprint for Survival.* New York: Simon & Schuster.

Park, Robert (2000). *Voodoo Science: The Road From Foolishness to Fraud.* New York: Oxford University Press.

Patman, Robert G. (1999). Reagan, Gorbachev and the emergence of "New Political Thinking." *Review of International Studies* 25 (Oct.), 577–601.

Paton, Boris E., Victor G. Baryakhtar, et al. (2003). The Chernobyl catastrophe in Ukraine: Causes of the accident and lessons learned. *Environmental Science & Pollution Research,* Special Issue 1, 3–12.

Perle, Richard (1987). Reykjavik as a watershed in U.S.-Soviet arms control. *International Security* 12 (1) (Summer), 175–78.

———(1992). *Hard Line.* New York: Random House.

Petrosyants, Andranik (1988). *Nuclear Engineering Before and After Chernobyl: Problems and Prospects.* Moscow: Progress Publishers.

Pious, Richard M. (1991). Prerogative power and the Reagan presidency: A review essay. *Political Science Quarterly* 106 (3) (Fall), 499–510.

Pipes, Richard (1977). Why the Soviet Union thinks it could fight and win a nuclear war. *Commentary* (July), 21–34.

———(1986). Team B: The reality behind the myth. *Commentary* (Oct.), 25–40.

———(2003). *VIXI: Memoirs of a Non-Belonger.* New Haven, CT: Yale University Press.

Podvig, Pavel, Ed. (2001). *Russian Strategic Nuclear Forces.* Cambridge, MA: MIT Press.

Potter, William C.(1985a). Nuclear proliferation: U.S.-Soviet cooperation. *Washington Quarterly* (Winter), 141–54.

———. (1985b). The Soviet Union and nuclear proliferation. *Slavic Review* 44 (5), Fall, 468–87.

———(1989). Soviet decision-making for Chernobyl: An analysis of system performance and policy change. National Council for Soviet and East European Research, Dec.

———(1991). The effects of Chernobyl on Soviet decision-making for nuclear safety. *Impact of Science on Society* 163, 257–67.

Potter, William C., and Lucy Kerner (1991). The Soviet military's performance at Chernobyl. *Soviet Studies* 43 (6), 1027–47.

Powaski, Ronald E. (2000). *Return to Armageddon: The United States and the Nuclear Arms Race, 1981–1999*. New York: Oxford University Press.

Powell, Colin L., with Joseph E. Persico (1995). *My American Journey*. New York: Random House.

Powers, Thomas (1996). Who won the Cold War? (Review of Robert M. Gates, *From the Shadows*, Simon & Schuster, 1996). *New York Review of Books* 43 (11), 20 June (online version).

Preble, Christopher (2005). The Uses of Threat Assessment in Historical Perspective: Perception, Misperception and Political Will. Threat Assessment Working Group of the Princeton Project on National Security. June.

Pry, Peter Vincent (1999). *War Scare: Russia and America on the Nuclear Brink*. Westport, CT: Praeger.

Pryce-Jones, David (1995). *The War that Never Was: The Fall of the Soviet Empire 1985–1991*. London: Phoenix Press.

Ramzaev, P. V., Ed. (1996). *Medical Consequences of the Chernobyl Nuclear Accident*. Commack, NY: Nova Science.

Read, Piers Paul (1993). *Ablaze: The Story of the Heroes and Victims of Chernobyl*. New York: Random House.

Reagan, Ronald (1990). *An American Life*. New York: Simon & Schuster.

——(2000). *Abortion and the Conscience of the Nation*. Sacramento, CA: New Regency Publishing.

Reagan, Ronald, with Richard G. Hubler (1965). *Where's the Rest of Me?* New York: Best Books.

Reed, Thomas C. (2004). *At the Abyss: An Insider's History of the Cold War*. New York: Ballantine.

Remnick, David (1991). Dead souls. *New York Review of Books* 38 (21), 19 Dec.

——(1994). *Lenin's Tomb*. New York: Vintage.

Rhodes, Richard (1995). *Dark Sun: The Making of the Hydrogen Bomb*. New York: Simon & Schuster.

——(1986). *The Making of the Atomic Bomb*. New York: Simon & Schuster.

Rippon, Simon (1986). The Chernobyl accident. *Nuclear News* (June) (LexisNexis Academic, accessed 3 May 2005), 87.

Robin, Corey (2004). *Fear: The History of a Political Idea*. New York: Oxford University Press.

Rodberg, Leonard S., and Derek Shearer, Eds. (1970). *The Pentagon Watchers: Students Report on the National Security State*. Garden City, NY: Doubleday & Co.

Rogers, Paul. (1988). *Guide to Nuclear Weapons*. Bradford Peace Studies Papers: New Series No. 2. Oxford: Berg.

Rosenberg, David Alan (1983). The origins of overkill: Nuclear weapons and American strategy, 1945–1960. *International Security* 7 (4) (Spring), 3–71.

Rosenberg, David Alan, and W. B. Moore (1981–1982). "A smoking radiating ruin at the end of two hours": documents on American plans for nuclear war with the Soviet Union, 1954–1955. *International Security* 6 (3) (Winter), 3–38.

Rosengren, J. W. (1983). Some Little-Publicized Difficulties With a Nuclear Freeze. Office of Internal Security Affairs, U.S. Department of Energy, Oct.

Rostow, Walt W. (1975). Robert S. McNamara Oral History Interview I, 8 Jan., Internet Copy, LBJ Library.

Roxburgh, Angus (1991). *The Second Russian Revolution: The Struggle for Power in the Kremlin*. London: BBC Books.

Rummel, Rudolph J. (1998). *Statistics of Democide*. Munich: Lit.

Sagan, Carl (1992). Between enemies. *The Bulletin of the Atomic Scientists* 48 (May), 24–26.

Sagan, Scott D. (1987). SIOP-62: The nuclear war plan briefing to President Kennedy. *International Security* 12 (1) (Summer), 22–51.

Sagan, Scott D., and Kenneth N. Waltz (2003). *The Spread of Nuclear Weapons: A Debate Renewed.* New York: W. W. Norton.

Sagdeev, Roald Z. (1994). *The Making of a Soviet Scientist.* New York: John Wiley & Sons.

Sakharov, Andrei (1990). *Memoirs.* R. Lourie, Trans. New York: Alfred A. Knopf.

———(1991). *Moscow and Beyond: 1986 to 1990.* A. Bouis, Trans. New York: Alfred A. Knopf.

Sanders, Jerry W. (1983). *Peddlers of Crisis: The Committee on the Present Danger and the Politics of Containment.* Boston: South End Press.

Satter, David (1996). *Age of Delirium: The Decline and Fall of the Soviet Union.* New Haven, CT: Yale University Press.

Sayle, Murray (1993). A reporter at large: Closing the file on Flight 007. *New Yorker* (13 Dec.), 90–101.

Scarry, Elaine (1991). War and the social contract: Nuclear policy, distribution and the right to bear arms. *University of Pennsylvania Law Review,* 139 U. Pa. L. Rev. 1257.

Scheer, Robert (1988). *Thinking Tuna Fish, Talking Death: Essays on the Pornography of Power.* New York: Noonday Press (Farrar, Straus & Giroux).

Schell, Jonathan (2004). Cold war to Star Wars. *Nation* (28 June), 7.

Schmid, Sonja (2005). Envisioning a Technological State: Reactor Design Choices and Political Legitimacy in the Soviet Union and Russia. Doctoral dissertation, Cornell University.

Schmidt, Helmut (1981). A policy of reliable partnership. *Foreign Affairs* 59(4) (Spring), 1–8 (online version).

Schneider, Barry R., and William L. Dowdy, Eds. (1998). *Pulling Back from the Nuclear Brink: Reducing and Countering Nuclear Threats.* London: Frank Cass.

Schwartz, Stephen I., Ed. (1998). *Atomic Audit: The Costs and Consequences of U.S. Nuclear Weapons Since 1940.* Washington, D.C.: Brookings Institution Press.

Schweizer, Peter (1994). *Victory: The Reagan Administration's Secret Strategy That Hastened the Collapse of the Soviet Union.* New York: Atlantic Monthly Press.

Shcherbak, Iurii (1989). *Chernobyl: A Documentary Story.* I. Press, Trans. New York: St. Martin's Press.

Sheehy, Gail (1990). *The Man Who Changed the World: The Lives of Mikhail S. Gorbachev.* New York: HarperCollins.

Sheldon, Robert (2004). Military Operations Research Society (MORS) Oral History Project interview of Alfred Lieberman, FS. *Military Operations Research* 9 (1), 57–73.

Shevardnadze, Eduard (1991). *The Future Belongs to Freedom.* C. A. Fitzpatrick, Trans. London: Sinclair-Stevenson Ltd.

Shultz, George P. (1993). *Turmoil and Triumph: My Years as Secretary of State.* New York: Charles Scribner's Sons.

Shvets, Yuri B. (1994). *Washington Station: My Life as a KGB Spy in America.* New York: Simon & Schuster.

Sigal, Leon V. (2000). *Hang Separately: Cooperative Security Between the United States and Russia, 1985–1994.* New York: Century Foundation Press.

Skinner, Kiron K., et al. (2001). *Reagan, In His Own Hand.* New York: Simon & Schuster.

Solomon, Fredric, and Robert Q. Marston, Eds. (1986). *The Medical Implications of Nuclear War.* Washington, D.C.: National Academy Press.

Steinbruner, John D. (1981). Nuclear decapitation. *Foreign Policy* 45 (Winter), 16–28.

Stelzer, Irwin, Ed. (2004). *The Neocon Reader.* New York: Grove Press.

Steury, Donald P., Ed. (1994). *Estimates on Soviet Military Power, 1954 to 1984: A Selection.* Washington, D.C.: Central Intelligence Agency.

Stockman, David A. (1986). *The Triumph of Politics: How the Reagan Revolution Failed*. New York: Harper & Row.

Stone, I. F. (1973). The Sakharov campaign. *The New York Review of Books* 20 (16), 18 Oct., 1–7 (online version).

Strober, Deborah Hart, and Gerald S. Strober (1998). *Reagan: The Man and His Presidency*. Boston: Houghton Mifflin.

Szporluk, Roman (2000). *Russia, Ukraine, and the Breakup of the Soviet Union*. Stanford, CA: Hoover Institution Press.

Talbott, Strobe (1984). *The Russians & Reagan*. New York: Vintage.

———(1985). *Deadly Gambits: The Reagan Administration and the Stalemate in Nuclear Arms Control*. New York: Vintage.

———(1988). *The Master of the Game: Paul Nitze and the Nuclear Peace*. New York: Alfred A. Knopf.

Tannenwald, Nina, Ed. (1999). *Understanding the End of the Cold War, 1980–87: An Oral History Conference, Brown University, May 7–10, 1998 (Transcript)*. Providence RI: Watson Institute for International Studies.

Thomson, James A. (1984). The LRTNF decision: Evolution of US theatre nuclear policy, 1975–9. *International Affairs (Royal Institute of International Affairs 1944–)* 60 (4) (Autumn), 601–14.

Tilly, Charles (2003). *The Politics of Collective Violence*. Cambridge: Cambridge University Press.

Todd, Emmanuel (1979). *The Final Fall: An Essay on the Decomposition of the Soviet Sphere*. J. Waggoner, Trans. New York: Karz.

Tonelson, Alan (1979). Nitze's world. *Foreign Policy* (35) (Summer), 74–90.

Tuchman, Barbara (1984). *The March of Folly: From Troy to Vietnam*. New York: Ballantine Books.

Tucker, Robert C. (1981–82). Swollen state, spent society: Stalin's legacy to Brezhnev's Russia. *Foreign Affairs* 60 (2) (Winter).

Turner, Paul R., David Pitt, et al., Eds. (1989). *The Anthropology of War & Peace: Perspectives on the Nuclear Age*. Granby, MA: Bergin & Garvey.

Turpin, Jennifer, and Lester R. Kurtz, Eds. (1997). *The Web of Violence: From Interpersonal to Global*. Urbana: University of Illinois Press.

Uhler, Walter C. (2003). There he goes again. *The Nation*, 3 Feb.

Ukrainian Weekly (1983). *The Great Famine in Ukraine: The Unknown Holocaust*. Jersey City, NJ: Ukrainian National Association.

Underhill-Cady, Joseph B. (2001). *Death and the Statesman: The Culture and Psychology of U.S. Leaders During War*. New York: Palgrave.

van Oudenaren, John (1990). The tradition of change in Soviet foreign policy. *McNair Papers (Institute for National Strategic Studies, National Defense University, Fort Leslie J. McNair, Washington, D.C.)* 7 (Apr.).

Vargo, George J., Ed. (2000). *The Chornobyl Accident: A Comprehensive Risk Assessment*. Columbus, OH: Battelle Press.

Velikhov, Yevgeni (1991). Science and scientists for a nuclear-weapon-free world. In *Physics and Nuclear Arms Today: Readings from Physics Today*, D. Hafemeister, Ed., 368–72. New York: American Institute of Physics.

Velikhov, Yevgeni, Roald Sagdeev, and Andrei Kokoshin, Eds. (1986). *Weaponry in Space: The Dilemma of Security*. Moscow: Mir.

Viola, Lynne (2001). The other archipelago: Kulak deportations to the North in 1930. *Slavic Review* 60 (4) (Winter), 730–55.

Volkogonov, Dimitry (1988). *Stalin: Triumph and Tragedy.* H. Shukman, Trans. New York: Grove Weidenfeld.

———(1998). *Autopsy for an Empire: The Seven Leaders Who Built the Soviet Regime.* H. Shukman, Trans. New York: Free Press.

Warnke, Paul (1975). Apes on a treadmill. *Foreign Policy* 18 (Spring), 12–29.

Waskow, Arthur I. (1964). Disarmament as a special case in military strategy (review of three books). *World Politics* 16 (2) (Jan.), 322–27.

Wasserstrom, Richard A., Ed. (1970). *War and Morality.* Belmont, CA: Wadsworth.

Weinberger, Caspar W. (1990). *Fighting for Peace: Seven Critical Years in the Pentagon.* New York: Warner.

Westad, Odd Arne (2001). Concerning the situation in "A": New Russian evidence on the Soviet intervention in Afghanistan. *Cold War International History Project Bulletin* 8/9 (in Documents on the Soviet Invasion of Afghanistan, e-Dossier No. 4, Cold War International History Project, Woodrow Wilson International Center, Washington, D.C., Nov.), 128–32.

Whelan, Joseph G. (1988). *Soviet Diplomacy and Negotiating Behavior—1979–88: New Tests for U.S. Diplomacy.* Special Studies Series on Foreign Affairs Issues, U.S. House of Representatives (Committee on Foreign Affairs), II. 3 vols. Washington, D.C.: U.S. GPO.

Wieseltier, Leon (1985). When deterrence fails. *Foreign Affairs* 63(4) (Spring), 827–47.

Wiesner, Jerome (1984). We Need More Piefs. SSI Conference Proceedings, SLAC, Stanford University.

Wills, Garry (1987). *Reagan's America.* New York: Penguin Books.

Wilson, Richard (1987). A visit to Chernobyl. *Science* 236 (4809), 26 June, 1636–40.

Winik, Jay (1996). *On the Brink: The Dramatic, Behind-the-Scenes Saga of the Reagan Era and the Men and Women Who Won the Cold War.* New York: Simon & Schuster.

Wirls, Daniel (1992). *Buildup: The Politics of Defense in the Reagan Era.* Ithaca, NY: Cornell University Press.

Wittner, Lawrence S. (2004). Did Reagan's military build-up really lead to victory in the Cold War? *History News Network,* http://hnn.us/articles/2732.html. (Accessed 12 Oct. 2006.)

Wohlforth, William C., Ed. (1996). *Witnesses to the End of the Cold War.* Baltimore: Johns Hopkins University Press.

Wohlstetter, Albert (1974). Is there a strategic arms race? *Foreign Policy* 15 (Summer), 3–20.

Wohlstetter, Albert, Paul H. Nitze, et al. (1974). Is there a strategic arms race? (II): Rivals but no "race." *Foreign Policy* 16 (Autumn), 48–92.

Wolf, Markus, with Anne McElvoy (1997). *Man Without a Face: The Autobiography of Communism's Greatest Spymaster.* New York: Times Books.

World Health Organization (1987). Nuclear Accidents and Epidemiology: Reports on Two Meetings. WHO 25.

———(2005). Health Effects of the Chernobyl Accident and Special Health Care Programs (Report of the Chernobyl Forum Expert Group "Health"). EGH. 5 Apr.

Yakovlev, Alexander (1993). *The Fate of Marxism in Russia.* C. A. Fitzpatrick, Trans. New Haven, CT: Yale University Press.

Yaroshinskaya, Alla (1995). *Chernobyl: The Forbidden Truth.* M. Kahn and Julia Sallabank, Trans. Lincoln: University of Nebraska Press.

Yeltsin, Boris (1994). *The View From the Kremlin.* C. A. Fitzpatrick, Trans. New York: Harper-Collins.

Zanzonico, P. B., and D. V. Becker (2000). Effects of time of administration and dietary iodine levels on potassium iodide (KI) blockade of thyroid irradiation by ^{131}I from radioactive fallout. *Health Physics* 78 (6) (June), 660–67.

Zaslavskaya, Tatyana (1984). The Novosibirsk Report. *Survey* 28 (1) (Spring), 88–108.

Zubok, Vladislav M. (2000). Gorbachev's nuclear learning: How the Soviet leader became a nuclear abolitionist. *Boston Review* (Apr.–May), http://bostonreview.net/BR25.2/issue.pdf. (Accessed 10 June 2005.)

ACKNOWLEDGMENTS

Anne Sibbald and Mort Janklow ably represented this third volume in what has evolved into a multivolume history of the nuclear age, with one more volume to go. Jon Segal and Sonny Mehta at Knopf saw its value and supported it enthusiastically across five years.

At length or briefly, I interviewed many people for this book. Thanks first and foremost to Stanislav and Irina Shushkevich, whom I met originally in Belarus while researching *Masters of Death* and who subsequently visited California as my houseguests. Their contributions were invaluable.

An evening with Elena Bonner in Moscow in 1992 helped me understand her ordeal and Andrei Sakharov's. I corresponded by e-mail with Yuli Khariton at that time as well.

Hans Blix gave me a day out of his life for a long, rich interview, conducted improbably in Las Vegas. Tom Graham sat for many hours of interviews that supplemented his books. So did Sig Hecker, an old friend. More will be heard from all three the next time around. Susan Eisenhower and Roald Sagdeev welcomed me into their home and offered valuable eyewitness accounts; I wish I had been able to include the story of their courtship—another marker of when the Cold War ended—but both have told it in books. Berry Blechman clarified the work of the Palme Commission, wise Jim Goodby his understanding of summits and leaders. Robert McNamara, Sam Nunn, Lee Hamilton, Jack Matlock, Jr., General Eugene Habiger, Rozanne Ridgway, and Richard Perle responded helpfully to questions. So did Georgi Arbatov through the kind agency of his son Alexei, whose work contributed in its own right. I benefited from several pleasurable luncheon conversations with Sid Drell and a long dinner conversation with Jonathan Schell.

My colleagues at Stanford's Center for International Security and Cooperation deserve special thanks for their warm support and encouragement, particularly CISAC's director, Scott Sagan, and associate director, Lynn Eden. Seminars and lectures there, and conversations with Herb Adams, George Bunn, Gail Lapidus, Mike May, Pavel Podvig, and Dave Hafemeister deepened my understanding of U.S.-Soviet relations and U.S. diplomatic politics. Sonja Schmid expertly vetted my Chernobyl chapter.

Nina Tannenwald generously made available the invaluable transcripts and documents from the Brown University oral history conference. James Prados offered guidance on ABLE ARCHER 83, Finn Aaserud on Niels Bohr and common security, Stan Norris on Soviet and American nuclear weapons, Dori Ellis on Sandia. Mike Keller allowed me to wander the Stanford Library. Glen Worthy supplied fluent translations from Russian. Randy and Terri Reese explored Iceland on my behalf. Cornelia and Michael Bessie, cherished friends, recalled their work with Mikhail Gorbachev and Alexander Yakovlev. Julia Penrose transcribed, alphabetized, extracted, and sorted, indefatigably.

My wife is Ginger Rhodes, Ph.D., now, a clinical psychologist and skilled psychotherapist. She was there for me, as she is always.

PERMISSIONS ACKNOWLEDGMENTS

Excerpts from William E. Odom, *The Collapse of the Soviet Military,* New Haven: Yale University Press, © 1998 by Yale University, and from Alexander Yakovlev, *The Fate of Marxism in Russia,* New Haven: Yale University Press, copyright © 1993 by Alexander Yakovlev, reprinted by permission of Yale University Press.

Excerpts from Thomas Graham, Jr., *Disarmament Sketches: Three Decades of Arms Control and International Law,* Seattle: Institute for Global and Regional Security Studies, copyright © 2002 by University of Washington Press, reprinted by permission of the University of Washington Press.

Excerpts from Emmanuel Todd, *The Final Fall: An Essay on the Decomposition of the Soviet Sphere,* New York: Karz Publishers, copyright © 1979 by Karz Publishers, and from Zdenek Mlynar, *Nightfrost in Prague: The End of Humane Socialism,* New York: Karz Publishers, copyright © 1980 by Karz Publishers, reprinted by permission of Karz Productions.

Excerpts from Lynn Eden, *Whole World on Fire: Organizations, Knowledge, and Nuclear Weapons Devastation,* Ithaca: Cornell University Press, copyright © 2004 by Cornell University, used by permission of the publisher, Cornell University Press.

Excerpts from Nina Tannenwald, Ed., *Understanding the End of the Cold War, 1980–87: An Oral History Conference, Brown University, May 7–10, 1998 (Transcript),* copyright © 1999 by the Watson Institute for International Studies, reprinted by permission of the Watson Institute for International Studies.

Excerpts from Mikhail Gorbachev and Zdenek Mlynar, *Conversations with Gorbachev on Perestroika, the Prague Spring and the Crossroads of Socialism,* New York: Columbia University Press, copyright © 2002 Mikhail Gorbachev, reprinted with permission of the publisher.

Excerpts from Mikhail Gorbachev, *Memoirs,* copyright © 1995 by Mikhail Gorbachev, English translation copyright © by Wolf Jobst Siedler Verlag Gmbh, Berlin, used by permission of Doubleday, a division of Random House, Inc.

Excerpts from Michael Ellman & Vladimir Kontorovich, eds., *The Destruction of the Soviet Economic System: An Insiders' History,* Armonk, NY: M. E. Sharpe, copyright © 1998 by M.E. Sharpe, Inc., reprinted with permission of the publisher.

Excerpts from Don Oberdorfer, *The Turn: From the Cold War to a New Era,* New York: Simon & Schuster, copyright © 1991, 1992 by Don Oberdorfer, reprinted by permission of the Joy Harris Literary Agency.

Excerpts from Svetlana Alexievich, *Voices from Chernobyl,* Normal, IL: Dalkey Archive Press, Copyright © 1997 by Svetlana Alexievich, translation copyright © 2005 by Keith Gessen, reprinted by permission of the Dalkey Archive Press.

Excerpts from George P. Shultz, *Turmoil and Triumph: My Years as Secretary of State,* New York: Simon & Schuster, Copyright © 1993 by George P. Shultz, reprinted by permission of Scribner, an imprint of Simon & Schuster Adult Publishing Group. All rights reserved.

INDEX

PHOTOGRAPHIC CREDITS

John Lehman: Defense Visual Information Center (DVIC).
Shultz/Weinberger: Terry Ashe/Time Life Pictures/Getty Images.
Peacekeeper warheads: © 1993 by Paul Shambroom.
Reagan as lifeguard: Ronald Reagan Presidential Library.
Reagan shooting scene: Ronald Reagan Presidential Library.
SDI illustration: U.S. Air Force.
SS-20 missile: ITAR-TASS.
Pershing 2s: Defense Visual Information Center (DVIC).
"The Day After" scene: ABC/Photofest.
Greenham Common arrest: Sahm Doherty/Time Life Pictures/Getty Images.
NATO exercise: NATO.
Gromyko/Gorbachev: AP/Wide World Photos.
Gorbachev on Lenin Mausoleum: ITAR-TASS.
Eduard Shevardnadze: Eastlight/Getty Images.
Anatoly Chernyaev: Dr. Svetlana Savranskaya.

PHOTOGRAPHS APPEARING IN INSERT III

Reagan/Gorbachev: Ronald Reagan Presidential Library.
Challenger disaster: NASA.
Olof Palme: AP/Wide World Photos.
Schmidt/Bahr: Robert Lackenbach/Time Life Pictures/Getty Images.
Yevgeny Velikov: Private collection.
Arbatov–Eisenhower: Private collection.
Garwin–Sagan: Richard Garwin.
Sidney Drell: Sidney Drell.
Andrei Sakharov: AP/Wide World Photos.
Paul Nitze: AP/Wide World Photos.
Sergei Akhromeyev: © Peter Tunley/CORBIS.
Gorbachev/Reagan at Reykjavik: Ronald Reagan Presidential Library.
Reagan/Perle: Ronald Reagan Presidential Library.
Reagan/Gorbachev leaving Hofdi House: Ronald Reagan Presidential Library.
Matthias Rust's plane over Red Square: unknown.
Lithuanian succession: © Pascal le Segretain/CORBIS SYGMA.
Gorbachev at the UN: John Chiasson/Liaison/Getty Images.
Celebrants on Berlin Wall: AP/Wide World Photos.
Wolfowitz-Sununu: George Bush Presidential Library.
Baker/Shevardnadze: AP/Wide World Photos.
Scrapped Soviet tanks: © TASS/Sovfoto.
Boris Yeltsin on tank: AP/Wide World Photos.
Kravchuk/Shushkevich/Yeltsin: ITAR-TASS.

Richard Rhodes is the author or editor of twenty-two books, including novels, history, journalism, and letters. *The Making of the Atomic Bomb* won a Pulitzer Prize in Nonfiction, a National Book Award, and a National Book Critics Circle Award. *Dark Sun,* about the development of the hydrogen bomb, was one of three finalists for a Pulitzer Prize in History. He has written about the roots of private violence (*Why They Kill*), the Holocaust (*Masters of Death*), the French-American artist John James Audubon (*John James Audubon: The Making of an American* and *The Audubon Reader*), mad cow disease (*Deadly Feasts*), and life on a family farm (*Farm*), as well as personal memoirs (*A Hole in the World, Making Love*) and four novels. An affiliate of Stanford University's Center for International Security and Cooperation, he lectures to college and professional audiences. He lives near Half Moon Bay, California, with his wife, Ginger Rhodes, a clinical psychologist. His Web site is at www.RichardRhodes.com.

A NOTE ON THE TYPE

This book was set in Minion, a typeface produced by the Adobe Corporation specifically for the Macintosh personal computer, and released in 1990. Designed by Robert Slimbach, Minion combines the classic characteristics of old-style faces with the full complement of weights required for modern typesetting.

Composed by North Market Street Graphics,
Lancaster, Pennsylvania

Designed by M. Kristen Bearse